Elementary Social Studies

Elementary Social Studies

A Practical Guide

Fifth Edition

JUNE R. CHAPIN
Notre Dame de Namur University

ROSEMARY G. MESSICK
San Jose State University

Allyn and Bacon
Boston ■ London ■ Toronto ■ Sydney ■ Tokyo ■ Singapore

Series Editor: Traci Mueller
Editorial Assistant: Bridget Keane
Executive Marketing Manager: Amy Cronin
Editorial-Production Service: Omegatype Typography, Inc.
Composition and Prepress Buyer: Linda Cox
Manufacturing Buyer: Suzanne Lareau
Cover Administrator: Kristina Mose-Libon
Electronic Composition: Omegatype Typography, Inc.

Between the time Web site information is gathered and published, some sites may
have closed. Also, the transcription of URLs can result in typographical errors.
The publisher would appreciate notification where these occur so that they may
be corrected in subsequent editions.

Library of Congress Cataloging-in-Publication Data

Chapin, June R.
    Elementary social studies : a practical guide / June R. Chapin,
Rosemary G. Messick.—5th ed.
        p.   cm.
    Includes bibliographical references and index.
    ISBN 0-321-08667-8
    1. Social sciences—Study and teaching (Elementary)—United States.
I. Messick, Rosemary G.   II. Title.

LB1584 .C47 2002
372.83'044—dc21
                                                            2001031806

Printed in the United States of America
10 9 8 7 6 5 4 3 2   06 05 04 03 02

Contents

Preface   ix

Chapter 1   **The Elementary Social Studies Curriculum**   1

Images of the Social Studies   1

Why Teach the Social Studies?   3

Standards, Standards, Standards: Control to the States   5

Affective Goals: Should We Teach Values, Moral Education, and Character Education?   12

Definitions of the Social Studies   18

National Curriculum Patterns   24

Importance of Textbook Series   27

Mounting Criticism: Scope and Sequence   28

Summary   31

Suggested Readings and Web Sites   31

Chapter 2   **Planning for Social Studies Instruction**   34

Planning   34

Goals, Long-Range Planning, and Standards/Instructional Objectives   37

Treasury of Resources for Planning   44

Units   46

Lesson Plans   63

Organizing and Scheduling   64

Summary   65

Suggested Readings and Web Sites   66

Chapter 3   **Instructional Strategies**   67

General Consideration of Methods   67

What Happens in Real Classrooms?   69

Direct Teaching: From Passive to Active Learning   70

Discovery Learning and Thinking   74

Specific Thinking Skills: Observation, Listening, and Questioning   82

Cooperative or Collaborative Learning   87

Role Playing   94

Simulations   97

Summary   99

Suggested Readings and Web Sites   100

Chapter 4   **Assessing and Evaluating Students' Progress in the Social Studies**   101

Perceptions of Evaluation   101

National Assessment of Educational Progress   105

State Testing   105

Assessment of Student Learning   108

Assessment Techniques and Tools   110

Evaluating Learning and Development   124

Summary   131

Suggested Readings and Web Sites   131

Chapter 5   **Social Studies in the Primary Grades**   133

Primary-Grade Social Studies Curriculum Using State Standards   134

Primary History State Standards   135

Primary Economics Standards   144

Primary Geography Standards   149

Primary Citizenship Standards   152

Guidelines for Integrating Social Studies in the Primary-Grade Curriculum   155

Classroom Environment and Scheduling in the Primary Grades   167

Summary   170

Suggested Readings and Web Sites   170

Chapter 6   **Social Studies in the Fourth through Eighth Grades**   172

Children in the Middle Grades   172

The Social Studies Curriculum: Content   173

Current Events/Current Affairs Programs   193

Teaching Controversial Issues   197

Summary   201

Suggested Readings and Web Sites   201

Chapter 7   **Elementary Citizenship Education**   **203**

Defining Citizenship   204

Classroom Citizenship   206

Instruction in Democratic Citizenship   215

Citizenship in School   219

Linking Schoolwide Citizenship to the Community   220

Global Citizenship   223

Summary   232

Suggested Readings and Web Sites   232

Chapter 8   **Social Studies and Diversity**   **234**

Describing Learning about Diversity   234

Classroom Organization and Learning about Diversity   236

Classroom Instruction about Diversity   239

Classroom Intergroup Problem Solving   254

Summary   259

Suggested Readings and Web Sites   260

Chapter 9   **Social Studies and the Literacy Connection**   **262**

Typical Social Studies Instructional Activities and Literacy   262

Meeting Special Needs: Mild Disabilities, ESL Students,
    and Struggling Readers   267

Reading Difficulties   271

Finding Information   272

Relating the Social Studies and Literacy   276

Summary   282

Suggested Readings and Web Sites   282

Chapter 10   **Teaching Social Studies Skills: Time, Space, Technologies**   **284**

Learning About Time and Chronology   284

Map and Globe Skills   289

Technologies for the Social Studies   297

Summary   311

Suggested Readings and Web Sites   312

Index   313

Preface

This edition has the most extensive revisions compared to previous editions. This is due to three important trends. First, the most significant change in social studies in the last few years is the state standards-based educational reform and the assessment of these curriculum standards (Chapters 1, 4, and 5). Therefore, new lesson plans and units pervade the text on how to implement state standards. The Arizona Primary Social Studies standards in the four areas of history, geography, economics, and civics are used as examples of using standards in a creative manner (Chapter 5).

Second, as *access* and *inclusion* have become more essential and significant, teachers are facing increasingly greater diversity in classrooms with ESL students, students with disabilities, as well as differences in ethnic groups, home cultures, and social class of their students (Chapter 8). The literacy chapter has new material on helping ESL students and students with mild disabilities, the need to balance the whole language and phonics approaches, reading difficulties in the social studies, finding information, and writing (Chapter 9).

Third, citizenship education (local, national, and global) in a diverse society is given more emphasis, realizing that social studies is not the only academic subject in the curriculum concerned with citizenship education. For civic education, there is new material on service learning and global education as well as attention to the NAEP Civics Report Card (Chapter 7). Civic education is also related to the new material on the teaching of character (Chapter 1).

In addition, the technology chapter presents the new computer literacy standards for students, more on Internet research, and types of CD-ROMs (Chapter 10). Technology is also interwoven throughout all chapters. Additional new material includes home-school-community partnerships, the status of integrated curriculum (Chapter 2), updating trends in history and the social sciences as to their impact in the schools (Chapter 6), new assessment content (Chapter 4), and appropriate Web sites for all chapters.

In summary, in this revision, we wish to reassert the primacy of citizenship education in a democratic society since there are too many students who grow into adults lacking or unwilling to use the knowledge and skills needed to become contributing civic members of their local and wider communities. We, as teachers, need to summon all the methods and resources necessary to teach participatory democracy to today's students.

We have made three assumptions in preparing the fifth edition of *Elementary Social Studies:* First, that you come to the professional sequence of your teacher preparation program with a general background in academic disciplines such as history, sociology, and geography that serve as a foundation for elementary social studies. Second, that you, like students in most professional programs, are scheduled for only a one-semester, one- to three-credit course in teaching social studies, or a core methods course in which social studies instruction is integrated. And third, that you have other courses in your program that expose you to learning theory, curriculum planning, the teaching of concepts and generalizations, and instructional technology.

To help you focus on important concerns, we have limited the scope of the text to topics that are *basic, specific,* and yet *critical* to teaching the social studies in the elementary years, kindergarten through eighth grade. Preparation of this edition has, however, made us realize that changes in current practice, in reform emphases, and in our society and schools require that we interweave new material that has now become basic, specific, and critical to this subject.

To conceptualize the core information on social studies education, we also present and analyze vignettes and provide additional textual exposition to enrich your knowledge about classroom instruction and curriculum in general. Chapter introductions and definitions of terms provide you with links to your other professional courses in the areas of curriculum and learning. Small group discussion topics, lesson plans, and other activities suggest instructional resources to pursue in your own teaching.

The small group and individual exercises integrated into all the chapters, if pursued as part of your class time, can position you to explore more thoroughly key issues that the text introduces. Time spent doing these exercises with your peers will certainly enrich your ability to think critically and reflectively about issues within social studies instruction. Lesson plans, unit outlines, and instructional resource lists throughout the text suggest activities you can try out as you participate in elementary classes and ideas you can build on as you plan more extended teaching sequences.

We continue to learn from the experiences of our own students, from classroom teachers with whom we work, and from our university colleagues throughout the country. Our reviewers, in particular, served an important role in improving and updating this text for the fifth edition: Gail Hickey, Indiana University, Fort Wayne and William W. Joyce, Michigan State University. We are grateful for the valuable additions of all our colleagues to this text.

Finally, between us, we have taught in the Midwest, Portugal, Spain, and Brazil and for many years in California. We have seen teachers make a positive difference in the lives of children and feel privileged to watch children gain opportunities through education. We believe that the social studies can help you make dreams a reality for the children you teach, and we invite you to work with us toward that goal.

J. R. C.

R. G. M.

Elementary Social Studies

Chapter 1

The Elementary Social Studies Curriculum

In this chapter we learn that the traditional social studies curriculum is being heavily criticized and that changes may be coming in the future. The following topics are covered here:

- Images of the Social Studies
- Why Teach the Social Studies?
- Standards, Standards, Standards: Control to the States
- Affective Goals: Should We Teach Values, Moral Education, and Character Education?
- Definitions of the Social Studies
- National Curriculum Patterns
- Importance of Textbook Series
- Mounting Criticism: Scope and Sequence

■ IMAGES OF THE SOCIAL STUDIES

Welcome to the world of social studies! What do you remember about your elementary social studies program? If any of the following activities seem familiar, jot down on a piece of paper whether the memory is pleasant.

Clipping out items from a newspaper for Friday current events
Doing a research report on Daniel Boone from your school's encyclopedia
Finding out the latitude and longitude of a long list of cities
Learning about the Pilgrims at Thanksgiving
Visiting a site where your state's Native American tribes lived
Writing a contest essay on American government
Answering the questions at the end of a textbook chapter
Writing to foreign consuls and embassies for information about your assigned country
Reenacting pioneer life
Making a papier-mâché globe

Writing a personal history book

Drawing neighborhood maps

Working on a committee that one person dominated

Learning about the immigrant groups from which you came

Seeing old films

Making a book report on a famous American

Role-playing a character

Finding new information

SMALL GROUP WORK	**WHAT WORKS BEST?**
1.1	

We have used this exercise with classes many times. Often we have heard I loved doing . . . , but sometimes it was I hated. . . . This exercise points out that your days as an elementary student years ago are influencing your image of the social studies. Your images act as a filter as you make judgments of what a good social studies program is and what methods should be used to achieve social studies goals.

    Now add to this list the activities that you remember experiencing in elementary social studies. Try to include both pleasant and boring times. Compare with others in your group your list of what you liked and didn't like. Are there activities that everyone remembers enjoying? Are there other activities that everyone disliked? Your image of elementary social studies stems mainly from your own experiences. Can you now draw a simple picture or graphic that summarizes either positively or negatively your experiences as a social studies student? What one descriptive word best pulls together your image of the social studies? Do you think teachers teach much in the way they were taught?

SMALL GROUP WORK	**HOW IMPORTANT IS SOCIAL STUDIES?**
1.2	

How do you rank the importance of social studies in the elementary curriculum? Look at the following list of traditional subjects taught in elementary school.

    Health/physical education (PE)

    Mathematics

    Reading/language arts

    Science

    Social studies

    Now rank these subjects, 1 through 5, in order of their importance to you. Share your list with other members of your group. Most elementary teachers and students rank social studies third or lower. If your ranking was within this range, what influenced your response?

Elementary teachers often have negative attitudes toward the social studies as a result of their own school experiences, perhaps because of the following:

Learning about social studies largely emphasized trivial facts.

The dominant instructional tool was the textbook.

Most social studies activities concentrated on large group recitation and lecture.

Emotional or affective objectives were not included as part of the curriculum.

In addition, although students on a national survey looked forward to social studies and were not afraid to ask questions in social studies, they did not think social studies was as useful as math, English, and science. Many students do not see the link between their social studies program and social participation in the classroom, school, community, nation, and the world.

Two other reasons may account, at least in part, for the less than enthusiastic attitude that many elementary teachers have toward the social studies: lack of preparation and lack of interest. Many of you have taken only a few social science or history courses in college. You may feel underqualified or reluctant to tackle the sometimes controversial subject matter of the social studies. Many of you may feel strongly that reading and math programs are basic in elementary education; however, a social studies program is also basic. In fact, a good social studies program can go far toward improving students' skills in other subjects, including reading, writing, and math.

The basic purpose of social studies is **citizenship education** because a good social studies program can contribute to producing good citizens. We believe in the *vital* importance of social studies instruction, both to prepare students to become responsible, thoughtful, participating citizens and to provide students with the basic skills that they need to function in our society. If we are successful in transmitting these beliefs to you, then social studies teaching at least in your classrooms may not suffer the neglect that otherwise often occurs at the primary level.

This text will help you find ways of teaching the social studies that you and your students will learn from and enjoy. Social studies *can* be taught creatively and thoughtfully. As a result of your efforts, students may find that social studies is their favorite subject. More important, through *your* social studies instruction, your students will acquire the necessary knowledge, skills, and values to participate as active citizens in our society and the global community.

■ WHY TEACH THE SOCIAL STUDIES?

The main purpose or rationale for teaching the social studies is citizenship education. To achieve citizenship education, there are four major **goals.** Goals are the overarching aims or desired outcomes of education. Goals are not achieved in one day, one week, or even one year. Goals such as good health and good citizenship are pursued by individuals for decades and in a certain sense are never completely achieved. Here are the four important social studies goals.

1. To acquire **knowledge** from the social sciences, history, and humanities
2. To develop **skills** to think and to process information
3. To develop appropriate democratic **values** and **beliefs**
4. To have opportunities for **citizenship/social participation**

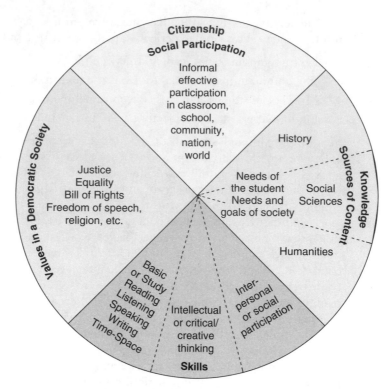

FIGURE 1.1 Goals of the Social Studies

These four goals are not separate and discrete. Usually they are intertwined and overlapping (see Figure 1.1). You may find in some state standards or frameworks that two goals are combined. Social participation may be regarded as a democratic value or the goal may be stated as "skill attainment and social participation." The knowledge goal can be referred to as "knowledge and cultural understanding" or "democratic understanding and civic values." Values may sometimes be called **civic** values to differentiate them from **personal** values. But regardless of how the goals are combined or written, together they form the basic goals of a social studies program. Although these goals may take several years of student learning, the schools can and should focus their social studies program on these four main social studies goals.

As these goals indicate, social studies is about people and, thus, builds on an inherently high interest. Each of us is concerned about self, family, and friends and social studies is designed to help us understand ourselves as well as our nearby neighbors and those who live halfway around the world. Creative social studies instruction offers the possibility of humane individuals who incorporate basic American values such as equality, freedom, and respect for property and who are able to put these values into action through effective participation in the classroom, school, community, nation, and the world. Again, this emphasizes the main purpose of the social studies curriculum: citizenship education.

Frequently, the process of learning has emotional values attached to it. Did you *hate* math in school? Did you *love* music? For example, when students study pollution, they usually acquire opinions or attitudes about it. Emotional concerns such as racism in the community can have a striking impact on both subject area and students' skill development. Certain skills such as writing or thinking may be taught in school, but there is no guarantee that students will make use of them. Unless students have a commitment to, a need for, or a willingness to use the skills they have learned, those skills will be of little value either to the students or to society. All this underlines the connections among the four main goals of a social studies education; although we may speak of each one separately, we must not forget their inherent interrelationships.

■ STANDARDS, STANDARDS, STANDARDS: CONTROL TO THE STATES

Prodded by the 1983 federal report, *A Nation at Risk*,[1] which questioned American students' ability to compete in a global economy, and conferences by the nation's governors in 1995, the fifty states in our nation embarked on a standards-based education reform effort. Reform implies something is wrong and changes are needed. **Standards** are what teachers are supposed to teach and students are expected to know (content) and be able to do (performance).

National Standards

Initially, it was thought that the federal government's voluntary standards and testing would be the most important player in the standards movement. Professional organizations related to the field of social studies then published their national standards. The National Council for the Social Studies (NCSS) had ten broad curriculum themes/standards with five process (skill) standards (Table 1.1). Four other groups immediately wrote separate discipline standards for history, geography, civics and government, and economics. (These will be discussed more in Chapter 6). Much later in 1999 the American Psychological Association published its standards for the teaching of high school psychology, which has had little impact except on high school psychology classes.

At the heart of the reform-based standards effort was the question: *What is the most essential knowledge of the discipline or the social studies?* Answering this question has led to a greater emphasis on students' understanding the major concepts of the subject area, the big ideas, and learning the ways of thinking of the discipline, the particular methods used for investigation.

---

[1] *A Nation at Risk: The Imperative for Education Reform*. Prepared by the National Commission in Education (Washington, DC: U.S. Department of Education, April 1983).

TABLE 1.1 NCSS Curriculum Themes/Standards

1. Culture (anthropology)
2. Time, continuity, and change (history)
3. People, places, and environments (geography)
4. Individual development and identity (psychology)
5. Individuals, groups, and institutions (sociology)
6. Power, authority, and governance (political science)
7. Production, distribution, and consumption (economics)
8. Science, technology, and society
9. Global connections
10. Civic ideals and practice

Source: Expectations of Excellence: Curriculum Standards for Social Studies, Task Force of the National Council for the Social Studies, Bulletin 89, Washington, DC, 1994.

The 1994–1995 political outcry over the proposed National History Standards ended any possibility of national consensus on history standards (Chapter 6). In addition, conservatives feared increased federal control over the state and local boards of education. Liberals, in turn, worried that the standards movement would stifle educators, be culturally biased, and lead to further standardization. These concerns shifted the development of standards to the states. So the states, not the federal government, are the key actors in the standards-based reform movement for the foreseeable future. It is the states that will take corrective action in the schools and districts that continue to lag in student achievement.

Raising standards presently has widespread approval and strikes a responsive chord with the public and political candidates. Who can argue for low standards? Parents want their children to be adequately prepared for the world of work in the twenty-first century, which means having knowledge and basic skills such as reading and math as well as being technologically literate. Parents are also exposed to the media focusing on urban and rural low-performing schools with little coverage on successful students and schools. These increased perceptions about the "failed public school system" have led to a debate about charter schools, vouchers, and home schooling. Parents want the power to make choices about the type of school for their children. Given these anxieties and fears, the standards movement to reform the schools by requiring students to demonstrate by tests certain knowledge and skills makes sense to parents and the public.

Teachers appear to be divided on the issue of the use of standards. Some welcome the guidance that standards give. Others get emotionally upset at the idea of having standards and are very negative about what they see as an imposition on what they can do in their classrooms. This raises the issue of how much compliance there will actually be in using standards in classrooms. Will some teachers continue to ignore standards and hope that standards will be a passing fad? Or will teachers work creatively within the system of standards? In practice, some teachers will probably be users and others nonusers of standards. However, for standards to be successful in reforming the schools teachers must support them. A feeling of ownership of the standards by teachers is necessary.

Testing of the Standards

High-stakes testing for students raises complex problems. (Testing will be discussed more in Chapter 4.) Will parents and students get upset and angered if too many students are retained in a grade or denied or given different types of diplomas? The answer is yes. How many opportunities will students have to retake the test(s)? Have students had the opportunity to learn what is being tested? These issues in many cases will be decided by the courts.

If the testing in a given state is considered unfair, the standards movement will probably suffer a decline in popularity. Simply enacting a standard is not enough and, in some cases, the demands are either unrealistic or out of line with the resources that are devoted to the task of meeting them. This issue is particularly acute in schools serving disadvantaged children. The tendency is to soften the requirement by lowering the score needed to graduate or adding other criteria. For example, in Wisconsin the all-or-nothing high school graduation test was replaced by a combination of students' portfolios of their work, including test scores, grades, and letters of recommendations.

However, the accountability of the standards based primarily on test scores seems here to stay for a number of years. This is especially true in states that have signed long-term contracts for the preparation and administration of tests. In addition, the standards assume there are no changes in content in academic fields such as history and geography.

State Standards

Now almost every state has adopted standards for the social studies. A state has faced two problems in developing standards for the social studies. First, should there be one set of interdisciplinary, social studies standards, such as Wisconsin's standards, or should standards be developed in each of the related areas, such as history, geography, economics, and civics? Probably more states choose to list four separate standards for history, geography, economics, and civics. Second, how should the standards deal with many value issues and political interpretations so common in the social studies? Here to avoid the firestorm of the detailed national history standards, most states have moved into broad statements. But they have also included more citizenship standards compared to the national standards.

The states' efforts for social studies often built on a compilation of national standards developed by NCSS and the four subject areas—history, geography, civics, and economics. The other behavioral sciences such as sociology and psychology were deemphasized. The work on the state's standards often was then repeated by a group in the school district that prepared its own local version of the standards because of the desire to keep local control, meet the needs of the community, and to give teachers a stake in the ownership of the standards. To avoid political controversy, the standards were often loosely defined.

Forty-nine states have also adopted mandated standardized tests, but in many states these only include reading, math, and sometimes writing. By 2003, twenty-six states will require students to pass a test to graduate from high school. Wide variations exist on grade-level standards. Although some states have written what is expected in the social studies on each grade level, more common are **learning benchmarks,** which are the progress indicators for measuring students' achievement of the standards. These benchmarks are typically grades 4 or 5, 6 or 8, and 10 or 11.

To understand this better, let us first discuss the many meanings of the term **curriculum.** In the most general sense curriculum consists of both the **plans** for learning and the actual **delivery** of those plans. Standards are really **curriculum or learning standards.** Your state with its standards or local district may have a **required or recommended curriculum,** which can be mandatory for all teachers. This required curriculum is typically written and spelled out and is often called the **official curriculum** or framework. It has been formally adopted by the state or local board. But what teachers actually do in their classrooms is the **taught curriculum.** The **tested/assessed curriculum** is the curriculum that is revealed in tests and other assessments given to students. Sometimes these are called **performance standards,** which measure mastery or levels of attainment in a given content topic or skill.[2]

Important Role of the Teacher

The teacher makes the difference in the implementation of or noncompliance with the standards because the quality of the teacher is the most critical factor in children learning in school. Three years with successful teachers can really move a child ahead in learning while the opposite is true if there is a succession of poorer teachers. A good teacher can enhance student learning, compensate for curriculum, overcome negative student attitudes, and refocus low expectations. This means that standards do not automatically flow down from the state capital into the hearts and minds of students.

As mentioned before, teachers are divided on using standards. In practice, some experienced teachers may disregard them and continue their habitual teaching. Beginning teachers who do not have at hand accumulated units and materials may be more likely to design their teaching with standards in mind. Regardless of your views on standards, please do not ignore them. In the worse possible case, you could be sued by parents for not following the prescribed curriculum. Instead, analyze care-

[2]Allan A. Glatthorn, *Curriculum Renewal* (Alexandria, VA: Association for Supervision and Curriculum Development, 1987).

fully the standards on your grade level but do not think of them in terms of being fixed, rigid mandates that rule out creativity. Then decide with your colleagues where in your curriculum you will teach each standard.

Ultimately, teachers will be the final decision makers in the classroom for any improvement in the quality of the elementary social studies program. The teacher is the primary agent of educational change.

Teachers are responding to their students' testing requirements. Where there is state testing, the standards-based reform movement is having an enormous impact. Teacher anxiety and stress have been heightened in some states as teachers and administrators examine what they presently teach and decide whether or how they should make changes in the curriculum to achieve higher test scores. If there is only testing in reading and math, some teachers unfortunately are focusing on only these two areas. Thus, there are reports of schools dropping physical education, art, and music, having reduced recesses, and so on to give more attention to the subject areas that are tested and dropping or slighting subject areas that are not tested.

Pros and Cons of the Standards Reform Movement

There are strengths and weaknesses to having social studies content standards. First, the standards movement has placed greater emphasis on the major concepts or key ideas along with the methodology of the discipline. This could help to focus the elementary curriculum. Second, by focusing on every student and not just the brighter students, the standards movement could improve education, especially if there were a financial commitment to create the proper educational conditions for achievement. Too often in the past, in a given state or even in the same district, two different classrooms on the same grade level had wildly different social studies content or too little content, violating students' equal access to the curriculum. There has been little consistency in how much time students spend on a given subject or the knowledge or skills emphasized within that subject area. The real challenge of reform is reaching all students. Some states have reported increased scores on achievement tests.

A good result of the standards movement is that standards have been the source of new lesson plans. Due to the Internet, these lesson plans are now more readily available. Teachers also especially like the assessment examples that appear in their state standards. The Wisconsin standards include a sample proficiency standard (what the student is able to do) and examples of actual student work that demonstrate their learning. In addition, some schools engage in promising practices such as upgrading and realigning curriculum, training parents to help their children, creating faculty committees to suggest plans for improvement, and providing extra help to struggling students, especially in summer school. However, critics of the standards movement cite negative consequences of the standards movement: teaching to the test, more student dropouts, rigid curriculum, cheating, more grade retention that does not help students' motivation, and more pressure on students who need the most help.

TABLE 1.2 Virginia's History–Social Science Standards, Grade 3

The standards for third grade students include an introduction to the heritage and contributions of the people of ancient Greece and Rome and the West African empire of Mali. Students should continue developing map skills and demonstrate an understanding of basic economic concepts. Students will explain the importance of the basic principles of democracy and identify the contributions of selected individuals. Students will recognize that Americans are a people who have diverse ethnic origins, customs, and traditions, who all contribute to American life, and who are united as Americans by common principles.

History

3.1 The student will explain how the contributions of ancient Greece and Rome have influenced the present world in terms of architecture, government (direct and representative democracy), and sports.

3.2 The student will study the early West African empire of Mali by describing its oral tradition (storytelling), government (kings), and economic development (trade).

3.3 The student will study the exploration of the Americas by
   a) describing the accomplishments of Christopher Columbus, Juan Ponce de Leon, Jacques Cartier, and Christopher Newport;
   b) identifying reasons for exploring, the information gained, and the results from the travels.

Source: Virginia Board of Education, *History and Social Science Standards of Learning for Virginia Public Schools* (Richmond, 2001).

It is in assessment that the biggest impact may come from the standards movement. Some states are changing their mandatory assessments with increasing emphasis on problem solving and on items with more than one right answer. These types of questions, moving away from the easy-to-score, objective items, will make the assessment process more expensive. However, they also may motivate teachers to have their students do well on these types of test items and this would have a lasting and good impact.

Teachers, however, have the following specific criticisms about state standards.

1. Standards are not age appropriate.
2. There is too much content specified for the grade level.
3. In contrast to being too specific in content, standards may be too general.
4. There is less attention to multicultural/global education.

Let us check some of these criticisms by examining Virginia's history standards for grade 3 as shown in Table 1.2. For the third grade in Virginia there were also geography, economics, and civics standards.

Another pattern is illustrated by Missouri in its content specifications for statewide assessment by standard.[3] Each school district develops and implements a

[3]Missouri Department of Elementary and Secondary Education, *Content Specifications for Statewide Assessment by Standard Social Studies Grades 4, 8, & 11* (Jefferson City, MO: Missouri Department of Elementary and Secondary Education, 1998).

curriculum with Missouri's content standards. Missouri has seven knowledge standards for social studies for grades 4, 8, and 11. Six of these standards are based on history and the social sciences, and one is called "Tools of Social Science Inquiry." A partial list of two standards for Grade 4 Benchmark is given in Table 1.3.

TABLE 1.3 Grade 4 Benchmark Standard 2. Knowledge of American History

1. Knowledge of the ways Missourians have interacted, survived, and progressed from the distant past to present times.
   • Knowledge about individuals from Missouri who have made contributions to our state and national heritage. Examples of a few such people include Lewis and Clark, Mary Easton Sibley, John Berry Meachum, George Washington Carver, Laura Ingals Wilder, Mark Twain, Harry S Truman, and Thomas Hart Benton.
   • Broad knowledge about the following developments, their importance and general sequence:
      • The habitats, resources, art, and daily life of Native American peoples (Woodland and Plains Indians)
      • Settlements in Missouri of people of European and African heritage
      • The Louisiana Purchase
      • The Lewis and Clark Expedition
      • The impact of westward expansion on Indians in Missouri
      • Statehood and the Missouri Compromise (when Missouri became a state, why statehood was difficult to obtain, Missouri as a slave state)
      • Westward expansion (people's motivation, their hardships, Missouri as a jumping-off point to the West)
      • Civil War (Missouri as a border state)
      • Changes in Missouri since the Civil War in education, transportation, and communication

2. Knowledge about the contributions of non-Missourians students typically study in K–4 programs (i.e., George Washington, Thomas Jefferson, Abraham Lincoln, and Martin Luther King).

Missouri's Grade 4 Benchmark Standard 6. Knowledge of Geography

1. Knowledge of how to read and construct maps, attending to such features as the map's title, key, and compass rose.

2. Knowledge of the geography of Missouri, the United States, and other regions using maps and applying the following geographic themes or concepts:
   • **Location**
      • Students can locate the cities of Kansas City, Springfield, St. Louis, Jefferson City, Columbia, and St. Joseph; the Mississippi and Missouri Rivers; and the world's continents and oceans.
      • Students can communicate location of a place by pointing it out on map, by describing its *absolute location* (description of a location using some grid system) and by describing its *relative location*.

ON YOUR OWN	**WHAT IS YOUR REACTION TO STATE SOCIAL STUDIES STANDARDS?**
1.1	*Looking at the brief descriptions of Virginia and Missouri's standards, do you think the standards are age appropriate? Too much content? Will the standards promote creative thinking? Or will they be a list of facts for students to memorize? Or will it depend on the teacher? Realize that you are seeing only a small part of the description of the standards and there is wide variation among the states in terms of their level of detail and degree of prescriptiveness. Check the social studies standards and state assessment (if any) of your state. These are usually available on the Internet. Search by using your state's name followed by Department of Education (e.g., Alabama Department of Education) or Department of Public Instruction (e.g., Delaware Department of Public Instruction). In a few cases the title may be different (e.g., Minnesota Department of Children, Families, and Learning).*

■ AFFECTIVE GOALS: SHOULD WE TEACH VALUES, MORAL EDUCATION, AND CHARACTER EDUCATION?

Role Model

You are an important role model. Your actions in and even out of the classroom are carefully observed by your students. Students make judgments on whether you really like them and whether you are fair. In effect, your behavior shows a "proper" way of how to act. Thus, a teacher has been described as a moral compass pointing out to students the accurate direction and the way to act. All values education approaches acknowledge the importance of the teacher as a role model.

Everything you do reflects your values. This leads to the importance of teaching **values,** the strongly held standards or criteria we use in making judgments about people, places, and things. Sometimes the phrases *beliefs and values* and *attitudes* or *dispositions* are used. Surveys show overwhelmingly that the public and parents want the schools to teach basic values such as honesty, respect, and responsibility. But how, as teachers, do you do this?

Values

Schools have always taught values and moral development through textbooks, teachers, and school rules. Values are presented by the way teachers treat students and the way students are allowed to treat teachers and each other. There is a **hidden curriculum** of what is right and wrong even when questions of right and wrong do not come up directly in the classroom. Every classroom has rules that embody values. "Children should put or store their possessions in certain places in the room." "Raise your hand if you wish to speak." These rules are more than just classroom management techniques. They communicate to children what is required to be good students. These rules teach important lessons about authority, responsibility, caring, respect, punctuality, working in teams, and so on.

Teaching values directly often becomes restricted to teaching broad, civic values such as justice and public responsibilities—voting, obeying the law, paying taxes, and serving on a jury. These public values have a high level of acceptance at an abstract

TABLE 1.4 Approaches to Major Values Education

Approach	Purpose	Method
Caring (Noddings)	Care for self Care for others	Modeling, dialogue, practice, and confirmation
Moral development (Kohlberg)	Students develop higher set of values	Moral dilemmas, small group discussion, teacher in devil's advocate role
Values clarification (Simon et al.)	Students become aware of their own values Students identify values of others	Variety of methods, self-analysis exercises
Social action	Students have opportunities for social action based on their values	Projects in schools and in community
Indoctrination	Values of students change in desired direction	Variety of methods, selective data provided
Analysis	Students use logical thinking to decide values issues	Rational discussion, research

Note: Difficulties arise when trying to place certain programs such as substance abuse approaches like the Drug Abuse Resistance Education (D.A.R.E.) program, which stress self-esteem and drug-free behavior. Some would classify these programs as indoctrination while others would put them in the analysis approach since they may use medical research as a data source. There is a similar problem with many of the character education approaches.

level by almost all members of the community, although concrete issues such as capital punishment and police rights engender wide controversy. The primary organization in the field of social studies, the National Council for the Social Studies, lists thirty-one democratic beliefs and values grouped in the following four categories.

1. Rights of the Individual (life, liberty, justice, security, privacy, etc.)
2. Freedoms of the Individual (worship, thought, assembly, etc.)
3. Responsibilities of the Individual (honesty, respect rights of others, etc.)
4. Beliefs Concerning Societal Conditions and Governmental Responsibilities (elections, civil liberties, minorities protected, common good, etc.)[4]

Few educators or parents would dispute the inclusion of teaching these general public values in the classroom, but more controversial are social-moral issues and personal values. The differing viewpoints of community members as well as different teachers make teaching controversial issues a contentious subject (see more in Chapter 6). Ultimately, it boils down to whose values will be taught.

There are many approaches to values education in the school (Table 1.4). Let us look at these various values education approaches.

[4]John Jarolimek, Chair NCSS Task Force on Scope and Sequence, "Social Studies for Citizens of a Strong and Free Nation," in *Social Curriculum Planning Resources* (Washington, DC: National Council for the Social Studies, 1990), 31–32.

Even though moral development has generally received little attention by educators (see Table 1.4), Nel Noddings and many others have advocated that more attention be given in the schools to developing caring individuals who have a knowledge of self and a moral recognition that they can do both evil and good. According to Noddings, restructured schools need to teach students not to harm each other.[5]

Lawrence Kohlberg sought to help students develop more complex reasoning patterns based on a higher set of values. Kohlberg called for students to discuss the *reasons* for their value choices, not merely to share with others, but to foster change in the students' stages of moral reasoning. His main method was to present artificial moral dilemmas (should you steal a drug to help some family member, should you tattle on a friend who has stolen a sweater in a department store, etc.). Students then would take positions (such as whether you should tell on a friend) followed by group discussion and relatively structured argumentation in a Socratic dialogue format.[6] Carol Gilligan criticized Kohlberg for omitting a feminine perspective. She believed that females had a different but equally valid way of arriving at moral decisions.[7] Critics of this approach have argued that the moral dilemmas were unrealistic and not the problems that most students presently face in everyday life.

However, the most severe criticism about values education in the schools was directed against Sidney Simon and his colleagues, who advocated a nonjudgmental approach called *values clarification*.[8] These authors wanted to help students become aware of and to identify their own values and those of others. They wanted students to communicate honestly with others about their own values even if their beliefs might be supportive of using drugs or other socially unaccepted values. Simon's methods included using both rational thinking and emotional awareness to allow students to examine their personal feelings, values, and behavior. Often these exercises were contrived situations (deciding who should be chosen to stay in a fallout shelter, writing your own obituary) and self-analysis exercises (writing about two ideal days, jotting down twenty things you love to do). While critics raged against the values clarification approach for not teaching "good" values and allowing any value system to be acceptable, teachers purchased handbooks of values clarification exercises by the hundreds of thousands and most students enjoyed working with the "fun" exercises.

Critics of the values clarification approach were also concerned about invasion of privacy issues as students talked about their own personal behavior. Some parents also felt that the schools were teaching the wrong values or not correcting students

[5]Nel Noddings, *The Challenge to Care in Schools* (New York: Teachers College Press, 1992).

[6]Lawrence Kohlberg, "Moral Education in the Schools: A Developmental View," *School Review* 74, no. 1 (Spring 1966): 1–30.

[7]Carol Gilligan, *In a Different Voice: Psychological Theory* (Cambridge, MA: Harvard University Press, 1982).

[8]Sidney B. Simon, Leland W. Howe, and Howard Kirschenbaum, *Values Clarification* (New York: Hart, 1972).

who had "bad" values; many were horrified at Simon's conception of values as relative rather than absolute.

In addition, the few teachers who implemented *social action*—changing or reforming the community—were also criticized when students were encouraged to take social action based on their values. Usually no one complained if the students cleaned up the local park, and student campaigns to protect the faraway whales usually did not engender much controversy. Citizens were upset, however, when the students began a public information campaign about a local factory that was polluting the environment or when students tried to protect local endangered species such as the spotted owl in an area with an economy dependent on logging.

All these approaches to values education—caring, Kohlberg's moral development, Simon's values clarification approach, and social action—raise the question of whether the values education classes in the schools really work (see again Table 1.4). The evidence is inconclusive partly because of the problems of doing research in the field. If you teach students to think and reason about important values, do they *behave* according to their reasoned values? Does formal teaching about values always translate into action? Measuring the effectiveness of any values education approach in the schools has always been difficult. What do you count? A reduction in the number of student referrals or suspensions? The number of children who report more smiling faces?

Character Education

We single out for further discussion **character or moral education,** an ethical approach that has received more attention in recent years. The same concerns of parents and the public who have supported the standards movement and drug abuse programs also buttress the character education movement. In particular, school violence, increases in the number of working parents, worries about the harmful influence of television and music, and the courts' rulings on sexual harassment by students have given character education more attention.

Character education programs can be controversial. Criticisms of character education formerly came most often from liberals who objected to the conservative Christian values they detected as being taught. These critics called the character education advocates "virtuecrats," referring to William Bennett's very popular book, *The Book of Virtues,* stories designed to help children to understand and to develop good character. More recently, conservatives have objected because they believe the schools are promoting values such as feminism and one-world government under the rubric of character education. Some social studies experts fear character education uses an approach that is too simplistic by ignoring cases in which "good" values are in conflict or in tension. For example, should minorities be given more preference to be admitted to highly rated schools? Fairness, equity, justice, providing equal opportunity, and so on are all good values involved in this case. In addition, character education previously had the image of being a single-minded, patriotic movement with an emphasis on indoctrination.

The definition of character education varies and one definition is not widely accepted. However, character education often has the following elements:

1. The moral crisis in society must be addressed by the schools.
2. Role models are important in character development.
3. Some degree of direct-learning instruction is desirable.
4. Students need opportunities to practice good character.
5. Schools must establish a positive moral climate.
6. Community input should guide character education programs.

Thus, the advocates of character education hold that there are widely shared, important, universal core ethical values—caring, honesty, fairness, responsibility, and respect for self and others—that form the basis of a good character. To promote character education, the school explicitly names and publicly stands for these core values. Students are to understand, care, and act on these values. The character education approach supports all effective methods to reach the goals of fostering good character. Programs use cooperative learning, direct teaching, problem solving, simulations, role playing, service learning, active participation in the school and community, and the like as well as good behavior modeled by all adults in the school from kitchen workers to the principal.

Because there are significant differences among programs and their implementation by teachers and staff in the school, it has been difficult to classify character education. It should be noted that when some public schools have adopted a set of basic ethical values, there has generally been widespread support from parents and the community. How effective character education programs have been is not clear. Like any program, a good character education program needs leadership from the staff, students, parents, and community to be successful.

Are there any particular characteristics of a school with a character education approach? Perhaps it is that literature selections in these classrooms are often used to prove a specified or implied moral. In some primary grades, this has taken the place of the social studies program or is the social studies program. In addition, typically, a list of rules for appropriate behavior is posted. Students are exhorted and rewarded to follow these rules for the good of themselves, the class, and the school. But character education programs may also have a great deal of discussion about the rules by the students using a variety of methods. For example, most schools have rules for students about using the Internet. "Do not use improper language or photos." "Never arrange to meet in person someone you know only over the Internet." Probably every teacher believes these computer rules and other rules are needed and spends time discussing why we have such rules. Thus, it is often difficult in actual practice to identify characteristics of character education classrooms because their methods are not unique but are practiced to some degree by all teachers.

Your Decision on Values

Your values influence how you teach. Your definition of the social studies, citizenship education, treatment of controversial issues, and culture education springs from

SAMPLE CLASSROOM EPISODE

CHEATING BY USING THE INTERNET: A VALUE QUESTION

Ms. Kim Camera, a teacher with a fourth–fifth grade combination class, has successfully taught the unit on "Early Explorers and Pioneers" for many years. But she has noticed that on student projects and reports that there is a growing number of students whose written language is way above their typical level. Ms. Camera thinks they are using whole paragraphs and even articles without getting permission from the source or citing the source. She suspects that the copying is from the Internet and CD-ROM adult encyclopedias, but she has no definite proof. Ms. Camera wants students to cite the sources of their information at all times and thinks copying without permission is a bad habit for students to get into.

Being careful not to accuse any student, Ms. Camera talks privately to each student she suspects of "cheating." Students grudgingly report the following: "Mom helped me." "I don't remember how I got the information." "I forgot to put down where I found the stuff." "The Internet is free and you just take it."

Ms. Camera then at parent conferences speaks to these students' parents about this alleged copying. Ms. Camera is amazed at most of the parents' responses. Most defend their actions with the following sentences. "You should be glad that I am helping Benjamin; I work long hours and I am giving him my time." "Get with it; there is a real world out there and that's the way the Internet works." "Other teachers do not object and are glad to see better reports." "Our Gina needs special accommodations to do the work you require." "Boys do not write as well as girls and they need the help from the Internet."

Ms. Camera realizes that there is a difference between her values and that of parents and their children. She is unsure what to do next. She is also aware that the principal wants to improve school–family relationships.

What steps do you think Ms. Camera should take? Speak to the principal? Bring the issue up at teacher meetings? Talk more to the students about not copying and needing to cite sources of information? What would you do? Does your opinion change if the teacher has tenure?

your position on values and the way they should be explored in the classroom. Are democratic values and how these values relate to living in a democracy central to teaching social studies? You will make the decision about whether you want to formally teach values, moral education, or character education.

ON YOUR OWN	WHAT ARE THE SOURCES OF YOUR VALUES?
1.2	*What do you think have been the main sources of your values? How do you think your values may affect your teaching?*

■ DEFINITIONS OF THE SOCIAL STUDIES

We have listed four main goals, but educators do not always agree on either the **definition** or **content** for the field of social studies. Look at your state's framework or curriculum documents. Is the title *Social Studies*? Or is it *History/Social Sciences*? *Social Studies* implies an integrated approach whereas *History/Social Sciences* connotes a separate subject approach.

In 1992 the National Council for the Social Studies adopted its integrated definition of the field.

> Social studies is the integrated study of the social sciences and humanities to promote civic competence. Within the school program, social studies provides coordinated, systematic study drawing upon such disciplines as anthropology, archaeology, economics, geography, history, law, philosophy, political science, psychology, religion, and sociology, as well as appropriate content from the humanities, mathematics, and natural sciences. The primary purpose of social studies is to help young people develop the ability to make informed and reasoned decisions for the public good as citizens of a culturally diverse, democratic society in an interdependent world.[9]

In addition, when NCSS published its national standards in 1994, it reaffirmed its commitment to an integrated approach drawing its content from seven disciplines: history, geography, political science, economics, psychology, sociology, and anthropology (Table 1.1). The first seven standards were based on the major concepts of the social sciences and history. The last three standards were broadly based themes that included several subject areas. An integrated approach assumes that many issues such as health care and crime are multidisciplinary in nature. In other words, you need knowledge from several disciplines, not just one social science or history, to think intelligently about the subject.

Critics of the integrated social studies approach believe too often that the separate disciplines get neglected. They especially think that history and geography get watered down. As a result, they feel that students do not have either the knowledge or the perspective that these academic disciplines have to offer. The history, geography, civics and government, and economic associations were eager to publish their national standards so that their respective fields would get more attention. Although the American Psychological Association has just recently written standards, the standards are coming too late for consideration from most states. The fields of sociology and anthropology did not produce national standards and are less likely not to be emphasized.

Presently, many states have separate standards for history (in some cases, one for American history and another for world history), geography, economics, and principles of government (civics). Although teachers may be tempted to use each standard as a unit of content, it is probably more desirable for elements of geography or civic education or economics to be distributed across the other units they teach. Thus, how standards are to be integrated both within the social studies field and with other themes and topics in language arts and science will have to be addressed. You can see both the challenges and why educators do not always agree on what content should be included in the social studies.

[9]Task Force of the National Council for the Social Studies, *Expectations of Excellence: Curriculum Standards for Social Studies*, Bulletin 89 (Washington, DC: National Council for the Social Studies, 1994), 3.

ON YOUR OWN	CONTENT FOR THE SOCIAL STUDIES
1.3	*Would you include subjects related to careers; consumer education; substance abuse; child abuse; law-related education; ethnic, women, and other minority studies; AIDS; or environmental education?*
	How do you think children define social studies? Ask a few students, ideally some in your own school or a school in which you are likely to teach, to tell you in their own words what social studies is. Do some have difficulty? When asked by his parents why he had a lower grade in social studies, a primary child replied that he did not know what social studies means.

Although definitions of the social studies may vary, the definition that *you* accept is important. All elementary teachers should be able to define their objectives in teaching the social studies as well as their own decisions about its content.

Robert Barr, a social studies educator, and his colleagues defined the first three main social studies traditions, shown in Table 1.5. Note that all the approaches emphasize the broad goal of citizenship education but differ on how to achieve this goal. Concrete examples are given to illustrate the differences of each.

Citizenship Transmission

What do you think the tradition of social studies taught as *citizenship transmission* means? Every nation or societal group brings up its children to reflect its own values and culture. All social groups—from the most primitive to the most advanced—attempt to socialize their children. For example, the French want their children to appreciate French culture; members of various religious groups want their children to practice their religious beliefs.

TABLE 1.5 Different Approaches to Citizenship Education

Approach	Goals of Citizenship Education
1. Citizenship transmission	Students are taught traditional knowledge and values as a framework for making decisions.
2. Social science/history	Students master social science/history concepts, generalizations, and methods.
3. Reflective inquiry	Students use knowledge and thinking to make decisions and to solve problems.
4. Personal development	Students develop a positive self-concept and a strong sense of personal efficacy.
5. Informed social criticism/reform	Students develop understanding and skills needed to critique and transform society; often a focus on injustice/inequality.

Source: Robert D. Barr, James L. Barth, and S. Samuel Shermis, *Defining the Social Studies,* Bulletin 51 (Washington, DC: National Council for the Social Studies, 1977). Reprinted with permission of the National Council for the Social Studies.

In the United States, children must be prepared to live in our common culture. They must understand our unique American heritage and our political and economic systems. In addition, they must speak English and participate in community life. Many institutions in our society, including the family and the media, contribute to our children's knowledge about mainstream culture. Our schools also play an important role in this process of teaching about our shared political and social values.

Social studies authorities such as James Shaver argue that the school *must* instill in students a commitment to democratic values. These basic values, called "the American creed," cement the nation together; they include, among other things, due process of law, respect for others, free access to information, freedom of choice (including multiculturalism), and respect for the value of rational thought. According to Shaver, it is crucial that social studies instruction be based on democratic values and that students accept the basic values of our society as fundamental and not debatable.[10]

But this position does not mean that the teacher has the right to indoctrinate students in every area. **Indoctrination** is the shaping of people's minds by providing information without permitting them to question or examine the information being transmitted. We are on shaky ground when we attempt to indoctrinate "correct" answers to questions and issues that raise difficult ethical choices. Here our role is to help students think about the issues rather than to attempt to dictate the right answers. Often the purpose of indoctrination is to make citizens subject to those in power or to influence individuals to accept a dictated solution to a problem. Indoctrination can also be considered a values approach similar to those already discussed, such as moral development or values clarification (see again Table 1.4).

As teachers, we are guilty of using indoctrination if we base our presentations on biased or incomplete data or if we do not allow students to question ideas offered as solutions to problems. Sometimes a teacher's motivation in such a case may be understandable or even admirable. He or she may not want students to express certain "wrong" ideas or opinions. Here's an example: Ms. Cherez wants the students in her class to collect funds for starving children in Africa. She would like to show a film or pictures demonstrating this great need. Ms. Cherez certainly does not want to receive comments from students suggesting that, according to their parents, donated money would be wasted because it would not get to the starving people or because developing nations should solve their own problems. If Ms. Cherez manipulates the discussion to prevent alternative opinions and comments, she is guilty of indoctrination—even if she feels it is indoctrination for a good cause.

However, the citizenship-transmission model of social studies often contains elements of indoctrination. One goal is to instill in students basic American values and not simply an understanding of those values themselves. In this process of cultural transmission, a teacher will emphasize the positive nature of our society's democratic values.

Many authorities want to teach children to be patriotic and to love their country. They want all students to know about our historical traditions and our nation's great

---

[10]James P. Shaver, "Commitment to Values and the Study of Social Problems in Citizenship Education," *Social Education 49* (March 1985): 194–197.

achievements and high ideals. How can this goal be achieved? Traditional methods include the recitation of the Pledge of Allegiance at the beginning of the school day, singing patriotic songs, and retelling legends and myths (e.g., George Washington never told a lie). Celebrating the birthdays of our presidents or outstanding citizens also makes children aware of the heroes and heroines of the nation's history. In these activities, teachers are not simply transmitting information from a textbook or a prepared curriculum guide; they are socializing for the desired value. Good literature or films can be used as well to invoke in students positive feelings about their heritage.

As students get older, however, they must begin to explore how the basic values of our nation should be interpreted to help solve the problems facing our society. The goal must be to create "good" citizens.

According to the citizenship-transmission tradition, social studies education has two main purposes: to instill in students a basic commitment to the values of our society and to help students develop an ability to *apply* those values to the issues facing our nation. Note that a vital component of our basic values is the application of rationality and critical thinking, or inquiry, especially among older children (see again Table 1.4).

Social Science/History

The social science/history model is a knowledge-centered approach that became popular in the 1960s, when a wide variety of new social studies curriculum projects were funded by various government agencies. Curriculum planners wanted students to understand how social scientists did their work and to grasp the major concepts of each social science discipline. For example, there were anthropology projects in which students were given actual artifacts from a particular culture and were instructed to study the objects and guess their purposes. In the study of history, students were taught the difference between primary and secondary sources. They might, for example, be provided with conflicting eye-witness reports of what happened on Lexington Green at the start of the American Revolution and be asked to compare these reports with the textbook description.

Social studies textbooks in the 1960s began to include more short selections from original source documents so that students might learn more about how historians actually go about writing history. Sociological Resources (the American Sociology Association's project for the social studies) designed inductive exercises in which students gathered data and then were led to form hypotheses from a more critical point of view. Students might be asked to complete sentences such as the following: "Parents are _____." "Rich people are _____." "Russians are _____." "Police are _____." Typically, students filled in the blanks with glib generalizations, often based on inadequate information, limited experience, and prejudiced views. After gathering data on the topics covered, they were made aware of their errors and assumptions. The goal of this kind of exercise was to show students how easily we all jump to conclusions rather than to treat general statements as hypotheses to be tested. These exercises also demonstrated how sociologists obtain data on stereotypes.

In some cases, the new curriculum projects focused on a single subject area—such as economics or anthropology—but in many cases they used an interdisciplinary approach such as Asian studies. On the whole, the new social studies curriculum projects included more sociology and anthropology than did more traditional approaches. But in the 1970s many questioned whether these new curriculum projects with their emphases on the structure of the social sciences were relevant. In numerous cases, students had difficulty with the reading and conceptual levels of these projects.

Reflective Inquiry

The social studies, when taught as reflective inquiry, emphasize the importance of motivating students to think. The teacher helps students use logical thinking and scientific investigation to decide on issues and values. One difficulty with this approach is the lack of a clear definition for **inquiry** or **reflective inquiry**. In general, with the inquiry approach, students engage in the process of discovering and thinking for themselves, weighing pros and cons, and interpreting the facts. Students are taught not merely to absorb or memorize materials but to evaluate them critically.

Reflective inquiry or analysis can be considered a value approach when students are helped to use rational, analytical processes in interrelating and conceptualizing their values (see again Table 1.4). The methods used for this values approach might include discussions requiring students to cite evidence, other analyses, and research to back their statements. For example, in a discussion of proposed health care plans, students might have to research the topic carefully, citing analogous cases and coming up with data to support their positions.

One variation is the **public issues–centered approach** in which units of instruction are organized around persisting public problems that are controversial—for example, the environment or poverty. Characteristics of this approach include an emphasis on in-depth understanding of a given topic, multiple points of view, insights from many fields of study, and skills in making decisions. Although more typically used in the middle grades and high school, if considerations are made for children's developmental level, younger students can learn as they study topics such as traffic congestion, drug dealing, water scarcity, or air pollution.

Another variation is the **real-world problems approach** in which thoughtfully designed, authentic learning experiences help students develop the understanding, skills, and values needed for success in school and beyond. This line of inquiry is associated with the authentic learning approach, the constructivist classroom, and performance assessment (discussed in Chapters 2–4). An example of a real-life project for students to tackle might follow this sequence: A group of students plans, prepares, and implements a way to assist the elderly in their community. Students might begin by asking questions: What do the elderly in the community need? What might our class do to enhance their lives? The class is structured so that students will understand what they are doing, why they are doing it, and how it relates to work in school and outside. Students have a chance to authentically exhibit their knowledge, skills, and attitudes during the whole project.

A Child-Centered Approach

The child-centered approach suggests that the purpose of social studies and other subjects should be student centered and directed toward personal development. The focus is on development of the student's unique potential by allowing for the fullest pursuit of creativity, personal integrity, love of learning, and self-fulfillment. Children should feel that they are competent and capable of making choices and that they can influence their own behavior as well as that of others. The child-centered approach, which concentrates more on the individual than on the needs of society, encourages children to gain an understanding of their own needs and to work with others to achieve their goals. This approach is sometimes followed by teachers in private schools.

Informed Social Criticism/Reform

Teachers following the informed social criticism/reform approach guide students to the understandings and the skills necessary to correct or to reform existing institutions in our world. Various perspectives—multiculturalism, feminism, global education, neo-Marxism—may be vehicles for organizing instruction. In general, students are challenged to critique the existing social institutions in our society using criteria such as justice, democracy, and human rights. Sometimes this approach is called critical theory or transformation theory.

Your Choice

Which of these five approaches or rationales (see again Table 1.5) do you prefer for teaching elementary social studies? Which model do you think reflects the most common practice in schools today? These questions may be difficult to answer because most teachers use some combination of all five approaches. They choose from various positions depending on the topic being taught. They do some indoctrination, especially of American values and patriotism, while also encouraging students to think about social policy issues. They teach one unit on a problem in the community using an inquiry approach and the next unit on local government using a traditional citizenship-transmission approach. Monday's lesson might be on making economic or consumer choices, whereas Tuesday's lesson might return to a structured textbook reading with questions at the end of the chapter.

You can see now that definitions of social studies content will vary depending on the value system or philosophical orientation of the teacher or curriculum planner. The citizenship-transmission approach tends to emphasize American history and our nation's high ideals and achievements. The social science/history approach uses content from the various social science disciplines and history with a view to understanding the major concepts and the respective methods of gathering data. The reflective-inquiry and informed social criticism/reform approaches use almost any content as long as it encourages thinking on the part of students.

ON YOUR OWN	MAKE A CHOICE
1.4	*Do you now have a tentative definition of the social studies? Which approach do you think is best for children? List the strengths and weaknesses of each model on a piece of paper. Which model do you think you would use most often in an elementary classroom?*

SMALL GROUP WORK	PARENT SURVEY
1.3	*Interview three parents and then three adults who do not have children in the schools. Ask them to define the social studies. Ask what they think the social studies should do for children. Bring your responses to class. What concerns does the public have about social studies education?*

Concerned parents, community members, and policymakers may be more concerned than some elementary teachers about which curriculum is implemented in elementary social studies classrooms. In fact, court cases indicate that many parents are very worried about the values and curriculum approaches that schools are using. Controversies over the adoption of social studies textbooks by districts confirm this indication. Some critics want a more traditional, fact-based history and are worried that their children are no longer learning the names of the presidents or significant dates in our history. Others want more diversity in the curriculum. Some states also had a bitter fight over social studies standards.

■ NATIONAL CURRICULUM PATTERNS

The United States has thousands of local school districts. Although each one is autonomous and can organize a curriculum to suit its own needs and meet state requirements, a national social studies curriculum exists. There are two reasons for this. First is the dominant role that textbooks have had in social studies instruction. In fifth- and eighth-grade classrooms across the nation, you will find in some form U.S. history being taught from books published by only a handful of large companies. About five probably control about 90 percent of the textbook market, which ensures a certain similarity in course offerings throughout the nation.

A second reason for national curriculum is that most teachers follow guidelines produced by their state, and the states have been influenced by the recommendations of the National Council for the Social Studies. In the past some state standards and frameworks were very broad, requiring only that history, geography, and the social sciences be taught in some manner from kindergarten through twelfth grade. The recent trend with the state standards-based reform is to provide standards with considerable detail for each or some grades.

State standards and frameworks in turn influence textbook publishers, who want as broad a market as possible. State frameworks of the largest states, particularly California and Texas, help to determine what focus textbooks have. For these interrelated reasons, we see a certain amount of uniformity in elementary social studies programs throughout the nation.

In 1980 Project SPAN (Social Studies: Priorities, Practices, and Needs, funded by the National Science Foundation) found the following social studies curriculum pattern in most U.S. schools:

Grade	Topics
Kindergarten/1	Self, family, school
2	Neighborhoods
3	Communities
4	State history, geographic regions
5	U.S. history, culture, and geography
6	World cultures, history, and geography
7	World cultures, history, and geography
8	U.S. history
9	Civics
10	World history
11	U.S. history
12	American government/problems of democracy

Is this the pattern that you followed when you were in school? The basic structure of social studies content at both elementary and secondary levels has changed little during the past fifty years, but a careful reading of the preceding list reveals some problems in the traditional social studies curriculum.

Notice first that U.S. history is taught at three grade levels. Too often all three courses are surveys, covering repeatedly everything from Columbus to the latest space shot. There is little differentiation of content and a minimal attempt to build from one course to the next.

How did this come about? It happened partially for historical reasons. In the early years of this country, children attended school for only a few years. Because it was important to teach children U.S. history before they ended their school careers, American history was taught in the fifth grade. Then, as more children remained in upper elementary school, the course was taught again in the eighth grade, just before students left school to go to work. Finally, as more students continued on through high school, educators again wanted to make sure that they remembered their U.S. history. So history was repeated in the eleventh grade.

Concerns about patriotism continue to favor the inclusion of the U.S. history in elementary and secondary schools. It would be unpopular for a local district or a state framework committee to suggest dropping a U.S. history course—how unpatriotic or un-American! Thus, the impact of tradition and patriotic concerns has led to the entrenchment of three separate U.S. history courses.

Notice also the problem area in the sixth and seventh grades. Both grades cover the same broad topics, but there is little agreement about what the content should be at these levels. In some schools, ancient civilization is taught in the sixth grade; in others, this topic is found at the seventh-grade level. Thus, world history/world cultures courses also have a similar problem of duplication as U.S. history courses. Usually the high school course covers everything again, from early human history to the latest world crisis.

Some social studies educators believe that the primary-grade topics are not sufficiently differentiated. The content is thin and redundant—repeating families and communities several times. Too often the textbook content is already known by students or likely to be learned through everyday experiences. Topics are stressed in the first, second, and third grades without new material being introduced or higher levels of thinking being required.

But perhaps the heaviest criticism of primary social studies content focuses on the "holiday curriculum." In many schools, holidays such as Thanksgiving, Christmas, Presidents' Day, Valentine's Day, Easter, and Mother's Day dictate what is covered in the primary social studies program. These holidays do offer the opportunity to explain much about our cultural heritage, but reliance on them suggests that many teachers feel more comfortable teaching these topics than ones that require more thoughtful preparation.

The holiday curriculum, however, need not be narrow. Holidays can be used as springboards for teaching about cultural diversity by showing how they are celebrated (or not celebrated) in this country and throughout the world. In many cases, though, holiday activities are simply repeated grade after grade, with little attention paid to learning beyond entertainment. Valuable social studies time is wasted. Furthermore, teachers are not always sensitive to the feelings of children from different backgrounds who may be offended or excluded by the holiday focus. In the same manner, children may not understand why particular religious holidays are not mentioned or are celebrated in ways unrelated to their religious meanings. The separation of church and state in the United States means that children may *learn* about different religions but religious beliefs may not be practiced in the classroom.

As you can see, there *is* a national social studies curriculum pattern. But your state's pattern may vary from this model in several ways. Each state generally requires that its own state history be taught at the fourth-grade level. Check on what your state recommends for the sixth- and seventh-grade levels as well. Information about social studies content guidelines can be obtained from your state department of education and the Internet. Your state may also have *legal requirements*—observance of holidays, positive and accurate portrayal of the roles of women and minority groups, or the protection and conservation of the environment—that dictate to some extent what will be taught in the social studies.

ON YOUR OWN	YOUR STATE CURRICULUM
1.5	*How does your state or local curriculum compare with the traditional social studies curriculum patterns? Is there more emphasis on diversity? On global education?*

■ IMPORTANCE OF TEXTBOOK SERIES

The adoption of textbooks has had a great influence on what is taught in elementary social studies. If you compare a new social studies textbook series with the one you had in elementary school, you will notice that today's textbooks are much more colorful and attractive.

There are other differences as well. Almost all textbook series now show pictures of a wide diversity of ethnic, gender, racial, and religious groups, in response to demands to eliminate racism and sexism in our society. The portrayal of the elderly and people with disabilities demonstrates an interest in presenting a more realistic view of American life. The primary social studies textbooks on the family now move beyond a traditional two-parent family; an illustration may show a mother remarrying with her two children looking on or a family headed by a mother, father, or grandparent.

Typically the large publishers offer a series (often called a *basal series*) of textbooks and related supplementary materials from kindergarten through grade 6 or 7. Even if you follow a basal series closely, you will have some choices about what you teach. One choice occurs at the fourth-grade level, where state history and geography are generally taught. The major publishers issue specially prepared state textbooks for large states, and regional books are available for smaller states. Smaller publishing firms may also offer state history textbooks.

The next choice occurs at the sixth- and seventh-grade levels. Because there is no standard curriculum pattern at these levels, publishers often offer two or more textbooks that can be used for either grade, thus providing a wide and varying range of topics—the Eastern Hemisphere, the Western Hemisphere, or the world, for example.

Far more supplementary material coordinated with the student textbook is now available than ever before. For kindergarten there normally is not a pupil textbook. Instead, the Big Book format is more widely used for the kindergarten as well as in the first and second grades. For all grades, there is a Teacher's Guide/Teacher's Edition. In addition, each primary grade now has available at least one set of literature books to purchase, some in the format of Big Books and others at the normal book size, including paperback books. All the rest of the grade levels have sets of literature books, adventure books, and library trade books correlated to the pupil text. For assessment there are unit tests, chapter tests, and performance assessments such as checklists. Technology abounds with music cassettes, videodiscs, videotapes, and CD-ROMs to enrich the delivery of content. Student workbooks, stickers, posters, and daily geography activities are all available. Teachers can even buy into a "Social Studies Center," which is updated monthly on their computer. There often is a Spanish edition to the materials and one publisher has summaries of the chapters in six languages.

Of course, all of the supplemental materials cost money as well as the initial purchase of the pupils' textbooks. Publishers' representatives informally state that if a teacher or district buys the supplemental materials, then the teacher is more likely to have and to use the materials. This will result in more time spent in achieving a better social studies program. But in many classrooms, teachers feel fortunate if they have enough pupil textbooks and a Teacher's Guide for their own use.

Some critics argue that the basal social studies textbooks are very similar. This concern may stem from the similarity of titles; the word *family,* for example, shows up frequently at the first-grade level. But a careful examination of the textbooks will show considerable differences. Some textbook series are better for slower learners. Others emphasize global education. Still others, although they bear recent copyright dates, really have changed very little from those of twenty years ago. Map skills are found in all textbooks, but some series also emphasize skills in reading, fact-finding, and thinking.

ON YOUR OWN	COMPARE THE SERIES
1.6	*At a curriculum library, examine three different social studies textbook series at one particular grade level. Note carefully what content is covered in the textbook. Also, look at the teacher's guide for suggestions on how to teach the program. How are the series similar? How are they different?*

Educators complain about overreliance on the textbook. Often it has been the only instructional tool used, and this limitation has resulted in narrow, restricted programs. Applied creatively, however, the textbook can be a very valuable resource. It is important for teachers and committees concerned with the selection of textbooks to look very carefully at the possible choices. There are many differences among the textbook series. The wide range of activities suggested in a teacher's guide may make a social studies textbook series unique. Teachers stuck with unsuitable textbooks for their classes work at a disadvantage in trying to provide a good social studies program.

■ MOUNTING CRITICISM: SCOPE AND SEQUENCE

Almost all elementary social studies textbooks use what is often called the **expanding communities pattern** or the **expanding horizons** or **widening world scope and sequence model.** All three terms are used interchangeably. **Scope** refers to the list of topics covered in a program. **Sequence** is the order in which these topics are covered. Usually, the two words are used together to indicate what is being taught, whether in the social studies or in any other area of the curriculum.

Scope and sequence issues are important. You need to know when students are ready for certain difficult concepts, such as time or chronology. Most primary students have great difficulty trying to imagine what life was like 2,000 years ago. They may think that we have always had television, airplanes, and cars. The eras B.C. and A.D. pose conceptual difficulty for most primary students. Determining at what grade level you might successfully try to teach time concepts is a scope and sequence issue.

The traditional scope and sequence pattern for the elementary grades—the expanding communities—is based on a consideration of the developmental needs of the child. Children usually learn better about real things and life around them than about abstract topics that they cannot see or feel. Therefore, the expanding communities concept begins where children are when they enter school. The focus in the primary grades is first the self, then families, communities, cities, the region, and finally the nation and the world (Figure 1.2).

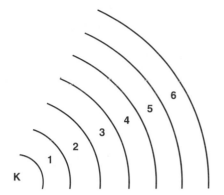

Key:

K	Self and Others	4	Regions
1	Families	5	United States and Canada
2	Communities	6	World
3	Cities		

FIGURE 1.2 The Expanding Horizons Curriculum

Source: Robert D. Barr, James L. Barth, and Samuel Shermis,
Defining the Social Studies, Bulletin 51. Reprinted with
permission of the National Council for the Social Studies.

This pattern of expanding communities made a lot of sense years ago. But at the present, with computers, mass media, and especially television, children are exposed to events and issues taking place far from their homes. Children also travel more. Primary-grade children are aware of international relationships and domestic crises, wars, terrorism, and pollution problems. They come to school with a greater knowledge of the world and a far wider range of interests than the expanding horizons curriculum envisioned.

Critics believe that the expanding horizons curriculum does not present an accurate view of the interrelationships among the different communities (e.g., family, local community, state, nation, and world). It may also discourage using current and controversial events that take place outside of the community being studied. For critics, the focus on the here and now can be replaced with other learning experiences if children can connect with the topic through personal experience or interest.

The 1990s were awash with new curriculum ideas. The national standards in history, geography, civics, and economics all stressed more attention to their respective fields including the primary-grade area. Some advocated a greater focus on children's literature integrated into the social studies curriculum whereas others wanted more integration of subject areas within a theme. Alternative assessment ideas also attracted attention. However, these recommended changes were all within the existing expanding horizons model.

Modifications of expanding horizons, however, were taking place in textbooks. In the first grade, information about families might include families in Israel and Zambia. A second-grade textbook on neighbors may focus on groups both in the United States and in other parts of the world. A topic such as where food comes from is more likely to expand into farming in other lands since the United States gets an increasing number of products from other parts of the world. Supplemental literature books usually stressed a multicultural/global emphasis as shown by books such as *Extra Cheese Please! Mozzarella's Journey from Cow to Pizza* and *Clothes from Many Lands.* In a similar manner, music cassettes focused on various cultures and time periods.

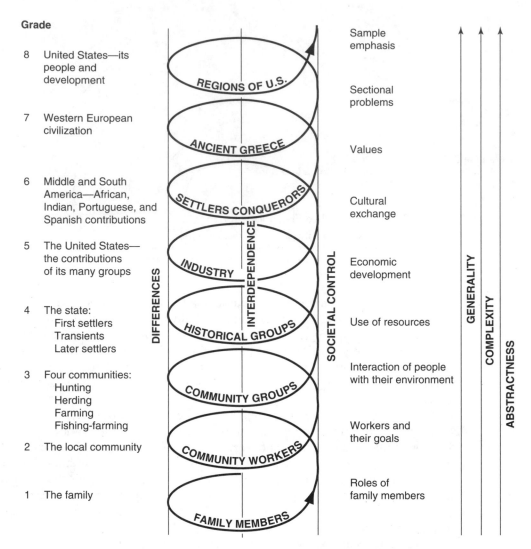

FIGURE 1.3 The Spiral of Concept Development

Source: Hilda Taba, Mary C. Durkin, Anthony H. McNaughton, and Jack R. Fraenkal. *A Teacher's Handbook to Elementary Social Studies,* 2nd ed. (Reading, MA: Addison-Wesley, 1971). Copyright © 1971 by Addison-Wesley Publishing Company. Used by permission of Pearson Education, Inc.

One older alternative pattern is the **spiral curriculum** advocated by Hilda Taba (see Figure 1.3). In this model, basic concepts and processes from the social sciences such as interdependence or cultural change are taught each year on a higher level of abstraction. For example, first-grade students might learn how families depend on one another for natural resources and manufactured goods. By the fourth grade, they might study the first pioneer families that settled in their state. Care must be taken in using this pattern to ensure that the topics are truly moving to higher levels and not just repeating topics such as "community workers" or "food." The spiral curriculum can be used to support the rationale for repeating U.S. history three times—each time it is taught at a more complex and more meaningful level. The NCSS ten learning themes are also an example of a spiral curriculum.

No matter what material you eventually teach, we would like to point out two important concerns: gender bias and the increasing number of different ethnic or racial minorities in many urban public schools. We must continually try to ensure that our social studies curriculum, as well as all school experiences, include women and minorities. Teachers who wish to improve student attitudes in these two areas should not limit themselves to a special unit taught once a year devoted to African American history, for example. The infusion of all assignments and materials with an antibias, pro-justice concern will have more impact than a once-a-year unit. In addition, you need to be very conscious of your own teaching behavior. Whom do you call on to answer questions? Who gets the hard-thinking questions? Far too often, teachers fall into patterns such as reinforcing boys to the detriment of girls and of not expecting high achievement from children of certain ethnic and racial groups.

SMALL GROUP WORK	**CHECK WHERE YOU STAND**
I.4	*Do you think any changes should be made in what is taught (topics) and when it is taught (specific grade levels)? Should there be a greater emphasis on certain disciplines such as history? Do you think the expanding community pattern is the best way to organize the elementary social studies curriculum?*

■ SUMMARY

A good social studies program should help students become informed citizens capable of making good decisions. Advocates of national and state standards encourage teachers and schools to strive for higher achievement and citizenship goals. The traditional social studies curriculum has been faulted by students, teachers, and reform reports as not being adequate to fulfill the goals of citizenship. The typical expanding community pattern that has been the basis of national curriculum patterns is presently under criticism. More history and geography in the elementary social studies curriculum is recommended. These trends are pushing educators to make the social studies in the elementary grades more challenging, with a greater number and depth of concepts and an inclusion of more content than what has traditionally been taught.

■ SUGGESTED READINGS AND WEB SITES ■

Barr, Robert D., James L. Barth, and S. Samuel Shermis. *Defining the Social Studies,* Bulletin 51. Washington, DC: National Council for the Social Studies, 1977.

Bennett, William J., ed. *The Book of Virtues.* New York: Simon & Schuster, 1997.

Hundreds of stories to help children understand and develop character. An example of building character education approach. See also Bennett's two other books: *The Book of Virtues for Young People: A Treasury of Great Moral Stories* (New York: Simon & Schuster, 1997) and *The Children's Book of Heroes* (New York: Simon & Schuster, 1997). Other advocates of the character education movement are the following: William Kilpatrick,

Why Johnny Can't Tell Right from Wrong (New York: Simon & Schuster, 1992); Thomas Lickona, *Educating for Character: How Our Schools Can Teach Respect & Responsibility* (New York: Bantam, 1992); Edward Wynne and Kevin Ryan, *Reclaiming Our Schools: A Handbook on Teaching Character, Academics, and Discipline* (New York: Macmillan, 1993).

Cuban, Larry. "History of Teaching in Social Studies." In James P. Shaver, ed., *Handbook of Research on Social Studies Teaching and Learning,* New York: Macmillan, 1991, pp. 197–209.

Summary of history of social studies teaching.

Evans, Ronald W., and David Warren Saxe, eds. *Handbook on Teaching Social Issues,* NCSS Bulletin 93. Washington, DC: National Council for the Social Studies, 1996.

Rationale and activities for issues-centered social studies.

Haas, Mary E., and Margaret A. Laughlin, eds. *Meeting the Standards: Social Studies Readings for K–6 Educators.* Washington, DC: National Council for the Social Studies, 1997.

Excellent source of journal articles designed to help teachers using the NCSS standards; other curriculum issues also discussed.

Jenness, David. *Making Sense of Social Studies.* New York: Macmillan, 1990.

A publication of the National Commission on Social Studies in the Schools.

Kaltsounis, Theodore. "Democracy's Challenge as the Foundation for Social Studies." *Theory and Research in Social Education* 22, no. 2 (Spring 1994): 176–193.

Democracy and democratic citizen education should be the logical foundation on which to structure the social studies program. Previous models of democratic education have failed.

Kirschenbaum, Howard. *100 Ways to Enhance Values and Morality in Schools and Youth Settings.* Boston: Allyn & Bacon, 1995.

Traditional methods for inculcating and modeling as well as the values clarification approach.

Munroe, Susan, and Terry Smith, The Casados Group. *State Geography Standards: An Appraisal of Geography Standards in 38 States and the District of Columbia.* Washington, DC: Thomas B. Fordham Foundation, 1998.

Authors funded by a conservative foundation find most state geography standards faulty.

National Commission on Social Studies in the Schools. *Charting a Course: Social Studies for the 21st Century.* New York: National Commission on Social Studies in the Schools, November 1989.

Rejection of expanding communities pattern by four organizations.

National Council for the Social Studies. "Fostering Civic Virtue: Character Education in the Social Studies." *Social Education* 61, no. 4 (April/May 1997): 225–227.

Policy statement on character education.

Noddings, Nel. *The Challenge to Care in Schools.* New York: Teachers College Press, 1992.

Alternative approaches to education organized around the theme of care.

Ryan, Kevin, and Karen Bohlin. *Building Character in Schools.* San Francisco, CA: Jossey-Bass, 1998.

Saxe, David Warren. *State History Standards: An Appraisal of Standards in 37 States and the District of Columbia.* Washington, DC: Thomas B. Fordham Foundation, 1998.

Author funded by a conservative foundation reviews state history standards and is very disappointed in their quality.

Social Education 49 (March 1985), article by S. Samuel Shermis and James L. Barth followed by response of James Shaver on indoctrination in the social studies.

Social Education 54 and 55 (November–December 1990 and January 1991), special issues devoted to pros and cons of *Charting a Course: Social Studies for the 21st Century.*

Task Force of the National Council for the Social Studies. *Expectations of Excellence: Curriculum Standards for Social Studies,* Bulletin 89. Washington, DC: National Council for the Social Studies, 1994.

NCSS's curriculum standards.

Journals

The three journals of social studies that teachers should become familiar with are *Social Education, Social Studies and the Young Learner,* and *The Social Studies.* In addition, publications such as *Learning* and *Instructor* may also have social studies materials.

Web Sites

Character Education Partnership

www.character.org

> Most important resource on character education maintained by Character Education Partnership. This site gives the eleven principles of effective character education plus other resources.

ERIC

http://ericir.syr.edu/Eric/

> ERIC is the world's largest source of education information with more than one million abstracts of documents and journal articles on education research and practice. For lesson plans in the social studies organized by subject area such as economics, geography, history, and so on, go to http://ericir.syr.edu/Virtual/Lessons/Social_St/index.html

National Council for the Social Studies

www.ncss.org

> Site of the most important organization in the field of social studies, the National Council for the Social Studies. Material on its associated groups, conferences, workshops, standards, and resources.

Chapter 2

Planning for Social Studies Instruction

The importance of planning for effective social studies teaching is emphasized in this chapter. Planning is organized into several steps including the unit approach, resource units, and lesson plans.

- Planning

- Goals, Long-Range Planning, and Standards/Instructional Objectives

- Treasury of Resources for Planning

- Units

- Lesson Plans

- Organizing and Scheduling

■ PLANNING

The teacher is the key to what the social studies program will be in any classroom. As a teacher, you will make many decisions: What units will you include during the year? How will you teach tomorrow's lesson on living in cities? In general, the more decisions you can make during the *planning stage*, the better prepared you will be. Your alternative is to make decisions on the spot, with a classroom full of students waiting for your instructions. Teachers need to do both daily as well as long-term planning.

How do you go about planning? First, assemble all available planning tools and resources. They include the following:

State standards and/or district curriculum guide(s)

Your adopted textbook, the teacher's guide, and ancillary materials

Media catalogs for your district and county

Computer resources including virtual field trips and simulations

Recommendations from your school media specialist (usually your librarian) for stories, trade books, reference books, map and globe collections

Ideas from other teachers in your school

Parent resources

Community resources, guest speakers, field trips, and local newspapers

Data on the background and ability of your students

Once your resources are assembled, you are able to begin making choices. Choose units and activities for which you have appropriate materials and which you think will interest your students and be appropriate for their backgrounds. It is equally important that you choose a program that interests *you*. Any lack of interest on your part will surely be conveyed to your students. Finally, prepare your plans in detail. Write down not only the names of the units you wish to cover but also the specific topics you plan to include and, if possible, some thoughts about how you will teach them.

Should you, as a beginning teacher, try to create original lesson plans or should you use plans designed by "experts" (e.g., textbook authors and curriculum designers)? Some local districts mandate that all teachers cover given units according to specific instructional modes. Other districts give teachers complete freedom to choose content and method of instruction. Most districts occupy a middle ground: They outline the general standards and content areas to be taught but allow flexibility for teachers to achieve content goals in any manner they wish.

Most beginners would panic at the thought of total freedom and move quickly to see how they could adapt an existing textbook program or other curriculum projects. Many experts would approve of this decision, arguing that often teachers, especially beginners, can best select and modify existing materials and ideas rather than try to create entirely new programs. This alternative makes better use of teacher time and is more likely to bring success. Developing an innovative social studies program on your own is difficult, and it ignores time-tested resources already available, including the teacher next door.

"Borrowing" creatively also provides for flexibility in your social studies program. Why, after all, do experienced teachers continue to attend conferences, workshops, and courses if not to get new ideas from other experts? Good teachers are continually modifying their programs, always on the alert for new and useful suggestions. In borrowing, however, you need to be certain that the new ideas and materials you adopt help you to achieve your desired objectives and that their appeal is not simply their newness.

SMALL GROUP WORK	YOUR CONCEPT OF PLANNING
2.1	*Concept maps are useful ways of organizing ideas. Jot down the words* teacher planning *in the center of a sheet of paper. Think of the various subtopics such as* lesson *or* books. *Now try drawing the relationships you see among the topics. Compare your concept map of teacher planning with the maps of others in your class.*

Sometimes elementary schoolteachers resist planning, especially writing out their plans, because they are so busy with immediate responsibilities—filling out forms, grading papers, checking homework. Planning is often a low-priority task. But there is an important psychological benefit to planning and especially to working out and writing down daily lesson plans: confidence. With a plan in front of you, you feel organized and prepared to face the class. A plan a day keeps disaster away! Planning can often help you anticipate management problems in the classroom, and it enables you to have better control of the situation.

Sometimes a new teacher will say, "I did a lot of planning for a lesson on our local transportation system, and the whole thing fell flat. But the next day I walked in 'cold' and taught a terrific lesson on neighborhoods. So why plan?" This can happen. Planned lessons do not always go as well as expected. Instead of abandoning planning, however, you should go over an unsuccessful lesson at the end of the day, when you are less emotionally involved. At what points did it go off track? Were the students bored? Unable to keep up? Confused? What actually was wrong with the lesson? Make notes on your lesson plan to help you with future planning. Using a word processor for your lesson plans is ideal because you can easily revise them. In effect, you are *reflecting* on your teaching, a highly approved method to improve your teaching.

Even if a lesson *is* successful, you should critique your written plan. What would have made the lesson better? Write down proposed changes so that you won't forget them. Having both the original plan and your notes on how to improve it will provide you with an ever-expanding resource file in years to come.

Good planners actively seek materials. You should systematically build your own collection or library of resources for teaching social studies. Continue this throughout your teaching career. Having a variety of unit plans and instructional resources for students will pay dividends. Organize your collection under standards or themes so that you can retrieve your resources as you need them.

Some teachers argue that planning encourages rigidity. Having a written plan, they suggest, prevents them from taking advantage of unexpected instructional opportunities. Serendipity is always welcome! Your lesson plan, however, is meant to be a guide, not a prison sentence. Always be ready to bend it to take advantage of student interest or some recent and unanticipated event.

You may find that you have no choice about writing out lesson plans. Some school districts and principals require teachers to submit lesson plans for the coming week throughout the year. Frequently, administrators ask only for brief statements of topics and textbook pages to be covered. Most plans written for administrators show very little detail. Written lesson plans are valuable to administrators if they need a substitute teacher for you or if there ever is a parent who challenges what you are teaching. The fact that a lesson plan must be submitted, however, acts as an incentive for many elementary teachers to plan ahead, if only to list the subject areas they will cover in a given week. Writing in topics under subject-area headings—science, social studies, math—may suggest areas of potential integration: How can language arts or science work with this week's social studies lessons?

There are often differences between what is listed on the plan handed in to an administrator and what actually goes on in the classroom. Some differences are inevitable, since lesson plans should always allow for flexibility. In a few cases, subjects are listed that are never taught. Frequently, this happens because the teacher does no planning in depth and, therefore, has no real plan to implement.

Successful planning needs to be detailed enough to help you organize what actually happens in the classroom. It is inaccurate to suggest that only drudges and drones plan; planning is a vital and basic skill for all effective teachers. Research indicates that teachers who plan are more likely to be satisfied with their teaching and are more likely to remain in the teaching profession. Poorly planned activities are frustrating to both teacher and students; valuable time wasted can never be recovered.

ON YOUR OWN	**ISSUES THAT AFFECT SOCIAL STUDIES PLANNING**
2.1	*Some of the many issues in curriculum planning that teachers think must consider are meeting the needs of an increasingly diverse student population, using technology in the classroom, and improving test scores. Note if these issues apply to where you are teaching or are expecting to teach.*

■ GOALS, LONG-RANGE PLANNING, AND STANDARDS/INSTRUCTIONAL OBJECTIVES

Let us now go through the process of planning a social studies curriculum following the outline in Figure 2.1. First, read carefully the standards or curriculum framework of your state and local district. These documents are published by your state education agency and/or your local school district. Then look at the framework's **goals,** which are the broad statements of desired outcomes.

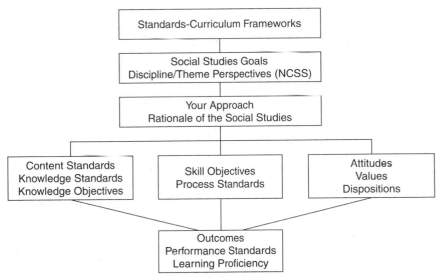

FIGURE 2.1 The Curriculum Planning Process

Promoting good citizenship, which is often found on district lists of educational goals, is also generally listed as a goal for social studies education. The social studies program does not have sole responsibility for teaching citizenship skills; other areas of the curriculum also contribute. But an elementary social studies program should be designed to do as much as possible to move students toward effective citizenship participation (see Chapter 7). As an elementary teacher, you will plan the entire day or most of the day for your students. In looking over the day's program, you will want to be alert to those activities that best promote both broad educational goals and specific goals of the social studies.

In Chapter 1, we mentioned the four basic social studies goals:

1. To acquire **knowledge** from the social sciences, history, and humanities
2. To develop **skills** to think and to process information
3. To develop appropriate democratic **values** and **attitudes**
4. To have opportunities for **citizenship/social participation**

In some states, instead of the term *goal*, **guiding question** or **fundamental question** is used. These interchangeable terms identify what is to be learned at a broad level. Regardless of the terms used, almost all districts have some set of general goals (lifelong learning skills and habits, health, responsible behavior at school, etc.) as well as goals for certain subjects.

These goals provide the framework for planning in the social studies and also fit easily into the general goals of most states and school districts. In some cases, the Ten Themes of the National Council for the Social Studies (NCSS) or the goals and standards of the separate social science/history disciplines might be included because they often list the key discipline concepts on which the social studies curriculum should focus.

The problem with goals is that they are so broadly stated that any social activity you plan to teach could be listed under at least one of them. Goals are useful in defining broad objectives but they lack the specificity necessary for effective day-to-day teaching.

Long-Range Planning

Most elementary teachers begin social studies planning by roughing out an outline of the entire curriculum. Given the number of weeks in the school year, how would you divide the subject matter normally covered in, say, the second grade? What would be the most important ideas or concepts? What would make reasonable, manageable sections?

Many teachers when planning for the year like to make a list under the three headings of Social Studies, Language Arts, and Science. As they think about the months of September and October, they see if correlations offer any possibilities such as literature selections or science experiments. As teachers do monthly planning, they again see if other subject areas can be correlated with standards, learning activities, and resources.

As you do this, your own approach or rationale to the social studies comes into play, whether it is conscious or not (Chapter 1). This affects how you make some decisions: Will you select only certain units from the textbook, or will you try to cover all of them? Will you use the district's curriculum guidelines, or will some of your units be from specific curriculum packages—an economic unit on choices, perhaps? Once you begin to make these basic determinations—what you will cover and how much time you will devote to each topic—you can focus your attention on the individual chunks of time, frequently called **units**. Long-range planning is vital because there is usually far more content (and resource material) available than there is time to teach it. Your first step is to examine what must be taught, according to state or local standards, at your particular grade level. Usually, grade-level standards are broad. What other criteria could you use for selecting topics for a year-long curriculum? You should consider all of the following:

National, state, district standards/frameworks/guides

The adopted textbook

Tradition (e.g., last year's units in your school)

State-mandated tests

What other teachers in your school are doing

Personal teaching style/strengths

Resources (books, media, speakers, etc.)

Suggestions from parents

Potential management problems

Need for efficient use of time in planning and developing materials

Student needs (children's ability, etc.)

Social studies experts' recommendations and standards

Your philosophy of education

We include the adopted textbook as a prime resource for instructional planning, acknowledging and agreeing with the criticisms leveled at textbook-centered teaching. In our view, a good program needs structure and topical direction. Most textbooks provide this. Taking advantage of the content outline, activities suggested, and enrichment ideas need not condemn you to a rigid chapter-by-chapter, lesson-by-lesson coverage. Instead of thinking of the text as a novel to be read from beginning to end, we need to see the text as a tool to help us conceptualize and speed up our long-range planning. If you use the textbook as your main guide in long-range curriculum planning, you should typically follow these steps:

1. Skim the text, looking at broad unit titles. Decide which ones you will use. (The author's recommendations about how much time a unit will typically take may be helpful.)
2. Decide which units will receive major emphasis or minor emphasis.
3. Examine the teacher's guide. Look for activities for you and your students.
4. Find other activities to supplement the text. The teacher's guide may suggest some; the publisher may also provide other materials, such as literature books.
5. Decide whether you will use the tests supplied by the publisher for evaluation.

Because a major part of your long-range planning will be done early in the school year or even before it begins, you probably won't know your students' full range of talents and abilities. Once you begin to learn more about your students, you will need to modify the learning activities in your curriculum to fit your classroom, where student abilities may range from those of special education students to the gifted. Following constructionist ideas, you will want to find out your students' prior knowledge. What do they already know about a topic or idea and what do they want to learn about it? Some teachers involve students in planning what is to be learned.

Content Standards and Instructional Objectives

Whereas a *goal* is a broad statement of purpose, *content standard* or *instructional objective* is a specific accomplishment that you want your students to achieve in a specific period. Often the terms *knowledge objective, knowledge standard, standard, content standard,* and *instructional objective* are used interchangeably. The standards movement has greatly increased the number of educational terms because states often have used different terms.

You know that a well-written objective specifies the level of acceptable performance and the conditions under which a student must perform. Typically, objectives are focused on specific content mastery or skills that are more easily measured or evaluated. Many teacher-training institutions advise their students to use Bloom's taxonomy. For many state standards the objectives are listed but without the level of acceptable performance necessary on the part of the students.

You are no doubt familiar with the general process of curriculum planning. Typically, there are three main questions to answer:

1. What are your objectives or standards?
2. What learning experiences will be used to achieve the desired objectives?
3. What evaluation procedures will be used to determine whether the objectives have been achieved?

You hear the term **alignment** more often. Pleas are made to teachers to align classroom instruction to the state/district standards in methods, materials, and assignments. Administrators want to ensure that all students are developing the knowledge and skills needed to meet the standards. In many cases, professional development is provided to help teachers in this process. This may indirectly reflect the desire to have higher test scores.

There is now also more attention given to the goal that objectives, instruction, and evaluation should all be connected or coordinated with each other. This is called **curriculum alignment**—meaning that both instruction and evaluation should be based on the objectives. Poor alignment can occur because of various circumstances—for example, when the objective is improved thinking skills but the learning activities do not involve the students in thinking, or when the objective is improved thinking but the students are tested with low-level factual questions that do not assess their thinking skills.

FIGURE 2.2 Instructional Cycle

As an example of the cycle in Figure 2.2 in the primary grades your **objectives** in a law-related education/citizenship education unit would be:

- To understand the need for rules and laws
- To understand the need for fair consequences for inappropriate behavior
- To develop rules appropriate in a given situation

Your activity to accomplish these objectives is to read *Goldilocks and the Three Bears* (any of the many versions) to the class. As an introduction to the story, have students make a sad face on one side of a paper plate. Tell them that you are going to read the story *Goldilocks and the Three Bears* and that they should raise a sad face each time Goldilocks does something they believe she should not do.

As you read the story, you notice that many children do not raise a sad face (the assessment) when Goldilocks does something wrong, such as entering someone's house without permission, breaking the chair, sleeping on the bed, and running away without an apology. This assessment/feedback alerts you to the fact that perhaps some of the students enjoy the charm of this old classic, especially as you change your voice for the three bears' dialogue, but they really do not understand the need for rules and laws.

This assessment/feedback leads you to engage the students in a discussion listing on the board what Goldilocks did wrong and why it is wrong. Ask students to suggest a fair penalty for each wrong action. Should Goldilocks's parents be involved? Does the fact that Goldilocks was hungry and tired excuse her actions?

As another activity, you might as an extension read another classic, *Jack and the Beanstalk*. Again ask if Jack did anything wrong. Has the giant done anything wrong. Discuss what has happened from the giant's point of view. Again the instructional cycle is repeated: the same objectives, activities of reading the story and discussion, with evaluation of students' responses to see if they truly understand the objectives. As another activity you could also discuss a variety of situations on "What's Fair." Some of these could be experiences from your own students. You could also ask the students to give a report card grade (A to F) on how good the characters were. You would then make an assessment based on students' responses to see if further changes in the curriculum were needed. Perhaps the objectives need to be modified if students still do not see that Goldilocks or other characters did anything wrong. New objectives would be formulated based on the previous feedback. Or you could conclude that the objectives for your students had been achieved.[1]

Evaluation/assessment should be both aligned and an integral part of the learning experience (Figure 2.2). It may occur during a given day's lesson. If assessment is embedded within a lesson, students receive immediate feedback and can better understand that testing is part of learning and that it is to their advantage to recognize their strengths and weaknesses.

[1] The activity described was adapted from *Goldilocks, The Trial*, video and leader's manual (Maryland State Bar Association, 1990).

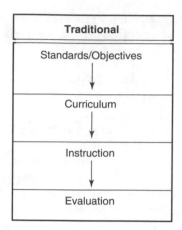
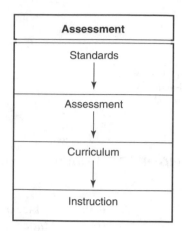

FIGURE 2.3 Planning Models

A more innovative approach is to turn the traditional planning model upside down (Figure 2.3). Let's see how this would work. Assume that you have chosen the following standard for your second graders.

West Virginia's History Standard 2.20

Investigate change over time that has occurred in the community.

This standard or closely related standards are found in almost all state standards. For example, California has the following Grade Three Standards:

Grade Three California Standard 3.3

Students draw from historical and community resources to organize the sequence of local historical events and describe how each period of settlement left its mark on the land.

Grade Three California Standard 3.5

Students demonstrate basic economic reasoning skills and an understanding of the economy of the local region.

Using West Virginia's standard, you must now decide what assessment you will use to determine whether your students have achieved this standard. You think that having the students produce a Community Almanac is a good idea. This will also fit in with literacy needs as well as using other standards for the social studies. In effect, the product, the Community Almanac, will be the assessment tool of how well students have achieved this specific history standard as well as other standards.

You have to make some additional decisions about the unit. First, you decide that you will limit changes in your community from 1940 to the present. Otherwise, the "Long Ago" period is confusing; students may think of the American Revolutionary War period or the Civil War, which are more popular images from the media for students. Choosing 1940 to the present also allows you to get data (maps, newspapers, etc.) more easily than for earlier periods. Using 1940 as a benchmark means also that students can interview older, long-term community members to gain data.

What activities will have to be done to achieve the standard? Students will learn that an almanac is a publication of miscellaneous information. You will share with them samples of different almanacs such as *The World Almanac* and *The Farmer's Almanac*. In addition, you need to write to parents that their help is needed for the Community Almanac project with photographs of their family and the community. Students then will be divided into groups and each group will produce two or three pages, including photographs, about their topic for the Community Almanac.

Here are some topics and in parentheses are concepts that students will use to compare the changes from 1940 to the present:

1940	Present
Population (migration/ movement of people)	
Land Use (human–land relationships)	
Transportation (economics, technology)	
Businesses (economic systems)	
Clothing (culture)	
Recreation (culture)	
Homes and Appliances (culture, human and environmental relationships)	
Time Line of Important National and International Events Such as World War II (change)	

Although the students will all have learning experiences in history as they compare the changes from 1940 to the present, you can see that students in this unit will also learn about other social studies standards and concepts as well as literacy skills. Thus, starting with selecting a specific standard and then choosing the type of assessment will lead into the topical development of the curriculum and instruction for this unit.

Let us review the steps we made in this example.

1. *Standard Number and Description* (in some states more description is given).
2. *Essential Key Concepts and Skills for This Standard.* The most important concepts are change, a history concept, and community, a civics concept. Skills include research skills for gathering a variety of primary sources for student topics, reading maps, interpreting photographs, constructing time lines, using the Yellow Pages to find specific types of businesses, working cooperatively in groups, and writing.
3. *Secondary or Optional Topics for This Standard.* Economic and geography standards are also used for the student topics such as location, land use and the relationship between geographic factors, available resources, and transportation in determining how people make a living.
4. *Interdisciplinary Opportunities/Connection.* Strong connection with writing.

TABLE 2.1 Los Angeles Unified School District

Guidelines for Developing a Standards-Based Instruction Model

1. *Culminating Task/Assignment.* What will the individual **student** produce to demonstrate achievement of the standard(s)? Begin the task with a verb. The student *will.* . . .

2. *Assessment.* What criteria will be used to evaluate/score **student** work/performance of the culminating task? The statement of the product to be scored is followed by a verb. Task to be scored by four levels (highest score to lowest score).

3. *Instructional Activities.* What learning activities will the student be involved in to acquire content knowledge and skills to achieve the standard? Consider alternative strategies and modifications to promote equal access for all learners. Begin each learning activity with a verb describing what the student is to do.

4. *Time.* How much time will be required for the **student** to complete each of the activities?

5. *Resources.* What materials, textbooks, supplies, documents, and so on will support the **student** doing each instructional activity?

Source: Model developed, refined, and field-tested by Task Force on Standards-Based Instruction (no date).

Of course, some districts will request even more detail. Examine the Los Angeles Unified School District Guidelines (Table 2.1). Whew! After glancing at the Los Angeles Unified School District's Standards-Based Instruction Model, do you want to teach there? It will take time to design an instructional unit using this standards-based instruction model. However, with such detailed planning and sharp focus, there is also a much better chance that the students will learn more. Note that this model is a combination of new ideas about standards and assessment with the older practice of instructional objectives using clearly defined verbs (e.g., student *will identify* . . . or student *will compare* . . .). In some schools, specific state standards are used instead of objectives. This appears to be a growing trend.

ON YOUR OWN	**EXPLORING POINTS OF VIEW**
2.2	*Do you like using state standards as a tool in curriculum planning? Jot down your thoughts, pro and con, about this approach to curriculum planning.*

■ TREASURY OF RESOURCES FOR PLANNING

In thinking about objectives, can you identify any factors unique to the field of social studies that should be considered in planning? Students and their families, the community, and other resources may help you with better planning of your social studies program.

Student, Parent, and Family Resources

Because the social studies are about people, students and their families can often be used as resources. A grandmother may be able to tell what it was like to live on a farm fifty years ago. A parent may be able to describe his or her job when the class is studying community workers or the job market. A student may have lived in another part of the country or the world. There may be artifacts from different nations in the homes of students that would be of interest to the class. Many teachers find that these resources add sparkle to the class. Use special events such as open house and media presentations by the class to talk to and ask for help from parents. Try newsletters or e-mails to parents outlining what is going to be covered in the coming social studies unit and asking if they can help in any way.

Community Resources

The community is the neighborhood beyond the family. There are three important community resources: local publications, field trips, and guest speakers. Use the community as a resource for field trips, especially if the students are able to walk to see something such as the local bakery or police station. If this is not feasible, resource people from the community (e.g., probation officers or park rangers) can come to the classroom. Community resources can also include free local newspapers or materials from the local bank or other community institutions, especially government agencies. In particular, community programs such as Healthy Start, After School Partnerships, Healthy Kids, and School-Health Connections desire more cooperation and attention from the school in their goal to improve the health of all children.

Your school may also have a partnership arrangement with a local company or institution such as the local college or university. This can be an important resource because the partnership often provides funds, tutors, and other resources. Explore in what ways the partnership could help your class. To be successful, however, partnerships must be a two-way street. Both sides need to contribute. Students should not just be on the receiving side. For example, can the teacher and the students put together a short musical performance or skit for the other half of the partnership? Communication with the partner as well as parents can also be increased by e-mail and Web sites of the school or the individual class.

In addition, students can serve the community in projects ranging from helping senior citizens to cleaning up local parks. Community service provides a bridge between students and the community and can be an important resource in building toward the goal of citizenship (see Chapter 7). Be certain to clear such projects with your school principal.

Media Resources

You need to look carefully at the videos, photographs, slides, and television series that can be obtained in your district. Typically, the sooner your order is placed, the better will be your chance of securing the items because other teachers also may want to use these resources. These media, especially with visual components, can add meaning to otherwise abstract ideas that a teacher's voice cannot provide. New technology such as the digital versatile disk (DVD) or digital video disk is also becoming more available, adding an additional resource to enrich your teaching (see Chapter 10).

Free or inexpensive posters and other materials may be obtained from the consulates of foreign nations in large U.S. cities. Order the materials as early in the school year as possible to allow time for shipment, and make arrangements well in advance for speakers, especially those on tight schedules, such as government officials.

Current Events/Current Affairs

The social studies are unique among elementary-school subjects because they deal with events that are continually happening in the local community and the wider world that have an impact on students and their families. Often these events are directly relevant to what you are trying to achieve in your social studies program. The goal of encouraging social participation in community affairs should lead you to consider how current events can be used to enrich the social studies program.

Weekly papers, prepared by publishers at the appropriate reading levels for students in different grades, can be helpful. But in real life, newspapers, magazines, and television are not as neatly balanced and objective as educational products, and students eventually need to become familiar with regular news reports. In addition, students living in an environment dominated by television must understand what the news reporters on television are talking about. Discussions on television are often incomplete. Students need more background to understand the issues. Also, television news is frequently weak on analysis. Teachers must teach students to understand how all elements of the mass media including the Internet are important and how the students can analyze the messages that are being given and received.

All these elements make the social studies unique among subject areas and should be part of your consideration in planning. See Chapter 6 for more detail on teaching current events/current affairs.

■ UNITS

A **unit** is the unifying structure with a focus around which lessons and assessment are prepared. Basically it is time allocated to teaching a major subdivision in the year's course. The unit is a plan that organizes a sequential progression of lessons related in theme, topic, issue, or problem, as well as how assessment will be handled. Typically, a social studies unit covers the main concepts of a particular subject area. In addition, the unit has provisions for teaching skills, values, and, if possible, social participation. A unit consists of three parts: (1) an introductory activity designed to activate students' prior knowledge and to stimulate interest; (2) a series of sequenced lesson plans; and (3) one or more culminating activities that reinforce, bring closure to the unit, and allow students to demonstrate what they have learned. Using this planning model, teachers can determine student strengths and weaknesses in the context of daily learning activities rather than waiting for the unit test/assessment.

Why do experts recommend teaching in units? Students learn less if on Monday they have a map exercise on latitude and longitude, on Tuesday they have a value exercise on twenty things they love to do, on Wednesday they visit their local fire department, on Thursday they read their social studies textbook on Native American tribes in the northeastern part of the United States, and on Friday they study current events. Each lesson may be worthwhile by itself, but the lessons do not build sequentially. A unit should tie skills and knowledge together under a theme so that learning is not isolated and fragmented. Learning is more likely to take place when topics are not fragmented or isolated. Learning takes place when we introduce a unit, have a progression of lessons to develop a theme, and conclude with an activity. We can characterize the many different types of units as textbook units, commercial units, and teacher-prepared units.

Textbook units are found in most texts in use today. Almost all social studies textbooks are organized by major units such as *Africa Today* or *The New Nation Faces Many Problems*. There are usually several big units in the book and under each unit are several chapters. Then within each chapter are several daily lessons. The publishers generally predict or project a given time for how long a unit will last and offer many suggestions for teaching or enriching the unit. Probably the greatest advantage to using the units in the textbook is that they reduce the amount of planning a teacher needs to do, especially if the teacher's background in the content is not strong or current. However, we should use textbooks with caution. Some students may not be able to read the textbook, or they may find the concepts are described too briefly, making the ideas seem artificial and abstract. Often the textbook's lessons and chapters are written in a repetitive format, requiring students to read and answer questions posed by the textbook. The students' reaction: boring, boring, boring. With few hands-on experiences or discussion of the topics, the social studies program is lackluster.

Textbook units cannot accomplish every aspect of planning in the classroom. Specifically, they may cause teachers to make the following instructional errors:

- Teacher makes all the decisions on what will be learned and when.
- All students must learn the same body of knowledge despite individual differences, prior learning, culture, and disabilities.
- Students do not always understand the purpose of an assignment.
- Texts may encourage fragmented connections with other subject areas.
- Content is not connected with students' interests and experiences.
- Texts may encourage the teachers to ask lower-level factual questions based only on the textbook.
- Texts may not focus on changes and problems in the students' real-life community.
- Students will see social studies as just facts and figures from a textbook.
- Texts may not be related to state and local standards.

Commercial units are similar to textbook units but are prepared by a specific group. For example, the Anti-Defamation League has prepared workbook units with the objective of reducing bias and discrimination in our society. Professional organizations also make units available for a fee. The Social Science Education Consortium, P. O. Box 21270, Boulder, CO 80308-4270, FAX: (303) 449-3925, phone (303) 492–8154, has many publications helpful to teachers. One of its publications, *C Is for Citizenship: Children's Literature and Civic Understanding,* has three thematic citizenship units based on children's literature along with detailed guides for using twenty literary works. The units incorporate such teaching strategies as a simulated talk show, small group discussion, and art projects that show the value of freedom of expression. The National Center for History in the Schools, University of California, Los Angeles, CA, 90024-4108, FAX: (310) 825-4723 sells units developed by teachers who have spent a summer developing and then trying out units. Units are also available from the ERIC Clearinghouse for Social Studies/Social Science Education, Indiana University, 2805 East 10 Street, Bloomington, IN 47408. Web site information for all three sources is found at the end of this chapter.

Often these commercial units are designed by teachers or consultants who are trying to meet a special curriculum need or a desire of the sponsoring group to get its point of view into the classroom. For example, changes in population and new state curriculum directions may suddenly ask sixth-grade teachers to cover Islam, a topic that has rapidly achieved high interest and importance. Many experienced teachers would feel unprepared to teach a unit on Islam or other unfamiliar topics. They are often willing to pay or have the district pay for a unit that can specifically help them to include a topic new to them in their program. Buying commercial units is common in the teaching of novels, especially classics such as *The Adventures of Tom Sawyer* and *Little House on the Prairie.* One company, Novel Units, has over three hundred titles, each available with vocabulary words, comprehension questions, and activities. If a teacher is trying to integrate literature with a social studies unit on the American antebellum period, he or she may be eager to buy a unit that summarizes a novel's chapters, gives good evaluation questions, and shows how to integrate the novel into a social studies unit. Groups such as those trying to introduce more economic education into the curriculum may find one of the easiest ways to do so is to produce a unit that teachers can immediately implement.

Commercial units, often free, are also produced by associations or companies with the goal of exposing students indirectly to the organization's ideas. Organizations ranging from the Dairy Council to the National Association of Newspaper Editors and the National Rifle Association produce units and free or inexpensive instructional materials. For example, Procter & Gamble for years has produced social studies units on ecology, the economy, and advertising. These free materials may include reproducible lessons, videos, teaching tips for each lesson, and colorful posters. A teacher, of course, needs to be aware that a given company may be introducing subtle bias into the unit and should carefully alert students to the source of the data. Commercially sponsored units or kits are especially common in the areas of nutrition, the environment, and the economy.

Teachers can develop or adopt from a variety of resources to organize their own units. Unlike the typical textbook or commercial units, *teacher-prepared units* can be based on the concepts, generalizations, and themes generated by the social sciences. For example, economics focuses on how individuals and groups use the resources available to them. Therefore, both individuals and groups make economic decisions every day. Using this major economic generalization, a teacher can ask primary students to keep track of what they spend their money on during a given time period. Then they can classify which expenditures were for goods and which ones were for services. Which is the larger category? Children often see their parents paying by check or money when they buy goods, but they seldom see them pay for the dentist, and they are even less likely to realize that their families pay indirectly through taxes for public services such as those given by teachers or other employees of the schools. Children can be asked to list people who provide services that are paid for by taxes. Shifting from services to goods, students can classify the materials that were used to produce the goods they purchased, such as candy bars, or the tools that workers used to deliver services. For example, what resources are needed to make candy or bread? Another resource is time. How are students spending their time when they are out of school? What choices are they making? What are the implications of their research? What do the data reveal about themselves and their community? This one economic generalization can lead to a variety of interesting lessons focused on the children's lives while also helping the children make sense of the complex world in which they live. Most textbook or commercial units would not be as focused on the lives of the students and their communities as would be possible with a teacher-made unit.

Teachers can experience several advantages from making their own units:

- Having a sense of ownership and pride in the unit if it is successful.
- Integrating the curriculum easily across subject areas because the teacher knows what will be taught during the rest of the day and can link subject areas.
- Individualizing the unit to match students' abilities and experiences.
- Using the teacher's own talents and experiences.
- Using local community resources.

Integrated Curriculum/Interdisciplinary Thematic Units

The Debate About Integrated Curriculum

The popularity of **curriculum integration** may be declining at the present time. One reason is that many state social studies standards are divided into specific, separate social science disciplines such as history, geography, economics, and civics instead of social studies themes (Chapters 5 and 6). In these states, the focus is on teaching the important knowledge and methods of the specific academic discipline such as history or geography and not on the integration of academic disciplines. Another reason is that the teaching of reading and math is seen by many as skills subjects that need to be taught separately. Reading and math are tested whereas an integrated curriculum is not tested.

This contrasts with the philosophy of **interdisciplinary thematic units,** which typically try to combine history and the social sciences with other academic subjects such as science, literature, music, arts, and other areas. An interdisciplinary thematic unit has a theme (or concept or generalization) that organizes the learning around the central ideas. Thus, in an integrative social studies unit, reading/language arts and mathematics are not seen as ends in themselves but should become tools students use to study the social studies content. Thus, some skill development in these subjects flows from the tools needed in the unit, such as reading the text or reference books and newspapers, lending to a more natural sequence of instruction. Thus, advocates of integrated curriculum want to avoid the compartmentalization in which subjects are taught during the day without students making connections about what they are learning. In other words, too often the science unit on plants or energy is not related to what students are learning about pioneer families' food production and their preparation of food. In addition, integration helps to cut down the "bloated curriculum" of the many different subject areas.

In an interdisciplinary approach, subjects are interwoven instead of being taught as separate subjects at different times of the day. This approach also goes by a variety of other names: *integrated curriculum, interdisciplinary curriculum, thematic instruction, multidisciplinary teaching,* and *integrated studies.* The terms *integrated curriculum* and *integrated instruction* are also used interchangeably. All of these terms and synonyms refer to a way of planning and teaching so that the separate disciplines are brought together in a meaningful unit.

Critics such as Brophy and Alleman[2] have raised questions about whether curriculum integration is a boom or a threat to social studies. They are concerned that social studies goals get lost in the process of integration and academic content is trivialized. In particular, important content is not taught when students read a literature book about an immigrant family or the Civil War and, thus, students do not have the background to understand why the historical events in the book are occurring. In other words, sometimes in practice an integrated curriculum often avoids difficult content and low-quality learning experiences are the result.

Another concern about integrated curriculum is that it leads to confusion on the part of students because they only partly understand the various subject disciplines introduced. For example, in studying about Benjamin Franklin, students may not understand enough about electricity to appreciate Franklin's experiments with electricity or have enough background in American history to comprehend Franklin's important roles before and during the American Revolution and his crusade in later life against slavery. He was just someone flying a kite during a storm. In some classrooms, Franklin might be best studied with the emphasis on the historical period.

These criticisms of integrated curriculum are worth taking seriously. There is little research presently on student learning from integration. The whole point of an integrated unit is how students' learning can best be encouraged. Does this happen most of the time? For example, a fifth-grade class studied a unit on the American Revolution by reading theme literature, but the students could not tell which side was victorious in the American Revolution. It did not appear that the students learned much

[2]Jere E. Brophy, and Janet Alleman, "Is Curriculum Integration a Boom or a Threat to Social Studies?" *Social Education* 57, no. 6 (1993): 287–291.

about history. A strong argument can be made that each discipline or school subject has important contributions to make to student learning and that an integrated unit is not always desirable.

These comments emphasize that during a given year all units do not have to be integrated or need to be taught as separate subjects. Professional judgment is necessary to evaluate when it is best to integrate a unit and how much integration is needed. Good interdisciplinary thematic units have many advantages if they are well thought out and result in high student interest and achievement. Normally in the social studies some degree of reading, listening, and writing is found. These skills then can be infused into the social studies unit. In many cases, social studies is the most logical area for integration of a theme. Reading/language arts as well as art and drama are often easily incorporated into an interdisciplinary thematic unit. But at times it is artificial to try to integrate a subject or subjects into a theme and the results are a jumbled mess in terms of students losing sight of what the theme or central idea is.

How are thematic units put together? In practice, units are integrated in varying degrees—ranging from some that are barely blended to completely integrated units with no subject boundaries.

Designing Integrated Units

Let us look at a possible primary grade topic: transportation. The major theme or generalization is that transportation is moving people or things from one place to another.

Sometimes changing the theme into a question makes planning easier. What kinds of transportation exist in the world today? By brainstorming ideas that fit this broad question, you will develop a list of concepts, definitions, and questions relating to the theme. Here are some possibilities:

Animals that provide transportation

People power, such as walking

Machines that provide transportation

Transportation on land, air, and water; different kinds; classification

Why it is important to have good transportation

Safety—roads and highways—traffic rules and signs

What is a vehicle? A wheeled vehicle?

What makes a vehicle run or go?

Trucks

Trains

Some teachers like to think in terms of subjects. How might art contribute to the theme? Science? Math? Language arts?

The next step is to look over these ideas. Which ones seem logically connected with each other? Drawing these connections on a large sheet of paper using the technique of schematic webbing will help you visualize ways that topics can be linked and sequenced. Once the topics or questions are diagrammed, the next step is to focus on what objectives you wish to achieve from the unit. They might be as follows:

1. Students will identify examples of transportation on land, air, and water (a content objective).
2. Students will create a graph of the different types of transportation their families use within a week (a skill objective).
3. Students will give reasons why it is important to have a transportation system in their community (content and appreciation objective).

Once the objectives are sketched, the next task is to think of all the learning activities and resources that will help develop each objective. Trade books, songs, tapes, and records need to be surveyed as a first step. You can then list other resources and activities:

- Possible guest speakers such as female pilots and male visiting nurses
- Class surveys of different transportation used by students
- Field trips to airports and truck depots to see these systems in operation
- Observation and discussion of correct ways of crossing streets
- Figuring out distances to school
- Getting lost, or the value of helpful maps

You can add a lot more. The difficulty usually comes in deciding when to stop and selecting the ideas you will use.

This type of unit would have the usual introductory activities as well as a final culmination activity. The learning activities and resources come from a variety of academic areas. With no artificial divisions between time periods in the classroom, students can put together and reconstruct their own ideas more easily. Students can express their ideas through dramatization, writing projects, visual arts, or music. Assessment and evaluation could include portfolios of student-produced projects and anecdotal records as well as paper-and-pencil tests.

The formal process for developing interdisciplinary thematic units can be summarized in a few logical steps:

1. Select a theme/important idea.
2. Brainstorm different ideas, activities, and resources that fit the theme.
3. Formulate unit objectives.
4. Locate resources.
5. Organize activities that allow students to make connections among ideas and experiences.
6. Evaluate and assess progress and achievement (may be done throughout the unit).

The sample unit plan "Grasslands: A National Resource" is an example of how the geography standard, *Places and Regions,* used Grasslands as an interdisciplinary unit. One key concept for the students to learn is *region,* an area with one or more common characteristics or features that give it a measure of unity and make it different from the surrounding areas.

Look carefully at this briefly sketched unit. Do you like it? Is it a good interdisciplinary unit? Its strengths are that the assessment is built into the learning experiences and is not divorced from it. There is also a beginning (providing background), a middle (with numerous sequenced activities), and a final culminating experience.

The designer of this unit, a teacher from Colorado, used Colorado as one of the two regions of grasslands. You might want to use the common characteristics of the region in which your students live and make some comparison with a similar or

SAMPLE UNIT PLAN

GRASSLANDS: A NATURAL RESOURCE

Overview

Grasslands are the world's best places to grow food. Grasslands have less than 20 inches of rain per year. Getting food becomes a problem as our population increases and land is plowed under to make room for people. This unit teaches about two grasslands (in Colorado and in Kenya) and ends with the class analyzing the future of one of the earth's most precious natural resources.

Integration

Social studies, science, language arts, art

Activities

1. Utilize a number of books/resources about the grasslands to provide background knowledge.
2. Begin dioramas that will be used in assessment. Plant grasses from Colorado prairie and Kenya savanna NOW so these will be growing at assessment time.
3. Review concepts of region. Discuss if grasslands are a region. Use primary atlases to investigate if (and where) grasslands are found on various continents.
4. Using a variety of resources, identify and analyze past and present use of both grassland areas. Develop a chart or graphic organizer to display information gathered.
5. Investigate what food products come from grasses.
6. Investigate and analyze how weather and climate affect grasslands in these two areas.
7. Discuss present use of both areas and theorize on the future. Discuss conservation/preservation practices.
8. Do the treasure map activity that takes students through a grassland to practice map skills.

Assessments

1. The task is to make the previously planted container into a recognizable ecosystem by adding plants, animals, people, homes, etc., in some art form. Each diorama is to be divided in half, to show both past and present.
2. Present diorama to class and justify contents orally using information gathered in this unit. Weather and climate are factors to be discussed. State why grasslands are a "region."

Source: Abridged version of a unit for grades 1–5 by Janet Pommrehn, Denver Public Schools Elementary Teacher.

different region. Some teachers have used different regions of their own state. You can identify the animal and plant life indigenous to your region, or the products your region produces and where they are marketed. Perhaps you may want more time to show that regions change or that a region has common characteristics. Or you may want to include more group work or to use photographs to describe ways in which your local area has changed. Note that any teacher can modify and emphasize different key ideas in the concept of region in this unit, especially through the selection of resources and materials.

SMALL GROUP WORK	**IDENTIFY ACADEMIC DISCIPLINES AND SKILLS IN GRASSLANDS**
2.2	1. *Make a list of the disciplines (science, art, etc.) that appear to be used in each activity and assessment.*
	2. *Write down the skills that are developed in each activity and assessment.*
	3. *Each group member should decide if this is a good interdisciplinary unit.*

What are some sources of themes? Besides traditional themes such as transportation, the American Revolution, and the environment from content areas, sources might include biographies, local events and history, world events, or family histories. Teachers have successfully used such themes as Egyptian mummies, architecture of a given community, or a book such as *Sarah Plain and Tall*. Popular primary themes are foods, friends, grandparents, folktales, and famous people. Themes for the middle grades might focus on immigration, courage, and prejudice. Themes could be selected by the teacher or could emerge from the experiences and current needs of students.

Beginners often ask how long a unit should last. There is no fixed answer to this question, but younger students probably profit more from shorter units, perhaps two or three weeks, and older students gain more from units that are longer, up to six weeks. If the unit goes on too long, students may lose interest. Some teachers, however, find that students beg for more after interesting units, such as the economic simulation called *Mini-Society*, which lasts a full six weeks. The ideal time depends both on the age of the students and the material being taught.

Units may vary in length depending on how many other areas of the curriculum are included in them. A social studies unit that incorporates art, music, literature, and science usually lasts longer than one that includes no other disciplines. In planning a unit, try to incorporate as many relevant curriculum areas and skills as possible.

Now let us look in more detail at some other units.

Elizabeth A. Gelbart reported about the unit "Travel Day to Hawaii," which she had designed, at a social studies conference.[3] In addition to the previous outline, Gelbert provided ten pages describing in more detail worksheets with topics such as "A Hawaiian Volcano Erupts."

---

[3]Elizabeth A. Gelbart, "Travel Day to Hawaii." Presented at the California Council for the Social Studies Conference (Los Angeles, 1986).

TRAVEL DAY TO HAWAII

The following unit is planned to last one week and is prepared for the primary grades. Usually, such a unit has a broad objective and specific daily objectives. Although it might be inappropriate to use verbs such as *know, value,* and *understand* in behavioral objectives for individual lessons, such words are appropriate at the beginning of a unit where they provide overall guidance and organization to the instructional process.

Unit Goals

1. Students will understand the geography, history, and traditional culture of Hawaii.
2. Students will identify different types of transportation.

Day 1

Objectives: Students will distinguish an island from a land mass.
Students will describe their experiences about Hawaii.
Students will draw the Hawaiian Islands.

1. Introduce the vocabulary term *island*. Brainstorm with the class: What is an island? Have the children look at a map of the United States and find a state that is a group of islands.
2. Discuss the history of Hawaii. Share past experiences of children or their parents who have visited there.
3. Tell the children that the class will go on a "pretend" trip to Hawaii in five days. Discuss different modes of transportation.
4. Draw the islands on brown butcher paper and label them according to shape. Have the children pin up the product on the bulletin board with a blue background for water.

Day 2

Objectives: Students will differentiate the various types of transportation.
Students will calculate distances from their state to Hawaii.

1. Brainstorm with the children as to the different ways the class could travel to Hawaii (airplane, ship, sailboat, etc.).
2. Design an airplane ticket. Include the date, time of departure, and so on.

Day 3

Objective: Students will describe the traditional cultures and history of Hawaii.

1. Read "Palm Tree" from *Young Folks Hawaiian Time.*
2. Discuss the term *luau,* as well as foods usually eaten, dances, and so on.
3. Have children make drawings of Hawaiian traditions for a mural.
4. Learn the hula from a community member.

(continued)

TRAVEL DAY TO HAWAII *(continued)*

Day 4

Objective: Students will depict the sequence of volcano formation.

1. Brainstorm the term *volcano*. Discuss how volcanoes formed the islands.
2. Have the children divide paper into four squares. Illustrate an eruption of a volcano in sequence.

Day 5

Objective: Students will simulate a travel day in Hawaii. This lesson plan is part of a full day's activity: a "pretend" in-classroom flight to another state. Hawaii is used as an example in this lesson, but other states or nations could be used as well. This travel day combines all subjects in a *fun* educational setting. The following is an example of such a day.

1. "Takeoff"
   a. Collect children-made airplane tickets at the door.
   b. Review the flight route (ocean to be flown over, etc.).
2. Math-macaroni leis
   a. Design a simple count pattern (two reds, one yellow, and repeat) with dyed macaroni and construction-paper flowers. Save for the luau.
   b. Count the number of leis made.
3. Language/letter-writing skills
   a. Write and design a postcard to a friend or family member.
   b. Discuss how to address a postcard, the purpose of a stamp, and how to use descriptive language.
4. Reading/vocabulary skills
   a. Share "Hawaiian Alphabet" from *Young Folks Hawaiian Time.*
   b. Complete a worksheet on Hawaiian terms.
   c. List terms in alphabetical order.
5. Science: parts of flowers
   a. Label a hibiscus flower.
   b. Discuss the climate needed for it to grow and the stages of plant growth in general.
6. Art and music
   a. Learn the hula and Hawaiian folktales.
   b. Design a scrapbook of the day's events. Draw scenes of Hawaii with brief written descriptions.
7. Social studies: culture and foods of Hawaii
   a. Finish with a luau in Hawaii. Poi, coconut, and pineapple juice are a few suggested foods to share. The children should eat with their fingers.
   b. "Reboard" for the return flight home.

ON YOUR OWN	**ANALYZE THE UNIT**
2.3	

ANALYZE THE UNIT

In the sample unit plan "Travel Day to Hawaii" are the theme and content appropriate for the age group? Are there provisions for teaching skills and values? Is there a variety of activities for the children? Is there integration with other subject areas of the curriculum? Do you think the class would enjoy the unit? Is there a progression of experiences and activities that leads to a cumulation in the unit?

The sample unit plan "Travel Day to Hawaii" has many strengths; many classes would learn from and enjoy it, especially the final day's culmination activity. Check how assessment is handled. Does it flow naturally from the activities? But there is one serious concern: Is the unit reinforcing stereotypes about Hawaii? Will students learn about the large city of Honolulu with its wide diversity of people? Will students find out about the problems Hawaii is facing today as its land usage changes? The unit focuses on the tourist world of Hawaii. Attractive as that may be, it is not the whole picture. Note that the basic plan of this unit could be used for other nations or even states within the United States, but a teacher must be certain that students understand there is more to a region than the tourist view.

SAMPLE UNIT PLAN

LIVING IN HAWAII

The following one-week unit is prepared for primary grades.

Unit Goals
1. Students will understand the geography, history, and traditional culture of Hawaii (same objective as first unit, "Travel to Hawaii").
2. Students will describe how contemporary life in Hawaii differs from their own and how it is the same (different objective compared to first unit).

Day 1
Objectives: Students describe their images and experiences concerning Hawaii.
    Students formulate questions to answer about what it would be like to live in Hawaii.
    Students locate Hawaii on a globe and relate it to their location.

1. Ask what the students think of when they hear about the state of Hawaii. Explore individual experiences. Locate Hawaii on the globe as well as the community of the class. Ask students to describe how it would be to live on one of the Hawaiian islands.
2. Ask students to imagine they were going to move to Hawaii. Ask "What would you like to know about Hawaii?" and record questions.

(continued)

LIVING IN HAWAII *(continued)*

3. Read *Hawaii in Words and Pictures* (Dennis B. Fradin, Children's Press, 1980) to find possible answers. Discuss where and what children do to play, what homes are like, how life is the same or different.
4. Have students draw individual pictures of their images of Hawaii to place in their Hawaiian unit folder.

Day 2
Objective: Students describe how islands are formed.

1. Share student drawings from Day 1, clustering them in subgroups such as food, homes, and play; display on a Hawaiian Life unit bulletin board under "First Images."
2. Have students write captions cooperatively telling the essence of each cluster. Ask students to cross-check these images with their initial questions as a bridge to formulating questions differently or to asking other questions.
3. Ask students questions on how islands are formed. Using pictures, videos, or encyclopedia visuals plus lava and coral samples, lead presentation of volcanic island formation. Introduce vocabulary—*volcano, lava, eruption, erosion, coral,* and so on—in explanation; review and copy for Hawaiian dictionary page of unit folder.
4. If available, present science lesson on volcanic eruptions including model eruption.
5. Display aerial photographs of actual inhabited islands to show varying water depth around the islands.

Day 3
Objective: Students recount how the islands came to be populated by a non-Western voyage of discovery.

1. Were there always people, plants, and animals on the new islands? Hypothesize how the islands came to be populated. Use globe, encyclopedia, and library resources to visualize the story of how the islands were colonized by Polynesians.
2. If possible, show video of a 1992–1993 voyage that replicated original voyages of Hawaiian settlement that began in South Pacific islands. Count out on calendar sheets the length of this voyage. What did the travelers eat? Where did they sleep? Mark the route on a globe. Have students draw their version of Polynesian discoverers for unit folders and write what their picture tells.

Day 4
Objectives: Students contrast traditional Hawaiian life with living in Hawaii today. Students contrast their own lifestyles with those of contemporary students living in Hawaii.

1. Students share pictures and stories. Teacher asks what students think children in Hawaii do to remember the early days of Hawaii.
2. Teacher shares sections of books on Hawaii that describe and picture ways of maintaining traditional cultural practices such as the hula, canoe teams, net

fishing, fish farming, weaving from palm and banana leaves, and making flower leis. Teacher directs viewing and listening of video and tape materials, such as annual hula contest broadcast on Hawaiian television, annual Lei Day, or uses promotional materials from local travel agent and recording of Hawaiian music.

3. Resource person teaches students short hula, speaking first in English, then in Hawaiian.
4. Teacher shows pictures from a book (John Penisten, *Honolulu,* New York: Macmillan Child Group, 1990) or video of people living in a city in Hawaii. Students discuss how Hawaii has changed since people first came to the islands; how it would be to live there now; how living there would be the same as or different from where they live.
5. Teacher provides newspaper or magazine articles of native Hawaiian descendants marching for sovereignty. Discuss what that might mean. What would be good and bad about recognizing Hawaiian land rights?
6. Students draw pictures of Hawaii "today and yesterday" with explanatory captions for display on the unit bulletin board.

Day 5
Objectives: Continued from Day 4.

1. Students take turns presenting "today and yesterday" pictures.
2. Teacher leads students in reviewing initial questions and drawing conclusions about what they have learned for a cooperative chart story for bulletin board display.
3. Teacher plans with students what they could do to share their unit with another class.
4. After practice, students give a presentation on the unit to another class, using bulletin boards, video segments, map displays, hula performance, and oral presentations.

ON YOUR OWN	**COMPARING THE UNIT**
2.4	*Using the same questions found in the On Your Own Exercise 2.3, analyze and compare the unit "Living in Hawaii" with "Travel Day to Hawaii" (pp. 55–56)." Notice that although the subject matter for both is Hawaii, there is a great difference in what students will learn, the skills they use and develop, and the attitudes or appreciations that they may acquire as a result of the unit. What are the strong points of the unit "Living in Hawaii"?*

Comparison of the two units certainly shows the variety and creativity that can be developed with the same topic. Both units encourage an integration with other areas of the curriculum and use skills and content from a variety of subject areas. Both also try to make the activities interesting and meaningful for students. By comparison, both can make connections with previous units.

Both units have the power to expand student knowledge. Compared with the first unit, "Living in Hawaii" goes beyond tourist stereotypes and pushes students beyond their first, and probably inaccurate, images of Hawaii. It uses a more *constructionist* or active role on the part of the learner. Constructionist instructional practices emphasize the following:

- Organizing learning and instruction around important ideas
- Stressing the importance of students' prior learning by asking what students already know
- Challenging the adequacy of the learner's prior knowledge
- Assessing a learner's knowledge acquisition during the lesson

Now check how often the foregoing constructionist elements are used in this unit. Students will also use higher-level thinking skills as they compare traditional Hawaii, contemporary Hawaii, and their own way of life. They will probably appreciate more the daring and brave Polynesians who made the trip to Hawaii and have more respect for their culture. The emphasis on the native culture and its history probably also reinforces a more multicultural view of world history. The unit also introduces the idea that Hawaii is more than a holiday paradise; real people live there facing real problems.

Are there any weaknesses in the "Living in Hawaii" unit? Checking your state standards might suggest using more economic standards such as "Understanding the economy of the local region." First, the teacher needs up-to-date data about the economy of Hawaii. The teacher implementing the unit on Hawaii can easily gain this economic information from *Encyclopaedia Britannica* CD or other reference books and Internet sources. There under "Economy" you will find that the major problems in Hawaii are the high cost of living, due in large part to Hawaii's dependence on imports, and housing costs.

How much economic data to present and the format to use must then be decided. Should students be introduced to the concepts of exports (sugar, canned pineapple, garments, flowers, and canned fish) and imports (fuel, vehicles, food, and clothing)? Will they understand that when almost all the building materials for a house must be imported that this increases the cost of building the house? Should students compare the prices of various modes of transportation from their own state to Hawaii? On the other hand, state standards may also emphasize contributions from past events and cultures (a history standard). This would suggest more attention to the Polynesian culture. These are just a few of the decisions that teachers will make looking at their own state standards and modifying existing units.

A second possible weakness is that the teacher may feel unfamiliar with some of the content or resources. This illustrates the importance of the knowledge and background that a teacher brings as well as the learners' backgrounds and experiences. Try to build on your own strengths; during your vacations as well as during the year, round up as many resources as possible for current and forthcoming units. Increasing use of the computer by the teacher should make access to both content and teaching materials easier, especially **virtual field trips** on the Internet.

Having more resources available has led in some schools to a more complex form of "Travel Day." It is called "Passport Day" when each classroom at a school represents a different country, state, or time period that students have learned about in their social studies program. For example, the sixth-grade class studied India while a third-grade class studied the Native Americans in their area. Students may wear attire representative of the culture on "Passport Day" as they explain their work and artifacts to visitors. Students holding passports in their hands visit the different classrooms according to an arranged time schedule. "Passport Day" makes a good culminating experience for completion of a unit. Exchanges between classes also encourage more of a school community feeling and students may even look forward to the next grade levels when they see the results of interesting social studies units. Increasing use of computer networks should make access to teaching materials easier (see Chapter 10).

Elements of a Unit

What does a unit contain? The typical elements found in a unit are shown in Figure 2.4. No set format exists for writing units. Some teachers prefer to divide a page into three columns—the first for objectives, the middle for teaching procedures, and the third for materials. Others like to put each lesson plan on a separate page so they can eliminate or modify the lesson plans more easily.

What criteria can be used to choose units? Here are some ideas:

- *Construction of knowledge:* Will students organize, interpret, or explain information? Will they consider different points of view and alternative solutions?
- *Thinking and other skills:* Will students use and extend their skills?
- *Value beyond school:* Will the knowledge and skills be used outside the classroom? Will citizenship skills and values be likely to increase?
- *Link to state standards:* Will the unit help students to achieve state and local standards?

Elements of a Unit

1. Description
   Title
   Description of grade level, target student population
   Rationale/overview for the unit; significance of topic; tie to standards
   Estimated time

2. Goals and objectives (number each for ease of referral)

3. Lessons
   Introductory and initiating activities
   Series of sequence lesson plans with enough detail on procedures
      so that the teaching strategies and activities are clear. Worksheets
      and similar handouts should be included.
   Concluding activities to encourage students to apply what they
      have learned

4. List of resources (textbooks, people, media, library books, speakers)

5. Assessment, including procedures used during the unit as well as tests

---

FIGURE 2.4 Sample Unit Format

SAMPLE UNIT PLAN

FOOD

The following resource unit, designed to promote global education, is from the *Indiana in the World* teaching activities packet.

Activities
The pupils may:

Draw a two-column chart. Head one column "Animals" and one "Plants." List in the columns the foods students eat that come from plants and animals.

Make a list of their favorite foods.

Make a collage of their favorite foods.

Make a list of junk foods.

From a list of favorite foods, categorize the foods according to the six groups of the nutritional pyramid, identifying those that qualify as junk foods.

Discuss the nutritional value of the food they eat.

List and discuss health problems that can be prevented through adequate nutrition.

Describe and discuss their individual family eating patterns and compare them with those of other members of the class.

Divide into groups, each group choosing a foreign country; research and list the foods of their chosen country.

Find pictures and make a picture chart of the foods of their chosen country.

Discuss the eating utensils of a country (e.g., chopsticks in Asia).

Visit a supermarket that features foods of many countries. List the foods that are featured from the country they are studying.

Take a field trip to a restaurant featuring food of a chosen country.

Research and make a picture story chart on the influence religion may have on the diet of a country.

Plan a balanced diet from the foods of their chosen country.

List five or more foods eaten by people of other countries. State the countries (e.g., octopus, Italy).

Research and report on the history of some foods eaten in the United States.

List some of the foods eaten in the United States that were brought here from other countries. Name the countries.

Find pictures of children suffering from malnutrition in other countries.

Research and report on the diseases prevalent in these countries because of malnutrition.

Write two story paragraphs, one explaining plankton and the other hydroponics.

What is the difference between units (sometimes called *teaching units*) and resource units? *Resource units* are units designed (e.g., by the Census Bureau to help teachers teach about the census) for use by a great many teachers. Districts may design a resource unit for a given topic. Usually resource units contain more ideas and activities than any one teacher can use.

TABLE 2.2 Lesson Plans for the Week—Social Studies

Monday	Tuesday	Wednesday	Thursday	Friday
Introduction of community images	Map of community	Telephone book used to locate businesses	Librarian to visit	Post office counter used

ON YOUR OWN	WHAT ARE THE STRENGTHS OF THESE ACTIVITIES?
2.5	*In many cases, teachers incorporate the ideas from resource units or guides into their own teaching. Do you think any of these ideas on foods are helpful? Might you incorporate them into your own unit?*

What are some special considerations that teachers should be aware of in designing and implementing units in the social studies? One is *variety*. Look at your lesson plans. Are you using the same techniques (e.g., worksheets) every day? Are you showing three videos three days in a row? Is content emphasized without consideration of the importance of skills, values, and citizenship education?

To spot these problems more easily, some teachers like to jot down in broad outline what they are doing throughout the course of a week (see Table 2.2). Seeing a whole week's schedule often points out the need for more variety in teaching strategies and more attention to skills and values.

After you have completed a unit, evaluate it from your students' point of view. What was their favorite activity? What did they like least about the unit? Most important, what did they learn from it?

■ LESSON PLANS

A *lesson plan* is an outline of what you expect to teach in a given day's lesson. (See the daily plans in the sample unit plan "Travel Day to Hawaii" for examples.) Many teachers begin by creating and photocopying a blank form with several headings (see Figure 2.5). This form can be filled in at the beginning of each week or each unit.

Subject Area _____ Date _____

- Objective:
- Initiating activity/motivation:
- Procedure/teaching strategies:
- Resources:
- Closure/assessment:

FIGURE 2.5 Lesson Plan Format

Lesson plans are constructed within the general framework of a unit and should reflect the goals of that unit. You need to be alert in constructing daily plans to how activities can move your students toward an understanding of the unit's general goals—how daily activities can make those goals more meaningful. This requires a careful match between student readiness and interest and the activities you plan.

The first consideration in making a lesson plan is the objective or purpose. Is there a special concept that you hope students will acquire? The next step is motivation. What can you do to capture students' attention? This may involve relating the experiences of students to your objectives. Student interest and involvement in the lesson may be triggered by an artifact, a learning game, or a planned classroom experience.

Beginnings are important. They help to shape the motivation of students. Teachers should try to effect a smooth transition from what students already know to the new material. In general, sequence your instruction from the simple to the complex. Sometimes a brief review by a student of what was done in yesterday's social studies lesson is helpful. Try to create an organizational framework for ideas or information so that students know where things are going. It is often valuable simply to state the purpose of the lesson. Some teachers turn lessons into guessing games for their students, who must figure out where they're going and why. This generally does not help the learning process, especially for slower students.

In writing out procedures, teachers often do not use enough detail. What does "read and discuss the textbook" mean? Read aloud? Read silently? Read one paragraph silently and then discuss? Will students discuss questions in small groups? You can see that "read and discuss the textbook" is open to a wide variety of interpretations. Often more planning could turn the lesson into an exciting and useful learning experience for the students.

During the lesson, be attentive to the responses of the students. Is there a sense of accomplishment among them? Finally, think about closure, or ending the lesson. Will you depend on the bell to close the lesson? That can leave students dangling in mid-thought. A better way is to draw attention to the end of the lesson, to help students organize their learning, and to reinforce what they have learned. Have a student summarize the lesson for the class, or do so yourself.

SMALL GROUP WORK	**LOCATING INTERESTING LESSON PLANS**
2.3	*It would be exhausting to develop all your lesson plans by yourself in the area of the social studies. Look at teachers' guides, professional literature, the Internet, and resource units for ideas for lesson plans. Find three lesson plans you like. Explain why they appeal to you.*

■ ORGANIZING AND SCHEDULING

Time for teaching is a valuable resource. Many elementary students attend school for more than five hours a day, and the trend in the reform movement is to increase the number of minutes that elementary students spend in school. But when you subtract lunch time and recesses, most teachers probably have only about four hours a day actually to teach.

How much time should be spent on teaching the social studies? Many school districts give recommendations. The minimum usually is fifteen minutes a day for the first grade with an increasing time allotment each year. By the fourth grade, around thirty-five minutes a day is usually recommended, and by the sixth grade, social studies usually occupies a full period of approximately forty to forty-five minutes.

These time allocations, however, presume that subjects are not integrated. Typically, first-grade language arts (reading, writing, listening, speaking, spelling, handwriting) are allotted *two to three hours* each day. This means that if you integrate different areas, such as language arts (reading stories about the culture you are studying, writing a thank-you note to a community worker who spoke to your class), you can greatly increase the number of minutes devoted to social studies instruction. Integrating science and social studies is also worthwhile; studying the geography of a given area lends itself easily to the study of that area's plants, animals, climate, and the like. Integrating social studies with music, art, dance, and drama is natural, especially when you are studying a particular culture. More middle schools are using **block scheduling,** a longer period of time.

When is social studies typically taught during the school day? In many schools the basic subjects, reading and math, are taught in the morning "prime-time" hours. Social studies is generally relegated to the afternoon in such programs. By integrating subjects, however, you can bring social studies content into the morning hours when students are fresher and better able to learn.

You may not have complete control over scheduling block time and subject areas. In most schools, physical education, music, art, and other such subjects are taught by specialists whose schedules will dictate part of your own scheduling. In addition, students are often grouped for reading and math and may go to different rooms for these subjects. Again, you may have to follow prescribed time allocations for such classes.

Most teachers, however, can make decisions on how to use the time available. You will probably want to set up a "normal" daily and weekly schedule. You may decide that you would rather teach social studies on Monday, Wednesday, and Friday for a longer block of time than every day for a shorter period. Time allocations may change depending on the activities. A field trip or a local guest may dictate changes in the normal schedule. However, most classrooms eventually move into routine scheduled times for different subject areas or learning periods. Teachers differ on how to schedule and organize their class time. As long as time is used wisely, these differences are probably not important.

■ SUMMARY

Planning is important for effective teaching. Teachers usually block out a year's social studies curriculum by determining what units will be taught during the year. The unit approach with a theme, sequential lessons, and assessment provides better learning experiences for students. Ideally, daily lesson plans should be detailed enough to make teaching of the social studies effective and interesting. Teachers also have to plan so that citizenship and multicultural education as well as other goals and skills are treated as a day-long concern (see especially Chapters 7 through 9).

■ SUGGESTED READINGS AND WEB SITES ■

Davis, James E., ed. *Planning a Social Studies Program: Activities, Guidelines, and Resources*, 4th ed. Boulder, CO: ERIC Clearing House for Social Studies/Social Science Education, Social Science Education Consortium, 1997.

Good tool for schools changing their social studies program.

Eisner, Elliot W. *The Educational Imagination.* New York: Macmillan, 1985.

Sees much of teaching as an artistic enterprise.

Fredericks, Anthony D., Anita Meyer Meinbach, and Liz Rothlein. *Thematic Units*. New York: Harper-Collins, 1993.

Theory of thematic approach and examples of thematic units.

Roberts, Patricia, and Richard D. Kellough. *A Guide for Developing an Interdisciplinary Thematic Unit*. Englewood Cliffs, NJ: Prentice-Hall, 1996.

Purposes, initiating an interdisciplinary thematic unit, developing objectives and learning experiences plus assessment.

Web Sites

A Curriculum Site
discoveryschool.com/schrockguide
Categorized list of sites useful for the curriculum.
Gateway to Educational Materials (GEM)
www.thegateway.org
Lesson plans, curriculum units, and so on by grade level and topic. GEM is the Education Department's responses for federal agencies to improve and expand access to teaching and learning resources on the Internet.
National Center for History in the Schools
www.sscnet.ucla.edu/nchs/
The National Center for History in the Schools has the national history standards and over sixty world and U.S. history teaching units of reproducible primary sources and materials. Best for fifth grade and above.
Social Science Education Consortium
www.ssecinc.org
Resource materials and free monthly lesson plans.
A Teachers' Web Site
www.teachers.net
A gathering place with lesson plans, curriculum, supplies, and chat center.

Chapter 3

Instructional Strategies

This chapter illustrates the use of various instructional strategies with social studies topics. One instructional approach is not appropriate for all types of content and all types of learning. Remember that teaching strategies should be challenging, flexibly applied, and responsive to students. The following areas are highlighted in the chapter:

- General Consideration of Methods
- What Happens in Real Classrooms?
- Direct Teaching: From Passive to Active Learning
- Discovery Learning and Thinking
- Specific Thinking Skills: Observation, Listening, and Questioning
- Cooperative or Collaborative Learning
- Role Playing
- Simulations

■ GENERAL CONSIDERATION OF METHODS

What methods or instructional strategies should be used to teach elementary social studies? Planning instruction is like planning a trip; you need to consider your goals, transportation that will be used, time, what places you wish to visit or what you want to do, and what to do if there are delays. In a similar manner, in planning teaching methods you need to give very careful attention to the wide range of your students' abilities and skills and their attention span and motivation, as well as their background in the topic.

The typical instructional sequence is shown in Table 3.1. Note the similarity to a daily lesson plan (Chapter 2).

TABLE 3.1 Possible Instructional Sequence

Introduction
Motivation
Development
Student Application of Knowledge and Skills
Culmination, Summary, Closure, Conclusions, Assessment

To teach effectively, you should have a wide repertoire of teaching methods. Using a variety of strategies will help you meet the varying needs of students who have different styles of thinking and learning. Howard Gardner's theory of **multiple intelligences** is of particular interest here.[1] Gardner identifies seven basic intelligences.

1. Verbal linguistic (language)
2. Logical/mathematical
3. Visual/spatial
4. Body/kinesthetic
5. Musical/rhythmic
6. Interpersonal (understanding of others)
7. Intrapersonal (understanding of self)

Gardner believes that individuals possess all of these intelligences but differ in the relative strengths of each of them. However, the schools tend to focus primarily on only the first two intelligences. This means that teachers need to provide experiences that use and extend all of the seven intelligences of children. Gardner also is critical of a curriculum based on facts and advocates more of a focus on depth and understanding.[2] Although critics of Gardner report his theory of multiple intelligence (M.I.) has not improved achievement in schools in formal research studies, his ideas that each child may have important abilities offers hope for children learning when teachers use a variety of methods.

To meet the wide diversity in student backgrounds and learning styles, it is wise to use a range of teaching methods. For example, with a fifth-grade class studying the history of the U.S. West, you could begin with an exercise on planning a trip to the pre–Civil War West. Have the students, organized in small groups, decide how much they should spend on various supplies and which articles they should put in the covered wagon. (There are computer programs such as *The Oregon Trail* that work on a similar theme, but if you do not have a computer in your classroom, the small group exercise can work very well.)

Ask students to analyze their findings. In a whole-class discussion, they can gain insights from the experiences of other groups about what is important for making the trip. The class can rank the priority items for moving west. (Discussion and list-making favor verbal students.)

Introduce literature and songs about the pioneers to enhance the students' understanding of the settlement of the West. Have students learn or listen to songs such as "Oh, Susannah" or "Sweet Betsy from Pike"; talk about the *Little House* books or television shows; teach students square dancing. To use another strategy, give a short lecture on abstract concepts such as freedom and lawlessness on the frontier. Have students read the appropriate textbook pages and do workbook assignments. Involve nonverbal students in a range of art projects or activities: putting together a short play on the West, making maps of wagon-train routes, and so on. More verbal

[1]Howard Gardner, *The Unschooled Mind: How Children Think and How Schools Should Teach* (New York: Basic Books, 1991).

[2]Howard Gardner, *The Disciplined Mind What All Students Should Understand* (New York: Simon and Schuster, 1999).

students might write "pretend" diaries, songs, or poetry on the West. All might gain from films that show the perspective of Native Americans whose land was being taken away from them. Finally, have students evaluate their own efforts to see how these projects could serve as stepping-stones for future learning.

The variety of activities in this unit on the West provides channels for a wide range of learners and their abilities. Students start with a concrete experience (planning a trip to the West) and move into concept development (lawlessness, freedom, etc.). Furthermore, the students find applications for the materials and concepts as they develop their own projects. In the process of evaluating their projects, the students engage in analysis and also move into the affective domain by sharing their projects with other members of the class. You will meet many needs in this series of lessons.

In addition to the learning needs of students, certain environmental factors may also influence your choice of teaching methods. Large class size might make some methods inappropriate. The physical environment of the school or the social climate of a given class may not be conducive to certain methods. Simulations, for example, may be noisy. If the walls are thin and a simulation would bother other classes, using this activity would not be a considerate choice. In addition, each class has its own personality. Often you hear experienced teachers say, "No group reports this year. My kids just don't mesh well enough." Each particular mix of students in a class is unlike any other. Experienced teachers know that one lesson or approach will not always work the same way in a different class. Each class has its own personality and its own needs.

■ WHAT HAPPENS IN REAL CLASSROOMS?

Most experts believe sound education practices include depth as well as breadth, student involvement, and connectedness to curriculum and life skills. We want students to gain critical thinking and problem-solving skills, effective communication skills, and responsible behavior toward self, community, and citizenship. But what happens in actual classrooms?

Teachers' Decisions

Teachers make many decisions daily regarding instruction or methods. In effect, they decide which roles they and their students play during a given activity. They may serve as **experts** as they lecture, do presentations, or orally quiz students to determine the accuracy of their understandings. They may act as **consultants** in student-directed activities as when students work individually or in groups on projects or presentations. They may **coach** students while students puzzle their way through a problem.

In their roles, teachers may provide whole group instruction, work with small groups, or work with individual students. A longstanding criticism of teachers is that they often have spent too much time on *recitation*, a combination of talking and asking questions of students. In fact, many studies have found teachers talking at students at least 75 percent of the classroom time. However, there are variations of time of teacher talk depending on grade level, subject matter, and student characteristics.

To counter the recitation method, experts from a wide variety of sources—teacher and academic professional organizations, government agencies (e.g., National Science

Foundation), and higher education faculty—have recommended the following four practices that directly relate to teacher methods and strategies.

1. Small group instruction such as cooperative learning at least once a week
2. Students' use of supplementary material other than textbooks at least once a week; less use of routine exercises commonly provided in textbooks, workbooks, and worksheets
3. Use of technology (computers, videotape, etc.) once or twice a month and manipulatives, or models, at least once a month
4. Classroom and homework activities to emphasize higher-order thinking as well as mastery in basic skills

In considering various practices, methods or strategies can be divided into two main categories: **direct teaching** such as lecturing in which the teacher has a prominent role and **indirect methods** of teaching such as cooperative learning, role playing, and simulations in which the teacher's role changes. Let us now examine these various methods in depth to help you make sound core curriculum decisions.

Many factors need to be considered when you think about teaching methods. Each method represents one possible route to more successful learning for your students, and different methods may be more appropriate for different topics and skills.

All teaching methods, however, have some common elements. Each one involves teacher direction of student thinking processes. All require preparation, concern with motivation, setting up of the learning experience, and the creation of some evaluative technique to assess whether students have gained in knowledge, skills, values, and social participation—the four goals of social studies.

ON YOUR OWN	**FINDING YOUR STYLE**
3.1	*With which teaching method are you most comfortable? Jot down the strengths and weaknesses of your "style." Is it one that engages most of your students?*

■ DIRECT TEACHING: FROM PASSIVE TO ACTIVE LEARNING

Lecturing is one of the oldest teaching methods but the "talk and chalk" method has its critics. To improve lecturing, a method called **direct teaching** or **direct instruction** is employed. Direct instruction presents information directly through lecturing, questioning, and demonstrating/modeling. It makes explicit to students at the beginning of the lesson what students are to learn. The main purpose of direct teaching is to present knowledge and skills that will enable *all* students to *master* the material being taught. Sometimes this method is called direct explanation teaching.

Direct-teaching advocates argue that this approach—which includes structured content, the carefully explained introduction of new material, demonstration, considerable student practice (both guided and independent), and frequent recall and comprehension questions—can improve achievement, especially for lower socioeconomic status students.

Direct teaching has been successful in part because it begins from a realistic assessment of what goes on in many classrooms, including social studies classrooms. It recognizes that the textbook is still the major vehicle for social studies instruction. Unfortunately, teachers often simply assign sections of text and worksheets without much explanation of the material covered. Direct teaching or lecturing can be used to help teachers convey content more effectively. A second reason for the popularity of the direct-teaching model is that it was developed at a time when some educators were questioning the value of the looser, less direct, or less structured teaching strategies, such as role playing, simulations, and value exercises, which relate more closely to the affective domain.

Figures 3.1 and 3.2 illustrate two models of the direct-teaching method: the five-step lesson plan and the direct-explanation and teacher-modeling method, which is a more constructionist instructional practice.

1. Anticipatory set
   a. Focus students
   b. State objectives
   c. Establish purpose
   d. Establish transfer (if possible)

2. Instruction
   a. Provide information
      Explain concept
      State definitions*
      Identify critical attributes*
      Provide examples*
      Model
   b. Check for understanding
      Pose key questions
      Ask students to explain concept, definitions, attributes
         in their own words*
      Have students discriminate between examples and nonexamples*
      Encourage students to generate their own examples*
      Use active participation devices

3. Guided practice
   a. Initiate practice activities that are under direct teacher supervision
   b. Elicit overt response that demonstrates behavior
   c. Provide close monitoring
   d. Continue to check for understanding
   e. Provide specific knowledge of results

4. Closure
   a. Make final assessment to determine whether students have met
      objective
   b. Have each student perform behavior on his or her own

5. Independent practice
   a. Have students continue to practice on their own
   b. Provide knowledge of results

FIGURE 3.1 Five-Step Direct-Teaching Plan

Note: The starred items are particularly critical when you are teaching an abstract concept (e.g., democracy). They may not be relevant or appropriate when teaching a practice-oriented concept (e.g., state capitals). Thanks to Bill Crandall for the development of this material.

1. *Anticipatory set:* Get students focused on the lesson. Use material relevant to the objective and related to students' past experiences or interests. Use when introducing new learning, after an interruption, or when changing to a new subject.
2. *Objective:* Tell students what they are going to learn.
3. *Purpose:* Tell students the benefit of the learning. Explain why you are teaching the lesson. (Objective and purpose are sometimes combined.)
4. *Input:* Analyze the knowledge and skills that need to be learned. Present the material.
5. *Modeling:* Tell students what to look for. Provide a perfect model. Demonstrate what the end product of the learning will look like.
6. *Check for understanding:* Monitor the learning. Adjust your instruction to accommodate where the students are.
7. *Guided practice:* Actively involve all students. Monitor their activity. (Understanding and practice are sometimes combined.)
8. *Closure:* Tie the learning together; recapitulate; summarize.
9. *Independent practice:* Assign classroom work and homework, to be done independently.

FIGURE 3.2 Direct-Teaching Model

What are the key elements of direct teaching? *Pacing* and *learning for mastery* are important. Students spend a high percentage of their time on tasks that they will successfully complete. In contrast, regular instruction too frequently skips many of the elements of direct teaching and leaves students frustrated, either because they are not sure *what* they are supposed to have learned or because they don't know *why* they are learning it.

The direct-teaching model may remind you of what a public speaking instructor would say: Tell them what you're going to say, say it, and then tell them what you've said. That is, in fact, a large part of direct instruction. In addition, the emphasis on *set* is an attempt to relate actual student experiences to the objectives—to bring students into a more active participation in learning. Direct teaching attempts to stimulate interest and involvement in the lesson by explaining to students the importance of what they are learning and by presenting the content clearly. Furthermore, the lesson is planned in detail, so the teacher avoids meandering along trivial or personal paths. Finally, direct teaching gives students an opportunity to practice what they have heard and then to reinforce it with further assignments.

When is direct teaching appropriate in the social studies? Certainly, teachers need to explain ideas and concepts to students whenever instruction begins on a new unit of work, a new concept, or a new project. Direct-teaching methods can help. Here is how direct teaching might work if a textbook is being used.

Mr. Smithy, a third-grade teacher, wants to explain the concept of *organization*—a group that has at least two members who have common interests and rules. His teaching objective is for students to distinguish organizations from nonorganizations. To *set* the lesson, Mr. Smithy points out that many members of the class belong to organizations: José is a Cub Scout and Sarah is a Brownie. What other students, he asks, belong to these or other organizations? Mr. Smithy explains that religious or after-school sports groups are also organizations.

Mr. Smithy then tells his students that they are going to learn about organizations, which form important parts of our society. It is, thus, useful for the students to be able to identify them. In other words, Mr. Smithy has explained the *objective* and *purpose*. In the *input* stage, he may give examples of organizations. The city council is an organization; it has more than two members, rules, and common interests. The local gardening club is also an organization. Members have common interests, pay dues, and come to meetings to find out more about how to garden. The Parent-Teacher Association (PTA) is another organization, as are computer clubs and after-school soccer teams.

Mr. Smithy then gives examples of *non*organizations. The local shoe repair store employs only one person. It is not an organization. A group of individual shoppers in a mall is not an organization; the group includes more than two people but the shoppers do not meet regularly or follow common rules.

Mr. Smithy explains to his students the main characteristics of an organization. He continues to provide examples of organizations and nonorganizations. He summarizes the main distinctions again, then has the class read the pages in their textbooks about organizations.

After the class finishes reading, Mr. Smithy *checks their comprehension* by asking questions about what is and what is not an organization. Then he gives a worksheet to the class and has students check the words on a list that represent organizations and those that do not. The list may include *people at a movie theater, the Sierra Club,* or *people walking in the park.* Mr. Smithy supervises this activity, providing *guided practice.*

After allowing time for this exercise, Mr. Smithy and the class go over the correct answers on the list. During *closure,* the students summarize again the main characteristics of an organization.

Finally, for homework, Mr. Smithy has students ask their parents what organizations they belong to (unions, churches, clubs, etc.). Students then create, independently, lists of organizations to which their parents belong. This provides *independent practice.* Mr. Smithy may check these lists to be certain that students have an accurate understanding at this point of what an organization really is.

In the foregoing example, Mr. Smithy assumed that all students could read a textbook, which is not necessarily true of all class members. By identifying the key ideas before giving students the reading assignment, however, he ensured that even students who were not good readers would find the assignment easier. In effect, he had built in "readiness" for the reading experience. He used the textbook to reinforce his own teaching and to help students understand a concept.

Simply creating all the elements of a good direct-teaching lesson is not sufficient. You must *communicate* those elements to your students. Breakdowns can occur in direct teaching as well as in any other teaching method. Because much of the instruction in this method depends on your speaking to your class, your vocal delivery is important. If you use poor diction, mannerisms, or digressions, or show a lack of clarity, these may interfere with your delivering the information effectively to your students. The level of abstraction may be too great for a particular group, and students may simply "tune out." Students may also ignore what you are saying if the lesson goes on too long. Their attention may be diverted by physical distractions in the room or by other students. Concrete examples will always help maintain student interest, as will having students use their other senses by employing visual aids or requesting a written response. Too often lecturing is a passive activity for students, who remember little of what they have heard. If you follow a direct-teaching model carefully, you won't fall into the trap of delivering a poor, ineffective lecture.

Direct teaching emphasizes the teacher, rather than the student, as a decision maker. However, used exclusively, direct teaching can stifle creativity in teachers and prevent them from exploring different teaching strategies in different situations. Direct teaching obviously has many good points. Whenever you explain a concept or lecture to a class, you would do well to check the steps of the direct-teaching model. Introducing lessons with clear goals and making ideas logical and cogent are helpful principles in conveying knowledge and skills. As with any teaching strategy, however, direct teaching should not be employed day after day in the social studies program. Daily repetition of the same process is dull for both student and teacher unless you are an exceptionally enthusiastic advocate of this method. Direct instruction may be particularly effective for teaching facts and skills to low-ability classes, but the teaching of higher-level thinking skills may best be done by other methods.

SMALL GROUP WORK	
	WHEN TO USE DIRECT TEACHING
3.1	*How did you learn to use e-mail or any other computer application? How did you learn about what to do in a power shortage or how to find information in a reference book? Make a list of student social studies knowledge and skills best learned by direct instruction. You may wish to refer to one of the units in Chapter 2 for a list of activities. Share your list with your group.*

■ DISCOVERY LEARNING AND THINKING

Problem-Based Learning

What do the words **problem-based learning, discovery learning, inquiry, problem solving, inductive thinking, thinking,** and **thinking skills** have in common? They all refer to the processes that everyday citizens as well as scientists and scholars use to discover knowledge, make decisions, and solve problems. The schools have always claimed to do more than just teach the three R's. One goal of education has been to foster the thinking skills that are universally needed outside the classroom by all members of society. Many critics believe, however, that thinking is a process rarely encouraged or manifested in most classrooms.

How many times have you wished you could have done something differently after things have gone awry? "If only I could do things over again" is frequently heard as we discuss our personal problems with others. This human capacity to learn from experience is our greatest potential resource for building a better personal future. Instruction in the processes of thinking is even more vital for the future of our lives as citizens. Teaching decision-making skills is essential in the curriculum of the social studies. When making decisions, ranging from minor ones such as what book to choose from the library for recreational reading to major ones such as evaluating what is the best way for the nation to have good health care services, children as well as adults must determine the alternatives and then choose wisely among them. Decisions made without careful consideration of the alternatives and the consequences of each can be costly in terms of the quality of our lives.

When thinking skills are not taught, many students (and inevitably, many adults) lack confidence in their own abilities as thinkers. For most, thinking is a *learned,* not an *innate,* skill. Those without it feel unsure of themselves and believe that they cannot generate good ideas. This lack of confidence is true even of those students who receive high grades in all subjects on their report cards.

A reform movement recognizing the need to teach thinking skills began in the 1960s. More than fifty new social studies projects were created at that time, and many of them had some emphasis on teaching thinking, most commonly called *inquiry.* Although educators in the 1970s showed greater concern with values and relevance of materials to students, an interest in teaching thinking skills has manifested itself again today for many reasons. Our society in general is more concerned about being able to compete in a global market. Only if our youth are educated to think, this argument goes, can the United States survive as a leading industrialized nation with a high standard of living. In addition, citizenship goals have always emphasized the need for teaching all children to think.

Thinking does not occur in a vacuum. Good thinking is a coordination of strategies and knowledge, a product of a number of factors interacting with each other—from well-developed language skills and short-term memory capacity, to well-controlled emotions and appropriate confidence. You can take a student's backpack, perhaps one borrowed from another classroom, filled with items. Exhibit the items one by one to the class. Have the students first by themselves make a profile of the backpack's owner and try to guess how the owner became separated from the backpack. Then move the students into pairs to discuss their ideas.

The constructivist model of teaching and learning places a high priority on the importance of thinking because understanding is developed through discussions in which problems are posed, clarifications are sought, and dialogue is promoted. The student tries to make sense of new information by relating it to prior knowledge and participating in discussions guided by teachers.

Although in practice, thought processes differ from one person to the next and the steps are not uniform, the following sequence outlined by John Dewey is a good starting point for "thinking about thinking."[3] The sequence shows the importance of dividing the problem into steps. Attacking the broad problem straightforwardly is too difficult for most children and adults. The first step may be to gain an understanding of what students know about the problem and what new knowledge is needed to solve the problem.

1. Define the problem.
2. Suggest alternative solutions to the problem; formulate hypotheses for testing.
3. Gather data to support or negate hypotheses. Try to use a variety of sources.
4. Select supportive hypotheses or reject unsupported ones.

[3]John Dewey, *How We Think* (Boston: D. C. Heath, 1933), 72.

This sequence translates into the following steps for teaching thinking skills:

1. Introduction—problem, question, or dilemma posed
   Example of activities:
      What are our images about Mexico?
         Small groups brainstorm; chairpersons report back to the class.
         Teacher presents items on Mexico gathered from media.
2. Development of a hypothesis (tentative answer)
   Example of activities:
      Teacher leads a discussion of ideas generated from brainstorming and teacher and class select the best one; hypothesis could be that our images of Mexico are not accurate or it could be the more specific hypothesis that Mexico is facing serious financial (or political or social) problems.
3. Gathering data
   Example of activities:
      Teacher presents data in charts.
      Students extract data from the textbook.
      Students collect data (group or individual research).
      Students classify and interpret data.
4. Hypothesis accepted or rejected
   Example of activities:
      Class or teacher evaluates data and methods of research.
      Class or teacher states a conclusion.
      Students suggest further questions for investigation.

We use these processes of problem solving in our everyday lives. Assume that you go to your car in the morning and it does not start. Definitely a problem! You listen and it seems to be making a funny noise as you try to start it. You form a hypothesis: The battery is dead. Then you get help from a friend or neighbor who charges the battery. It works! Your hypothesis (the cause of the problem was a dead battery) has been supported.

Students also face decision making or problem solving on many different levels in their own lives. They may make plans for a birthday party and have to decide whom to invite or what activities to plan. They need to decide how to use their leisure time. Should they watch television, read a book, or play soccer? They may need to resolve problems in getting along with classmates or siblings. They may need to figure out a way to earn money. Students may also have more weighty concerns about how they should behave in school or outside the classroom.

Problem-solving skills, then, have universal value. Anything that the schools can do to sharpen students' thinking skills now will have a big payoff in the future. Certainly, our society and its citizens face many problems that can be solved only through informed and logical thinking. But developmental stages are important, and there are limits to what children can do in thinking and problem solving. Young children, for example, cannot think abstractly. In addition, children who are impulsive and not motivated toward intellectual tasks may not show much interest in thinking activities in school. In teaching students to think, you need to consider the formal process as well as the specific needs of your students.

Defining the Problem

To resolve any problem, we must first be able to recognize it and define it. This is a thinking ability that you should encourage in your students. A good way to approach this first step at the elementary level is through *inductive reasoning*, in which an individual perceives a particular pattern of relationships based on a finite number of items or events. It is a way of generalizing from experience or data. The inductive model gives students the opportunity to construct their own ways of learning by building on what they already know.

To encourage inductive thinking to help students recognize that culture influences art, you might bring in pictures or show filmstrips on the art and architecture of a particular society such as that of the Mayans or the ancient Greeks. After they have seen a series of art "products" from that culture, have the children try to state something about that culture's beliefs. How are women and men depicted? Does most of the art represent gods and goddesses? What does that suggest about the importance of religion? By beginning with the concrete objects and encouraging students to generalize from them, you will help students grasp the concept that culture influences art. In contrast, simply asking your students how cultural beliefs affect a society's art will present a far more difficult problem for them. Other inductive activities include bringing in artifacts from earlier time periods such as buttons, toys, tools, photographs, postcards from various states or nations, and full wastepaper baskets to allow students to make inferences about the culture.

Many forms of problem solving begin with inductive reasoning. Teachers often try to trigger student thinking by presenting a discrepancy between what students *think* they know and some new data. Ask your students what images they have about a given nation. Contrast this with actual data. Or raise a controversial question such as what a community should do about housing the homeless or controlling pollution. Contrast the students' solutions with what is actually being done.

Generating Ideas

The second step in thinking is to generate ideas or hypotheses (tentative answers) to help explain why a problem is occurring. Try to draw forth as many ideas as possible without making any judgments. Even silly ideas should be accepted to encourage all students to participate.

You might ask individual students to jot down as many different ways as they can think of to improve the common bathtub or, for more of a social studies flavor, their local transportation system. We recommend that students work by themselves for a minute or two before moving into small groups to share ideas. Always have students do some individual thinking first. Students should not get into the habit of believing that they can think only when they are part of a group. A good strategy is to have students think alone, then form pairs or small groups and share ideas. This is called the **Think-Pair-Share strategy.** The steps are first to brainstorm yourself by making a list. Second, compare your list with that of someone nearby. Third, make a whole class list from the contributions from the pairs.

Within each group, students will usually encounter a variety of ideas. Some students might think that public transportation should be increased; others might think that workers need to arrive at their places of employment at different times to avoid commuter congestion. It is good for students to learn that not everybody perceives the world and solves problems in the same way. In some exercises, especially at the beginning, you may not want to focus on determining the *best* ideas. In fact, students should be encouraged to brainstorm and generate ideas without making judgments about which ones are best. Students who are accustomed to questions with only one right answer (e.g., what is the capital of Chile?) may find the notion of many right answers both confusing and exciting.

All students bring into the classroom their ways of looking at the world that have been formed by their environment and personal experience. Students may come from homes in which the teacher's authority of telling and directing students is considered more important than promoting students' exploration or alternative solutions. In addition, some groups freely incorporate emotion and personal beliefs to come to a conclusion instead of developing arguments based on evidence and logic. This does not mean that students cannot generate ideas or do problem-based learning but may need to be explicitly taught how to do so.

Class activities can help students learn to select good ideas, decisions, or solutions. In the sample lesson plan that follows, students take the role of an explorer and try to determine solutions to particular problems. The exercise encourages cooperation rather than competition. Notice also that the lesson plan tries to break down the steps of thinking. It does not simply pose the problem but first provides background information. Unfortunately, teachers often pose problems too broadly. In this exercise, the student is led step by step through the process to see which ideas will work best in the particular situation.

SAMPLE LESSON PLAN

DECIDING WHICH IDEAS ARE BEST

In 1542 the Spanish had a claim, or right, to the land in California. This was a land in which 300,000 Native Americans lived. But in the 1700s the Russians were moving down from Alaska. They wanted the rich otter fur trade. The British were also coming closer to "Spanish" land.

Around 1700 the Spanish had settlements in Baja, California (now part of Mexico). To protect its claim, the Spanish government decided to send soldiers and missionaries to California to teach the Californian Native Americans and to create a permanent Spanish settlement.

The military leader of the group sent to California was Captain Gaspar de Portola, the governor of Baja, California. The religious leader was Father Junipero Serra, a Spanish priest and missionary.

Captain Portola had to decide how to move his group to San Diego, 640 kilometers (400 miles) north of Baja, California. He had two choices: to go by water or by land.

1. Put yourself in Captain Portola's place. List the most important consideration he should think of in making his journey. _____
_____

Ships at that time were small, about thirty meters (100 feet) long. A crew might number twenty. The winds might blow the small ship off course. The captain had poor maps. The crew and passengers might get ill from not eating the proper amount of fruits and vegetables, especially if they were at sea for a long time.

By land there was possible danger from the natives. The group had to bring enough food since they could not depend on living off the land.

They had to find water. The trip was also slow since most people walked only a few miles (kilometers) each day. There were not enough mules and horses available to carry everyone and all the group's supplies.

2. Captain Portola had to consider an additional problem. In 1769, the year the trip was to start, Father Serra was fifty-five years old. He was short and walked with a limp. How do you think Father Serra should travel? Why? _____

_____

3. Captain Portola also wanted to bring some cattle and horses with him to California. The animals would be useful in the new settlement. What would be the best way for them to travel? _____

_____

4. Now, with these considerations, what choice do you think Captain Portola should make on how to travel to California? Why? _____

_____

5. Captain Portola decided to "hedge his bets." He would use three ships and two land groups, one land group going ahead of the other land group. Was this the best plan? Why? _____

_____

6. Captain Portola had to decide whether he, the leader, should go by land or by the sea route. Portola was a skilled army leader. Which way would his talents be best used? _____

_____

7. Captain Portola and, surprisingly, Father Serra went by land. Walking with much difficulty and riding, Father Serra, with great determination, made it to San Diego. There the land group met the group that had gone by sea. One of the three ships was lost at sea, and many from the voyage were sick and died. The land party also had lost men from illness. But even with these hardships, Captain Portola was successful in establishing the first permanent European settlement in California. Had he used the best ideas in his decision making? What would you have done differently? _____

_____

_____

Another thought exercise is to ask students about the effects of this exploration and settlement on the lives of the Native Americans.

SMALL GROUP WORK	**TAKE THE STUDENT ROLE**
3.2	*First, pretend you are a student. Work out the exercise on Captain Portola. Then share your responses with a small group or with the class. Do you think the foregoing exercise helps students to think? What if a student decides that Portola should have done something other than what he actually did? Should the student's idea be accepted? How would you respond? What if the student takes the perspective of a Native American?*

Students need a lot of practice in generating ideas and then in deciding which ones are best. Usually, if a student's explanation of events or situations considers all the relevant facts, it is an idea worthy of consideration and should not be rejected. Ask your students to make sense of or to generate ideas out of puzzling things, such as why Stonehenge in England was built or why Native Americans called Mound Builders built their large structures in certain parts of the United States. Most students will enjoy thinking about and looking at data on the Bermuda Triangle and drawing conclusions about the possible explanations of these sightings. Or children's own experiences can be used to generate ideas. What can be done about the big kids in other classes who bully younger children? Or what do we do when all children want to paint at the easel at the same time? Students can also be given more formal social studies exercises, such as trying to account for the growth of large cities in their state. All these examples can serve as springboards for thinking and for generating ideas (i.e., hypotheses) to be tested.

Gathering Data

After identifying the problem and suggesting promising ideas to explain or solve it, the third important step in problem solving is gathering data to support or reject the hypothesis. It is important for students to acquire data from a variety of sources. Finding information often involves skills best taught directly, as with the direct-teaching model. Thus, in teaching the more creative thinking skills, you may find yourself using direct-teaching methods.

Information Skills

1. Finding information in a book
   Using a table of contents
   Using an index
   Using a glossary
   Using an appendix
2. Finding information in a library/media center
   Using online computer reference services and Web sites
   Using a card catalog or a computer to find books
   Using the Dewey decimal system

Using an encyclopedia
Using an atlas
Using an almanac
Using other reference books
Using a telephone directory

In many cases, before students can find information and data to support their hypotheses, they must be able to use the library and a computer appropriately. Usually, a school librarian will be helpful in explaining how to use the library and how to collect information, including using a computer. In today's elementary schools, the traditional library resources are still dominant but more current and diverse material will increasingly be available via computers. Knowing how to gain access to computer sources will become even more important. For example, the Boston school system requires all fourth graders to produce a travel brochure about Boston, retrieving information from computerized encyclopedias, paper reference books, and, in schools with an online connection, the Internet. Students need to know how to use both traditional as well as computerized sources of information, and they should always be encouraged to think how the "experts" got their data. This is especially important in looking at the data from some Web sites. In other words, students need to blend computer and library skills along with using critical thinking skills to evaluate data.

The importance of evaluating the data was shown in a study when a group of students investigated unsolved "mysteries" such as the Loch Ness Monster, Bigfoot, Alien Autopsy, and Stonehenge by using computer searches. Nessie is on the Net! The children reported that they found most sites were convincing in the way they presented information or, as one said, "If you didn't believe in Bigfoot, why would you waste your time creating a Web site for it?" The conflicting information made the students look at "expert opinions" on the Internet and how to determine which ones are truthful and honest. In addition, students reported that they liked visual images more than text and tended only to scan the written information, which could influence their conclusions. To do this exercise using the Internet as with all Internet searches, students must have good reading skills. Students also did not like the long wait time to gain access.[4] Even with these limitations, it appears in the future more data will be accessed by the use of the Internet.

Even without a computer to encourage information skills and inquiry, ask students to think about the following:

Once people "knew" that washing, especially with soap, was likely to make one ill. Now we "know" that keeping clean helps us stay healthy.

Once people "knew" that the earth was the center of the universe. Now we "know" that the earth revolves around the sun, which is one of billions of stars.

In other words, how do you "know" what you "know?" Ask students to find information on these or similar topics. They will become more aware of why we trust the data of some people and not others and also that often our knowledge changes when new ideas replace older ones.

---

[4]Mark E. Brown and Tracy L. Riley, "Internet Investigations," *Learning and Leading with Technology* 26 (November 1998): 28–34.

Here are other examples of activities that encourage information skills. Photocopy for each student the one-page Quick Reference Index of *The World Almanac and Book of Facts*. Then ask students to give the *category* in which you would look to learn about major earthquakes, the population of Canada's provinces, where nuclear reactors are located in the United States, and so on. Similarly, prepare an abbreviated copy of the telephone numbers of government offices. (In real life, people often need to telephone government agencies about such things as how to fill out an income tax form or how to secure a dog license.) Then explain how to find government office telephone numbers in the pages of a telephone directory. Finally, ask students to find and write down the telephone numbers for offices such as Animal Control, Birth Records, or Boating or Building Permits.

Students may also assemble their own data from interviews and questionnaires, but they must be taught to ask questions in an objective manner and to communicate clearly what is being asked. Most students will need your assistance in designing an interview sheet or questionnaire to gather data, for example, on how local residents view traffic problems in their neighborhood. Poorly designed interview forms and questionnaires may yield misleading information that is of little value in proving or disproving a hypothesis. Such questionnaires may also reflect unfavorably on the school and the teacher.

■ SPECIFIC THINKING SKILLS:
OBSERVATION, LISTENING, AND QUESTIONING

Let us look at some skills that may be needed for students to learn. *Observation* is a systematic approach requiring careful examination of behavior and phenomena. Teachers constantly direct the observations of children, teaching them how to see which object is larger, the differences between two geometric shapes, and how deciduous trees lose their leaves as weather turns cooler in the autumn. Science for young children places a heavy emphasis on the skill of observation. Another type of observation related to the observation of behavior of people is associated with the social sciences. Observation may sound deceptively easy, but it is hard to "tell it like it is." Students must be aware of the distinctions related to an action they observe, the *inferences* or meaning they attach to the action, and the value judgment they place on the action. An inference carries a student beyond the observable and into the realm of speculation. However, this speculation should not be just guesswork. The problem of looking at (and listening to) people and then making some inferences about their behavior is quite complex and filled with pitfalls. It is difficult to observe objectively people we know well. Objectivity may not be easy in reporting behavior and then making inferences about it when the activity involves family and friends. Frequently, both children and adults are unwilling to be harsh or make negative comments about friends and family; however, not everyone has the same degree of charity or kindness in judging behavior. Some are more severe in their judgment of a situation, whereas others are more lenient.

Thus, it is important to have many opportunities not only to observe a given person or group but also to get some agreement among the observers on the action being observed. An observation by just one person may be very perceptive but again it could be misleading. Thus, ideally two or more observers are necessary.

Even having more than one observer does not completely solve the problem. Children as well as adults respond differently even while looking at the same behavior. You may "see" hostile behavior if you are ready to believe a person is hostile. In a certain sense, you have a set or perspective that focuses your observation. Human behavior can also be studied from many points of view. From similar observations, two individuals will stress or see different actions, or make different inferences. Some observers report a great deal of detail while others see only gross actions. The site where the observation takes place is also important. The observer may be influenced by the crowd or the general atmosphere.

Yet observation can be a source of data in problem solving. What are the most likely examples that elementary school teachers may use? Usually they are school problems. How are children acting on the playground? Are they friendly or unfriendly? Are children recycling by putting their glass bottles, paper, or cans in the right containers? Ecology offers many possibilities for observation. How much food is wasted in the school? What do the trash cans show after lunch? Students can observe the wastepaper basket within their own classroom. Are paper and other supplies being wasted? Do students reuse their paper lunch bags by putting them into their backpacks? In all these examples, students might observe which of their practices are contributing to caring for their environment and which are not. In structuring observations, teachers can assist students to look for actions, not people, that contribute to creating or solving a problem.

With technology becoming increasingly available to schools, students know that not all direct observation has to be limited to the look-see-record variety. Videotapes and recordings can also be used as ways of collecting data on behavior. Recording behavior makes it available to be restudied and rechecked as needed. However, all students know from watching television that when the camera pans a group of people who know they are being observed, the people often will behave differently from the way they would act if they had not known they were being observed or recorded.

Teachers must help students define peer pressure if they are observing how groups may try to influence individuals. Students generally must be directed to look at specific aspects of behavior and move away from generalizations about individuals—she is a wonderful, friendly person or she is a lonely nerd; he never wastes food and is protective of the environment or he is a complete slob and never recycles.

Teachers can help students *before* they go out to observe by having them role-play what is to be observed and use guide sheets to record their observations. Checklists or rating forms are often very useful. After students agree on what they have observed, they can discuss the inferences and judgments they can make on the basis of the data. Should the class work with the rest of the school to reduce waste and recycle more? Taking action reminds students of the value of thinking and makes the action more likely to be successful.

Observation skills are also used constantly in viewing media, in role playing, and on field trips. Having students become critical about television—one of the most pervasive sources of information for many students—is especially important. Constantly check what reaction students have to a film or a photograph you have shown or what they may have seen at home; they may differ on what they remember seeing or hearing, the inferences they make, and their judgment or evaluation of the material. By continually making students aware of the skills they need to use in observation, you can help many of them become more careful observers. Observation skills should not be a hit-or-miss activity; students need to be given instruction and help to use the observations skills as they interact with people.

Listening skills are similar to observation skills and are also critical in learning. A great deal of the school experience involves listening. Listening is stressed in many reading/language approaches. As children learn to listen, they can learn from others and expand their world. As in reading, the goal in listening is to grasp the main ideas. Students need to remember the most important things they hear.

Students must be encouraged to listen for the main theme—the major idea or thought that runs through the material. After students identify the main ideas and understand what has been said, the second stage in listening is to evaluate the content and ideas. Children often do not recognize that others may have a different frame of reference. When listening to a different frame of reference, students must identify the feel of the situation and see the problem the way the speaker sees it. This skill is called sensitivity or empathy. Before students hear a tape or record, assign to some of them roles such as those of labor leaders, Native American tribal leaders, or Asian immigrants. Ask students to listen and react to the song or poem the way the individual in their assumed role would react. Compare their reactions to those of the rest of the class; in this way, many students become more aware of how their own frame of reference (also true in observation) allows them to hear certain messages and ignore others. In addition, students realize that different people speak in different ways.

Teachers often use the rumor exercise in the classroom to illustrate how easily meaning can be distorted. The original message is whispered to one child or group and each person repeats this to the next person. The last member repeats the message as it has been received. Typically, the message, having passed through many versions, is likely to be very different from the original. This activity can be followed by a discussion of the difficulty people have in transmitting messages accurately, and of the effects of poor listening habits and the insertion of bias.

The difficulty is that students think listening is boring; it's more fun to talk. In addition, biology works against attentive listening. Most people speak at a rate of 120 to 150 words a minute, but the human brain can process more than 500 words per minute, leaving time for inattention. (This has been pointed out as a disadvantage of direct teaching.) Furthermore, gender differences may play a role with females being more sympathetic listeners than males and their interruptions more supportive than intrusive.

What can teachers do to encourage students' listening skills throughout the whole school day? Sometimes it is necessary to take time out for teaching these skills, as in debriefing in cooperative learning groups, to encourage students to be courteous listeners and not talk all the time. Check the amount of listening required in your class; young children have short attention spans. Try to vary the amount of listening with the opportunity for them to interact with others. Help students see the importance of listening by having them record the amount of listening they do both during the school day and outside school. Initially, tell your students what to listen for or to focus on and to look at the nonverbal clues of the speaker to help in understanding; later they can learn to listen without your assistance.

Questioning

Questioning is such an integral part of thinking and learning that it is common to all methods (see also Chapter 5 for the Taba method). Teachers need to ask a variety of appropriate questions—multiple responses as well as application, evaluative, and factual questions. Frame the questions carefully so that they are adapted to the cognitive levels and affective needs of your students. Use wait time of at least three seconds to give more students time to reflect. Remember that such wait time has payoffs for students: Participation increases, responses are longer and more complex, and confidence rises along with academic achievement. Teachers also gain by not having to repeat questions.

Handle incorrect responses with prompts such as restating the question at a lower level; and avoid negative statements and nonverbal cues. The modeling of questions should in turn encourage students to ask their teacher as well as classmates questions as they work in small groups with discussion, simulation, and role playing (Figure 3.3). However, teachers should avoid always asking low-level factual questions because they do not stimulate students to think. Students should be encouraged to ask questions even if they appear to be obvious to the rest of the class. Unfortunately, most questions asked of the teacher are housekeeping questions: Where do put our worksheets? What page do we read? Teachers, thus, need to encourage and praise students who do ask meaningful questions that generate good thinking among all the students. Students should also be reminded that the data or facts cannot be ignored, that they need to understand what is being discussed before they can think on a given subject.

Questions of clarification
What do you mean by _____?
Can you give me an example?
Can you explain further?
Why do you say that?
What do you think Ellen meant?
Can you summarize what Jose said?
Jose, is that what you meant?

Questions that probe for reasons and evidence
Do you have evidence for that?
Why do you think that is true?
How can we find out whether that is true?

Questions about viewpoints or perspectives
How would other groups respond?
What objections might these other groups make?
Can you see this in another way?
What would someone who disagrees say?

Questions that focus on consequences
Which individuals/groups will gain? Which individuals/groups will lose?
What will happen if that goes into effect?
Will this always happen?

FIGURE 3.3 Questions to Improve Thinking

Accepting or Rejecting a Hypothesis

After students gather data and ask questions, they need to classify and organize the information. Finding relationships and classifying facts under main headings requires skill. Students must be able to see, for example, that data on immigrants might belong in several categories, such as the problems immigrants face and the successes they have had. In addition, students will often have to analyze and interpret their information to decide what it really means. Only then are they in a position to accept or reject their hypothesis, the final step in the thinking process. Do the data support the hypothesis? Discuss and debate the conclusions.

We have shown here that you will probably have to use a variety of methods to teach problem solving or thinking. Questioning is almost always part of the process as well as discussion. Discussion, either in small or large groups, requires skills in observation (seeing the nonverbal communication), listening, and questioning. Discussion can take many formats. Some elementary teachers like using the **council discussion format.** Here students sit in one large circle and a talking stick is passed from student to student. You can speak only if you have the stick. The speaker's comments are usually brief and limited to one minute.

Thus, sometimes students will work in small groups; other times, they will work alone. In some cases, your role will be indirect as you try to encourage students to generate as many promising ideas as possible. In these cases, your role is not to judge but to encourage an atmosphere in the class in which ideas are welcome and not subjected to ridicule by other students. On the other hand, for specific skills, such as how to find information in an atlas, direct teaching may work best. But it is not enough just to drill students in these skills. Worksheets or other teaching material should be as entertaining as possible so that students will want to use the skills after they do the required assignments. Teaching skills that students will not use in the future is not beneficial for either the students or the school.

In teaching thinking, then, present a variety of open-ended problems or questions that students can use to practice their thinking skills. Make sure the students become interested in the problems, and don't pursue a problem if most children seem bored by it. Also, don't foster dependency in students by giving them too much help. Be positive about their ideas, and remember that many children have not had much experience in thinking and will not become creative thinkers in merely a few weeks. Remind students that making mistakes is part of the learning process and that they should not be discouraged if their first ideas do not work out. Finally, make the encouragement of thinking a goal in everything you do and every lesson you teach, throughout the year.

In summary, here are some hints for teaching thinking.

- Teach for meaning, not just memorization.
- Ask thought-provoking questions.
- Explain your thought processes.
- Have students explain their thought processes; promote metacognition—knowledge of when and where to use thinking strategies.
- Encourage and accept all ideas and viewpoints.
- Summarize main ideas.

ON YOUR OWN	JUST THE FACTS!
3.2	*How much thinking do you believe goes on in a typical social studies classroom? Does it occur during the whole day? If you believe that little thinking takes place in most classrooms, list three reasons that you believe lead many teachers to concentrate on having students recall facts instead of emphasizing thinking.*

■ COOPERATIVE OR COLLABORATIVE LEARNING

Cooperative learning is a popular instructional strategy in which small groups work together toward a common goal. In the literature, it can take a variety of forms such as Jigsaw, Student Team Learning, Group Investigation, Complex Instruction, and Learning Together. Common characteristics of cooperative learning are holding each individual in each group accountable for his or her learning, assigning complementary roles and tasks to each individual, and communicating with each other and rewarding members for achieving their goal. In contrast, **collaborative learning** is a more unstructured process in which the group members negotiate goals, define problems, develop procedures, and produce knowledge. Collaborative learning is probably best done at higher levels of education but in usage the terms *cooperative* and *collaborative learning* are interchangeable.

There are compelling reasons for using cooperative learning. Students may learn from their peers and increase their academic knowledge. They may increase and learn skills in listening to others, offering ideas, asking questions, compromising to resolve conflicts, and improving intergroup relations. Although not necessarily the only way to teach, and certainly not a panacea to all the problems of education, cooperative learning is a viable strategy you can use to deliver content and to teach skills.

Cooperative learning has many definitions. Some educators include peer teaching and cross-age tutoring as examples of cooperative learning. But these forms of tutoring lack an important element of cooperative learning: individual accountability. In cooperative learning, each member of the group must learn the subject matter or complete the task and is evaluated on his or her performance. This accountability seldom occurs in tutoring, as the tutor is normally not tested in the subject area that she or he is teaching. Tutoring also implies an unequal status relationship in which the tutor knows the material while the person being tutored is presumed to be less able academically.

In contrast, cooperative learning presumes that all students will make distinct contributions to the group's task. In other words, they are *all* members of the group and each is dependent on the other group members (i.e., one member of the group does not have all the answers).

Some definitions stress the size of the group. Cooperative learning consists of three or more students who are united in a common purpose to complete a task and to include every group member. Elizabeth Cohen (see suggested readings at the end of the chapter) suggests that the group size be limited to no more than five members.

TABLE 3.2 Teacher Evaluation of Cooperative Learning

Group	Work		Presentation	
Name	**Used Time Well**	**Encouraged Others**	**Quality of Information**	**Effectiveness in Delivery**
1.				
2.				
3.				

In summary, cooperative learning is a method in which a heterogeneous group is given a task to do that should include the efforts of all the students in the group. Students directly interact with each other. They do not just sit silently working on their own assignments. In addition, cooperative learning includes the element of individual accountability. There should be no "free ride" in which any student does not contribute to the group's efforts. Instead, each student is held accountable for learning the subject matter or contributing to the task. Lack of student accountability is probably the biggest problem in using cooperative learning. Accountability is often determined by tests or teacher evaluation of group work and presentations (see Table 3.2). To encourage the group effort, some teachers assign a group grade on a test as well as the presentation (if given) so that the more able members of the group take some responsibility for teaching the material or skills to all members of the group.

Why do experts recommend cooperative learning? During the typical classroom discussion, the average student has only one chance out of twenty-five (or whatever the class size may be) of having the opportunity to speak at a given moment. But if she or he is in a small group of four, the probability of speaking goes up to one in four. This means that there is more interaction among students, an important factor in learning both content and social skills.

Adults spend a great deal of time in small groups. Most of us interact with our families and friends. In community affairs, organizations, and clubs, a task is frequently assigned to a small committee. For teachers, it is almost impossible to avoid being put on a committee to work on some project to help improve the school.

In order to function in our society, everyone needs the skills to participate in small groups. Usually the activity is pleasant; most of us enjoy the socialization and companionship. But this is not always true. Have you ever been in a three-person group in which the other two members "ganged up" on you and tried to impose their views? In real life, three-member groups are often unstable regardless of the setting—three persons sharing an apartment or three people on an outing. Or have you been in a small group that was unpleasant because one person knew all the right answers and would not listen to others? Just putting individuals or students into a small group is not a guarantee that students will automatically become more involved, thoughtful, tolerant, or responsible when working with a group.

With these cautions, the first task for a teacher is to identify the lessons that are appropriate for cooperative learning. Ideally, there should be more than one answer or more than one way to solve the problem. If just factual answers from a textbook are asked, students will look to the brightest member of the group for all the answers and the rest of the group will just copy them. The task must be challenging and rewarding, requiring a variety of skills such as reading and writing.

The teacher's second task is to make organizational decisions in five areas: group size, team formation, use of roles, room arrangement, and materials. Group size, as noted previously, is an important characteristic of cooperative learning. In the past, some group work has divided the class into three more or less equal groups, typically with seven to ten members. This is far too large for effective small group work. In general, younger children profit most from smaller groups. In fact, two children is the proper group size for many primary children. Groups of three, four, or five are appropriate for more mature children. Group members must be able to see the non-verbal clues that other group members give as well as hear what everyone is saying. If the group is too large, members cannot monitor what is happening. Five should probably be the largest size for a group.

In assigning groups, especially early in the year, you need to look carefully at the academic achievement and the personalities of the class members. Initially all experts recommend heterogeneous grouping—mix students by ability, gender, ethnic groups, and so on. One way to do this is to make a list of students by academic achievement, from the highest to the lowest. If there are to be groups of three, put into each group a high-ability member, a middle achiever, and a low achiever. Some experts think it may be wise not to put high- and low-ability students in the same group if the differences are too extreme. Here the recommendation is to mix lower and middle students in small groups and middle- and high-ability students in other groups. Ensure that the gender and ethnic distributions are mixed. That means there should be a fairly equal distribution of girls and boys and of minority students. If you know that two students don't get along, do not, at least initially, place them together. However, later in the year, after their small group skills improve, you might *want* to assign them together. Avoid placing best friends on the same team. They will tend to talk and interact only with each other and ignore other members of the group. As a final suggestion, many teachers color code the groups. The names of all members of the blue team or group are under blue. These color-coded materials are posted so that all students can easily see to which team they belong.

The traditional approach by experts was to recommend heterogeneous grouping. But now tentative research findings have pointed out some dilemmas for teachers. The below-average student gains by achievement test scores if she or he had access in the group to a high-ability student who has correct answers and high-quality explanations. However, in general high-ability students gain more if they are grouped with other high-ability students.[5] In addition, high achievers grouped together are more focused on getting work done, offering better conceptual explanations, and engaging in superior problem-solving strategies. This may be due to the high-ability students having greater oral facility and more experience in providing explanations than other lower-ability students. The net result is that teachers will have to make deci-

[5]Norren W. Webb, Kariane M. Nemer, Alexander W. Chizhik, and Brenda Sugrue, "Equity Issues in Collaborative Group Assessment: Group Composition and Performance," *American Education Research Journal* 35 (Winter 1998): 646.

sions and struggle with balancing the needs of low- and high-achieving students in their classrooms. It may also be a problem if there are not enough experts, or high-ability students, to spread around to each group.

However, teachers who deliberately used a mix of criteria in forming groups by taking into account students' achievement levels as well as compatibility and interest reported stronger outcomes. This suggests you get inferior results by using grouping strategies such as random assignment (count off 1, 2, 3, etc.), groups of convenience (seated near each other), and self-selected groups. The teacher's judgment in forming groups increases achievement levels of the small groups.

Even with your best judgment in assigning groups, some groups may have difficulty working together. There may be personality clashes, ranging from minor bickering to insults that end in tears. Another problem is lack of participation. Often there are recognized stable hierarchies of "smart" and "slow" students. Most students in most classes within a short time categorize every member of the class as smart, average, or dumb, usually based on a verbal ability (such as reading). These attitudes about ability can carry over into students' small groups. Groups frequently take less advantage of the contributions and skills of students who are labeled dumb, despite your plea that everyone participate and that all work together.

Thus, students may quarrel about who is to do what and who should make decisions. In effect, they play power games, just as adults do. Higher-status students want to have leadership roles, and lower-status students resist being in a group that does not seem to appreciate their talents. In many cases, "slower" students withdraw by physically moving away from the group or by disrupting it.

To mitigate these problems, some teachers assign roles to each member of the group. This is the third organizational decision. One student is the chairperson, another is the secretary, a third is responsible for getting the supplies to the group, and a fourth is charged with seeing that the group stays on task. Some teachers prepare cards with the title of the role—"chairperson" or "secretary"—to emphasize that each member of the group is to perform a certain role.

Here are some roles that students can play in small groups:

Chairperson or Facilitator
 Organizes the group's work
 Makes sure the group understands its job
 Takes the group's questions to the teacher *after* trying to get answers from
  the group

Recorder or Secretary
 Writes down the group's answers on the group's answer sheet

Checker
 Checks that everyone can explain and agrees with the group's answer

Supporter or Encourager (eventually all members should be this)
 Keeps people feeling good about working together
 Shows interest and excitement about the group's work

Some teachers include other roles such as reporter, but often it is easier for the secretary to read his or her own writing than to give it to another student to try to decipher. Of course, these roles should be rotated throughout the group so that

TABLE 3.3 Group Self-Evaluation

	Usually	Sometimes	Never
1. Every group member participated.			
2. Our group used its time wisely.			
3. Every group member did his or her job.			
4. Group members encouraged each other.			

each student has a chance to assume each of the roles. You need to monitor what is going on. Occasionally, students do not take their assigned roles and, thus, allow leadership, for example, to pass on to another student who has not been assigned that role.

Roles may have to be taught and evaluated. You should explain clearly what is expected in each role. Sometimes a teacher may want to use the role of a student observer who checks carefully what is happening in the group. Another way is for group members, at the end of the work session, to process how they have worked together. One way to do this is for the teacher to ask whether everyone in the group participated and to ask the group to consider this question; another way is by using a group self-evaluation form (Table 3.3). Students should be given an opportunity to process how the group is working. This does not have to be done every day but is often a neglected element in cooperative learning.

The teacher's fourth organizational decision concerns the room arrangement for the groups. Ideally, the groups should be in a circle, preferably without tables or other obstructions. The group members should be close enough to each other to communicate and be removed enough from the rest of the class so that they do not get distracted by the noise and activities of the other groups. In addition, the teacher needs to be able to circulate among the groups without encountering physical obstacles.

You should consider what materials are needed for the group to complete its task. Will the members have to share one set of materials per group or will there be a textbook for everyone? Do students need a place to write or will oral discussion be the focus of the group's activity? Your decisions can influence the amount of interaction that the students have in their group.

These are the general steps for implementing cooperative learning. Usually it is wise at the beginning of the year to set up group learning experiences so that students can get to know one another better. Some teachers find it wise to start gradually with students in groups of two (dyads) for several weeks and then move into larger groups. At this point, the lessons do not have to include academic social studies content. Have the students in groups make collages, illustrating things they like to do, or have them share information about themselves with other members of the group. A favorite task is to develop a team name or sign to identify the group such as "The Experts" or "All-Stars of Room 2." Small groups might make poems on topics such as birthdays or a holiday. To do this, have individual students first jot down ideas or short phrases on the topic. These ideas can be incorporated into the group poem, which one member of the group might then read to the class. You might also want to post a copy of the poem, signed by all members of the group. The purpose of these activities is to teach students to use the ideas of *everyone* in the group and to take pride in *the group's final product*. In effect, this is team building in which each member develops a respect for everyone in the group.

As students get to know each other in the group, you may want to move into different formats of cooperative learning. One is group investigation, which requires each student to find material and decide how to communicate his or her learning to the remainder of the class. Perhaps you have decided that for the whole class to cover all the material in the textbook on Native Americans would take too much time. Instead, you decide to divide the students into cooperative groups, having each group study in depth a single nation or tribe. You can assign the nation or tribe, or let the group, with your approval, select the one they want to study. After being directed to the appropriate sources of information (with the help of your school librarian), the groups share with the rest of the class what they have discovered.

A more complex form of cooperative learning utilizes the *Jigsaw Technique* (Table 3.4). Here students teach each other factual content. Each child is assigned to both a learning team (the original home team) and a study group. Typically, content or a textbook chapter is divided into sections. On the elementary level, this probably should not be more than four pages. On the topic of the American Revolution, content could be divided into the following sections: the American Army, the American Navy, Foreign Aid, Loyalists, and Prisoners. Often the teacher prepares a list of questions to be answered on each section.

In every home team, each team member is assigned a number. For example, all of the "1's" get together to study the same materials, such as the content on the American Navy. All of the "2's" study the content on foreign aid. Each group becomes an expert in the content it has been given and thinks of ways to teach its content. Then these experts return to their home team to teach the information related to their topics to the other home team members. Within the group members take turns teaching the information in which they have become experts. Thus, each member teaches his or her assigned content to the rest of the group and learns from the others the content they were assigned to teach. Finally, after studying the content in their own home group, all students in the class are tested on content from all of the chapter sections.

TABLE 3.4 Jigsaw

Steps
1. Design a lesson with a clear objective for the task. The task should be communicated both orally and in writing.
2. Choose the group size and composition.
3. Assign roles, divide learning materials into small portions.
4. Have students do individual reading of information of their group.
5. Have each expert group study the information and decide how best to teach other groups.
6. Send experts back to home teams to teach their information.
7. Assess learning on all the material.
8. Process how well the groups did (expert and home teams).

Typically, each student receives two grades from the test: an individual score as well as a team score. Realizing that their grades are partially dependent on the achievement of the home team, students are encouraged to do their best in group work.

The teacher acts as a timekeeper; sometimes this can be a problem in the expert group, in which material may not be covered. Students often request more time. Each phase of Jigsaw need not be done on the same day.

In Jigsaw as well as other forms of cooperative learning, grading can be a problem. Sometimes the "smart" students overparticipate, and the less able students contribute little (or find their contributions undervalued by the group). Often students see as unfair the teacher's insistence that all members of the group be given the same grade. If you explicitly require that all students in some way participate in the group's efforts, the "able" students will be more likely to make sure everyone is included so their grades will not be lowered. Some teachers use the whole group's score on tests to determine whether there is improvement and give extra points to the groups that improve.

Teachers also have to decide how long a given group stays together. Some teachers like to change the groups after a number of weeks so that students will learn to work with a variety of different personalities. Others keep the same groups for months, especially if the focus is on teaching social participation skills, such as having members encourage each other. These skills take time and practice, and often they can be applied more effectively if the group members already know each other.

Cooperative learning, like any other method, can be used in inappropriate ways. In the worst cases, cooperative learning can exacerbate status differences and create dysfunctional relationships among students. When teachers do spend the time needed to teach the skills of group work, specify tasks, and use time allotments and roles for group work sessions, cooperative learning can be a productive and powerful method. The class atmosphere may improve as students get to know one another better and learn to work together. Everyone enjoys the class more. Furthermore, the academic achievement level of the class may increase.

Cooperative learning does require special attention and planning by the teacher. Make your assignments and instructions clear so that the group does not take too much time trying to determine what has to be done. In addition, you must monitor carefully what is going on and that the group is on task with all the students participating. Are some students passive? Is one group constantly bickering? Is one student always ordering the other members of the group around? If these problems persist, even after processing, you may have to show students how to make improvements in the group. Role playing at "being bossy" or demonstrating other problems can also provide a rewarding opportunity for students to become aware of how to improve their small group skills.

Teachers also need to think about students who have Attention Deficit Hyperactivity Disorder (ADHD) when using cooperative learning. It is important that all students understand the team rules. Team rules alert all students to expected behavior without targeting students with ADHD as potential "troublemakers." You may need to prepare and alert students to an alternative assignment or "time-out" area for students needing to remove themselves temporarily from their groups.

SMALL GROUP WORK	**TRYING OUT SMALL GROUP TASKS**
3.3	*The best way to learn how to use small group or operative learning is to do it yourself. Experience firsthand what it is like to be a member of a small group. Try the following formats and see how you like the experience. First, brainstorm in a group for a few minutes on the advantages and disadvantages of small group work. The rule here is that no one is allowed to discourage any ideas. Then write down a few ideas on how you think small group work could be used in teaching social studies. Now convene a second group and try to move toward consensus by choosing the three best contributions. How were the experiences different?*

■ ROLE PLAYING

What is role playing and how does it work? *Role playing* is a method of problem solving that enables participants to explore alternative solutions to a given problem. It is an *unrehearsed* dramatic presentation, usually more appropriate for children age 9 or older. Role playing is especially useful for dealing with controversial issues.

The impetus for role playing can be provided by reading the class a story or a law case or by having students view an open-ended film or photograph showing conflict. Classroom problems such as lack of sharing or breaking school or class rules can also be used for role playing. When you use problems in your own class such as dealing with the class bully, however, do not use actual names, and disguise the incident on which the group is focusing.

The basic steps in role playing are outlined in Table 3.5. Role playing can be a safe way of exploring alternative behavior. It allows us to express feelings or opinions without risking disapproval. Many of us, when we are driving on the freeway or sitting at our desks at the end of the day, have said to ourselves, "If only I had said this or that, the situation would have been better." Students need to know that sometimes alternative ways of acting lead to better solutions. Role playing offers a safe opportunity to explore.

Role playing also can help prepare students to cope with conflict resolution and problem solving. Role playing is used, for instance, to help students "say no to drugs." Proponents of this approach in substance-abuse education believe that it is not enough just to tell a student to say no to drugs. It is better to act out situations, such as a party at which one student offers alcohol to another student. Showing different ways in which a student can refuse alcohol while still remaining "friends" with the offerer may be important to students. In addition, this approach can suggest to the "straight" student that it is possible to find activities other than alcohol use to share with the user—a step to help the substance user.

Using role playing in substance-abuse education also illustrates another value of role playing. Role playing can deal directly with issues on which students might be

TABLE 3.5 Steps in Role Playing

1. Present the open-ended problem. Set the stage by asking, "Have you ever . . . ?" or "How did you feel when you were . . . ?" Then say, "Today we're going to hear a story about Kyle (or any name other than that of a member of your class) who got into a similar mess. Think about how you would feel if you were in such a situation." Next, read the story up to the conflict point. Encourage students to identify the problem and talk about how the people in the story feel.

2. Select the participants or role players. Ask for volunteers to play the various roles. The rest of the class will serve as observers.

3. Begin the role play. Enact an ending for the story. Have students pretend to be characters with the feelings and ideas of the people in the specific situation.

4. Discuss the solution, especially in terms of its realism. Ask the observers if there are alternative ways of solving the problems.

5. Explore the alternative possibilities in further role playing.

6. Discuss the several role-playing experiences and, if possible, summarize what has been learned.

---

reluctant to give their opinions in other formats, such as what to do if you see two children fighting or if you meet a friend after you have heard that this friend has told lies about you. By providing a situation in which students are and yet are not themselves, you give them a chance to bring out feelings and opinions they might otherwise not be willing to express.

Most students enjoy participating in and watching role playing. It provides an opportunity for more active involvement than many other classroom learning experiences, and it is more personalized. Acting out the dilemma of a pioneer child who must decide if he will report to his Native American friend that the tribe's camp will be raided the next day involves the students in what has happened in the past. Many teachers say they are using role playing to play out historical events (e.g., the Constitutional Convention of 1787) much as they actually occurred. Technically, when students act in a prescribed fashion and merely duplicate the historical event, they are doing *dramatic play,* not role playing. Mock trials, often used with older children who are already familiar with the procedures used in courts, are also an example of using drama. For example, students can reenact the Salem witch trials, Socrates' trial, or other important trials in history. To be successful, students need a good background in the time period as well as knowledge of court procedure. *Readers' Theatre* is another dramatic presentation in which the lines of the students, as in a play, are already fixed and not given as alternatives. This is not to deny the value of reading a play or script, especially if students themselves have made the script. It merely points out the differences in dramatic play and role playing. The focus of role playing is the concept of *alternatives,* or other ways the story or historical event might have ended (see Figure 3.4).

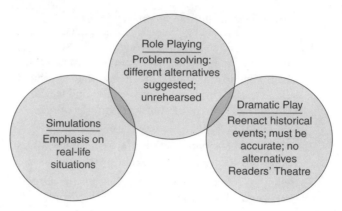

FIGURE 3.4 Interrelationships Between Interactive Teaching Strategies

You may encounter students who are reluctant to volunteer to role-play, especially at first. Others are often born hams who want to play roles every time. Do not let these "actors" take over the stage completely. Start with less controversial or emotional issues so that students become more at ease in role playing. Continue to encourage the shy students to volunteer, and as students get used to the format of role playing, they will become more eager to play a role. However, be careful not to cast students in the roles they occupy in the minds of their classmates. Do not put the class clown in a role in which he or she plays the class clown. Instead, put each student in someone else's shoes. The class bully should play the role of the weaker student who wants to have a turn in a game. Continually emphasize the role that the student is playing and avoid calling the student by his or her real name. Refer to the police officer or the landlady rather than to the specific student.

Sometimes students have a difficult time maintaining their roles. They start to giggle and often are distracted by the response of their audience. Members of the audience, too, must play their role appropriately. You may want to comment on this before or after the exercise. Usually, with time and practice, students are better able to maintain their roles.

Initially, you may find that many students want to play the enactment as it "should" be. In other words, they will play a role in a kind and loving manner and do all the right things. You need to ask if this is how it really happens. Some teachers are bothered if students enact negative, although realistic, behavior. They think that the class may model the wrong pattern. This is especially true, for example, if a student role involves pretending to take drugs or acting according to some other behavior that the community strongly opposes. But this should not be a major concern if you have an appropriate discussion and debriefing on what was going on. You can ask students who acted in negative roles how they felt. Often they will say that they were uncomfortable about how they acted. Thus, the debriefing stage is one of the most important parts of role playing. By sharing feelings and answering questions at the end of the enactment, students may see further alternative ways to act.

Teachers sometimes believe that they must force a generalization from the role-playing experience. They want the group to come to a conclusion—for example, "If you are not hostile in a situation, there is more chance that you can solve a problem."

But sometimes students are not yet ready to reach that conclusion. In those cases, it is best to drop the matter. Perhaps in a later experience, the group will come to that or a similar conclusion.

Role playing in the social studies offers the possibility of moving into the affective domain. It can help teach children to empathize with others by showing them how it feels to be in someone else's place. It can tap the emotional responses of students to certain situations while still moving toward a rational solution to a problem. This is one of the values of role playing. Often role playing can be a springboard for further study on a given topic. For this reason, it can be a successful method for the social studies teacher.

SMALL GROUP WORK	DEVELOP A ROLE PLAY
3.4	*Try role playing in your class. You might use the scenario of a principal walking into a class when everything is confused and disorderly. Assign roles of the principal, student teacher or teacher, and a few students in the class.*

■ SIMULATIONS

Simulations are learning activities that present an artificial problem or event. The situation described tries to duplicate reality but removes the possibility of injury or risk. Pilots, for example, learn to fly by using a simulator, whereas both the military and business worlds may use simulations to learn how to win a campaign or where to locate a new factory. In many cases, a computer records the responses of the trainees or participants in the simulation.

Like role playing, a simulation allows the trainee or the player to try out a role and make decisions in a safe environment. But unlike role playing, which focuses on problem solving, simulations have a gamelike quality in which there are players, roles, and an end goal, such as winning. Because of this, many students think that simulations are fun, and they are motivated to do their best. Often they are put in a conflict or crisis situation, such as a political situation in the Middle East, and are asked to play high-ranking political and military leaders or other important roles. Usually, they compete with others. Simulations such as "Seal Hunt" encourage cooperative behavior, but most simulations are based on competition.

In education, simulations were used initially without a computer. Students played simulations such as "Star Power," which set up an unequal division of power and resources, and students were supposed to learn what it was like to be a member of certain power groups. In another social studies simulation, "Farming," set in western Kansas in three different years, students acting in teams of two made economic decisions on what to invest in—hogs, wheat, livestock, and so on. The simulation tried to duplicate the reality of farming in the 1880s, and at the end of the simulation, many of the couples (students) found that they had lost their money. Part of the purpose of this simulation was to bring to life the problems that farmers were facing after the Civil War. One of the advantages of well-designed simulations is that they can make abstract concepts such as oversupply or power more meaningful for students.

In addition, simulations provide almost immediate feedback to the students on how they are doing, which is a key to motivation.

We are now seeing more computer-based social studies simulations. In most of them, the individual student interacts with the computer program, playing the role of the king-priest of an ancient city making economic decisions, for instance, or trying to win a political campaign in the United States. Other examples are the well-known "Oregon Trail" or the "New Oregon Trail," where players travel on the Oregon Trail making decisions faced by the original pioneers. There are many variations of this as children pretend to travel on the "Santa Fe Trail" or go to the gold mines of California ("Golden Spike"). In a few games, such as "Geography Search," students act in teams to try to locate valuable resources. In these cases, there is often competition between different teams in the same classroom.

Neither computer nor noncomputer simulations in the social studies are usually designed commercially for the primary-grade levels; they are for middle grades and beyond. However, primary teachers may design their own simulations, setting up, for instance, a post office, hospital, or other community institution.

Along with many advantages, there are also pitfalls in using simulations in the classroom:

1. In some cases, especially at the middle school level, students may have to learn complex rules in order to play. They may be unable or unwilling to listen to a long explanation, and you may find it best to have students learn by doing, even if some encounter frustration.
2. Some students are motivated in simulations only when they have important roles to play. They find it unfair that they have to play poor people or members of a group who are discriminated against. You may find that students are reluctant to accept these roles, although the roles are necessary to the simulation.
3. Simulations can have management problems. They are often noisy. Occasionally, students get so involved in playing the simulation that they actually become hostile and even start fights. You must constantly scan the classroom to monitor what is going on.
4. Teachers sometimes believe that simulations misinform students by oversimplifying. If a student plays the role of a United Nations delegate, for example, the student may then believe that he or she knows all about the United Nations. Some teachers also worry that simulations encourage unethical or immoral behavior, as when students choose to drop bombs and start wars or to take resources from poorer players.

As you can see, some of these concerns are similar to those associated with role playing. As with that approach, discussion and debriefing are essential to clarify what actions players choose to take and what effects those actions have on other players. Thus, in "Seal Hunt," students must realize that their decision not to share resources may have forced other students to starve. In the "Mercantilism" simulation, which is set in colonial America, students, eager to make money, find they are often engaging in both slavery and smuggling. It is important in debriefing to clarify what the students are actually doing and to explore the consequences of such behavior.

The strong advantage of a simulation is that students are often highly enthusiastic and motivated. There is a minority of students, however, who would rather read the textbook and answer the questions at the end of the chapter; not all students are the same. You must, therefore, determine whether a simulation has achieved the desired objectives. Do the students now know more about understanding different cultural groups? Do they feel more empathy for disadvantaged people or developing nations? Like any other method, a simulation is worthwhile only if it conveys knowledge, skills, or changes in feelings and attitudes.

ON YOUR OWN	RESEARCH BY DOING
3.3	*Acquire a simulation. Your curriculum library or computer library may have some to choose from. Good sources of what is available are Interact, P.O. Box 997, Lakeside, CA 92040 (www.interact-simulations.com) or Social Studies School Services, 10200 Jefferson Boulevard, Culver City, CA 90232-0802 (800-421-4246; FAX 800-944-5432; www.socialstudies.com). Secure the teacher's manual. Review the simulation, step by step, to see how it works. Do you see possible difficulties? What does it seem to teach? Secure reviews, if possible, from teachers or from computer journals on how the simulation is rated.*

Other methods do exist for teaching the social studies. Some teachers individualize instruction and set up learning centers. Others assume the role of a coach to the students. The teacher as a coach helps students master particular skills through the use of practice and prompts such as questioning. Sometimes questioning is listed as a distinct method, although questioning is part of almost all methods. In particular, the Taba approach, which uses teacher questions to move students to concepts and generalizations, is often recommended. (See Chapter 5.) Different methods are more appropriate for certain students and for achieving certain objectives; no method will work all the time for all teachers and all students. Since you are the decision maker, you must decide what combination of methods is best suited to achieving your objectives.

■ SUMMARY

Teaching strategies should be challenging, flexibly applied, and responsive to students' needs. Each teaching method has certain advantages. The direct-teaching learning model can be useful to impart certain information and concepts. Discovery and problem-solving methods are extremely important in teaching students how to think. Cooperative learning or other small group activities can teach knowledge *and* social skills. Role playing and simulations are more interactive methods that can touch the affective domain. Questioning skills are an integral part of all methods. The choice of methods depends partly on what you are trying to achieve. In general, by using variety in your teaching methods, you will be more successful in adapting to the diverse learning styles of your students and content differences.

■ SUGGESTED READINGS AND WEB SITES ■

Borich, Gary D. *Effective Teaching Methods*, 3rd ed. New York: Merrill, 1996.

Reviews teaching methods.

Chance, Paul. *Thinking in the Classroom*. New York: Teachers College Press, 1986.

Excellent overview of several types of current thinking programs.

Clegg, Ambroise, A. "Games and Simulations in Social Studies Education." In James Shavers, ed., *Handbook of Research on Social Studies Teaching and Learning*. New York: Macmillan, 1991.

Reviews games and simulations for the social studies.

Cohen, Elizabeth G. *Designing Groupwork*, 2nd ed. New York: Teachers College Press, 1994.

Good pointers, step-by step approach.

DeLisle, R. *How to Use Problem-Based Learning in the Classroom*. Alexandria, VA: Association for Supervision and Curriculum Development, 1998.

Freiberg, H. Jerome, and Amy Driscoll. *Universal Teaching Strategies*. Boston: Allyn & Bacon, 1996.

Divided into three main sections on organizing, instruction, and assessment.

Hunter, Madeline. *Mastery Teaching*. El Segundo, CA: TIP Publications, 1982.

Advocate of direct teaching.

Johnson, David W., and Roger T. Johnson. *Learning Together and Alone*, 4th ed. Englewood Cliffs, NJ: Prentice-Hall, 1994.

Excellent on cooperative learning techniques.

Joyce, Bruce, and Marsha Weil. *Models of Teaching*. 5th ed. Boston: Allyn & Bacon, 1996.

Different chapters on various models/methods used in teaching.

Orlich, Donald C., Anne L. Remaley, Kevin C. Facemeyer, Jerry Logan, and Qin Cao. "Seeking the Link Between Student Achievement and Staff Development." *Journal of Staff Development* 14, no. 3 (1993): 2–8.

A critical report on the effectiveness of the Hunter model.

Shaftel, Fannie R., and George Shaftel. *Role Playing in the Curriculum*, 2nd ed. Englewood Cliffs, NJ: Prentice-Hall, 1982.

Best text available on role playing.

Slavin, Robert E. *Cooperative Learning—Theory, Research, and Practice*, 2nd ed. Boston: Allyn & Bacon, 1995.

Reviews research, theory, and applications of cooperative learning.

Stahl, Robert J., ed. *Cooperative Learning in Social Studies: A Handbook for Teachers* Menlo Park, CA: Addison-Wesley, 1994.

A set of fourteen articles on cooperative learning as applied to the social studies.

Stahl, Robert J., and Ronald L. Van Sickle, eds. *Cooperative Learning in the Social Studies Classroom*, Bulletin 87. Washington, DC: National Council for the Social Studies, 1992.

Good examples.

Taba, Hilda. *Teacher's Handbook for Elementary Social Studies*. Palo Alto, CA: Addison-Wesley, 1967.

Excellent on thinking strategies.

Web Sites

Center for Problem-Based Learning
www.imsa.edu/team/cpbl
Center for Problem-Based Learning, Illinois Math and Science Academy

This site defines and describes problem-based learning and provides examples. Teachers from all grade levels will find this site valuable. Links to other problem-based learning sites.

Score
http://score.rims.k12.ca.us/

A good source for lesson plans is the Schools of California Online Resources for Education (SCORE). Lessons and resources are organized by grade level as well as topics. Although the Web site is organized for the standards and framework of California, most of the content is valuable for all teachers.

Many of the Web sites for problem-based learning or problem solving may be too advanced for some primary students and only appropriate, if at all on that level, for middle school students.

Chapter 4

Assessing and Evaluating Students' Progress in the Social Studies

In this chapter we describe from various perspectives the purposes and functions of assessment and evaluation in the social studies. We discuss techniques for gathering data for the assessment of learning. We also explore ideas for communicating these data to parents and students. The following topics provide the focus for this chapter.

- Perceptions of Evaluation
- National Assessment of Educational Progress
- State Testing
- Assessment of Student Learning
- Assessment Techniques and Tools
- Evaluating Learning and Development

■ PERCEPTIONS OF EVALUATION

Evaluation is something like beauty: Defining it depends, in part, on who is viewing it. As teachers, we play the pivotal role in this process. By examining the motivation of the other actors—the student, the parent, the school system, the public—in the process, we can get a better sense of the power and potential that our own role offers.

The Student

Remembering your own experiences or those of your children is a good place to begin when you examine the impact that evaluation can have on a student. How many of us remember report-card day as a positive experience in our lives? Did we have a clue about why we got the grades we did? Was the report card itself important, or was the response of our parents and friends to it what we remember?

From the perspective of a student, evaluation is synonymous with grades and report cards. Unfortunately, the connotation is too often pejorative. Students understand very early that grades represent a mysterious power over their lives. They know when they are grouped for instruction by ability. They are tuned in to any indication that a teacher may, or may not, like them and, seeking confirmation of their suspicions, they connect that indication to the grade they receive.

When questioned, students often do not establish a connection between work habits and grades. They usually do not link final results to a series of smaller steps in preparing for a test, project, or presentation. They see evaluation as something outside their control. For many students, grades have little to do with learning or pride of accomplishment.

The Parent

All parents want their child to succeed. They want you as a teacher representing the school to recognize their child for the special person he or she is. They want assurance that you know their son or daughter. Parents are often amazed to learn about aspects of their child's behavior that they have not seen at home.

Grades and reports worry parents because they represent judgments about their child—the first indications about how that child will do in life outside the home. They want to know whether their child measures up to others of the same age. Most parents see reports and grades as stepping-stones or barriers to "the good life."

Parents want to know what their child is supposed to be learning. Many will want suggestions from teachers about how they can help their daughter or son achieve what is required. Some may use reports as ways either to punish or reward their child at home.

The Teacher

Most teachers look upon evaluation as a necessary but uncomfortable task. It is a function they are forced to perform as a way to communicate how students are doing to the students, their families, and the school system.

Teachers try to treat each student fairly as they collect impressions of her or his progress. They are channeled by their school system to work toward instructional objectives according to grade level and subjects, even if these objectives may not be the most appropriate for every student. They are frustrated by lack of time and energy and their inability to attend more adequately to every child's needs.

Teachers are held accountable by parents to inspire in their children a love of learning and growth in all aspects of their social, cognitive, and physical knowledge and skills. They are expected by the school to produce the best possible test-score results. Sometimes it seems as though no one, not even the student, is accountable to the teacher. Yet teachers are being held responsible by the parents and the school for producing the results they both desire while not being given enough support from either group.

The School System

Evaluation is the principal means of quantifying how students are doing in school. Methods of authentic evaluation that are tied to student performance—checking students' actual work rather than separate or standardized tests against instructional objectives or performance criteria—represent an ideal toward which schools must work. In reality, however, moving systems toward more holistic ways to assess student progress by looking at performance requires expensive teacher training and curriculum revision that few schools can afford. Keeping records of individual student progress is an essential way to communicate with parents and other schools about that student. Reducing the data to grade-level equivalents and numbers or letters seems to be a more efficient way to communicate about individual progress.

The more evaluative data teachers collect on students, the better their program analysis can become. Decisions about new curricula cannot be made without data on student progress. Other factors are important, but test scores can offer insight to the performance of a school system over a long period. Comparing one district with other districts is difficult without demographic, funding, and standardized test data.

The Public and the State

Increasingly, there are other important players concerned with evaluation of the school achievement of children. This includes the local neighborhood whose residents know that their property values are influenced by the reputation of the local public school. Parents want to send their children to "good" schools and are reluctant to buy or to rent housing in a neighborhood with "poor" schools where tests show that children are not achieving as much as expected. Because of its importance, many real estate agents have on hand the published scores of tests of the schools to show to prospective buyers or renters.

The results of state test scores are now available from many sources—newspapers, online, real estate offices, local school offices—because of mandated state testing in many subject areas. Reforming education is considered an important issue for state government leaders who have responded to these concerns by a mandated standards-based educational reform. As a result, the annual publication of test scores of schools can be a hot item and an important public issue.

The Experts

Broad views about the value of evaluation suggest that it should serve all participants on the school-achievement scene—the student, the parent, the teacher, the public, and the school system. Elliott Eisner, a well-known education professor at Stanford, listed five functions of evaluation:[1]

1. To diagnose what a child knows and thereby point toward appropriate instruction;
2. To provide data for the revision of curriculum both for the classroom teacher and the system;
3. To compare what children can be before and after instruction and with and without instruction;
4. To anticipate educational needs of children as they progress through a curriculum;
5. To determine if instruction objectives are being met.

[1]Elliott Eisner, *The Educational Imagination*, 2nd ed. (New York: Macmillan, 1985), p. 192.

Even though we may empathize with the perspective of each of these groups, it is also important to be informed about and take advantage of the potential benefits everyone involved stands to gain from an effective assessment and evaluation process. All these perspectives are interrelated. Notice that in each perspective, evaluation is a decision-making tool, not an end in itself. No one would object to a process in which evaluation is an integral part of instruction, providing the momentum for instructional effort toward some agreed-on direction.

Experts want to change aspects of each perception described. They want children to participate more in decisions about their learning. They want parents to understand that evaluation is part of a process, not a final judgment about their child or a weight to be held over a child's head. They want teachers to make greater use of assessment results to guide their instructional planning. They want school systems to collect evaluation data in the most unobtrusive, least time-consuming way possible. And they want systems to refuse to test students with instruments inappropriate to the goals the systems have set, or in ways that were not part of the natural activity of learning. And most important, they would urge teachers first to invest their energies developing curricula with contemporary, significant content delivered in motivating and meaningful ways.

Everyone wants schools to test students fairly according to the goals the district has established, and ideally in ways that are part of the natural dynamics of classroom learning. What a marvelous idea it would be if students found assessment to be a lively, active, exciting experience! Or if teachers thought standardized tests or those given by the district or state were a fair assessment of their students.

You will remember from Chapter 1 that almost all states are asking for greater accountability for student learning from the schools. With increased attention to standards, it is clear that test results will continue to be used as arguments in the debate about how to reform education. Assessment can be used to determine if the individual, the teacher, the principal, and the whole school are successful in meeting the standards. What should happen if the student or school or district has low performance and is not improving? You can see how important assessment is.

Paralleling the growing momentum for state testing is the growth of interest and experimentation with alternative forms of assessment. These seek to move away from using only multiple-choice objective test items to judge student achievement. Critics of standardized tests charge that they inadequately and unfairly measure nonwhite, nonmiddle-class students. They also argue that the formats of these kinds of tests prompt all students to learn that there is only one right answer to every question or that their job is to get the answer by guessing. The debate about the forms and adequacy of achievement assessment has caused educators to become more critical of how they evaluate student achievement. For all types of assessment, there is general consensus that they should attempt to meet these criteria:

- Encourage high performance standards.
- Be gender, ethnic, and class-bias free.
- Promote critical thinking and effective citizenship.
- Be useful for diagnosis to improve student performance.
- Help students apply what they have learned to real-life situations.

SMALL GROUP WORK	**ACCOUNTABILITY**
4.1	*How do you feel about being accountable as a teacher for the test scores of your students? Do you think this type of accountability improves teacher performance? Do students work harder if they know they are to be tested?*

■ NATIONAL ASSESSMENT OF EDUCATIONAL PROGRESS

Besides the wide publicity given to international test score comparisons of American students to students in other nations, throughout the years you may have heard about the Nation's Report Cards, the **National Assessment of Educational Progress (NAEP)**. Since 1969, NAEP, as mandated by Congress, measures student growth in various areas of the school curriculum by doing testing on a very large sample of American students at the fourth, eighth, and twelfth grades so that the results can be generalized to the whole nation. It is the nation's foremost and only national ongoing educational survey, allowing all to see the strengths and weaknesses of American students.

NAEP has two assessments: the main NAEP in various subject areas, such as history, geography, and civics, and the long-term-trend NAEP in four subject areas: reading, mathematics, science, and writing. These two assessments use distinct data collection procedures, separate samples of students, and test instruments. Student and teacher background questionnaires also vary between the main and long-term-trend assessments. Since 1990, many states but not all have elected to have their individual NAEP state test scores released to the public.

Has your state chosen to release NAEP test results?

■ STATE TESTING

As you know, many states have mandated state testing in the social studies. But there are wide differences in what types of tests are used and what the consequences of test results are in the various states. Still, twenty-three states led by the Missouri Department of Elementary and Secondary Education, the Council of Chief State School Officers, and American College Testing are cooperating to develop high-level thinking assessments in history, geography, civics, and economics. This may lead to better questions on state tests.

Let us first carefully define the terms used in the state's accountability assessment program.

High stakes means that rewards and penalties are directed at students, administrators, schools, and districts tied wholly or in part to test scores. The groups that are affected vary among the states. For students, this could affect high school graduation or grade-level promotion at certain grade levels such as fourth and eighth grades. For administrators, it could mean a transfer, or in states that do not have tenure for principals it could mean the loss of their position. For schools and districts, continued low scores without improvement could mean that the state takes over control of the school or district. In most states, the high-stake focus is directly on students and individual schools and indirectly on districts.

Types of Tests

What tests will a state use to test social studies? One choice is **off-the-shelf tests.** Off-the-shelf tests are basic, generic, national tests such as the Iowa Test of Basic Skills, Stanford Achievement Test, and TerraNova, which are available by catalog. Their questions are based on national standards, regional curriculum, and testing research. In the politically charged education environment at the present time, publishers are very careful in the development of their tests. Lawsuits, especially if the test is unfair to minority students, make publishers mindful of the consequences of having a poor test. But even with carefully constructed questions, a particular state's standards may not be aligned to a national test, meaning it is not truly measuring what is being taught.

Of course, the advantage of off-the-shelf testing is the relative cheapness of the test. To create a custom-made test for states is expensive but is being done, for example, in Wisconsin for its social studies tests. A custom made test can use the state's own standards, control the rigor of the test, and adjust to any distinctive customs and mores. Some of the states are putting increasing emphasis on problem solving and on items with more than one right answer. These are desirable goals and may be the most important impact of the standards-based reform. The traditional tests have been criticized for prompting teachers to emphasize basic, factual information and for providing few opportunities for students to learn how to apply knowledge.

As a compromise, some states such as California are now using off-the-shelf tests augmented by additional questions or separate tests that are aligned with the state's own standards. Teachers in these states then have to balance teaching and learning for both types of tests.

Most national tests are scored by **norm-referenced testing,** which compares students' results with a national norm. The results for the individual students are expressed in percentiles such as the 84th and the 45th percentiles, which are comparing how students performed to a national sample of students on the same test. To determine norms, test makers give exams to a representative national sampling of students. Typically the norms are reconfigured every seven years. This means that progress toward state standards cannot be assessed with norm-referenced exams because they test how students compare with each other and not how much of the standards they know or can perform.

In contrast, **criterion-based testing** or **performance testing** measures students' performance based on standards of what they should know. Such tests can answer the question of how particular students compare with the criterion or standard that educators expect them to know or to demonstrate. An example of criterion-based testing is NAEP tests. Frameworks for the subject area are established by educators and state education officials and reviewed by a wide range of committees, public hearings, scholars in the fields, and so on to establish the subject standards. Test items are then produced that elicit if the student knows or can perform according to the standards. Scores are then reported as levels—not proficient, basic, proficient, advanced. Although performance scores are a better measure of what students know than percentile scores, they are also somewhat arbitrary and subject to the judgment of the experts who establish the cutoff points. The cutoff score that is used to indicate failure or nonproficiency is extremely critical because it influences the number of students who fail the test.

Let us remember that among students individual differences are immense. Some can easily pass a social studies test whereas others will have difficulty. Furthermore, the accuracy in testing means that there is always a small degree of error. The problem is to **set standards that are high but obtainable.** Holding all students, however, to the same standards will lead to lowering standards or untenable retention and failure rates. Just as Goldilocks wanted something not too hard or too soft and not too warm or too cold, standards should not be set too high or too low. This is easier said than done. This also means that students need the opportunity to learn the content and skills and teachers need professional development opportunities so that their students can meet the standards. Professional opportunities allow teachers and administrators to analyze instruction, assessment, and achievement. They can learn about effective practices and set goals for improvement. In addition, options such as untimed tests need to be examined.

Role of the Teacher

What, as a teacher, can you do if your state has a social studies test or other tests? A concern for high test scores should not drive the curriculum, but there is an overlap of good teaching of social studies and good social studies test scores. In fact, teaching higher level skills improves test scores. It is wise to become familiar with the test. First, analyze the test to understand the knowledge and skills needed to succeed. For example, in a fourth-grade test, what proportion of the test has geography items and what proportion of the test has economic items? Second, what is the format of the items? Multiple choice? Bar graphs? Time lines?

Then infuse the goals of the test in your ongoing social studies program. Through reading, listening, speaking, and writing activities plus instruction, test preparation occurs throughout the school year. In contrast teachers who confine their test preparation to the week or two before the test focus more on how to take the test rather than on how, over time, to actually gain and retain the knowledge and skills that underlie what is being tested. Also in your regular assessment give your students the opportunity to become familiar with the content, skills, and formats of the test items. Students should not be exposed to a new test item format on the day of the exam. They should be able to meet the challenge of the predictable test items they will face.

Check if some or all of your LEP students or those students with disabilities (SD) will be required to take the test. The trend is for more inclusion in testing except for those with severe disabilities. Press for all the possible accommodations for these students so they can show what they know.

SMALL GROUP WORK	**WHAT ARE THE EFFECTS OF STATE TESTING?**
4.2	*What effects is state testing or district testing having in your area? Examine both good and negative effects. On the negative side, state testing should use multiple measures of achievement rather than depending on a score from one test to make important decisions, there are errors in measurement, it encourages cheating, and it may increase the dropout rate of high school students. On the positive side, students are motivated to work harder, all in the system are held accountable, and state testing forces more attention on lower-achieving students.*

■ ASSESSMENT OF STUDENT LEARNING

Assessments are the ways we use to collect data for student learning. Assessment should reflect the goals, standards and objectives, and emphasis given during instruction. Students ought to be assessed in multiple ways that allow them to show what they have learned. If there are state standards, assessment needs to show evidence of achievement of the standards.

SMALL GROUP WORK	**WHAT ARE YOUR IMAGES OF ASSESSMENT?**
4.3	*What do you think about when you hear the term* assessment? *Is it negative? Why?*

Performance-Based Assessment

As the school-age population has become both more diverse culturally and linguistically and with the necessity for higher-order thinking skills, assessment tools must expand beyond multiple-choice or short-answer tests in order to measure students' progress accurately. These techniques are known as **authentic** or **performance-based assessment,** based on the idea that students should perform tasks that replicate the standards and challenges of adult life. Sometimes the equivalent terms are **performance assessment** and **authentic assessment.**[2] But regardless of the term used, performance-based assessment requires students to create products or to perform, not simply to answer paper-and-pencil tests. The assessment may call for writing (the familiar "term paper" used in higher education) or problem solving, or the students' learning may be measured from the oral presentations or projects they produce as a result of their studies. Although performance-based assessment is not new, in the past it has been pretty much reserved for art, music, and physical education teachers who have always evaluated their students on the basis of their products and performance and not on paper-and-pencil tests.

Portfolios

Probably the most popular form of performance-based assessment in the social studies is the **portfolio**—a file or folder of selections of student work collected over a period of time that provides evidence of student learning, achievement, and progress in the social studies. Portfolios can furnish a broad picture of individual performance assembled over time. Although not without controversy, portfolios have been promoted as an assessment strategy that allows teachers to evaluate higher-order, complex skills and also to provide opportunities for student goal setting and self-evaluation of

---

[2]Some do not like the term *authentic*, which implies that such assessments are superior to more conventional assessments and fear that *authenticity* denigrates the importance of knowledge and basic skills as legitimate educational outcomes.

TABLE 4.1 Elements of a Portfolio

- learner goals or objectives/standards
- guidelines for selecting material—example, best work
- a table of contents—valuable to find work
- work samples chosen by student, usually good work
- work samples chosen by teacher—not all agree this should be done
- teacher feedback, sometimes tests
- student self-reflection pieces
- clear and appropriate criteria for evaluating work (rubrics)

progress. Portfolios are now very popular in classrooms with reports of almost three-quarters of primary-grade teachers and 60 percent of intermediate-grade teachers using portfolios in at least one subject area. They are most common in writing and language arts.

What should a portfolio include? Look at Table 4.1.

You may see different items in some portfolios. This depends partly on the purpose and the audience for the portfolio. Roughly, portfolios can be teacher centered (or administrator) when they serve in school accountability and grading. Or portfolios can be student centered in which students collect most of the items and are involved in self-assessment. Mixed models seem to be becoming more popular. Self-assessment by the student is still encouraged but more teachers are combining portfolios with traditional assessment strategies such as students' tests, worksheets, and homework assignments so that multiple measures will be offered by the student to her or his parent(s). The portfolio might also include peer assessments by fellow students. In the future, electronic portfolios containing a student's work for several years may really demonstrate growth over time.

SMALL GROUP WORK	**WHAT ARE YOUR EXPERIENCES WITH PORTFOLIOS?**
4.4	*In what classes were portfolios a requirement? What did you like about the experience? Was it fair? Any disadvantages?*

Which is better? In summary, multiple-choice and other objective tests are often clearly inadequate as the *sole* indicators of school outcomes (see Table 4.2). Performance assessment can measure some important kinds of outcomes but often does not have the potential for generalizability. If a student does well on one particular problem-solving exercise, will he or she do well on the next one? Even advocates of performance assessment point to difficulties and limitations. Performance assessment tends to rely heavily on students' ability to read and to write Standard English. This is a particular

TABLE 4.2 Comparison of Assessments

Authentic Assessments	Paper-and-Pencil Tests
Examples: essays, open-ended problems, portfolios, hands-on problems	*Examples:* short answer, matching, true-false, multiple choice
Subjective evaluation	Objective evaluation
Small sample of tasks	Can tap a large number of content items
Time-consuming evaluation	Easy to grade
Student directly involved in own learning/assessment	Tend to separate assessment from learning

problem for students learning English as a new language or those who come from non–Standard English backgrounds. They may know the content but not be able to express it adequately. In conclusion, we probably need many forms of assessment to enable all students to demonstrate accurately their knowledge and abilities.

Because of cost, most states are using multiple-choice items with a short writing sample. It may be that more authentic forms of assessment will continue to become a larger part of classroom-level and individual student assessment whereas states and districts will require standardized achievement tests. In actual practice, it appears that teachers are combining both performance assessment and the traditional paper-and pencil tests.

Perhaps in the future there will be more online computer testing using multiple-choice items. This already is being done for tests by ETS (Educational Testing Service) at the university level. The advantage of online testing in the classroom can be that students would immediately be provided with feedback so they can improve.

■ ASSESSMENT TECHNIQUES AND TOOLS

As teachers, we need to be familiar with both the traditional and newer approaches to evaluating student achievement. Here, we examine first paper-and-pencil tests and then performance-based assessment techniques that might be used by the classroom teacher in evaluating social studies.

Paper-and-Pencil Tests

Paper-and-pencil tests are the most suited for assessing social studies goals in the knowledge and thinking skills area. In our test-dominated age, the use of paper-and-pencil testing in the social studies is often taken for granted, almost as a cultural imperative. Furthermore, tests provide a relatively easy means to gather data on what children know and what they are able to do. The data from objective-type test items are easily counted for ranking and averaging. Tests included in textbook-series materials make the chore of preparing tests easier. In addition, tests accompanying texts often have better coverage of textbook content and are written more clearly, especially the multiple-choice questions, than most teacher-made tests because of the time and energy required in test construction.

Most teachers use the commercially prepared tests that accompany textbook series. Feeling compelled to provide numerical evidence of student progress pushes many teachers to rely on textbook-related tests. Thus, the content of their instruction tends to be tied to the textbook. You may think this technique for selecting and assessing content is too narrow and limiting. Or you may believe that the content of texts you use is appropriate as a definer of instructional content. Either way, you need to be a critical consumer of prepared commercial tests or tests that accompany a social studies textbook series.

There are several criteria for selecting tests or test items. The principal criterion is to verify that the items are aligned with your instructional objectives. They should be consistent with both the content covered and the level of thinking about the content you have led the students to experience. Providing sufficient items to check individual objectives is still another criterion. That is, we can learn more about a student's mastery of a concept if the student has several opportunities to answer questions about it.

Beyond the general criteria for test and item selection, each type of test brings special considerations.

Short Answer

A short-answer item is typically a statement with a key word or phrase missing. Which of the following pairs are the better items?

> a. Mexico, Canada, and the United States are _____.
>
> b. The three largest nations of North America are _____, _____ and _____.
>
>
> a. _____ invented the _____ in _____.
>
> b. The inventor of the cotton gin was _____.

Both "a" examples are inferior. Neither cues the student to the desired content. For short-answer items, the content cue is best presented at the sentence beginning and its completion at the sentence ending. The first example requires students to invent, and they may give semantically correct answers such as "fun" or "big" or "all purple on the map" that have no relation to the content studied.

Short-answer items, and all pencil-paper items, can be criticized as testing reading more than knowledge of the social studies content. Should we give children a grade in the social studies that is really related more to their reading ability than, perhaps, to their social studies knowledge? Most teachers are more concerned with learning what a child knows about the social studies content. They find that poor readers of English can respond correctly to the items if these items and the possible answers are read aloud.

Matching

Using the process of elimination is a good thinking strategy. Matching items should prompt students to use this strategy. As with all test-item types, students need practice with this kind of item before they are tested.

Which of the following three sets of matching items is best?

a. You have read about Native Americans, white settlers, and the buffalo. Now, draw lines below connecting the part of the buffalo with the way that part was used by the Plains tribes.

hair	bow strings
hide	food
horns	mattresses
meat	spoons
sinew	

b. Match the following countries with the continents in which they are located.

Mexico	South America
Chad	Africa
Finland	Europe
Chile	Asia
India	North America

c. Match the example with the economic category it fits best.

services	skateboard
goods	trip to Disney World
resources	haircut
	gold coins
	farmland
	sleeping
	running a race

The best item is "a," according to test makers, because it has uneven lists. The student must use the process of elimination as well as either direct recall of what has been studied or analysis of what might be possible. Note that in "a" but not "b" or "c" the choices are listed in alphabetical order. Alphabetical order saves the student time when rereading the list. Other pointers for this type of item include not making the list too long and not mixing categories within the lists. Item "c" commits both of these errors.

True-False

Items that are true or false invite students to guess and afford them a higher probability of being correct than any other type of test item. For this reason, and because this type of item tends to be written at a low level of cognitive difficulty, most test-construction experts do not favor true-false tests as reliable measures of what children know.

Writing good true-false items is more difficult than answering them. It is easy to "give away" the answer to this type of item. Even though experts criticize these items, teachers continue to use them, recognizing that they require less time to check. Below is a list of development rules compiled by researchers that you can refer to when evaluating true-false items.

Checkpoints for True-False Items[3]

1. Avoid using specific determiners (*always, never, only*).
2. Avoid use of negatives or double negatives (*not impossible*).
3. Limit statements to a single idea.
4. State ideas as concisely as possible.
5. Avoid exact wording of the text or source material.
6. Make the statement clearly true or false.
7. Test only important ideas.

To extend true-false items beyond the level of factual recall, you can ask students to rewrite false items to make them true, or to tell one more thing they know about true items.

Selected Response or Multiple-Choice Questions

The term **multiple-choice questions** evokes such negative images to some students and teachers that publishers are now calling them **selected response questions**. Multiple-choice questions have a poor reputation because they have often focused only on rote memorization. But they can be designed to test the ability of students to think. The advantages of multiple-choice questions is that they can provide a broad and balanced coverage of the unit. They can also give poor writers a better chance to show what they know.

A multiple-choice question consists of a *stem* (the body of the question before the choices are presented), the incorrect responses, and the correct answer (known as the *key*). Publishers report that they have moved away from old fashioned multiple-choice testing that isolates factual recall to using more test items that test higher thinking processes.

Multiple-choice items are commonly found on various state-mandated tests. Many states release the spring test items to help teachers and the public to understand that the history/social science test and other subject area tests were based on the learning standards and core knowledge topics required by the state. For example, the released test items of the Massachusetts Department of Education in 1999 gave the specific

---

[3]Adapted from a twenty-one-item list developed by David A. Frisbie and Douglas F. Becker, "An Analysis of Textbook Advice about True-False Tests," *Applied Measurement in Education* 4, no. 1 (1990): 69.

learning standard and particular core knowledge topic as shown by the following items for grade 8.[4]

> 9. A historian in the 1990s is researching life in the Massachusetts Bay Colony in the 1630s. The historian finds a sermon and a diary written in the 1630s and includes them in a textbook. Both the sermon and diary are examples of a
> A. primary source.
> B. chronology.
> C. secondary source.
> D. biography.
>
> *Study Strand* and Learning Standard: *History:* **Research, Evidence, and Point of View (p. 286)**
>
> Core Knowledge Topic: *The United States:* **Early America and the Americans (Beginning to 1650) (p. 289)**
>
> 17. By 1815, the United States' land bordered all the bodies of water except
> A. the Pacific Ocean.
> B. Lake Erie.
> C. the Gulf of Mexico.
> D. the Atlantic Ocean.
>
> *Study Strand* and Learning Standard: *Geography:* **Places and Regions of the World (p. 287)**
>
> Core Knowledge Topic: *The United States:* **Expansion, Reform, and Economic Growth (1800 to 1861) (p. 289)**

Note that in Question 9, the student needs to know the meaning of a primary source and apply that knowledge. Use of primary source documents has received increased attention in the past few years and so the question is probably appropriate in terms of content. In Question 17, the student must be able to make a mental map of the United States in 1815, identify major bodies of water, and remember historical knowledge such as the Louisiana Purchase. Both questions require some thinking, an advantage of good multiple-choice questions. They also are tied in or aligned to certain Massachusetts standards.

Look carefully at the time line question (Figure 4.1) from NAEP for fourth graders. A test item that requires the student to interpret a primary source, a map, a chart, a time line, or a graph is called an *enhanced multiple-choice test item*.

To be able to select the correct option, students had to be able to read and understand the time line, which indicated that the First Thanksgiving was celebrated in October rather than in November as it is today. In order to eliminate the first two options, students needed to understand from the time line that the *Mayflower* was at sea for about four months and that it arrived in America before the beginning of 1621.

Only a third of the fourth graders were able to answer this question accurately, showing that they were able to read the time line, understand the negative phrasing

---

[4]*The Massachusetts Comprehensive Assessment System: Release of Spring 1999 Test Items* (Malden, MA: Massachusetts Department of Education, 1999).

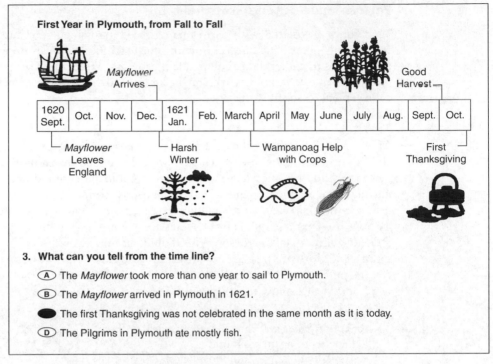

First Year in Plymouth, from Fall to Fall

Mayflower Arrives

Good Harvest

| 1620 Sept. | Oct. | Nov. | Dec. | 1621 Jan. | Feb. | March | April | May | June | July | Aug. | Sept. | Oct. |

Mayflower Leaves England

Harsh Winter

Wampanoag Help with Crops

First Thanksgiving

3. **What can you tell from the time line?**

   Ⓐ The *Mayflower* took more than one year to sail to Plymouth.

   Ⓑ The *Mayflower* arrived in Plymouth in 1621.

   ● The first Thanksgiving was not celebrated in the same month as it is today.

   Ⓓ The Pilgrims in Plymouth ate mostly fish.

FIGURE 4.1 Sample U.S. History Question
Grade 4—Time Line: *Mayflower* and Thanksgiving

Source: Evelyn Hawkins, Fran Stancavage, Julia Mitchell, Madeline Goodman, and
Stephen Lazer, *Learning About Our World and Our Past: Using the Tools and Resources
of Geography and U.S. History: A Report of the 1994 Assessment* (Washington, DC:
U.S. Department of Education, National Center for Education Statistics, 1998), p. 100.

of the correct response option, and relate it to their outside knowledge that Thanksgiving today is not celebrated in October. Why do you think students found this difficult? Probably most do not really understand how to read a time line.

Look again at these three multiple test items. Do you see any problems with them? Remember these tips in writing and using multiple-choice questions. Use clear language in the stem. Avoid double negatives. Always emphasize important individuals, events, or ideas, not trivia. Avoid choosing or making test items with excessively long sentences or a reading level that is too high for your students. Eliminate trick responses, such as "both *a* and *b*" or "neither *a* nor *b*."

When you use objective test items, or any other assessment, it is important for students to find out what they got wrong and why they got it wrong. An error and the right answers must be analyzed as soon as possible for each student. Try not to wait too long to grade tests. Returning tests given two weeks ago reduces the incentive of students to see their mistakes and to learn from them. Taking too long to correct tests also robs teachers of the opportunity to do reteaching right away in areas in which many students are having difficulties.

Performance-Based Assessment

Techniques associated with performance-based assessment are integrated in social studies unit plans. The natural flow of unit teaching produces opportunities as the unit evolves to gather data about student progress. Following are several of the ways that authentic or actual work can be organized to provide a picture of student achievement in social studies.

Essay

After a long period of eclipse, the essay is emerging as a technique for assessing a child's knowledge. Previously, teachers were persuaded that a more objective assessment of children's knowledge was one that could be counted and quantified, permitting them to compare individuals and groups. Some teachers welcomed objective tests as a time-saving way to avoid correcting essays. We now recognize the centrality of written expression in all curricular areas for assessing higher levels of thinking. Students who can talk about or write about facts and ideas show that they have structured new information. They not only recall and classify information as an objective-type test item would require, but they can also put the information into a context.

Look at the following essay question:

You are Columbus. Write a letter to King Ferdinand and Queen Isabella to convince them to finance a voyage. Be sure to include the following points:
- Benefits to Spain from trade
- Spreading Spain's Catholic religion
- How technology has improved safety on voyages
- Increases in Spain's power

Notice that the essay question is not vague but helps the student to focus on what should be covered in the question. In a similar manner, look at this essay question.

Benjamin Franklin was known as a "man of ideas." He was influential during his time and well respected. Explain how he contributed to the people of his time in the following roles:
- Inventor/scientist
- Writer
- Diplomat

This question could also be changed from Benjamin Franklin to Thomas Jefferson or some other historical figure by easily adding or subtracting categories.

Some essay questions are called *short-answer essay questions*. These often ask students to justify or explain their answers within a specified length, normally one paragraph or so. Here are some examples:

Explain why Americans did not want their new leader to be called a "king."

Explain why most Native Americans lost control of their lands.

Why was Anne Hutchinson banished from her home town?

All of these formats illustrate the value of good essay questions to promote student thinking and reasoning.

Teachers using holistic scoring estimate the overall impression of the quality of the performance. They then assign a grade, often A–F rating scale, or three divisions (such as below average, average, and clearly outstanding) to that quality rather than assigning specific points for specific aspects of the performance. Holistic scoring may be easier for the teacher to do compared to rubrics or rating scales but may not be as reliable and not provide as much feedback to the students.

Holistic scoring of a learning product such as an essay, map, videotape, or audiotape is useful when the goal is an overall assessment of student performance. As with a rating scale, the assessment must focus on the most important instructional goals that prompted the learning product. One way to use the holistic approach in evaluating essays and other open-ended learning products is to separate them into stacks of good, average, and poor, and then to reread or review each stack, further separating products into smaller stacks according to the grading scheme. When evaluating learning products, teachers must decide how to disentangle the evaluation of content, or "message," from form, or "medium." One way is to assign two grades, one for content and another for form.

To assist students, models of excellence should be made available and analyzed. Saving good examples of student work from one year to the next can assist you in aligning instruction with evaluation. When students analyze an excellent student product, they learn what is expected of them in a very concrete sense, and they recognize that these expectations have been met by others at their level of instruction. Cooperative analysis of excellent learning products empowers students to recognize the characteristics of quality. Even more important than sharing examples and recognizing what is good about them is a teacher-led discussion of how the former students went about producing the product. For some students, understanding the process of how to do the "assignment" is sufficient motivation. For even more students, participation in the dialogue about how their work will be assessed is crucial to their motivation to do the work. For nearly every student, participating in cooperative assessment of their own work and that of their classmates is highly motivating. Furthermore, students probably will be gratified that a teacher values student learning products enough to show them off.

Self-Evaluation

Taking responsibility for their own independent learning is one of the major goals of schooling for students. You can assist them toward this goal by providing frequent occasions for self-evaluation. This technique is appropriate in all the major social studies areas. Ask students to assess their knowledge and skills through questions such as these:

> What do you need to spend more time on?
>
> What areas of this topic do you feel you know?
>
> What did you learn today in your research reading?

Continuing self-evaluation can lead students to formulate plans for themselves based on what they see as significant.

Teachers find that self-reports about study habits and citizenship skills are useful data to collect periodically. A sample form that students can use for these reports is shown in Figure 4.2.

Self-evaluation reports can also be tied to specific units in which tasks and choices have been specified. Often known as a "contract," this kind of listing helps

My Work Habits and Study Skills				
Name:				
	Poor	Fair	Good	Comment
Turn in work on time				
Plan my work before the last minute				
Seek help when I do not understand				
Use my time to get work done first				
Help others in my work group				
Know where my supplies are				
Help keep the room clean				
Take my turn doing chores				

FIGURE 4.2 Self-Evaluation Form

some students stay focused on what they need to do (Figure 4.3). Forms such as this give students an overview of a topic and often help to make a unit more coherent and cohesive. The goal of self-evaluation is an increased sense of responsibility. Teachers hope that by lengthening students' view of school tasks from the period or day to the week or unit, students will begin to take more responsibility for completing their work.

Contract for Desert Study			
Name: _____ agrees to complete this work			
Task:			
	DATE	DONE	COMMENTS
Read my text section and teach my group.			
View group film and contribute to summary.			
Write safari card on desert animal.			
Complete desert map and identify major deserts.			
Contribute 2 items to Desert Trivia.			

FIGURE 4.3 Individual Contract for Social Studies

TABLE 4.3 Written Assessment Tasks

Advertisement	Autobiography	Biography	Book review
Character portrait	Crossword puzzle	Dialogue	Diary
Editorial	Essay	Game	Invitations
Journal	Labels/captions	Letter	Log
Memo	Notetaking	Newspaper article	Persuasive writing
Poem	Postcard	Questionnaire/ survey	Reader's Theater
Research report	Rules	Script	Story
Test	Time line		

Source: Courtesy of Dr. Priscilla Porter's Handout at the California Council of the Social Studies State Convention, San Diego, 2000.

Written Assessment Tasks

In designing assessment tasks, what student **products** can provide evidence of student learning in the social studies? You can see all the great possibilities in Table 4.3.

In addition, many times the written is combined with the visual as shown in the following: cartoon, chart, data table, graph, map, model, outline, Venn diagram, and webbing/mind map. Any of these assessment tasks can indicate what the students have learned. Essential is a rubric so that students know what is expected and for students to be graded fairly.

Short Constructed-Response Questions

Along with the wide diversity of products possible for assessment, probably the most commonly used product for formal authentic assessment is a short constructed-response question test item or short write-in item. Sometimes it is called a short-answer question. A **constructed-response question** requires students to produce an answer to a question. A short constructed-response item is a good compromise between the multiple-choice question and an essay. It can test for factual knowledge and critical thinking without putting a heavy writing burden on students or a time-consuming grading task on the teacher. In constructed-response items, questions may have just one correct answer or they may be more open-ended, allowing a range of responses. Common in the social studies are **identifications**. Here in a few sentences students need to describe why the person, event, or idea is significant. Try to encourage students to write more about Columbus to tell of his importance as an explorer.

Look at the following fourth-grade NAEP test item.

Your teacher has asked you to teach your classmates about *one* of these famous places where an important event in American history happened:
the Alamo
Pearl Harbor
Gettysburg
Roanoke Island

My famous place in American history is _____.

Write down three facts about the place that you have chosen that will help you teach your classmates about this work.

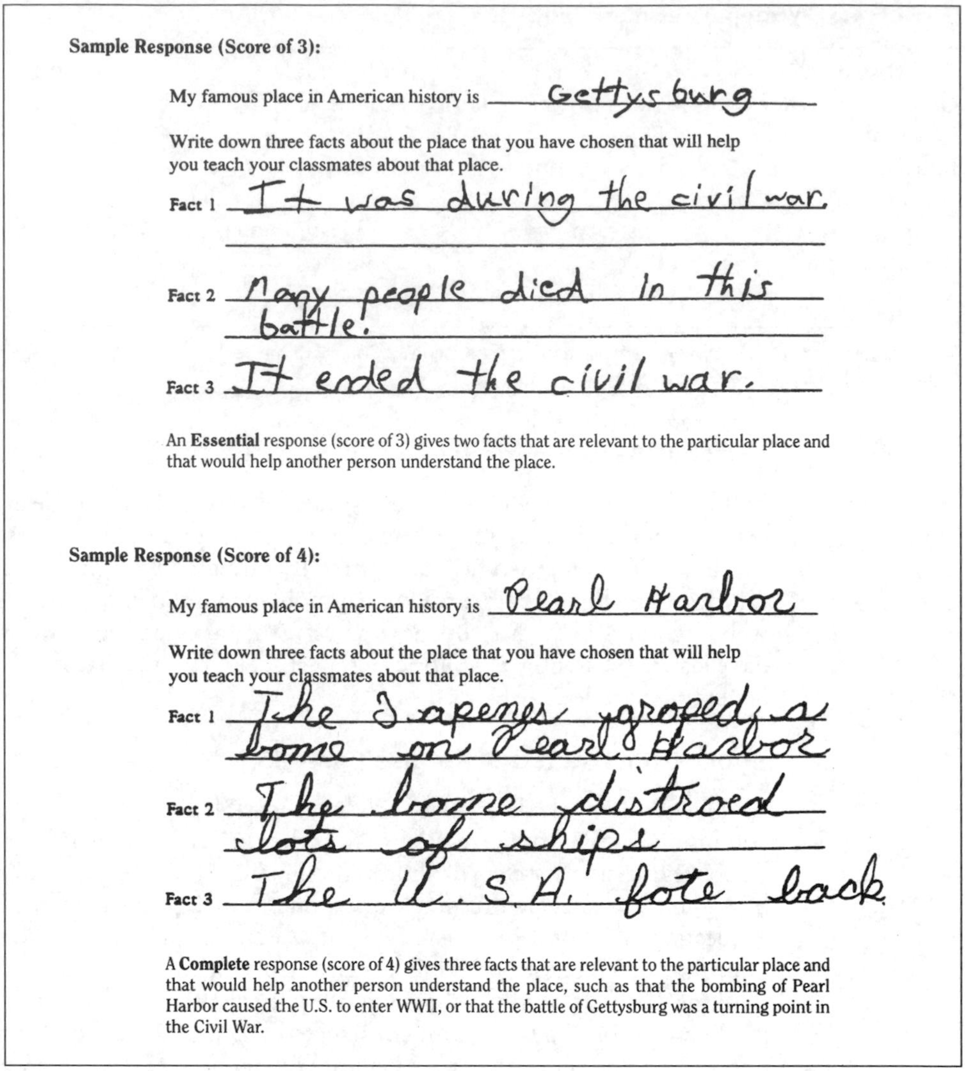

Sample Response (Score of 3):

My famous place in American history is ___Gettysburg___

Write down three facts about the place that you have chosen that will help you teach your classmates about that place.

Fact 1 ___It was during the civil war.___

Fact 2 ___Many people died In this battle!___

Fact 3 ___It ended the civil war.___

An **Essential** response (score of 3) gives two facts that are relevant to the particular place and that would help another person understand the place.

Sample Response (Score of 4):

My famous place in American history is ___Pearl Harbor___

Write down three facts about the place that you have chosen that will help you teach your classmates about that place.

Fact 1 ___The Japenes proped a bome on Pearl Harbor___

Fact 2 ___The bome distroed lots of ships___

Fact 3 ___The U.S.A. fote back___

A **Complete** response (score of 4) gives three facts that are relevant to the particular place and that would help another person understand the place, such as that the bombing of Pearl Harbor caused the U.S. to enter WWII, or that the battle of Gettysburg was a turning point in the Civil War.

FIGURE 4.4 NAEP Short Constructed-Response History Item

Source: NAEP 1994 U.S. History Report Card: Findings from the National Assessment of Educational Progress (Washington, DC: U.S. Department of Education, National Center for Education Statistics, 1996), p. 99.

Again, as in all performance assessment, the use of a rubric is essential. Responses to this question were scored according to a four-level rubric as (1) inappropriate, (2) partial, (3) essential, and (4) complete. Look at Figure 4.4 to see how the responses were marked. Note the format which forces the student to answer in terms of three separate sentences. This makes it easier to score.

As a compromise between a full essay questions and a multiple choice item, the short-constructed response test items are becoming more popular with their inclusion of a few short-constructed response test items on state examinations.

SMALL GROUP WORK	**YOUR REACTION TO "MY FAMOUS PLACE IN HISTORY"**
4.5	*Do you like this question? Is it too hard for fourth graders? Do you agree with the scoring? Did you see that the student with the high score of 4 has many spelling errors? Are the three facts accurate and their relevance and chronology deserving a high score even with poor spelling?*

Observation

Teachers continually make judgments based on observations. They move a child so that he or she can do quiet work. They give more practice examples of how to calculate map distances when they see that several children need it. They compliment a child for straightening up the project work area without being reminded. Rarely, however, do they keep records of these observations for purposes of communicating social studies progress.

It would be impossible to record every incident of a child's behavior for evaluation purposes! But for assessment of progress in positive social behaviors, often reported under the rubric of citizenship on primary-level reporting systems, there is a useful middle point between recording nothing and recording everything. Objectives for this goal may be general and year-long, such as "being responsible for myself and my things," or they may be related to a specific unit that involves small group work with an objective of "sharing information for the benefit of the group" (see Chapter 3, Table 3.3). Some districts are defining social learning outcomes that will prompt teachers to record more careful evidence of growth in this domain.

For this type of objective, teachers can keep a note card file that records the child's name and the date and a sentence reporting the behavior related to the objective (see Figure 4.5). Some teachers like to send these "Super Citizen" cards home

> Super Citizen News
>
> Name: Evan   Date: Oct 8
>
> By sharing his materials, Evan made Brad feel more comfortable as a new student in our class today.

FIGURE 4.5 Note Cards Can Be Used to Record Good Behavior

FIGURE 4.6 Group Skills Can Be Observed and Monitored on a Prepared Form

with children as they note the child's behavior. Others prefer to accumulate the notes in a folder to be used with parents at conference time. To benefit from this evaluation tool, keep a few specific objectives in mind and focus on them over time and/or incorporate one or two to guide a specific unit of instruction.

Observation by tallies is a convenient technique for gathering data on particular behaviors (see Figure 4.6). Once the form is prepared, you can carry it about on a clipboard during the monitoring of group work and record what individual children do. In a similar fashion, students can observe the on-task behaviors during their small group work and then use the data they collect as an evaluation guide in planning how to improve their individual and group productivity.

Checklists can be used whenever the assessment goal can be divided into a list of items or traits or a set of procedures that are present or absent. Rating scales, often called **scoring rubrics,** permit a greater assessment of quality than does the yes/no format of checklists. A **rubric** provides specific criteria for describing student performance at different levels of proficiency. Students typically receive a number of points that represent minimal to high-quality work, depending on the type of response. In some cases, teachers establish criteria for district or state standards and train scorers to be consistent in their grading. A well-constructed rubric lets students know in advance what is expected of them and helps teachers grade students' work fairly. Checklists and rating scales can help align instruction and assessment when they are presented to students in the initial phase of an instructional unit. Discussing checklists and rating scales with the class helps students understand what is expected of them. As instruction progresses, students can refer to these lists and rubrics as a means of self-assessment.

"Catching" Observation Data

Important for social studies is collecting data on oral performance. Some of the oral performances that you may have to assess and evaluate include oral presentations and oral reports, skits, newscasts, dramatizations, and class and small group discussions. How can you proceed to assess these areas?

The State of Michigan's Authentic Assessment Project uses skits as a method to set up authentic assessments (see Table 4.4 for a primary-grade example)[5]. It is suggested that after viewing the skit, students in small groups will discuss the focus and public policy questions. Do you think this will be interesting to primary students? If you use it, how can you assess it?

[5]Michigan Department of Education, *Social Studies Authentic Assessment Project: Conducting Investigations, Group Discussion, Responsible Personal Conduct* (Lansing, MI: Michigan Department of Education, no date), p. 35.

TABLE 4.4 Wearing Hats in School

A boy and a girl both wear hats to school. When they come into the classroom, the teacher tells the boy to take his hat off. The teacher says it is polite for boys and men to take their hats off indoors. The girl's hat matches her outfit. The teacher does not say anything to the girl.

The boy asks the teacher why he has to take his hat off but the girl is allowed to leave her hat on.

*Introduce the scenario as a skit, which you rehearse in advance with a boy and a girl from the class.

Related Core Democratic Values: Diversity, Rule of Law, Freedom of Expression

The Focus Question

What should the school do about letting boys and girls wear hats in the classroom?

The Public Policy Issue Question

Should schools allow boys and girls to wear hats in school?

Here is the **rubric,** the criteria used for assessing student discussion at different levels of proficiency (Table 4.5). Do you think the rubric is clear? The Michigan Department of Education recommends using a mechanism for recording the discussion, either audio or video, to help with the evaluation. It also suggests that students could be instructed to conduct self-evaluations. But you can see the problems of trying to

TABLE 4.5 Group Discussion Rubric for Early Elementary

	Made a Relevant Statement	Responded Appropriately
Performance Level 4	Participated in the discussion by making many relevant and elaborating statements throughout the discussion.	Responded appropriately at all times and made a concerted effort to invite and acknowledge the contributions of others.
Performance Level 3	Participated in the discussion by making at least one relevant statement that supports their point of view or clarifies the issue.	Responded appropriately at all times.
Performance Level 2	Participated in the discussion but statements were only marginally relevant to the discussion or did not support their view.	Responded inappropriately but made some appropriate comments.
Performance Level 1	Did not make any relevant statements during the discussion.	Responded inappropriately and made no appropriate comments, *or* did not take part in the discussion.

The Michigan Department of Education gives further examples of what is appropriate and inappropriate behaviors, p. 20 in *Social Studies Authentic Assessment Project.*

"catch" all the behaviors that are going on in the many groups. In the future, hand-held computers already coded with names of the students and an appropriate rubric will allow teachers to gather this type of assessment quickly and be able to get feedback to students after they finish their discussion.

Conferences

Talking individually with children about how they are doing is a powerful assessment and evaluation technique. It enables teachers to bridge the distance between the student and his or her efforts. Initially, many students are timid about discussing their work with teachers in a conference setting, but by the second round of conferences, students usually become accustomed to this kind of scrutiny. Individual conferences should focus on work samples and self-evaluations and any observational data that teachers may have collected. Leading students to see their work in terms of the goals and objectives often sheds a new light on the "why" of school assignments.

Conferences or interviews may be scheduled or they may happen spontaneously when opportunities arise. Here are some sample questions you could ask.

Do you like social studies? Or the unit you are working on? Why or why not?

Do you think social studies is important? Why or why not?

What do you do when you have a problem understanding social studies?

Through interviews, teachers can better understand how students see the unit and what difficulties they are encountering.

Increasing emphasis on cooperative learning does not eliminate the need for individual conferencing between teacher and student. Conferencing should also be about each student's production and contribution to group activities. However, individual teacher-student conferences must not be used to "evaluate" another student's participation in group activity. Rather, part of the cooperative group routine should be group assessment. Groups should critique their accomplishments and make plans for how to improve their work time together. Teachers should conference regularly with each group regarding the group's self-assessment and assist the group in devising ways to improve.

■ EVALUATING LEARNING AND DEVELOPMENT

For purposes of organizing a clear presentation, we have separated our discussion of the kinds of tools and techniques we use to collect learning data from our examination of how we use these data. In actual practice, these activities are not sequential nor are they separate or engaged in by the teacher alone. Remember that **evaluation** is a judgment on how much students have learned. It is telling students how well they are doing. Terms such as *excellent, good progress,* and *needs to improve* come to mind as we discuss evaluation.

Relating Objectives and Process Levels

Checking standards and objectives against a sequence of processes ordered by levels of difficulty will assist teachers in thinking about evaluation. The higher categories of the taxonomies require more practice and greater emphasis on projects that stu-

TABLE 4.6 Taxonomies and Instruction

Knowledge Level	Within Text Example (from "The Little Red Hen")	Curricular Example
Recall: Names, lists, locates, repeats, describes	Names animals in story	Pledge of Allegiance; names 50 states; retells native myth
Comprehension: Tells meaning, interprets, gives examples	Tells why hen ate the bread	Defines family; explains map symbols; tells ways Sojourner Truth showed courage
Application: Explains sequence or process, solves problem, demonstrates	Shows how hen's lesson applies to classroom	Shows how to find east in morning; demonstrates how to make tortillas
Analysis: Outlines, categorizes, relates events or causes	Tells why hen acted as she did	Puts clothes and shelters into climate groups
Synthesis: Revises, investigates, creates, presents	Tells a different ending to story	Presents a play about the beginning of the Revolutionary War
Evaluation: Ranks, judges, compares using criteria	Discusses whether each animal was treated fairly	After listing basic needs, chooses items for survival in desert
Values		
Receiving: Listens, observes	Attends to story as teacher reads	Attends as teacher explains project
Responding: Participates, complies	Reenacts part of story according to role assigned	Takes turns in cooperative group task
Valuing: Initiates	Repeats hen's line to remind classmate of classroom responsibility	Volunteers to help sort paper for recycling in classroom

Source: Partial list adapted from Benjamin Bloom et al., eds., *Taxonomy of Educational Goals. Handbook I—Cognitive Domain* (New York: McKay, 1956); David R. Krathwohl, ed., *Taxonomy of Educational Objectives: The Classification of Goals, Handbook II—Affective Domain* (New York: McKay, 1964).

dents organize and present. Higher levels of thinking need to be supported by instruction and practice on equivalent levels as well as on the cognitive levels that precede them before evaluation at that level is appropriate. For example, asking students to interpret weather information on an outline map of the United States requires that they (1) know the locational geography of the United States and (2) recognize the weather symbols and their meanings.

Cross-checking objectives with these taxonomies can alert you to instructional gaps. In the case of exploring written text or information presented in oral or visual form, the questioning sequence teachers design for children will be more successful if discussions begin at the more basic knowledge level. If the objective is for students to create an ending that shows the animals with different characteristics, then questions need to bring out the basic facts of the original story—such as who the animals were and what characteristic each represented and how the story might have ended if one or all the animals had behaved differently. The whole group needs to hear this information before they are asked to perform a creative task. If the objective requires students to create shoebox dioramas of pioneer life—a synthesis-level task—the children must understand what is involved. For diorama-making to be a meaningful task, not a copying task, students must first gather information about the activities—for example, the ones that were performed inside a settler's cabin. They must see pictures and hear and read stories about candle making, wool spinning, storing food in the root cellar, cooking at hearthside, and conserving food by drying, soaking in brine, and larding.

Cross-checking or analyzing what students must know or be able to do before they can complete an activity is known as *task analysis*. Planning for assessment and evaluation should include this step. It is an essential way to examine unit and lesson objectives. Once teachers are aware of the prerequisite knowledge and skills students need to perform an assignment, they can design a more realistic, meaningful, and successful sequence of instruction. A further benefit is that this exercise produces a structure that can be used to make objectives clearer to students.

Relating Goals, Objectives, and Instruction

Another indication of what kinds of data teachers need to collect comes from the learning goals and objectives themselves. If students are to learn the names of local landmarks and their locations, they need opportunities to visit the actual sites, view photographs, compose collages that replicate what they have seen or read about, and practice with blank maps, map puzzles, and spelling drills. Pencil-and-paper techniques for mastery may be indicated. If the learning goal is for children to work productively in a group, they need to be taught appropriate group behaviors and to be given practice working in group situations. Teacher observation complemented by group and self-evaluation and conferences may be necessary. If the objective is for children to be able to distinguish between valid and invalid conclusions, the students must be instructed in supporting conclusions with data and argument and must have guided practice with appropriate reading exercises. To assess student progress for this objective teacher observation of student discussions as well as writing samples that support or argue against conclusions are appropriate.

The sample unit plan that follows illustrates alignment of social studies learning goals and objectives with assessment. Every student receives a handbook that outlines what is expected and how the student's performance will be evaluated. The sample includes two of the fifteen pages designed to clarify what is to be learned in the unit and how student performance will be evaluated.

Scheduling Data Collection

Deciding when to collect evaluative data is a third element of the organizing task. Benjamin Bloom's ideas are useful for this task as well. He distinguished between **formative** and **summative evaluation.**[6] **Formative evaluation,** the collection of data about

---

[6]Benjamin S. Bloom, George F. Madaus, and Thomas Hastings, *Evaluation to Improve Learning* (New York: McGraw-Hill, 1981).

SAMPLE UNIT PLAN

INSTRUCTIONAL ALIGNMENT FOR FIFTH-GRADE UNIT: LIFE IN THE COLONIES

The Social Studies Task

Key Question

How did the life of the colonists depend on the physical environment in which they lived, on the culture that they brought with them, and on their interactions with one another?

Goals of This Performance Task

Doing a performance task gives you an opportunity to show how well you can meet Palo Alto school outcomes. You will be asked to carry out a project that demonstrates to teachers and community members how well you can:

- demonstrate your knowledge and understanding of key facts and concepts about the American colonies;
- communicate your ideas clearly and effectively, orally and in writing;
- plan, design, and carry out a multiday project;
- work cooperatively and effectively with other group members; and
- reflect thoughtfully on what you did and learned.

Overview

This is an exciting opportunity for you to use your historical detective skills. To do this task you will:

- Research a particular colony to answer the key question.
- Choose one of several possible projects to demonstrate your knowledge and understanding of the physical environment, culture, and colonist interactions in that colony.
- Keep a log of your work and a list of resources you used.
- Present your project to your classmates.
- Take notes on presentations made by other groups.
- Evaluate your own and your group's work and learning.

Questions About Your Colony:

Where did the people come from originally?

What did they bring to the Colonies (beliefs, culture, language, special skills, or arts)?

What kinds of work did they do and with whom did they trade?

What kinds of community activities were important to them?

What were their homes like?

How did they adapt their lifestyle to the weather and climate?

How did they use the natural resources they found?

Can you tell about a day in the life of an adult in this community?

Can you tell about a day in the life of a child in this community?

Source: Excerpted from the fifth-grade unit handbooks of the Palo Alto, CA, Unified School District. This provides an overview of the extensive descriptions of expectations from curriculum goals to performance assessment that students receive at the beginning of a unit on the American Colonies.

how the student is doing as he or she works through an instructional sequence, is crucial if teachers are to strive for mastery learning by every student. Formative evaluation gives teachers information about what they need to reteach for which individuals. This approach to evaluation tends to place the burden of the student's learning progress in the teacher's hands. It suggests that teachers should revise instruction as students proceed according to the progress the children make. A more constructivist view of instructional planning would alter this scenario to engage students in verbal description of what they understand as a way for both teachers and students to go forward based on the student's level of understanding.

Data on what children know about a topic should be collected at the beginning of a unit. For middle grades, this may be done using a pencil-and-paper pretest or an attitudinal technique—to determine how they feel about a subject or issue. For primary students, teacher observation and group discussions are the preferable tools. These data can be used to select students for cooperative learning groups, placing some of the more informed students with each group, or they may indicate that teachers should spend more direct-teaching time working with students on vocabulary items and providing more concrete and visual experiences.

Data collected during the unit are also useful to formative evaluation. Individual worksheets, student comments, class discussion, and student projects need to be monitored so that reteaching time for individuals or groups can be scheduled as needed. Work habits and cooperation in group efforts need to be evaluated on an almost daily basis.

Formative evaluation benefits both group and individual efforts. By coaching and monitoring group projects, teachers can guarantee better final projects and presentations. The same is true for individual efforts. Formative evaluation of both content and process objectives serves to keep the unit dynamics intact and flowing.

Summative evaluation is the point in instruction when there is a collective pause to calculate and reflect on what has been learned. It is the moment when projects are presented or when tests are taken. It should be the moment when individual children are asked to assess what they now know or can do or feel and compare it with what they knew or could do or felt at the beginning of the unit. This is the point at which a cumulative grade or assessment is given. In our view, the more deeply each of these assessment moments is integrated into the natural dynamic of unit of instruction, the more authentic the evaluation can be.

We have seen that organizing assessment and evaluation means finding a match between our learning goals and objectives instruction and student activity; it also means we must decide on the kinds of student data to collect and when to collect them if we are to determine the additional instructional steps students need to progress toward the objectives.

Communicating About Individual Progress

Informing students and parents about instructional objectives helps set expectations for learning. Long-range or one-year objectives as well as grade-level performance criteria are set by the school, district, and the state. These objectives and additional ones you diagnose as essential for the class or individuals should be clear to everyone involved. Many of the long-range objectives will have only a tangential relation to the social studies. For parents, seeing the subject matter designation is probably less important than getting a global picture of the year's expectations. Teachers can communicate these objectives through a letter sent home with the students or during the open houses for parents, usually held near the beginning of the school year. Unit objectives are best communicated by letter or e-mail at the beginning of each new unit.

The written format used to report student learning progress varies greatly from one district to another. Besides grades, it is now more likely to have subgrades that break each subject into specific skills and knowledge, linked to content standards. These often include precise descriptions of the knowledge, skills, and projects a student has mastered and those he or she must tackle next. They may use a rubric with four levels of achievement to indicate what the student has mastered. Absolutely essential is a statement showing the student's current status with respect to passing or failing state or district standards examinations.

As a teacher, you will decide on what various aspects of student performance are important in determining student grades or formal progress reports. In general, teachers look at effort, individual improvement, achievement relative to the rest of the class, absolute achievement, and portfolio items. Some teachers count behavior and cooperation in their grades. How important do you consider any of these factors in determining grades?

An important issue is whether all students will be required to meet the standards. Especially important is how you grade ESL students and students with mild disabilities. The recommendation is to rely more on the teacher's descriptive evaluation of student growth, including qualitative and anecdotal observations. You need to consider the obvious and hidden messages that are conveyed by the assessment data you have collected. Is it a message of support? Is it a message of your cooperation and willingness to work with the child and the family?

You should begin conferences with both the student and parent(s) present by clarifying areas of growth toward the specified objectives. Often parents are not helped just by seeing samples of their own child's work without showing samples of work that reflect grade-level expectations. Otherwise, parents may think all is well when it is really necessary to do some goal setting to help the student to succeed. Who should lead the conference? Advocates of performance assessment believe that a student-led conference is best. Teaching students to assess themselves well may be one of the best things a teacher can do. Others think that the teacher can make an enormous contribution by suggesting how to plan for further growth.

With regard to grades, ideally a classroom would have no "bad" or low grades. If there are low grades, it is essential that the students and the teacher recognize that low grades should be viewed as temporary and students will have the opportunity to improve their grades. This sets the tone for internal motivation to "do well." Otherwise, students may think they cannot do anything to improve.

Evaluation of Instruction

Using student data to evaluate instruction should guide what happens next with individual students and the entire class, in addition to providing evidence for future ways of organizing instruction for the teacher. There are several ways to examine student data for the purpose of improving instruction.

One of the problems with state standardized testing is that the results often do not get back to the teachers in time to help them in their teaching of the class that was tested. However, assuming that next year's class will be similar in many respects to the class that was tested this year, looking over the results is worthwhile. The correct and "wrong" answers should be analyzed to determine why the students succeeded or failed the individual test item. Was the material or skill taught during the school year? If taught, how frequently was it taught? Does more time have to be spent on certain topics and skills? For many skills, multiple instruction is necessary for success.

Examining the class trends in paper-and-pencil assessments enables teachers to check for their own flaws in instruction or item construction. If the majority of the class misses certain items, several possibilities need to be entertained. Is the item itself ambiguous or tricky? How about the instruction? Was there congruence between the item and variables such as the cognitive level at which instruction about it was presented? Was the amount of time devoted to content sufficient? Did the students have the general readiness necessary to understand the idea or perform the skill?

Another perspective on the appropriateness of instruction is examining the consistency between the amount of work assigned and the amount of work students actually complete. A poor rate of project completion may mean that aspects of the classroom management, such as reward systems and motivation, need to be reconsidered. Social rewards, such as being part of a group that is supportive and sharing results with others in a nonthreatening manner, are relevant considerations. Typically, students will complete a task that has personal significance.

When children do not complete individual projects, a task analysis to find out which skills the students need more instruction on will help teachers carry out similar projects in the future. Report writing from various sources is a classic obstacle for middle-grade students. Consider a fifth-grade assignment in which students are to choose and write about an explorer of the Americas. To do this, a student needs to combine several skills. Each skill in the following list requires mastery of the preceding skills. Often we assume that students will figure out how to handle the dynamics of report writing, as most of us did when we were that age, by trial and error and intuition. Commonly, steps 2 through 5 are not taught directly to the class, or they are taught for one report and assumed to be mastered for use in all succeeding reports. Looking at the report quality of completed reports and the rate of report completion can indicate which of the skills may need to be emphasized in future instruction.

Task Analysis of Report Writing

1. Locate topic using index and table of contents.
2. Prepare questions or main topics to research.
3. Read for main ideas and supporting details.
4. Take notes in own words to answer research questions.
5. Review notes and organize outline for first draft.
6. Write first draft using outline and notes.
7. Edit first draft for topic flow and organization.
8. Rewrite first draft.
9. Edit for spelling, grammar, and mechanics.
10. Prepare final draft.

SMALL GROUP WORK	**TASK ANALYSIS PRACTICE**
4.6	*Imagine that you teach the third grade and want your class to make a map of your county that shows major landforms and roads. Make a list of what students would have to know about mapmaking and the county before they could do this project. Share your list with a colleague. Do you both agree? Isn't it daunting to become aware of how much we assume when we ask students to do projects? Given this list, discuss how you would prepare the students for this project.*

■ SUMMARY

Classroom teachers must become knowledgeable consumers of prepared assessment instruments and adept designers of procedures and tools for evaluating individual student progress and their own instruction. As modes of assessment evolve and student achievement of subject matter standards is given increasing attention, teachers will be required to focus on assessment more than in the past. With increased attention on assessment, teachers must be clear about the relationship between the kinds of data a particular technique or instrument yields and the questions the data are used to answer. Some techniques and instruments are most appropriate for assessing group achievement and some are more appropriate for the assessment of individual learning. Furthermore, teachers need to understand the limitations of using classroom group averages as data to evaluate their instruction. Assessment of student progress is a continuous process, an integral part of instructional planning.

Authentic student assessment and evaluation is unobtrusive and instructionally integrated. Planning social studies units requires that teachers elaborate ways of collecting evidence about each instructional objective before beginning the unit with students. When assessing student progress, teachers must collect enough evidence to reflect on and communicate about a student's progress toward specified objectives. Evaluation can be made meaningful to students to the degree that they become knowledgeable about what is expected and have opportunities to select, explain, and evaluate their work. Whatever the tools and techniques used, the results of evaluation should be that students recognize their accomplishment and increase their desire to strive for further growth.

■ SUGGESTED READINGS AND WEB SITES ■

Adams, D. M. K., and M. E. Hamm. "Portfolio Assessment and Social Studies: Collecting, Selecting, and Reflecting on What Is Significant." *Social Education* 56 (February 1992): 103–105.
Survey of necessary issues to consider when using portfolios as an assessment tool.

Athanases, Steven Z. "Teachers Report of the Effects of Preparing Portfolios of Literacy Instruction." *The Elementary School Journal* 94 (May 1994): 421–439.
Participant-observer research probing assessment of teacher quality through teacher's own analysis of response-based literacy instruction.

Cervone, B., and K. O'Leary. "A Conceptual Framework for Parent Involvement." *Educational Leadership* 40 (October 1982): 48–49.

Suggestions for involving parents in school learning.

Cramer, Susan R. "Navigating the Assessment Maze with Portfolios." *Clearinghouse* 67 (November–December 1993): 72–74.

Presents rudiments of portfolio content design and use as assessment tool stressing importance of previously agreed on criteria for assessing quality.

Darling-Hammond, Linda, Jacqueline Ancess, and Beverly Falk. *Authentic Assessment in Action: Studies of Schools and Students at Work.* New York: Teachers College Press, 1995.

Case studies of classrooms and how five schools have developed authentic performance-based assessments of students' learning.

Doremus, Vivian P. "Forcing Works for Flowers, but Not for Children." *Educational Leadership* 44, no. 3 (November 1986): 32–35.

Represents argument against excessive testing of children's achievement and reliance on academic achievements to exclusion of other developmental areas.

Glazer, Susan Mandel. "Assessment: How You Can Use Tests and Portfolios Too." *Teaching K–8* 25 (August–September 1994): 152–154.

Brief discussion showing significance for students of portfolios in teacher-student interactive assessment.

McKeon, Denise. "When Meeting 'Common' Standards Is Uncommonly Difficult." *Educational Leadership* 51 (May 1994): 45–49.

Brings educational equity concerns to bear on standards movement that shows little consideration of learners from minority cultures and languages.

Simmons, Rebecca. "The Horse Before the Cart: Assessing for Understanding." *Educational Leadership* 51 (February 1994): 22–23.

Deals with demonstrating how to interpret evolving jargon used to describe assessment ideas when outcome-based education replaces mastery learning.

Tucker, Mark S. and Judy B. Codding. *Standards for Our Schools: How to Set Them, Measure Them, and Reach Them.* San Francisco: Jossey-Bass, 1998.

Good examples of seeking high standards.

Wiggins, Grant P. *Educative Assessment: Designing Assessments to Inform and Improve Student Performance.* San Francisco: Jossey-Bass, 1999.

Guidance on how to design performance-based assessments for use in classrooms.

Web Site

National Assessment for Education Progress
http://nces.ed.gov/nationsreportcard/site/map.asp

Can get information on the assessment of several subject areas. Data also organized for different audiences such as principals and teachers.

Chapter 5

Social Studies in the Primary Grades

Curriculum considerations for primary-grade social studies are divided into the following sections in this chapter.

- Primary-Grade Social Studies Curriculum Using State Standards
- Primary History State Standards
- Primary Economics Standards
- Primary Geography Standards
- Primary Citizenship Standards
- Guidelines for Integrating Social Studies in the Primary-Grade Curriculum
- Classroom Environment and Scheduling in the Primary Grades

Although the goals, standards, and strategies outlined in the previous chapters provide general guidelines for social studies curriculum and instruction at all levels, you will want to focus specifically on the particular needs and competencies of the younger child when you consider social studies issues to be presented in the primary grades. Children's statements such as, "The moon was at my house last night, not yours," and "My bike is going faster than that airplane!" reveal the many ways in which young children commonly invent explanations for the complexity of our world. Children from ages five to eight are just beginning to accumulate the information and experience that we take for granted in the intermediate-age child. They are becoming aware of their individuality. They are exploring interaction and cooperation with others. They are grasping for explanations of their vast, challenging physical environment.

An effective social studies curriculum for the early years is rooted in an awareness of the cognitive, psychological, and social tasks specific to the five- to eight-year-old child. All the academic knowledge about child growth and development and personal wisdom you have gained through experience with young children will help you as you organize initial plans for social studies instruction.

As a brief reminder, however, of the crucial nature of guidance from these sources, let us restate three precepts before looking at specific elements of the social studies curriculum for early grades. First, the content of the social studies program as well as the ways the social environment of the classroom and school are structured can have significant impact on the child's social vision. Second, young children are capable of, indeed require, discussion of moral and controversial issues as prompts to taking different perspectives and learning about people and situations that have multiple roles and meanings. Third, young children need learning strategies that activate their various kinds of intelligence—linguistic, musical, logical-mathematical, spatial, bodily-kinesthetic, personal, and social—and evaluation strategies that build on individual strengths as well as work toward developing all the intelligences.[1] Using these general principles as compass points can help us chart rich and well-founded social studies curricula for young children.

■ PRIMARY-GRADE SOCIAL STUDIES CURRICULUM USING STATE STANDARDS

To explore the elements of a social studies curriculum for young children, we will examine state standards recommended as essential content. We discuss guidelines for integrating social studies with other curricular areas. Finally, we consider various materials for implementing the curriculum, and we outline the specifics of organizing the classroom environment and scheduling social studies activities.

Content Design Alternatives

As we saw in Chapter 1, content for primary grades generally elaborates on the developmental needs of children. One approach to content organization that attempts to meet developmental needs is known as the **expanding horizons model.** According to this model, the curriculum extends gradually from the individual to wider social circles. This approach, popular since the 1930s, attempts to build on the child's growing awareness of the world beyond the self.[2] The family, school, neighborhoods, and communities were familiar topics in the traditional primary social studies program. Critics said that the children already knew from their own experiences what was being taught in the traditional social studies program. Usually concepts from history, geography, civics, and economics were not explored in any depth.

As an example, let us examine the topic of shelter or homes. Usually in the primary grades children learn and see pictures of various shelters around the world ranging from tropical straw-thatched huts to pictures of people who live in caves. But typically little is taught about economics in depth and especially as applied to children's own lives. Brophy and Alleman interviewed primary children and reported that most of the children understood that people have to pay for shelter and most people prefer homes to apartments.[3] Most children had difficulty understanding why some people prefer apartment rental to home ownership. Some confused apartments with

[1]Howard Gardner, *Frames of Mind: The Theory of Multiple Intelligences* (New York: Basic Books, 1993).

[2]Lavone Hanna, Gladys Potter, and Robert Reynolds, *Dynamic Elementary Social Studies,* 3rd ed. (New York: Holt, Rinehart, and Winston, 1973).

[3]Jere Brophy and Janet Alleman, "Primary-Grade Students' Knowledge and Thinking About the Economics of Meeting Families' Shelter Needs." Paper presented at the 1999 annual meeting of the National Council for the Social Studies, Orlando, Florida.

hotels and most were vague about what is involved in renting apartments. Only a few understood that most people get a mortgage loan to allow them to buy a home when they have not accumulated the full purchase price. The students possessed only limited and spotty knowledge of the economics of housing.[4]

SMALL GROUP WORK	**SHOULD WE BE TEACHING ABOUT MORTGAGES?**
5.1	*How valuable do you think it is for primary students to learn more about the expenses associated with where they live? It certainly could make children more realistic about the economic world in which they live. Another idea is to ask children to find out how much is spent in their family on water, gas, electric, phone, and cable bills. Is it an invasion of privacy to have primary children go home to ask their parents if they rent or own their own home? How do you think most parents would respond? How comfortable would you feel about teaching such economic concepts? There is evidence that young children have many misconceptions about money and the economic world.*

Improving Reading Achievement

Before looking at the history, geography, economics, and civics standards for primary children, let us reinforce some principles in improving reading achievement, which is the major focus of attention in the primary classroom. Instructional activities that promote growth in word recognition and comprehension include guiding reading and writing, strategy lessons, and conversations about texts children or the teacher have read. Students need opportunities to apply what they have learned to reading and writing. In successful classrooms, children write stories and keep journals. These events are monitored frequently by the teacher to ensure that time is well spent and that children receive feedback on their efforts. All of these activities to improve reading can be applied to the social studies. Reading achievement can be improved through the vehicle of teaching social studies. You need not fear that you are taking time away from reading instruction when you teach social studies.

Using social studies, proficient reading is improved by the acquisition of new knowledge and vocabulary, partially through wide reading but also through explicit attention to acquiring new concepts through instruction. Children need to understand the ways textbook writers organize the content. Explicit attention is needed to assist students in reasoning about the text. More attention to literacy is found in Chapter 9.

■ PRIMARY HISTORY STATE STANDARDS

Having standards does resolve what content teachers should develop as well as reinforce the crucial nature of content from history and the social sciences for the earliest years of schooling. Remember that *standards are the major concepts or the big ideas* of an academic subject. Whether the standards should be taught directly and

---

[4]Ibid.

indirectly in a unit or integrated into the life of the primary-grade classroom, or both, is an issue that the standards do not resolve. Let us look first at history standards.

The intent of these standards is that history content in the primary grades be alive and centered on people, not events or dates. The focus is on the children's personal histories and the histories of their own families and of people, ordinary and extraordinary, who have lived in the children's own community, state, nation, and the world. It is suggested that stories, myths, legends, and biographies be used to study these histories. There is also an emphasis on historical skills such as understanding chronology and using primary sources even in the primary grades.

The typical state's social studies standards for the primary grades list four core discipline standards in history, geography, civics, and economics. In addition, other social studies standards in skills and values are also normally listed. Technology skills are also sometimes highlighted.

As just one example, let us examine Arizona Social Studies History Standards in Table 5.1. Arizona's standards were chosen because they appear to be typical of what is recommended for the primary grades and they also possess the virtue of brevity as

TABLE 5.1 Arizona's History Standards Grades 1–3

1. Demonstrate the ability to place events in chronological sequence, with emphasis on: (*Note: Historical research and analytical skills are to be learned and applied to the content standards for grades 1–3.*)
   1. Using a time line to place in order important events in a student's life
   2. Recognizing a sequence of events

2. Describe everyday life in the past and recognize that some aspects change and others stay the same, with emphasis on:
   1. Using primary source materials, including photographs, artifacts, interviews, and documents to trace the history of a family long ago
   2. The economics, symbols, customs, and oral traditions of a Native American community of Arizona, including the significance of the Eagle Feather, trade networks, decorative arts, housing, songs, and dances
   3. How past cultural exchanges influence present-day life, including food, art, shelter, and language

3. Use stories to describe past events, people, and places, with emphasis on:
   1. Contributions from past events and cultures
   2. Examples of individual action, character, and values
   3. Descriptions of daily life in past time and different places, including the various roles of men, women, and children

4. Describe the stories of important American heroes and their contribution to our society, with emphasis on:
   1. Those who secured our freedom, including George Washington, Benjamin Franklin, and Thomas Jefferson
   2. Those who fought for the rights and freedoms of others including Chief Joseph, Chief Manuelito, (Navajo, the Long Walk), Abraham Lincoln, Harriet Tubman, Martin Luther King, Jr., and Cesar Chavaz

compared with Indiana's social studies standards for all grade levels taking 288 pages. In addition, there is more uniformity among the states on the primary level for social studies standards than on other grade levels, allowing insight into primary social studies from the one case study, Arizona. In Arizona, under each standard are subheads listing content to be covered. However, differences in the state's format in describing the standards range from almost grocery lists with everything appearing to be of equal importance to very detailed, complex outlines. Remember that you are seeing just an excerpt from the primary history standards. Arizona also has standards for geography, civics, and economics for the primary as well as other grade levels.

Compared to the traditional social studies program, notice in the Arizona history standards that there is specific recognition of the importance of time lines, historical research skills, and the use of primary source materials with an emphasis on individual action, character, and values plus a wider range of American heroes than has been taught in the past. Skills are also integrated with the content. In the sample unit plan on Historical Thinking Grade 1, we see how a teacher tries to meet these standards.

SAMPLE UNIT PLAN

HISTORICAL THINKING GRADE 1

Arizona History Standards 1 and 3
Emphasis on time lines, sequence of events, examples of individual action, character, and values

Unit Goals
1. Place the events of a story, a day, or the school year in chronological order.
2. Listen to, read, and act out fables, myths, folktales, hero/heroine tales, biographies, and other stories from different cultures to answer the following: What happened? Who did it? Why did it happen? What was the consequence? How might things have ended if a character had behaved differently?
3. Use literacy links to reading, listening, speaking, and writing.

Day 1. Beginning the Unit
Objective: Students will use time lines to place important events in order.

1. Ask students, "What are some things that happen each day in our classroom?"
2. Read the book *My Day/Mi Dia* by Rebecca Emberly (Little, Brown & Co., 1993). The English/Spanish text describes activities in a child's daily routine. Record the text in sentence strips and have the students sequence the events of the day.
3. Take photographs of events that occur each day in class or ask students to draw pictures of three to five events that occur each day. Make time lines and post times for the events.
4. Assign homework (parent letter home) asking for significant events in their child's life to use in a time line. Earlier photographs encouraged.
5. A "Time Line of the Day" is then produced each day along with a monthly and, finally, yearly accumulation and evaluation of time lines. Use TimeLiner software for creating and printing time lines.

(continued)

HISTORICAL THINKING GRADE 1 *(continued)*

Day 2. Consequences

Objective: Students will understand the meaning of *consequences.*

1. Discuss with students and identify in real life the meanings of *problem, solution,* and *consequences.*
2. In pairs students brainstorm other problems they might face and list them on the following chart.

   Problem/Solution/Consequences Chart

   Event
   Problem
   Solution
   Consequences
   Alternative Solution
   Alternative Consequences

Day 3. Interpret a Fable

Objective: Students will interpret a fable in terms of story and value.

1. Read the classic story of "The Lion and the Mouse" from the textbook *I Know a Place* (Houghton Mifflin).
2. By asking questions, go through the sequence of event, problem, and so on.
3. Ask students what this story tells us (e.g., importance of friends, friends help each other, friends come in all sizes).
4. Brainstorm what lesson the lion learned.
5. Develop class moral for the story (e.g., everyone needs a friend).
6. Two students dramatize the story.
7. Students draw three pictures to show three events in the story, which they then paste in order on a strip of paper. Share with the class.
8. Students draw a picture of a time when they had a problem and a friend helped them.
9. Introduce *value.* Ask students what values are presented in the story and list the values in the story on the chart.

Story	Values

10. Introduce *fact* and *fiction.* Ask students if this is a true story. How do they know? Chart responses. Discuss characteristics of factual stories: names, dates, places, and actions that can be verified. List these student responses on a Fact/Fiction Chart. Divide into three parts: Story, Fact or Fiction, and Reasons.

Day 4. Developing the Topic

Objective: Students will apply skills in interpreting a new story: (a) Identify a problem and solution by discussing events in story; (b) identify and chart values as they discuss stories; and (c) make time lines for characters.

1. Read the story *Paper Bag Princess* by Robert Munsch (Annick Press Ltd., 1980). A girl rescues her prince from a dragon and then decides he may not be as princely as she had first thought.
2. Ask students about the problem, solution, and consequences. What else could he or she do? Enter responses on Problem/Solution/Consequences Chart.
3. Ask students what values are presented in the story. Who has these values? List on the Story/Values Chart.
4. In pairs have students compare the characters of Ronald and Elizabeth on a Venn diagram.
5. Have students use three illustrations from the book and write a caption for each picture and place in sequential order.
6. Have students tell the story from the perspective of the dragon.
7. Discuss possible alternative endings and places in the book where such alternatives might occur. Use small groups for the activity.
8. Have a "hot seat" where one student is chosen to portray one character in the book and have the other students ask the character questions.

Day 5. Interpreting Stories

Objective: Students will apply skills to interpret another story.

1. Discuss what a hero or heroine is. Students discuss a story of a child who was a hero long ago in Holland. Locate Holland on the map and show canals.
2. Read the story "The Little Hero of Holland" from *The Children's Book of Virtues* edited by William Bennett.
3. Discuss the problem and what Peter did. Fill in class the Problem/Solution/Consequences Chart.
4. Discuss whether this story is fact or fiction. Introduce the term *legend.* Make an entry for the story on the Fact/Fiction Chart.
5. In cooperative pairs students discuss why Peter acted as he did. Ask students which values are presented in the story.
6. Use individual student clocks to demonstrate how long Peter had to stay in one position.
7. Pass out 9" × 12" sheets of construction paper in which a small hole has been made. Ask students to put the paper on a chair and kneel on the floor with their finger in the hole for 5 minutes. Discuss and chart responses.
8. Have students fill out the chart on Peter. I am . . . I hear . . . I see . . . I want . . . I say . . . I am. . . .

(continued)

HISTORICAL THINKING GRADE 1 *(continued)*

Next Days

Continue with other stories. Only a few are listed; you could substitute others.

Read *The Rough Face Girl* by Rafe Martin and David Shannon (Scholastic, 1992), an Algonquin Indian telling of the Cinderella story.

Read *The Story of Ruby Bridges* by Robert Coles (Scholastic, 1995). For months, six-year-old Ruby Bridges confronts the hostility of segregationists when she becomes the first African American girl to integrate Frantz Elementary School in New Orleans in 1960.

Culminating the Unit

Review each of the class charts and recall stories. Ask students to discuss, write (or dictate) new stories, and fill out the charts.

I am deeply indebted to Elizabeth Rickett, Montebello Unified School District, who explained this unit at the California Annual State Conference, February 19, 1998. This is a brief summary of a thirty-three-page unit that does not do justice to all the excellent ideas.

Look carefully at this briefly sketched unit. Do you like it? Will students meet the state standards of historical thinking and have a better understanding of chronology? Do you like the values emphasis on how actions have consequences and there can be other alternatives? Are there many opportunities for assessment built in throughout the unit?

SMALL GROUP WORK	**CONTROVERSIAL ISSUES FOR THE FIRST GRADE?**
5.2	*Check how multicultural this unit is. Also notice that there is a discussion of a moral and controversial issue, segregation, in the Ruby Bridges story. The author of this unit also suggests the use of* The Lily Cupboard: A Story of the Holocaust *by Shulamith Levey Oppenheim (HarperCollins, 1992). This story tells of when a young Jewish girl in German-occupied Holland is forced to separate from her parents and hide with strangers in the country. It is a sensitive portrayal and powerful story of ordinary people who are heroes. Do you think controversial issues should be brought up in the first grade?*

History in the primary grades can be taught with a variety of methods even with the same topics. A third-grade class studying the community used computer skills when they created a database of historical places and markers in their community. These included historic buildings, the oldest homes, and other items of historical interest. Any community would appreciate this publication as a guide for community members to use in visiting historic sites. Second-grade students studied the older forms of transportation used in their communities about 100 years ago including foot, animals, steamboats, and the early trains. They compared the older with the newer forms of transportation such as automobiles and airplanes. They also created a database for their information, allowing students the opportunity to categorize, arrange, sort, select, and display information. These and other projects show that primary students can meet history standards in different ways.

Time and Chronology Skills Related to Student Lives and Histories

As indicated by state standards and the unit "History Thinking Grade 1," time and chronology are, in part, social studies skill areas. Most programs usually introduce "telling time" using a clock and sometimes a calendar. Telling time in periods longer than a day needs to be part of the primary-grade daily routine. A year-long journal of class events along with a year-long time line can help students with this skill. One classroom job can be to record student-selected significant events from yesterday on the class time line or in the class journal. Computer software for making time lines can make this activity easier. This practice helps students build a sense of continuity and recall.

Studies have found that many young children are unaware of or fear change. Teachers need to involve children in activities that call attention to change as a natural part of living that they experience as they grow. Here are key questions that you can use to focus students on changes: Is something different? What is changing? What is causing the change? What do you think might happen because of the change?[5]

Observing change in their own height and weight by keeping individual charts helps children see change in themselves. Collecting weather and seasonal data on temperature, rainfall, snowfall, the length of days and nights, the changes in the moon, and the changes in vegetation and animal habits helps children see the cyclical nature of some changes.

Change in the human life cycle also needs to be illustrated. Contact with older people as classroom helpers or storytellers as well as books about growing, changing, and dying assist children to become more comfortable with the idea that, even with change, there is a continuity of life provided through our families and that change, including the loss that comes with it, is necessary for growth.

Fantasy and Story Line

As you have seen in the sample unit plan "Historical Thinking Grade 1," an additional perspective in the selection of social studies content for young children also arises from the developmentalist point of view. Arguing that children bring to school an intuitive knowledge of how their world works, proponents of this approach emphasize the importance of exploring values as the essential foundation for any content design. Myth, legend, and tale as social studies content sources, rather than insistence on engagement with reality, are materials used to capitalize on the interests of young children. Recognizing the significance of fantasy and story line in the thinking of young children,

[5]C. Sunal, "The Child and the Concept of Change," *Social Education* 45, no. 6 (October 1981): 438–441.

the examples we provide them need to be seen as "sense-making tools"[6] for building a more conscious understanding of their social lives. Using fantasy sources to discuss good and evil, kindness and cruelty, selflessness and greed can provide safe avenues for the young child to ponder human behavior and values. This approach resonates well with many experienced teachers of young children and some social critics calling for a curriculum that teaches values. It is possible to make any topic more satisfying to young children by emphasizing its storytelling potential.

SMALL GROUP WORK	**USING FANTASY AND STORY LINE AS CONTENT SOURCES**
5.3	*Everyone knows the tale "The Little Red Hen." How can this story be used for a social studies lesson? What human qualities do the characters represent? Is the hen justified in doing what she did at the end? How could everyone be satisfied in this story? Is the red hen's approach a value you want to inculcate or question? Can you think of a contemporary or home version of this story? Explore the global possibilities using versions of this story and comparing different kinds of bread—tortillas, chapatis, pita, fry-bread. Discuss with your classmates your ideas about using this kind of content for social studies.*

Storypath is a commercially available American spin-off of the story line approach.[7] This set of materials uses the basic components of a story—setting, characters, and plot—to help organize the social studies curriculum. Students work to solve problems presented as critical incidents embedded in each unit. In a unit on the neighborhood, for example, students develop a mural from the description provided by the teacher reading from the unit guide. As students work, they contextualize the setting with their own visual representation, oral descriptions, and chart stories. Once students have constructed their setting and character identities, they are presented with a plot-instigating incident such as litter in the neighborhood. As the group discusses how the neighborhood can solve the litter problem as well as other critical incidents—a child almost being hit by a speeding car and pizza delivery not working because no street names and numbers and maps exist—additional concepts and skills are developed, all flowing from the students' construction of identities and settings. Students are prompted to seek information from various sources that are pertinent to the topic being dealt with in the unit. Unit topics—the marine world and the Great Barrier Reef, communities and their decisions, the Wampanoags and the first thanksgiving, a safari to Kenya, independence, the presidential election, the medieval castle—are multidisciplinary. Most unit topics are general and recognizable as traditional primary content; however, some topics are seasonal and others are specific to a historic event or geographical environment.

[6]Kieran Egan, "Individual Development in Literacy," in Suzanne de Castell, Allan Luke, and Kieran Egan, eds. *Literacy, Society and Schooling: A Reader* (Cambridge, England: Cambridge University Press, 1986), p. 250.

[7]Storypath is produced by the Everyday Learning Corporation, Chicago, IL, Tel. (800) 382-7670; fax (312) 540-5848, http://www.everydaylearning.com

Some teachers take issue with approaches built on fantasy. They feel that social studies should specifically incorporate social issues with which young children are most concerned. They argue that teachers must help children with real problems, not concentrate on situations and settings that are unrelated to the reality of the class. In contrast, proponents of story line approaches maintain that even though the topics begin with the suggestion of fantasy from the teacher, in constructing the topic setting and character identities, students automatically utilize the experiences and social issues they bring from their daily lives in solving the critical issues. There is merit in both attitudes. Perhaps the difference is one of the pedagogical direction preferred to reach the issues related to students' lives. Teachers are not counselors trained to do therapy. They feel that school should be a safe place where the child can be exposed to knowledge that provides hope, which comes from finding out about other worlds. However, choosing social studies topics in the hopes they will not be upsetting or offensive to young children will almost surely guarantee that students see no connection between school social studies and their own lives.

There is renewed recognition that in any content design, the starting point should be topics that are elaborated with a specific understanding of the lives of the students in a specific class. Whether these concerns come directly from their lives or indirectly through the media, young children need social studies content that helps them grow in their abilities not only to survive and cope but also to seek ways of improving their lives and their communities. And fantasy sources or fiction may permit the necessary distancing from children's real situations to initiate exploration of these concerns.

As an example, children can explore family roles that reflect families of children in the class. Many children have caregivers who may be single, or older relatives, or not biologically related, or in same-sex relationships. Whatever the home constellation of caregivers may be, young children need to feel that they and their situation are respected as they are. Furthermore, they need to see that even though what they may have or do at home is different, all children have learning tasks in their home lives. Another way to explore the child's role is by looking at it from a historical perspective. Awareness of immigrant or pioneer children's responsibilities in an earlier time provides present-day children with important samples to draw from in seeing themselves and their situations as part of a social process that others have passed through successfully. Thus, the first rule of content selection is that it must lead from or be related to the group of individuals in a given class. Every class is different. Sometimes a class is different from one day to the next; topics and units taught last year will need to be rethought and redesigned if they are to be used as content for this year's class.

Again, we should underscore four points. One is that learning activities about social studies topics can be organized in formal, teacher-planned sessions or they can flow informally from an event that catches student interest. A second is that social studies content can come from nontraditional sources, and it may, but does not need to, come from a textbook. In fact, content does not have to come from a bookbound source. Third, choosing topics requires that the teacher perceive how familiar with the topic children are, and what potential the topic has to assist children to grow in problem-solving ability. Finally, some topics are more important than others to children. This does not mean selecting topics according to the results of a student opinion poll. Rather, it means that teachers are responsible for helping children connect to their lives a foreign or apparently insignificant topic. Important topics are those that offer children the concept of belonging to a diverse world, the context to understand who and where they are, the tools to resolve issues, and a sense of caring that prompts striving for better conditions for all people. Topics that meet these criteria can be defended as part of the social studies program.

■ PRIMARY ECONOMICS STANDARDS

The primary economics standards build on what students already have learned about economics from their family, school, and community experiences. Looking at Arizona's standards as an example, the kindergarten economics standard states, "Describe the way families produce, consume, and exchange goods and services in their community," with emphasis on descriptions of work that people do, the need to make choices because resources are limited, recognition of various forms of U.S. money (also a math correlation), and how money is used to purchase goods and services. For grades 1 to 3, two economics standards are shown in Table 5.2.

At first glance, these standards might seem too advanced for young children. How can they be made more in line with the lives of students? Remember you do not have to have separate units on each of the four basic primary social studies standards: history, geography, economics, and civics. Often you can combine two or more social studies standards with language arts or other standards.

Teaching About Costs and Benefits

Let us look more closely at the first primary economics standard on making decisions or choices with a comparison of additional costs with additional benefits.

Here are some suggestions for students to write about or discuss. First, find out how many have pets, what kind of pets they have, and the costs associated with a pet.

TABLE 5.2 Arizona's Economics Standards for Grades 1 to 3

---

1. Describe how scarcity affects students' daily lives, with emphasis on:
   1. The opportunity cost of a choice
   2. Natural resources, human resources, and capital resources, and how they are used to produce goods and services
   3. The costs and benefits of personal spending and saving choices
2. Describe the characteristics of production and exchange in an economy, with emphasis on:
   1. The use of money and barter in the exchange of goods and services
   2. Why some things are made locally, some elsewhere in the United States, and some in other countries
   3. The work that people do to manufacture, transport, and market goods and services
   4. The interdependence of consumers and producers of goods and services

---

Some may forget that caring for pets usually requires purchasing special food for them and taking them to the vet. Then go through these examples.

I. Pets
   A. List the costs of buying and caring for a pet.
   B. List the benefits of buying and caring for a pet.

Ask the children to tell you on Monday what they did on the last weekend or other weekends.

II. Use of their own time on a Saturday afternoon
   A. Costs and benefits of earning money selling lemonade, raking leaves, and so on
   B. Costs and benefits of riding bikes with friends
   C. Costs and benefits of going shopping for groceries with parent
   D. Costs and benefits of helping with housework

If you do not wish to ask directly if your students get allowances or earn money, or the amounts they receive, use characters in stories. What do you think Jack in "Jack in the Beanstalk" should do with his money? How about finding the "pot of gold?" What would you do if given a large sum of money?

III. Use of their own money
   A. Costs and benefits of saving all or part of their money
   B. Costs and benefits of spending all or part of their money

After doing a few of these exercises, most students will better understand the importance of making decisions that provide the greatest satisfaction for them. For example, a child must make a choice of what item to buy for his or her mother on Mother's Day. Given the amount of money available, if the child buys cut flowers from the local supermarket, then he or she cannot buy a small plant. One choice eliminates other possibilities. Or a child must make a decision at a fast-food outlet on what to order. A parent will normally not allow a child to order every single item on the menu. To make these decisions, a child must weigh the costs with the benefits. For example, what are the opportunity costs of sleeping late on Saturday morning? Being late to school? Choosing snacks? In most cases, choices involve doing a little more or a little less of something. Few choices are all-or-nothing decisions.

Songs also can be sung to illustrate economics concepts.

"Oh, Give Me a Choice"[8]
(Tune: "Home on the Range")

Oh give me a choice,
Oh, a difficult choice,
And I'll think about what I could use,
I'll have to decide,
With my eyes open wide,
What I'll give up and what I will
   choose.

Opportunity cost!
It's the thing you give up when
   You choose.
   It's the price that is paid
   When a choice must be made
   It's the thing I that I surely will lose.

[8]Teaching Strategies K–2, Economics America.

Teaching About Production and Exchange

As a teacher you may want to do more to get your students to meet the second economics standard (i.e., understand characteristics of production and exchange in an economy). How might this be done in a way that can build on your children's experiences? Appropriate economics books, teaching strategies, and resources for classroom use are available from the National Council on Economic Education.[9] Another way is to take a specific food item and see how it is produced and finally arrives at the table. Good choices might be pizza, cereals, tostadas, pita bread, noodles, biscuits, pancakes, spaghetti, pretzels, and orange juice. You could also investigate other items, such as how teddy bears or books are made in a factory or how subways are built. For each food product, make flowcharts with the class showing the sequence of events in planting, growing, harvesting, processing the crop to become a food product, packaging the food product, distributing (transporting), and selling the ingredients of the food or the product at a market.

An example of available trade books is *Bananas—From Manolo to Margie* by George Ancona (Clarion Books, Houghton Mifflin, New York, 1982), a story that follows a crop of bananas from a plantation in Honduras to the breakfast table of a child in the United States. Along the way the bananas are handled by many workers and carried by different forms of transportation. Both economics and geography objectives can be stressed, such as having students trace the route of the bananas, finding out why Central America is an ideal place for growing bananas, and making a list of the workers necessary for us to get bananas to eat.

Another popular choice is pancakes, partly because of the wide variety of related books available.

Pancake Books

Little Bear's Pancake Party by Janice Brustlein

Pancakes, Pancakes! by Eric Carle

Pancake Boy by Lorinda Cauley

Miss Mable's Table by Deborah Chandra

Pancakes for Breakfast by Tomie De Paola

Critters of the Night-Mummy Pancakes by Mercer Mayer

Curious George Makes Pancakes by Margaret Rey, H. A. Rey

Journey Cake, HO! by Ruth Sawyer

Pancakes and Pies: A Russian Folk Tale by Carole Tate

Although each book has value and students may enjoy the antics of good-hearted but mistake-prone Curious George in his attempt to make pancakes, some books lend themselves better to exploring the economics concepts. *Pancakes, Pancakes!* is a beautifully illustrated book about Jack, who wakes up hungry for an enormous pan-

---

[9]National Council on Economic Education, 1140 Avenue of the Americas, New York, New York 10036. Phone 212-730-7007; www.economicsamerica.org.

cake for breakfast. But before he can enjoy his pancake, he must get flour from the miller, an egg from the black hen, milk from the spotted cow, and butter churned from fresh cream. The book provides a step-by-step guide to making a pancake from scratch and introducing all of the people and their special work that are essential parts of its preparation, showing the ways in which we are interdependent in our world. After the teacher reads the book aloud, students could make a sequence chart of the steps described on how to make pancakes long ago. Headings could be the following: Ingredient; Source; Who or What Involved; Trade. Ask how Jack gathered the ingredients. Who helped? How did they get "paid"? What was exchanged in "payment"?

There are also other trade books illustrating economics concepts on such topics as how a child's coat is produced (*A New Coat for Anna* by Harriet Ziefert). Students follow the steps Anna and her mother take to get a badly needed winter coat for Anna though money is in short supply in their home town after World War II. Students learn the process involved in making a coat—from shearing sheep to buying clothing. Trade books can also illustrate how cotton, silk, and synthetics are made into clothing and how clothing has changed.

Then display a box of Bisquick and its recipe for pancakes—today's version of the story—or use a recipe from a cookbook. Students can also compare the cost of making a product from scratch or purchasing it. Make a class chart about making pancakes today using the same headings as earlier. Compare the two charts—then and now! How are they alike and how are they different? Why is transportation so important for our pancake breakfast today? Review the economics concept of trade as an exchange of goods and services. Discuss money and what we know about it. How do we get it? What work do our parents do to earn it? Do we earn money? How? How do we use our money? How does money substitute for swapping items or working to pay off a debt?[10] Using flowcharts, show transportation, marketing, and workers needed to get food to the table. Notice that this unit about pancakes also helps develop historical thinking about now and long ago.

Depending on your class, more lessons could be developed on facts about wheat, a staple food item throughout many cultures, and where it is found. If your state grows wheat or produces dairy products or eggs, write to your state for free materials from such organizations as the Dairy Council of California or the California Wheat Commission. Wheat could be a springboard to teaching about the basic needs, structures, and functions of plants. You could bring in a variety of flour samples or wheat stalks from the dried flower sections of your local stores. You may refer to the food pyramid and the placement of grains on the chart. Or you could discuss basic health measures for handling food and hand washing. You could read more books on how pancakes are made and eaten around the world. All of these are interesting activities, but in the process don't forget that your purpose is to teach economics concepts. Sometimes the main objective can get lost.

---

[10]Idea based on Julie Hume, Orange County Department of Education, presentation entitled "Literature Line-Up, A Standards Based Approach" at the California Annual State Social Studies Conference, February 2000.

TABLE 5.3 Making Pancakes

Ingredients	Utensils	Steps for Making Pancakes

Then comes the fun part—a cooking experience of a pancake party. Have your students in small groups fill out the chart headings in Table 5.3, Making Pancakes. Always inform other school personnel, including administration, food service, maintenance, and parent volunteers, about an upcoming cooking experience. Encourage their assistance in any available capacity, such as obtaining supplies. Organize the logistics of the cooking activity with stations, groups, and adult helpers. Make sure that the atmosphere for both making and eating the pancakes is pleasant. Some classes have had a pancake party for others than themselves: another class, parents in the evening, or for mothers before Mother's Day. For these occasions, the children have often made thinner pancakes like crepes so that fruit like strawberries can be rolled into the crepe to serve to guests. Children learn that by varying the amount of liquid in pancakes makes a thicker or thinner pancake and that tastes vary on what is the best type of pancake. Students also learn that, when serving guests, as a cultural preference we want our pancakes and the food serving to look as attractive as possible.

If making pancakes is not suitable, teachers can use the old favorite of making butter. Buy whipping cream at the store and pour it into a clear pint-sized jar with a tight-fitting lid. Have students take turns shaking it until it turns into butter. Serve on crackers, or serve the butter along with the pancakes.

Teachers also have reported success with a Gingerbread Man curriculum, using the folktale as a starting point and ending up making gingerbread men and gingerbread cookies. Students learn about the resources needed to produce gingerbread products, the opportunity cost of choosing one cookie decoration over another, and the goods and services produced in the community. They can try a division of labor with one child or a small group of children putting just the eyes on the gingerbread man versus doing all of the decorations. What are the advantages and disadvantages of having a division of labor? If they sell their products, they become aware of earning income, prices, and their productivity.

These examples of economic activities show the value of concrete experiences and examples. Too often young children have inaccurate ideas about the economic world. They think that buying things in stores is a ritual, not an exchange involving profit. They do not see that work and income are connected. Try to make learning about economics meaningful and memorable for children by focusing on children's own real-world experiences, thereby correcting economic misconceptions. There is also a treasury of children's literature to help meet the economics standards.

SMALL GROUP WORK	**HOW DID YOU LEARN ABOUT ECONOMICS CONCEPTS?**
5.4	*Do you recall how you learned economics concepts? Were they explicitly taught in school? Informally at home? Do you think the school should do a better job of teaching economics concepts?*

TABLE 5.4 Arizona's Geography Standards Grades 1–3

1. Construct and interpret maps and other geographic tools, including the use of map elements, to organize information about people, places, and environments, with emphasis on:
   1. Identifying the characteristics and purposes of maps, globes, and other geographic tools
   2. Identifying and using symbols, the compass rose, cardinal directions, and a grid system to locate places of significance on maps and globes
   3. Making a map using a title, compass rose, legend, scale, and grid system
   4. Using a spatial perspective to plan a safe route from home to school
   5. Using a globe and an atlas to locate a student's city and state
   6. Measuring distance on a map
   7. Labeling the continents, oceans, and major mountain ranges on a map

2. Identify natural and human characteristics of places and how people interact with and modify their environment, with emphasis on:
   1. Natural characteristics of places, including landforms, bodies of water, natural resources, and weather
   2. Human characteristics of places, including houses, schools, neighborhoods, and communities
   3. The relationship between the physical features and location of human activities
   4. How people depend on the physical environment and its natural resources to satisfy their basic needs
   5. How people can conserve and replenish certain resources
   6. The ways in which people have used and modified resources in the local region, including dam construction, building roads, building cities, and raising crops

■ PRIMARY GEOGRAPHY STANDARDS

Although for generations students have spent time on learning to read maps and globes, the newer emphasis goes beyond these two skills. The national geography standards emphasize six major concepts that the student knows and understands: The World in Spatial Terms, Places and Regions, Physical Systems, Human Systems, Environment and Society, and the Uses of Geography.[11] These standards require more than just memorization of the capital of China and its location. Geographers go beyond the "where" and ask why it is there and what the consequences are of its being there. Students are to see the effects of interactions of humans on the environment, the migrations of human populations, economic interdependence, changes in resources, and the like.

The two Arizona primary geography standards for grades 1 to 3 show both the traditional and new emphases. The first standard emphasizes students learning traditional map-reading skills whereas the second focuses on the interaction of natural and human characteristics as shown in Table 5.4.

[11]National Council for Geographic Education, *Geography for Life: National Geography Standards 1994* (Washington, DC: National Geographic Society, 1994).

In the primary grades, students can understand the human and environmental interaction by seeing how people in their community are "changing the land" by tearing down old structures and building new ones, converting agricultural lands to urban use, or through irrigation turning nonfarmlands into agricultural ones. Are any new streets, roads, or highways being built in the community? Students can investigate why these changes are taking place.

An important geography concept is migration. Migration of people, especially large numbers, into a community causes enormous changes in the environment by the building of houses, schools, hospitals, and government buildings such as the police station, fire department, and businesses. This changes how the land is used. Usually a transportation system is needed for the movement of people as well as goods and services. Increased numbers of people can put a strain on local transportation systems and other public services. In turn, a decline in population in a community can also have serious consequences. Focus on how people, increasing or declining in number, change the land. What is influencing the size, location, and population of the community?

To explore this topic and to build on the children's own experiences, distribute and explain the following "Family Migration" questionnaire to students. Ask and role-play the interview process for students to conduct an interview with a parent, older relative, or guardian to determine:

- When did your family or you come to _____?
- Where did your family or you come from?
- What mode of transportation was used to get here? What route did you or your family take to get here?
- Why did your family or you choose to come to this area?

Then have students record the information from the questionnaire on a chart such as the following:

My Family's Migration to _____

Date Arrived	From	Reasons for Migration

For the route taken by their family, have students write their name and where the family came from on a Post-it note and affix it to a U.S. or world map. Discuss the migration of different families. Are there any patterns shown on the map? Another activity related to historical thinking is to make a time line of the arrival of the children's families. This could be organized by decades starting with the first family's arrival.

Most important is a discussion of the reasons for migration—the push-pull factors. With each decade on the time line, ask students if they know of any major events in the local community, state, or nation that might have influenced families to move into this area. Did World War II draw more people into the community? Were changes in technology such as computers having an effect on migration?

Conduct a class discussion explaining the push-pull factors that promoted migration. *Push factors* are those that help convince people to leave an area whereas *pull factors* are those that attract people to a new area. Some push factors may include lack of jobs in their old community or discrimination. Some pull factors are better jobs, educational opportunities, and prospects for improved standards of living.

Ask students who have moved how they felt about moving. Why did their family move? What were the good things about it? What were the things that they did not like?

After these activities, students, using their own families' experience, will have a better understanding of the concept of migration, the movement of humans, and their interaction with the environment, which is an important geography concept.

Map and Globe Skills from Immediate Surroundings

Map- and globe-reading skills are among those specific to the social studies. Younger children need concrete experiences in spatial awareness before they are presented with maps. They need to practice, as is done on *Sesame Street,* the locational prepositions, for example, *under, around,* and *beside.* Songs and games such as "Simon Says" or "Mother, May I?" can help them learn *down, up, over, under, through, around, behind, between, left,* and *right.* Students must grasp these concepts firmly before they can learn about cardinal directions. Learning north, south, east, and west is best pursued outside at varying times of the day with the sun as a guide by which students can orient themselves to local landmarks. Once the students have learned that they can use the sun to find directions, and that their interpretation of the sun's position will vary according to whether the time is morning or afternoon, they are ready to transfer the skill anywhere. When they learn, for example, that the swings are to their east as they stand outside their classroom door, they are ready to name the direction of other landmarks from that point. After a series of varied, real experiences with finding direction, students are ready to transfer the idea of cardinal direction to the pictures they make of their classroom, school, route from home to school, and neighborhood.

Pictures and models that translate real physical space to a representation of it present conceptual challenges to any age. Young children can best begin this process by manipulating blocks and toys on a sand table or a floor area to replicate the classroom, the playground, a room, or a city street or block. Movable objects permit students to be experimental and free from worrying about ruining a painting or drawing with a mistake.

After miniatures of concrete settings are arranged, the further abstraction of representing them on paper begins to make sense. Before replicating the concrete, teachers may organize activities calling for pictorial representations or clay models without requiring that they be to scale or oriented to the proper direction. Software that permits manipulation of objects on a street grid or fictive landscape can be useful as reinforcement but not as a substitute for activities that engage children with physical, not "virtual," reality.

A globe is a model of our planet. Kindergarteners need exposure to this concept. After they learn their location on the model, they can begin learning names and shapes of continents as well as locations for places in the news they discuss. Outline globes that portray relief, landforms, and bodies of water with no printing are best.

Accumulating an index card file of place names as these are introduced and the places are located on the globe provides an excellent set of material for "changes of pace" and "filler" games during all-class sharing or activity change times. The cards can help students build verbal cues to incidental sight vocabulary and geographical locational skills. If these cards are numbered to coincide with numbers fixed on the globe, the globe can become one of the activity station choices for individuals or small groups during work periods.

SMALL GROUP WORK	HAVE YOU MIGRATED?
5.5	*In your group, using the Family Migration chart, tell the group why you have migrated or moved. After going through this activity yourself, do you think your students will enjoy this activity?*

■ PRIMARY CITIZENSHIP STANDARDS

Perhaps of all of the standards, citizenship/government standards are the most important yet most difficult to achieve. We want to move students toward responsible citizenship behavior in the community. It is not just enough for them to parrot back to us who the president or the governor is. Merely moving down civics content formerly taught at upper grades will not help students to appreciate our form of government. The goal is that students become committed to our democratic form of government and its rights and responsibilities. Arizona's general standard on civics/government states the following:

> Students understand the ideals, rights, and responsibilities of citizenship, and the content, sources, and history of the founding documents of the United States, with particular emphasis on the Constitution and how the government functions at the local, state, national, and international levels.

How are these lofty ideals to be achieved? Should you have a separate unit on developing social skills and citizenship responsibilities? You could have a unit on "School Rules, Now and Long Ago" to use as a vehicle to ask questions about whether certain rules are "right." How do you think most primary teachers would do this?

Some of the skill areas pertinent to the social studies should be taught throughout the day. Citizenship is such an area. Younger children need special guidance in citizenship skills. They are dealing with the idea of authority in their lives. Their parents, teachers, the traffic patrol guard, the school yard aide, and older children give them orders and rules to follow. Unless you highlight the need for rules and order, children may believe that authority is magical or capricious, not to be questioned, and resident with whoever has the most power and size.

Discuss why we have specific rules. Once the reasons for the rules are clarified, you should play the devil's advocate to help children learn to question authority using a principle or reason. For example, if students agree that the traffic patrol guard lets them cross after he or she has checked that traffic is stopped, ask them what they should do if they are told to cross while the patrol guard is laughing and joking with someone and has not checked the traffic, or if a friend crosses against the wishes of the guard, or if the guard keeps the children waiting when there is no visible reason.

Posing dilemmas such as what to do if a baby-sitter exceeds his or her authority is a natural prelude to role-playing alternative consequences (see Chapter 3 for a basic explanation of role playing). Teachers find that young children are more easily involved in trying out ideas when they can act through simple stick puppets. The puppet moves the direct focus of the audience from the performing child, which seems to ease the child's anxiety about self-expression.

Making up rules and practicing the use of authority open a child's understanding of justice and fairness. When children have real experience in rule making, they should be led to discuss how rule making and enforcement happen in the adult world. You can promote these exploratory conversations by bringing a newspaper to class and talking about what the president, or another public figure with power, is doing and what that person's role is in rule making.

To extend the exploration of concepts of authority and power beyond the immediate experience of the students, you should discover what they know about figures in authority. In this diagnostic phase of theme development, teachers need to interview the students: Who is the president? How does a person get to be president? What does the president do? Why is the president important to us? Can a president make a rule by himself or herself? Is the president's power limited? Or relate the idea of authority to the class: Who should decide what we do in this class? Why do teachers get to organize what we do? Why do teachers follow rules? How are these rules made? Should rules ever be changed? Should teachers ever be changed?

Student answers can help us know where to start our current events discussions. Typically teachers will need to "go with the flow"—that is, we need to extend our students' information by bringing in pictures and stories based on what they give us as starting points. The information students offer should be taken at face value and with seriousness. Laughing or finding fault with what a student offers will guarantee that the student will be less genuine the next time you ask what he or she thinks or knows.

Our ultimate goal is to help students see that those who have power in our system are real people. They retain their authority by following established rules and are subject to losing it if they do not adhere to these rules. Discussions in the classroom about situations that involve civic values, such as the consent of the governed and rights that have responsibilities, will help students understand the bits and pieces they gather from television. We are helping them build a background for interpreting events, a vital citizenship skill. Citizenship skills can be enhanced within the classroom as well. Chapter 7 details a middle-grade approach that sets up a class government, treating the classroom as a microsociety. Primary-grade children can also profit from assuming classroom responsibilities, devising classroom rules and procedures, and solving problems. Allowing students to organize classroom procedures and rotate classroom responsibilities gives them practical experience in citizenship skills.

In teaching citizenship as well as other subject areas, thinking skills are a high priority. The degree of sophistication in children's thinking has long been the subject of research and debate. Developmentalist theory suggests that children move through stages in their thinking abilities. Critiques of developmental perspectives suggest that young children are capable of complex and philosophical thought. Bringing this thought to a level of consciousness is second nature to some teachers. Others find they need models and suggestions to offer instruction in the processes of thinking. Among the several strategies devised to help children develop skill in organizing ideas is the simple scheme developed by Hilda Taba, an outstanding elementary educator who made significant contributions to social studies teaching.[12] This by now classic strategy has three basic steps:

1. Teacher enumerates and lists students' responses to an opening question.
2. Students group the responses.
3. Students label or categorize their groupings.

In this strategy teachers promote large or small group discussion through questions that follow these steps. For example, to explore the concept of rules, a teacher might ask, "What comes to your mind when you hear the word *rules*?" Recording student responses as they are given, the teacher tries to elicit a variety of responses, accepting all without regard to whether they are accurate. Working from the original responses, the next question according to the strategy would be "Can we group any of these?" "What is the reason you put _____ and _____ together?" Finally, "What title can we give to this list?" This line of questioning can also be used for guiding students in the formation of generalizations.

Recall teachers in your experience who prompted you to think. What kinds of questions did they ask? Weren't they always asking how we knew something to be true? To explain how we arrived at a conclusion? To give a reason(s) for a decision? This probing attitude should become second nature to teachers when dealing with individuals or group discussions. If you learn specific approaches for prompting student thought, these techniques can help you internalize this mode of verbal interaction with students. Teaching thinking skills must be a permanent instructional activity.

In looking over state primary standards, we have included both the content and the skills listed for each standard because in most cases these two areas are combined. Of course, some skill areas are also developed in other subjects. Lists of reading skills include research and study skills. Math skills include problem solving, critical thinking, telling time, and locational skills involving work with grids. Children are gaining study skills when they gather information for a report by observing how groups solve conflicts at recess or by interviewing a parent on the tools that the parent uses in his or her work. They are growing in decision-making skills when they compare several solutions to the issue of how to distribute the playground equipment during recess. They are growing in problem-solving skills when they test their predictions about which is the most productive way to get classroom jobs done. In some cases, specific skills will need attention, such as understanding a time line.

---

[12]Hilda Taba, *Teaching Strategies and Cognitive Functioning in Elementary School Children,* Cooperative Research Project no. 2404 (Washington, DC: U.S. Office of Education, 1996).

■ GUIDELINES FOR INTEGRATING SOCIAL STUDIES IN THE PRIMARY-GRADE CURRICULUM

From the various units already presented, you have seen that typically a unit includes content and skills from more than one social studies standard (e.g., history and geography together) as well as content and skills from other subject areas such as language arts. In fact, it is almost impossible to avoid using some language arts as children read, listen, discuss, and write about social studies. Let us look more closely at guidelines for integrating primary social studies.

Developmental psychologists tell us that materials used with young children should prompt them to interact, create, and manipulate. We are also told that children respond best to stories that are related to integrated themes. When we look at the kinds of topics suggested for the primary grades in social studies content designs, we sense two dilemmas. One is the apparent distance between the learning-mode prescriptions and the nature of social studies topics. The second is the difference in orientation between the separate subject tradition of curriculum designs and the more child-centered approach to organizing early school programs. How can we help children learn about families in other parts of the world or about how groups use resources? How can we manage to teach the crucial basics of literacy and still include all the other subjects? In the first apparent dilemma, we have topics that may be distant from the children or represent abstract ideas that are difficult to present in a concrete manner. In the second, we become overwhelmed by the expectation that long lists of topics be covered in the ever more crowded school day.

Integrated Thematic Instruction Connects Students to Curriculum

The scheme for organizing curriculum known as integrated thematic instruction is recognized as a way to build on the child's mode of perceiving the world while providing a rationale for reducing the segmented-day approach to curriculum organization. Organizing activities around a theme or problem allows development of basic skills as they flow from and make sense in relation to the chosen theme. Organizing programs around integrated themes represents a departure from the practice of listing skills and then organizing activities that develop them following a logically derived sequence from simpler to more difficult. Furthermore, integrated theme instruction does not necessarily observe the chronological approach to organizing topics, nor does every theme lend itself to including all the traditional ways of social science knowing.

Several general questions are important when you are planning for integrated thematic instruction:

- Is the theme one that will interest and extend the knowledge of students?
- Are there facets of the theme that can incorporate various ways of thinking and knowing derived from various kinds of information?
- Can adequate resources be located to provide students with adequate input that represents more than one point of view?
- Does development of the theme incorporate working with a variety of skills and modes of expression?

One planning device for this approach to organizing instruction is a brainstorming technique known as the idea or theme web. Typically, a theme web is developed by a grade-level teaching team. The chosen theme may come from the social studies topical guide—community, cooperation, family, heroes, changes, farms, celebrations. In a first meeting, using free association, members of the team jot down ideas and subtopics of the theme on a large, shared sheet of paper or chalkboard. The second phase of this process is to group ideas and subtopics into clusters. From this first sort, new ways of naming or grouping emerge as the group discusses what each cluster means. Working groups need to appoint a scribe who will record their ideas on a chart or chalkboard that the entire group can see. This listing will capture the resources and activities mentioned as the discussion evolves. Eventually the group settles on a set of subthemes or questions radiating from the larger theme. The third phase of this meeting is to review the general questions/criteria and decide whether to proceed with planning based on the theme or to revise or to abandon it.

In preparation for a second meeting, team members work individually to put together resources that can be used to "teach" the theme. This search takes teachers beyond the text, gathering sources from children's fiction and nonfiction books, reference books, maps, films, and videos. The list could also include manipulables, costumes, pictures, artifacts, resource people, computer software, newspaper files, and local field trip possibilities. Sorting through resources in a team meeting naturally brings to mind the kinds of activities that would be appropriate to help students to learn from these sources. Involvement of school media center personnel and municipal librarians is essential.[13]

SMALL GROUP WORK	**BRAINSTORMING THEME DEVELOPMENT AND SUBJECT INTEGRATION**
5.6	*With a partner, brainstorm primary-level ideas about the theme of water. Use the idea-clustering web based on questions children might ask about the theme "Water, a Basic Resource," beginning your discussion with the questions on the left side of Figure 5.1. Follow these steps: (1) Add more questions as you survey those already listed. (2) Discuss what kinds of ways of knowing or what subject matter sources are implicit in each and whether you need more variety. (3) Evaluate the possibilities of actually gathering the resources required to let students investigate this theme. (4) List the kinds of skills and modes of expression this theme would elicit from students, assessing whether it presents enough variety.* *Now, develop the second set of ideas that comes from the questions about the second theme web, "Looking for Our Roots." Do you find the same subject connections? Would the theme promote different ways of knowing? Of expressing? You need to discuss the questions this exercise raises as you explore integrated thematic instruction with your classmates. Does this kind of content organization promote social studies standards?*

---

[13]Integrated theme instruction is part of the integrated language or whole-language curriculum perspective. See Christine C. Pappas, Barbara Z. Kiefer, and Linda S. Levstick, *An Integrated Language Perspective in the Elementary School: Theory into Action,* 3rd ed. (White Plains, NY: Longman, 1999) for an extensive elaboration of this approach.

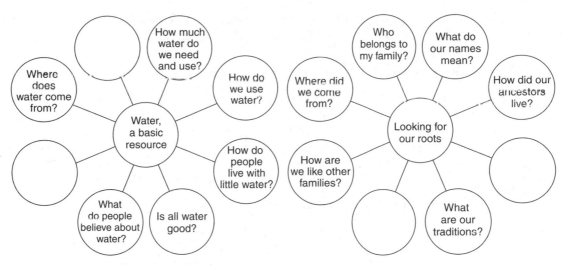

FIGURE 5.1 Sample Themes and Questions Children Might Ask About Them

Doing the preceding small group activity probably gave you a sense of the freedom you can have in planning the integrated approach. There is not one best or only answer to what is included as part of the theme. With this freedom comes the responsibility for choosing a worthwhile theme. Some themes that have been frequently used with young children deserve to be reconsidered. Think of the topics or themes you recall from your own primary-grade days. Would they meet the criteria for integrative themes you have just been considering? Would these same themes relate to the real concerns many children have today? Integrated theme planning can also relieve teachers who are worried about covering a long list of topics. Broad topics, rich with content possibilities, will engage students in various kinds of skill development and occupy them profitably for longer stretches of time, relieving teachers' concern for covering specific, lengthy topical lists. Did this exercise bring up questions about skill exposure and practice? Teachers need to be sure to build in adequate time for teaching and reinforcing beginning decoding and numeracy skills. Striking a balance between success of thematic exploration that permits integration of social studies and science while providing impetus for development of literacy and math skills is crucial to the success of thematic approach to instruction.

There have been criticisms also of the integrated approach. One is that often children really do not learn the major concepts or understandings of the topic. In turn, many primary teachers spend far more time constructing the activities than the children spend doing the activities. This is also true of other curriculum approaches. In other words, the teacher takes a half-hour to design an activity, often involving the children filling in something, which the children whiz through in a few minutes without much understanding. They just get it done. The focus of many activities is on skills or skill reinforcement and learning about the content is relegated to a minor position.

Another criticism is that children's choices are not honored. Children can brainstorm after the first week or so their ideas on what they want to know and learn about a topic. The teacher needs to see the links between the topics the children want to study and what standards their state or district requires. It is especially important to find out what children already know about a topic and their misconceptions.

Using Passive Media in Primary-Grade Instruction

Choosing a topic that follows traditional grade curriculum or flows from an integrative theme approach does not resolve the issue of opening vistas beyond students' immediate experience of that topic. Most social studies topics require the unlocking of information conveyed by print or voice or video. There are some guidelines that teachers can follow when using passive media materials with young children so that profitable interaction occurs between the children and the material.

Instructional Checklist for Using Books and Media in Primary Grades

Keep input session short—ten to twenty minutes.

Elicit predictions (What do you think will happen?) or questions (What does this [picture or title] make you wonder?) to set direction and focus.

Use explicit objectives (Let's read to find . . .).

Explain new and/or important vocabulary.

Break up exposition by asking children to answer questions, demonstrate, predict.

Provide visuals to accompany print information.

Conclude with discussion, chart making, predicting, and summarizing.

Follow with a related activity that prompts the children's expressions about the topic read or viewed.

These are general instructional steps in reading or viewing for comprehension. Teacher's editions of social studies texts usually contain such guidelines. Using them when you work from library or trade books and visual media will also increase student focus and engagement.

Children who are learning English as a second language ELLs (English Language Learners) can benefit from all these suggestions. In addition, they will require repeated interactive exposure to visuals plus individual and small group tutoring and discussion with other students and adult aides that permit them to hear and imitate vocabulary as well as to use gestures, movement, and art to show and extend their comprehension. It is good to keep in mind that learning another language takes time. Typically, social usage precedes academic-related expression by several years.

Having surveyed the general guidelines for primary social studies instruction, let us examine the various traditional sources—textbooks, unit materials, trade books, holidays—of the social studies curriculum for young children.

Role of Textbooks and Reading Materials

Textbooks from social studies series can be used as a resource—not the principal element—of primary social studies programs.

Newer textbooks come enriched with "Big-Book" illustrations that facilitate teacher-led group "reading" and "re-creating" with chart story writing. Beyond the more traditional reinforcement of content through group production of a chart story, researchers in English as a Second Language (ESL or ELLs)[14] suggest that teachers can help children comprehend content embedded in print and visual texts by creating additional visualizations. This can be done by developing categories, constructing time lines, developing flowcharts or cycle outlines, clustering ideas using webbing from a main topic, or building charts to be filled with data as part of group instruction. A listening-post center through which children rotate can be used to bridge aural and visual decoding. For this activity many teachers record the text passage, including management directions and questions or comments they want children to reflect on as they follow along in their books.

Helping ESL children, and all children, acquire language and understand the ideas expressed by the printed words requires teachers to assemble a rich diversity of reading materials around the themes being studied. One way is to present sources that range in difficulty from picture books to items for independent reading, and to offer a variety in genre—from fiction to poetry, letters, reference materials, and other non-fiction sources. Teachers can also include all kinds of visual aids such as photographs, films, and audiotaped and videotaped materials. Teacher presentation, individual study, reading teams, and learning centers can be organized as strategies for children to gain information.

Using Trade Books for Theme Development

The extensive use of trade books for primary children can be a natural strength for social studies topics. Check the NCSS children's literature reviews. The annual notable social studies trade books of new books for each year is found annually in the May/June issue of *Social Education*. Children love to listen to stories. They empathize with stories more easily than with video or film. Stories are an easy and malleable way to deliver social studies content. Stories are more accessible and personalized than most text and video treatments. Levstik argues that children's historical fiction, because of its narrative or storytelling format, makes historical understanding much more accessible to children than do social studies textbooks or other media treatments.[15]

The unit plan that follows, designed for third graders, focuses on the topic of continuity and change as a preparation for the study of local history. Relying heavily on a set of trade books as the primary content input, it is intended to emphasize student outcomes in historical and geographical literacy, particularly the concepts of time and chronology, cause and effect, reasons for continuity and change, human and environmental interaction, and human movement. As you study this unit plan, think about these questions to discuss with a colleague or your class.

1. What literacy skills are developed?
2. How are trade books linked to where students are?
3. What strengths and difficulties do you detect in using trade books as the input material for social studies units?

[14]Margaret Early, "Enabling First and Second Language Learners in the Classroom: Language Arts in English-as-Second Language," *ESL* 67 (October 1990): 567–575.

[15]Linda S. Levstik, "Mediating Content through Literary Texts," *Language Arts* 67, no. 8 (December 1990): 848–853.

SAMPLE UNIT PLAN

HOW THINGS CHANGE

Sequence

Lesson 1: Read aloud *The Little House.* Find instances of change in story. After students understand the story's feelings about change, assign activity to create paper house puppets and write how the Little House would feel about these changes. Share student products.

Lesson 2: Display eight pictures from portfolio, *The Changing Countryside,* around room. Explain that pictures show same land area over twenty years. Students view pictures silently, then do cooperative group work to list ten changes they note. Share findings with class. Call attention to details of pictures.

Lesson 3: Read aloud *I Go with My Family to Grandma's.* Students compare transportation in the 1900s with that of today. Discuss how families still visit as continuity. Use last page to discuss how family photos are a record of change. Share own family photos that show changes in dress, toys, cars, houses.

Lesson 4: Students bring and share family pictures, clippings, or belongings that demonstrate changes in their lives.

Lesson 5: Read aloud *Bayberry Bluff* eliciting ideas as to why Bayberry Bluff is changing. Encourage students to predict what will happen next. Discuss why people came: Vacation? Farming? Fishing? Making movies? Mining?

Lesson 6: Students view pictures from *The Changing City.* Ask questions about what has changed and why changes occurred. For example, widening street indicates growth and more traffic, protection from fire; the new businesses and freeway alter community character and purpose. Ask what things remain the same in all pictures.

Lesson 7: Share the picture book *New Providence,* emphasizing how community strives to restore and preserve landmarks and structures. Student pairs choose something in own community worth saving. Discuss why it would be important to save as pairs share choices. Ask how preservation is good for a community. Compare and contrast the effects of change in *New Providence* and *The Changing City.*

Lesson 8: Students make up stories and pictures depicting how a place changed and stayed the same over time. Must include reasons for change in stories. Share with class. Discuss why changes were good or bad.

Closure: Read aloud *The Sky Was Blue.* Ask students what has been learned about change and continuity.

Bridging: Read *The House on Maple Street* as a prompt for next unit on studying local geography, indigenous peoples, early settlers, and community development.

Assessment

Students react by writing to changes in *The Little House*.

Students in a group note visual change from pictures.

Students share changes in personal history.

Students select and give reasons for place in own community worthy of preservation.

Students create pictures depicting change and explain reasons for them.

Resources

Burton, Virginia Lee. *The Little House*. Boston: Houghton Mifflin, 1942.

Lent, Blair. *Bayberry Bluff*. Boston: Houghton Mifflin, 1987.

Levinson, Riki. *I Go with My Family to Grandma's*. Illustrated by Diane Goode. New York: E. P. Dutton, 1986.

Muller, Jorg. *The Changing City*. New York: Atheneum, 1977. This portfolio consists of eight full-color, foldout pictures done by Swiss artist Jorg Muller.

———. *The Changing Countryside*. New York: Atheneum, 1977. A companion portfolio to the above title.

Pryor, Bonnie. *The House on Maple Street*. Illustrated by Beth Peck. New York: William Morrow, 1987.

Tscharner, Renata von, and Ronald Lee Fleming. *New Providence: A Changing Cityscape*. San Diego, CA: Harcourt Brace Jovanovich, 1987.

Zolotow, Charlotte. *The Sky Was Blue*. Illustrated by Garth Williams. New York: Harper and Row, 1963.

Source: California Council for the Social Studies Annual Conference.

The field of childrens' historical fiction and nonfiction gains new titles every year. We need assistance in selecting new titles and knowing which older titles are appropriate for our instructional purposes. In the past, we have unintentionally used trade books that contain stereotypical portrayals of individuals and groups according to all kinds of traits—age, race, body type, gender, class, ethnicity, abilities, sexual orientation, religion, region. Studies of the past three decades have done much to alert teachers to the biases, omissions, and shortcomings of many titles. Civil rights interest groups have worked to get more diverse portrayals to appear in children's trade books. Professional organizations have supported instructional materials that portray history more accurately, conflict more specifically, and diversity more clearly.

As a result of these consciousness-raising efforts, we now have yearly recommended lists from the National Council for the Social Studies in the journal *Social Education,* publications such as *Teaching Tolerance,* and organizations such as the Interracial Books for Children Council's *Bulletin.* School district resource specialists and children's librarians are also worthwhile sources for developing theme-related trade book bibliographies.

Perhaps more difficult than locating theme-appropriate trade books are the issues of acquiring them and teacher evaluation. Few schools have the luxury of classroom sets of trade books. Teachers eager to reap the instructional dividends of using trade books use a variety of tactics—from fund-raising to sharing classroom sets with other teachers on a rotation schedule; from reading aloud to the class to using one copy of a trade book for each cooperative group or distributing different trade books related to the unit theme to each cooperative group. All these tactics are valid, but the economic fact is that building a theme-related library of trade books should be looked at as a long-term project best done cooperatively by the entire teaching staff of a school. There is much to be said for the slower approach of one book per classroom as it allows for teacher evaluation. Books highly recommended by a professional organization's list may not provide the instructional fit for the unit theme plan or the type of students in your classroom. Newer books may appear that better fit the instructional purpose and the changing of social attitudes.

There are teacher-instigated remedies for trade books that do not conform with instructional purposes. For older books, teachers can ask students to reflect on the changes that have taken place since the books were written: How would we do this today? Would we think about this in the same way? How would we say this today? For biased books, teachers can ask, How would the [*group being misportrayed*] feel about this situation? Who was the writer and what do you think made him or her feel this way? It can even be argued that out-of-date and biased books are good materials to promote critical thinking skills. To take advantage of these opportunities for developing critical habits of mind, teachers must be aware of them and know how to use questioning strategies that promote critical thinking.

Using older books may be valuable in teaching students to take a different perspective. Think how the story entitled *The Three Little Wolves and the Big Bad Pig* would be written. Or ask students what advice they would give to a character(s).

Unit Planning for Active Learning

Textbooks and curriculum guides may present excellent content. To bring that content to life for most young children, you will need to collect and present material that your students can enjoy for its intrinsic merit while you use it to take students into expressive activities that engage them in exploring, appreciating, interpreting, organizing, and valuing the content. Units of instruction that include manipulation of materials help students internalize ideas. They involve children in a multidisciplinary exploration of a topic. Variety in modes of intake as well as recapitulation, discussing, and creative expression keep children's interest high and provide for accommodating individual differences in students. In planning a unit, check to see that activities include variety from listening, viewing, painting, writing, and classifying, to touring, community action, and dramatic expression.

Look at the kinds of activity designed to flow from the sample unit plan that follows. A unit outline on the hospital is presented here without listing the objectives. The story line, using the hospital as setting, hospital workers as characters, and a child with abdominal pain as the critical incident similar to the story path approach, is presented by the teacher using a curriculum guide supplemented with trade books and photographs. Note the kinds of materials that would be needed to carry out this unit.

ACTIVE LEARNING: THE HOSPITAL (SECOND GRADE)

Story Line	Activities	Skills
Feeling sick	Poem	Describing words
	Sick faces on wet pastel	Painting
How do we know when we are sick?	Drama in pairs: mother/child, doctor/child; nurse visits	Problem-solving discussion using descriptive words and medical instruments: thermometer, light, stethoscope, etc.
Accidents	Medicine precautions	Labeling; poetry writing
	Collage figures of accidents	Painting
	List preventable, nonpreventable accidents	Discussion; classifying; list cause-effect
	Design working body	Cutouts fastened with brads
Serious illness	Design ambulance	Cut-paste model
	Admission	Fill-in form; writing
	Hospital layout	Draw floor plan
	Dialogue nurse/patient	Role playing
Hospital life	Ward pictures	Labeling
	List hygiene rules	Discussion
	Patient's diary	Sequence drawings
	Diets	Classification
Hospital workers	Collage figures	Painting
	Job descriptions	Classification
People going home	How people get better, worse	Discussion
	Healthy faces	Compare sick-well
	Rules	Creative writing

In this unit the materials were chosen to foster artistic and written expression and to provide a positive, open-ended forum for discussion of fears about acquired immune deficiency syndrome (AIDS) appearing in young children. The teacher used storybooks, pictures, some medical instruments, and a visiting nurse in addition to the curriculum guide. Materials resulting from this unit would be voluminous. They would include word cards and lists of pertinent vocabulary, chart stories, a collage of figures representing kinds of accidents and kinds of hospital workers, model ambulances, drawings of hospital interiors, paintings of healthy and sick faces, poems about feeling well, and stories about the hospital. Each visual product of the unit topic can be used to help children discuss what they are learning, thereby assisting them to organize their thoughts.

After looking earlier in this chapter at the economics standards, do you think anything is missing in the hospital unit? You are correct if you think of expensive hospital bills. Should children learn that a day at a hospital is very expensive? The hospital is providing services and in turn must charge patients and their families. Phone your local hospital to get some idea of daily rates. Check also if it is a city or county hospital and who owns the hospital. You and your class might want to discuss why a hospital stay is so expensive.

The cost of a hospital stay prods us into the topic of insurance. Children may have heard their parents talking about home insurance, car insurance, or that they have a health insurance policy or HMO. Because of the cost of fire, other disasters, and misfortunes, and because health problems are so expensive, people pay into a pool (an insurance company) so they can be reimbursed if these problems occur. Should health insurance be added to the unit on the hospital? You can see how similar this issue is to teaching about home mortgages and other topics. How much in-depth economics do you want in your unit?

SMALL GROUP WORK	**BRAINSTORMING AN ACTIVE LEARNING UNIT OUTLINE**
5.7	*Here is another possible story line for a first-grade unit on transportation. Without gathering specific materials, develop a hypothetical activity sequence on this topic. You need not elaborate the skills that relate to these activities. Your goal is to provide activity variety that assists children in understanding the story line and subtopics. Compare your list with that of a colleague.*

Story Line	Possible Activities
My favorite way of travel	
Wheels that move things	
Wings that move things	
Moving big and little things	
People who work in transportation	

Holidays as Social Studies Curriculum

Holiday units are often a major component of social studies for young children. Decorating classrooms around holiday themes is a tradition in many primary classrooms. Children learn to associate symbols such as cupids, shamrocks, turkeys, and pumpkins with certain months of the year. Too often, however, children receive little or no explanation about the meaning of these symbols. They may be read a poem or story about the folklore of the holiday followed by an art project replicating the holiday's symbols. They may not gain any substantive information about the symbols they are reproducing. They do not know that the shamrock represents the Christian trinity of the Father, Son, and Holy Ghost or that the rabbit and the egg have been associated since pre-Christian times in Europe with the coming of spring and fertility. Extending our holiday and symbolic repertoire beyond the Eurocentric tradition into other cultural traditions must become part of our agenda. We must learn that the meanings of the animal symbols of the Chinese zodiac may vary from one Asian culture to another as do the celebrations of the New Year based on it. We need to respect religious positions, such as the Muslim aversion to portraying illustrations other than geometric abstractions in ornamentation because of the Koranic requirement of avoiding images, or the Seventh-Day Adventist aversion to having their children participate in school holiday celebrations that are not sacred times according to their reading of the Bible.

Using holiday materials that explain these symbols and their lore is part of cultural literacy that children deserve to have. Where do we begin educating ourselves about the significance of familiar symbols and the meanings of holidays not part of our own cultural experience? The religious composition of a class is the place to start. If the group has Christian, Jewish, Muslim, Hindu or Sikh, Santeria, or Buddhist students, a note to parents at the beginning of the year inquiring about special religious dates they wish their children to observe can begin to personalize the holiday calendar for your class. Ask these questions of parents: Are there special religious days for which your child needs to miss school or have special considerations at school? Would you or a member of your faith like to share a story or symbol of a holiday with the class? Does your child celebrate a birthday?

Next you need to consult a basic reference book such as an encyclopedia to inform yourself about the religion and sacred days parents mention. Some parents are reticent about requesting special attention or consideration regarding their religious practices. If they are not Christian, they often feel that American schools will not include learning about their beliefs in a school program. Devout Muslims may assume teachers know that their children are to eat little or nothing during the days of Ramadan and may be tired at school during this month as they eat a large meal at a family gathering late in the evening.

Some holidays are particularly American and, as such, deserve special note. Days appropriate for young children to commemorate are Columbus Day, Veterans Day, Thanksgiving, Martin Luther King Day, and Presidents' Day. Most of these days are best commemorated with a brief story followed by a creative activity.

Young children can understand the significance of Martin Luther King with few materials beyond a photograph and a recording. Barbara Green of Olinder School, San Jose, California, began by asking her class of second and third graders how they would feel if some of them could not come to this class because of the color of their skins, because of their religion, or because of how much money their parents have. After the children responded, Mrs. Green introduced a photograph of King. She told them his name and the story of his fight to end racial discrimination by allowing blacks to have the same access as whites to public places and jobs. Following recess,

Alex

I have a dream that

one day everyone gets

together black and white

that they make new

rules and Throw away

weapons and burn nuclear

bombs and we would

have no more war.

FIGURE 5.2 Child's Writing Sample

The content of this writing sample may be surprising; it reveals that young children, in their own way, do think about our most crucial issues.

Mrs. Green played a recording of King's "I Have a Dream" speech, and the children discussed King's dream. Mrs. Green asked if they had dreams of their own that they would like to see happen to make this a better country for everyone.

The floodgates opened! Children expressed dreams about eradicating poverty, unemployment, violence, and war that were far beyond Mrs. Green's expectations. This discussion led to a writing assignment in which the children expressed their dreams of social justice (see Figure 5.2). The results were read and discussed with another classroom group. This four-part experience gave these second and third graders a personalized, age-appropriate understanding of why King is honored with a national holiday.

Celebrating Columbus Day and Thanksgiving is a tradition in nearly every primary grade. With our growing sense of revisionist history, most elementary teachers have come to rethink the approach they take in presenting the historical background of these days by taking into consideration points of view of Native Americans. Knowing, for example, the fuller story of Squanto makes him the complex, star-crossed hero of the folkloric feast. Squanto was a translator for the Pilgrims as a result of a long series of misfortunes with Europeans. Squanto's European contact included being captured, enslaved, taken to Spain to work, escaping to England, earning his freedom, and coming back to his land in order to be with his own tribe only to discover they had all been killed in battles or died of diseases introduced by the Europeans. In his legendary role as peacemaker between two groups that did not understand each other, Squanto was probably doing what he thought necessary for his own survival. Squanto was the last Patuxet.[16] Although his people did not survive, commemorating his story is important as a tribute to those who are peacemakers.

Multiple points of view and critical thinking about the meaning of Columbus Day that evolved from the 1992 quincentennial of the European discovery of America have led us to see that the ways we traditionally related this event to young children and the children's literature we used to assist us are full of one-sided perspectives that may gloss over or contain errors of historical fact and its interpretations.[17] Older versions of the Columbus story ignore the fact that the Americas were settled long

[16]When possible, the names of the Native American nations should be used. Recognizing the proper tribal names helps young children internalize that not all Native Americans are alike.

[17]See William Bigelow, "Once upon a Genocide: Christopher Columbus in Children's Literature," *Language Arts* 69 (February 1992): 112–120.

before the "discoverers" arrived, that native groups had their own religions and cultures and social organizations, and that European contact was a genocidal experience for some native groups. Young children can understand the arrival of Columbus as a problematic situation about territory that was resolved in favor of those who had the deadliest weapons. Before you recount the Columbus story, you can lead young students to ponder the influence of European explorers by hypothesizing what America would be like today had the Europeans not come seeking resources and trading opportunities here. These guesses should be recorded and evaluated as to how they might be positive or negative. Or, in sharing an old version of the Columbus story, ask students to think how each part of the story would be told if a native of the island had written it.

By presenting national holidays such as Columbus Day and Thanksgiving in ways that promote valuing the complexity of historical events instead of passing along myth and stereotype, we are integrating critical thinking about historical events into school holiday commemorations.

Social studies instruction in the primary grades is not confined to a set daily time. It occurs in several continuous and simultaneous strands throughout the school day and year. Instruction organized in units is the formal strand. This is supplemented with instruction scheduled around the celebration of holidays. As we shall see in Chapter 7, social studies is supported by the ways in which the classroom is organized to function. The ways students are prompted to plan and evaluate individual work and class behavior may be the strongest forces for internalizing the civics and government goals of social studies.

■ CLASSROOM ENVIRONMENT AND SCHEDULING IN THE PRIMARY GRADES

Implementing the social studies in the primary classroom involves more than presenting the subject matter. Ideally, the goals of social studies teaching will be furthered by the manner in which teachers arrange their classrooms, schedule social studies experiences, and take advantage of student-initiated topics.

Classroom Environments That Support Social Studies

To organize your classroom space for optimal learning, take into account the variety of activities and positive social groupings young children need. Children need spaces to call their own. Designate a "cubby" or locker-type space for each child where he or she can keep snacks, lunches, clothes, and personal supplies. This removes the necessity of assigning a permanent table space or desk for each child, and allows you to arrange tables to serve a variety of purposes in spaces children can rotate through during the day.

Teacher-led large group activities usually occur in an area near a chalkboard that has floor-sitting space for the children and a chair for the teacher. Teacher-led, small group activities often have a special corner with chalkboard, pocket charts, teacher chair, and semicircular arrangement of children's tables and chairs. Seat-work groupings are usually in the middle of the room. Other activity sites include an easel or art area, a listening-post center, a dramatic play area with clothing and props, a writing-reading center with books displayed, computers, and a construction area with art and model-building supplies. Folders for accumulating children's work, portfolios, and boxes for keeping workbooks and text materials are arranged within the children's reach near the areas where the materials will be used.

Social studies teaching in the primary grades involves only three permanent materials: a globe, a picture of Earth taken from space, and a map of the world. Textbooks and workbooks may also be part of the materials. Most of the teaching aids in vibrant social studies programs are those the teacher has located and selected. As unit topics and seasons change, different materials are needed. Build files that assist you in bringing new stimulation to your classrooms that can be introduced throughout the school year.

Materials related to social studies topics can be placed in any of the activity areas—the globe and maps and the daily class journal can be in the reading-writing area, textbooks and related tapes can be in the listening area, community helper or other theme props can supply the dramatic play area—and can be renewed as topics change. Classroom display areas such as bulletin boards can be used to build collages and murals of social studies topics as children produce them. Teachers who provide a background for murals and collages or work displays find that children can be put in charge of arranging the rest of the displays. Materials purchased for bulletin board displays may be neater and more attractive to the adult eye. Student-produced murals, maps, and displays have more instructional power and are proof of active learning.

Scheduling and Instructional Approaches

In the way they schedule the school day, teachers express their values about what is important for a young child to learn and how that learning takes place. Some teachers follow a more traditional early childhood schedule by breaking the day into work periods. Each period is separated by a snack, recess, physical education, or another large group activity. Children rotate from one activity center to the next during different work periods. While the teacher directly instructs a small group on something such as reading, other groups of children might be engaged in seat work or might be at the listening center or in the easel area.

Each day begins with planning that suggests what each child must accomplish that day and what options each child has in choosing activities. Children manage their own movement by placing their names in pocket charts for option centers at the beginning of each work period. Then, as a child finishes, he or she makes a place for the next child in line.

Most teachers also want to balance quieter times with noisier times, sitting and listening time with movement time. Or they may want to provide large chunks of time for individual and small group activities and shorter amounts of time for whole group activities. Other teachers may want to have some time in which children choose and make decisions about how to structure their personal time.

Another pattern designates periods for each subject throughout the day and week. Social studies may be scheduled three days a week, from after lunch until the afternoon recess. There are benefits and disadvantages to this pattern. Designating a specific time for social studies guarantees that each child will receive some exposure to the subject. For younger children especially, however, that kind of exposure may seem unrelated to other areas of the curriculum and other times of the day. Also, it may limit strategies of instruction to large group intake of reading or visual information and limit responses to completing worksheets. Young children need to be engaged actively. For learning to be significant for them, their listening or viewing needs to be followed by opportunities to build, dramatize, or participate in some other expressive activity.

Ideally, from our point of view, social studies for young children should be seen as part of an integrated day in which a social studies or science theme provides the informational focus for activities in reading, writing, drama, and art. Basic programs in reading and math skills would continue to be part of the child's daily experience. But language arts, music, art, and physical education would be organized around the current topic under study in the social studies or science. Film and videos would continue to be shown. They would be part of an ongoing study. That is, they would be preceded and followed by intake and expressive activities and would not be merely an afternoon filler or reinforcement of a reading assignment.

Informal Teaching and Social Studies Curriculum

When children are asked to participate in sharing, they often introduce topics that may influence your scheduling and instructional plans. Through the informal method of capitalizing on children's interest, teachers construct social studies-related experiences. For example, if a child tells the class that his pet was hit by a car, you might turn the discussion to the general theme of what we do when we lose someone we love. The following day, you could bring in Judith Viorst's *The Tenth Good Thing about Barney,* a story about a boy's grief when his cat dies, to read to the class and discuss. Some critics, however, think that *The Tenth Good Thing about Barney* shows an evasive and inadequate solution to a child's loss. Sensitive teachers attempt to respond to these teachable moments.

Developing an extended instructional sequence based on such a teachable moment requires much planning and scheduling flexibility. Certainly, organizing instruction based on children's interests is an honored early childhood ideal.

There are several issues to consider in deciding whether the teachable moment merits further class time and attention. First is the issue of attention span. Sometimes when children ask questions, they want only a "yes" or "no" answer, not an elaborate response. We must develop a sixth sense for determining which questions and issues children can sustain with a more detailed exploration. Even when we believe the topic is within the children's attention span, our judgment about which topics really will add to the growth and development of the group is essential.

A second factor in determining how far to pursue a child-initiated topic is the issue of dignity or trust. Children may reveal confidences or home situations of abuse within families. Teachers, by law in many states, must follow up such confidences and suspicions by reporting them to the school or legally authorized personnel charged with defending children's safety and health. However, to elaborate a mini-unit on child abuse based on concerns about an individual child or a group of children would most probably abuse that child's or that group's dignity within the classroom. This could also damage the children's trust in the teacher.

On the other side of the argument is the need to provide children with proactive models rather than perhaps leaving them helpless by ignoring a topic or denying the appropriateness of a topic for young children. Issues concerning unfairness should not be ignored. Exploring ways to seek justice through discussion, conflict resolution, and role playing that probe different sides of an issue offer valuable, enduring experience and insight to children. Seeking justice through group action such as requesting to speak to the principal or writing letters to the editorial section of the newspaper or to an organization or politician is indelibly instructive to all children.

Adding to the daily schedule social studies–related explorations that spring from children's interests is a laudable practice. The same is true of holiday-related social studies schedules. Both types of scheduling are enriching. Neither, however, can replace deliberately planned social studies programs. Reliance on holidays and student-initiated issues for social studies content most surely will short-circuit exposure to the comprehensive understandings and thorough skill development guaranteed by more formal social studies instruction. There is no substitute for a teacher-planned curriculum that systematically engages young children in learning more about who and where they are and the world in which they live.

■ SUMMARY

The content and processes associated with the social studies are as essential to the young child's growth and development as any curricular area. State standards support the importance of including history, geography, economics, and civics strands in content for the primary level. Curriculum at the state and local levels as well as in published textbook series will incorporate these emerging expectations. Effective instruction in the social studies for children in the primary grades is experiential and integrative. Concepts are presented in ways that involve children in exploring who and where they are and in thinking critically about what they explore to construct and reconstruct their understanding. Materials and strategies expose children to a variety of people and cultures and problem-solving possibilities. Informal teaching that capitalizes on children's concerns is an enrichment of the basic social studies program that intentionally involves children in exploring facets of their world.

■ SUGGESTED READINGS AND WEB SITES ■

Alleman, Janet, and Jere Brophy. *Social Studies Excursions, K–3. Book One: Powerful Units on Food, Clothing and Shelter.* Westport, CT: Heinemann, 2001.

    Units on cultural universals for the primary grades.

Bigelow, William. "Once upon a Genocide: Christopher Columbus in Children's Literature." *Language Arts* 69 (February 1992): 112–120.

    Critically reviews Columbus biographies from perspective of natives.

Boutee, G. S., Sally La Point, and Barbara Davis. "Racial Issues in Education: Real or Imagined?" *Young Children* 49 (November 1993): 19–23.

    Presents African American adult perspectives of young children's "playful" ethnic and racial interactions with suggestions for addressing them positively.

Derman-Sparks, Louise, and the A.B.C. Task Force. *Anti-Bias Curriculum Tools for Empowering Young Children.* Washington, DC: National Association for the Education of Young Children, 1989.

Broad view of curriculum inspires this essential early childhood publication.

Egan, Kieran. *Teaching as Storytelling: An Alternative to Teaching and Curriculum in the Elementary School.* London, Ontario: Althouse Press, 1989.

New interpretation of how and what children of different ages learn about their social world.

Feldkamp-Price, Betsy, and David Lee Smith. "Teaching About Indians? Use the Real Stuff!" *Teaching K–8 25* (October 1994): 57–59.

Lists sources and activities to confront misconceptions about Indians.

Lamme, Linda Leonard. "Stories from Our Past: Making History Come Alive for Children." *Social Education* (March 1994): 159–164.

Uses familiar, quality children's trade books to demonstrate how to lead young children to discover links between the books and their own lives.

Matthews, Gareth B. *The Philosophy of Childhood.* Cambridge, MA: Harvard University Press, 1994.

Critique of Piaget and Kohlberg suggests developmental hurdles not precise and sees more similarities than differences between adult and child thought processes.

Paley, Vivian Gussin. *Kwanzaa and Me.* Cambridge, MA: Harvard University Press, 1995.

Long-time kindergarten teacher-writer of University of Chicago Laboratory Schools illustrates use of storytelling method as way of letting children reveal their concerns that permits teacher to supply creative alternatives to problems as she recounts encounters with racial and social problems that informed her reflective teaching.

Pappas, Christine C., Barbara Z. Kiefer, and Linda S. Levstik. *An Integrated Language Perspective in the Elementary School: Theory into Action,* 3rd ed. White Plains, NY: Longman, 1999.

Well-grounded curriculum/methods text for realistically implementing whole-language approach.

Parker, Walter C. *Renewal in the Social Studies.* Washington, DC: Association for Supervision and Curriculum Development, 1991.

Outlines directions in curriculum development and the need for it.

Seefeldt, C. Social *Studies for the Preschool Primary Child,* 6th ed. Columbus, OH: Merrill, 2001.

Methods text focusing on early social studies instruction from developmentalist, whole-child perspective.

Winston, Linda. *Keepsakes: Using Family Stories in Elementary Classrooms.* Westport, CT: Heinemann, 1997.

Each chapter describes how family stories can enhance curriculum.

Web Sites

The National Council on Economic Education
www.economicsamerica.org

Resources, standards, lessons.

National Geographic Society
www.nationalgeographic.com

The national geography standards; atlas, publications, and so on.

Busy Teacher's Web site
www.ceismc.gatech.edu/busyt/

Lesson Plans and Resources for Social Studies Teachers
www.csun.edu/~hcedu013/

Lesson plans and resources for social studies teachers.

Use Web sites of local government agencies, such as your city hall, to gain information about your local government.

Chapter 6

Social Studies in the Fourth through Eighth Grades

In this chapter we discuss the teaching of social studies from grades 4 through 8 with special emphasis on strategies and materials that move beyond the basal textbook:

- Children in the Middle Grades

- The Social Studies Curriculum: Content

- Current Events/Current Affairs Programs

- Teaching Controversial Issues

■ CHILDREN IN THE MIDDLE GRADES

Teachers who have experience with both the primary and middle grades are very clear about the developmental differences between these age groups: "I love teaching fourth graders. They can think and they enjoy discussion." "My first graders are so loving! They still confuse me with their mothers." "Kindergarteners are so active. They need to change activities every twenty minutes."

Cognitively, middle-grade children are ready to incorporate a wide span of spatial and temporal relationships in their thinking. Just as middle graders are extending their personal range of familiar space by roaming farther from home on their bikes and scooters, they are ready to learn about unfamiliar places in social studies. The contrasting ways of rural and urban or desert and rain forest life interest them. Middle graders are able to see themselves in the context of time. Their curiosity about prehistory and earlier human times grows. They are eager to conjecture about the future.

Psychologically, middle-grade children are focused on personal competency. They like recognition for what they can do, whether as an outstanding speller or a whiz at drawing or a standout in recess team sports. Middle graders like quick-paced and varied activities. Class or small group games such as baseball and Twenty Questions or trivia contests are appealing as content-review strategies. Projects that involve them in producing concrete products such as graphs, models, and murals gratify their need for variety and evidence of their competence.

Socially, middle-grade children are entering the age of reciprocity in friendship and human relations. They comprehend the social consequences of their actions. When they are in a group, they are eager to seek fairness. They relish opportunities to make rules, to enforce them, and to establish consequences for breaking them.

All these children are growing and developing, but there are individual differences in their rates of growth. The areas sketched earlier are, nevertheless, some of the typical changes in the ways that middle-grade children see and interact with the world, and that should influence how you orient your social studies program. As you examine content, strategies, and materials for middle-grade social studies, keep these general characteristics in mind.

Remember two other points when you begin teaching social studies to fourth through eighth graders. The first is that developmental levels may vary dramatically within each grade and, as with any teaching, you need to be aware of these variations and adapt your presentation of content and methods to the readiness of your students. The second point is that at some time in this grade range, probably at the sixth- or seventh-grade level, students will enter a middle school where, typically, schedules will be divided into specific periods for each subject. Students may even begin changing classrooms for different subjects, as they do in high school.

The advantage of this environment is that the teacher will often be a specialist in his or her field and, therefore, will have more background and interest in the subject matter. The disadvantage, however, is that subject matters tend to be even more compartmentalized, with less and less integration between them. To avoid these difficulties, more middle schools are scheduling one teacher for an extended period—a core class for two or three periods. The intent is that "kids in the middle" will get both basic academic and exploratory subjects in a setting with a wide range of extra or cocurriculum and guidance services. But even in middle schools, some teachers tend to split the core period into separate subject content times.

Almost all experts recommend some degree of integration, particularly the integration of language arts into the social studies. We strongly encourage you to include language-arts content and methods in your social studies teaching, no matter what the organizational structure of your classroom time, since the two areas both complement and reinforce each other. See Chapter 9 for specific tips on using language arts in teaching social studies.

■ THE SOCIAL STUDIES CURRICULUM: CONTENT

What is currently taught in a typical fourth- through eighth-grade social studies program?

Grade 4:   State history, geographic regions
Grade 5:   U.S. history
Grade 6:   World cultures, history, and geography
Grade 7:   World cultures, history, and geography
Grade 8:   U.S. history

As you can see from the topics, history and to a lesser extent geography have been emphasized at these grade levels. Concern about effectively covering the range of topics in U.S. history—from Columbus to the latest president, or ancient civilizations to the most recent war—in one year has made social studies curriculum designers of the California Framework and other states try to divide up the content and not repeat it. Thus, in California the framework in the teaching of U.S. history gives the fifth grade the Colonial-Revolution period, the eighth grade the nineteenth century, and the eleventh grade the twentieth century. A division of content allows more depth and detail than are presently possible with the typical broad coverage of hundreds of years of content in one academic year.

History and geography have traditionally been emphasized at these grade levels, although there has been an attempt in the past twenty years to include more of the social sciences—political science, sociology, economics, and anthropology. Similar to using themes for integration of several subject areas (science, art, etc.), often an *interdisciplinary* social science approach is very worthwhile. In this approach, several of the social sciences and history are used to explain a topic. To consider nearly any problem—unemployment, poverty, crime, health care, changes in the family, violence in our society and in the world—requires using data and research methods from several of the social sciences and history. No one academic discipline such as economics can give the full picture. Areas of the humanities such as film and novels further personify and visualize social studies topics. This curriculum approach works especially well in a theme- or issues-centered approach in which students examine topics such as world peace or population trends.

Broadening of the social studies framework reflects a similar broadening in historical research. In recent years, history has expanded by giving more attention to women, ethnic/racial groups, the lives of ordinary people and their culture, and the effects on the environment as people interact on the nonhuman world. In other words, history more reflects the wide range of human diversity. It is more than politics, military, and social leaders and their institutions. It includes those with power as well as those without power. Usually this has meant seeing the darker side of American history and has resulted in a wide variety of perspectives or different voices. In effect, there are now more interpretations of what has occurred in the past. This means that the idea of a common history appears to be breaking down.

Historians regard revision and reinterpreting history as what historical scholarship is all about. The cold war, the dropping of atomic bombs on Japan, the Tonkin Gulf incident (Vietnam War), Christopher Columbus, and Presidents Thomas Jefferson, Ronald Reagan, and William J. Clinton are just a few of the personalities and events subject to constant revision and reinterpretations that take place in American history. Revision is part of the process in which history enlarges its perspectives and enriches its insights. This also means that future historians will question the current historical scholarship. The history that students will learn about in twenty years will not be the same as it is today.

History

As you are probably aware from the media, the kind of history that features a particular people's story of the past is a controversial issue for the schools. There is a national debate on what history should be taught. In general, liberals advocate multiculturalism in history, trying to include the experience of all Americans by expanding the traditional Eurocentric perspectives. In contrast, conservatives see "extreme" multiculturalism as a rejection of Western culture and a fragmentation of U.S. society. Thus, the following questions arise: Whose history is to be presented? How much attention should the various groups receive? Should multiple perspectives be presented, such as showing how immigrant women or white male managers saw the growth of the industrial revolution in the United States? If more attention is given to various individuals and groups, will all students be exposed to the core values and cultural heritage of the American society as well as the global society?

There are no easy answers to these questions. Part of your response depends on your values. In general, more conservative educators usually advocate teaching all children a core of historical knowledge to maintain the mainstream culture and the democratic values that tie together all Americans and give us our shared heritage and national identity. This group is concerned that there is now too much emphasis on diversity and not as much on teaching about mainstream American history. However, more liberal educators tend to believe that the histories of too many groups have been left out of American textbooks and the children from these groups do not see themselves or their groups in the textbooks they study. Thus, they believe that not enough attention has been given to the various individuals and groups that make up the diverse American society and more multiple historical perspectives from people of color and women are needed. In a similar manner, the debate continues over whether the world history/world culture course has too much of a European centered focus. Should non-European history/cultures be given more attention?

Another issue is curriculum integration in social studies. Some argue that history should be taught mainly as a separate subject in the social studies program. The proponents in favor of the separate subject approach believe that the teaching of history has been so diluted during the past twenty years by concentration on other social sciences that students no longer learn history as history. They cite research about students' gaps of knowledge, such as when the Civil War took place. Currently some curriculum experts value greater integration in all subject areas, while other advocates and scholars recommend teaching academic disciplines primarily as separate subjects, believing students will learn more with this approach. These advocates, if they do recognize other subject areas and the humanities, generally want their subject area to be the primary focus or the "queen" of the area, with the other social sciences and the humanities in a more subsidiary role.

A controversy about the teaching of history immediately arose with the publication of three books in 1994 presenting history standards:

National Standards for United States History: Exploring the American Experience (5–12)

National Standards for World History: Exploring Paths to the Present (5–12)

National Standards for History: Expanding Children's World in Time and Space (K–4)

What history to teach and how to teach it were examined carefully by the National Center for History in the Schools (History Center), which produced the National

History Standards Project (see Chapter 1). The History Center proposed an integration of historical thinking (skills) and historical understanding (what students should know).

Even before the publication of the *National Standards for United States History* in November 1994, conservatives and other individuals and groups protested against the report, stating that it was a "politically correct" document concentrating on "multiple perspectives." Lynne Cheney, former head of the National Endowment for the Humanities, in a *Wall Street Journal* editorial October 20, 1994, criticized the document as a too "gloomy" picture of America, one that is too critical of all things white and too uncritical of all things, brown, black and other.[1] As evidence, she reported the number of times historical subjects were cited in the *National Standards*. According to her count, Senator Joseph McCarthy and/or McCarthyism is mentioned nineteen times, the Ku Klux Klan seventeen times, the Seneca Fall women's rights convention nine times, and Harriet Tubman six times whereas important male heroes such as Paul Revere, Daniel Webster, Robert E. Lee, Alexander Graham Bell, Thomas Edison, Albert Einstein, Jonas Salk, and the Wright brothers were not mentioned at all. She and other critics felt that not enough attention was being given to the positive aspects of U.S. history in its long struggle for liberty, equality, justice, and dignity and too much emphasis was placed on the country's failures.

The media and its commentators picked up on this controversial topic. Headlines in the leading newspapers and magazines had such titles as "Conflict over a New History Curriculum," "The Hijacking of American History," "Instead of Western Civ, It's Multiciv," "History According to Whom: Let the Debate Continue," "History Rewrites Itself," and "History without Heroes?" In general, the critics condemned the standards for being manifestations of left-wing "political correctness" and extravagant multiculturalism. The criticism also focused heavily on the American history document (at the fifth to twelfth grades) and then the world history standards. The comments were almost exclusively devoted to the examples given of student achievement (the bulk of the document) and not on the standards. Hardly anyone commented on the five historical thinking standards that were to be used from grades K through 12 except to say that they demanded more critical thinking of students than what had typically been required in most history courses.

Responding to the harsh criticisms and the recommendations of the Council for Basic Education, the History Center revised its standards, dropping all student achievement examples, and condensed the three separate volumes into one that focused just on standards.[2] It had been the examples of student achievement that had brought about most of the criticism. However, for teachers the examples were probably the most useful part of the three volumes. In terms of practicality of the standards, teachers believe there is not enough time for most students in most schools to meet these ambitious standards. One social studies expert stated that an average fifth-grade teacher would have to teach nothing but history all day long for three years to meet the fifth-grade standards. In addition, some believe that the performance stan-

[1]Lynne V. Cheney, "The End of History," *Wall Street Journal,* October 20, 1994, p. A22.

[2]National Center for History in the Schools, *National Standards for History: Basic Edition* (Los Angeles, CA: National Center for History in the Schools, 1996).

dards have emphasized what students should "know" at the expense of what they should "do," a direction that might lead teachers to require students simply to memorize a lot of facts. Proponents of the standards respond that the purpose of the standards is to raise the level of teaching and learning in U.S. schools.

The history standards do reflect more multiple points of view than most teachers now use, and this is a concern of the conservatives who feel that too much of traditional American history and Western civilization is being left out. On the other hand, the history standards may not be extensive and complete enough to satisfy those who want even more attention to diversity. These standards, thus, clearly illustrate the debate in our society on what children should learn about American and world history. The teaching of these subjects is inherently controversial. As teachers attempt to interest students in how the knowledge of the past informs their present, we would hope that the content selected will illuminate the ideals that attract and connect us while honoring the diverse experiences of individuals and groups seeking to enjoy the promises of these ideals.

SMALL GROUP WORK	**WHY STUDY HISTORY?**
6.1	*Did you like history when you were in school? Do you think the study of the past is important to students? What might they gain?*

More research continues to be done on children and their thinking about history. According to the constructionist theory of learning, children learn a great deal of history outside of school from sources such as family stories, historical films, television fiction, and holiday celebrations, as well as local architecture and museums. However, students' prior knowledge of history tends to be overlooked. Often there is little connection with what has been learned outside of school and the typical textbook learning in the classroom. Check students' prior knowledge with a short questionnaire asking students what they know about the Salem witch trials, Patriots, Loyalists, or the Underground Railroad.

Elementary teachers have different goals while teaching history. For decades experts have emphasized teaching for understanding of history rather than just transmission of historical facts. To increase understanding, teachers must decide on the following planning issues in teaching history.

Coverage Versus Depth

Typically, the early primary grades have little history and then suddenly from the fourth grade on, teachers are covering vast amounts of historical content. In many situations, pursuing an in-depth approach built on a few powerful ideas, instead of broad chronological coverage, can be a worthwhile goal. The difficulty in implementation is that the teacher needs to know more about the topic chosen for in-depth study. Remember not every unit has to be in depth. Examples of in-depth topics might be the Native Americans who lived in your community in the past or the earliest schools in your community.

Multiple Voices from the Past: Primary Sources

Primary Sources: You need to decide how much attention you wish to give to multiple perspectives, especially of women and minority groups. Related to this is the use of primary documents such as diaries, newspapers, old photographs, maps, and record albums. If selected with care, primary documents can provide differing viewpoints. If you use written primary documents such as diaries or newspapers, remember that the reading level will be difficult. You should, thus, make sure that the excerpts are short and that you have given enough content and skill development to your students. Try to include as many visuals as possible that will enrich students' mental pictures of peoples, places, and objects and show them that there may be different interpretations of historical events—from the killing of buffaloes on the plains to the Oklahoma Land Rush.

Doing History or Being a Historian

Will any of your units give students a hands-on experience of dealing with a historical problem, gathering data, and then reflecting on it? This approach has the potential of teaching valuable skills such as sorting and evaluating the evidence of historical events.

In addition to the foregoing issues, we can never be certain that every elementary student has a mature sense of historical concepts that are not easily understood, such as time and change. Therefore, your teaching of these abstract concepts should include as much specific, concrete material as possible. Specific help in teaching chronological skills is included in Chapter 10. There are several other practical possibilities that can lead you beyond reliance on a textbook, however. Texts are important; they provide basic information and are a handy resource. But part of the problem in teaching history is that students cannot see how the material relates to their daily lives and their relationships with the larger world. You can help them broaden their perspective by using the following techniques.

Oral History

Students enjoy exploring the past through the collection of oral histories, a method that historians are using increasingly, especially with groups such as immigrants who tend not to leave traditional written records. Historians obtain oral data not only from famous or powerful people but also from members of a given community (an Indian pueblo), from a given period or national background, or from people who observed or participated in a specific activity (a strike or a protest march). These kinds of firsthand accounts fascinate children.

To use oral history in your classroom, first determine a topic that is relatively narrow—what life was like in an elementary school twenty, thirty, or fifty years earlier, for example. Don't expect students to question people about their whole lives; instead, define the topic clearly, focusing on a short span of time. Together with your students, create a short list of questions and have these printed out. Students might ask, for instance, what subjects were taught, how large the classes were, if students in a single classroom were all the same age or different ages, how long the day lasted, what games were played, and how the teacher enforced discipline. The questions should be clear, and each child should have his or her own printed copy.

Practicing interviews in the classroom often helps. Have your students role-play. At first students tend to ask only the questions on their list, ignoring any possibilities of interchange that might arise during the interview. You can encourage them in the role playing to move beyond the interview questions while still being certain that they gather the required material.

You need to determine whether students will tape the interview or take notes. In either case, role playing in the classroom will help them develop their skills. Taping requires good equipment that should be tested before use. It also requires the permission of the respondent. If students will take notes, tell them that they cannot expect to take down every word; you will need to work with them on listening skills. A form with the questions and spaces provided for answers is very helpful to many students. They can take notes directly on the form, or if they tape the interview, they can transfer the information onto the form later.

Children can interview anyone who fits the category for the information required—parents, grandparents, community members, even the school principal. You can also use a **graphic** or **advanced organizer** using categories such as buildings, furniture, lessons, and lunchtime and compare "Long Ago" with "Today." Students can compare and contrast information. How were students alike and how were students different long ago? When the data are gathered, you can use the information not only to help your students understand history—what went on in elementary schools in past years—but also to help your students understand the work of *historians*. How do historians weigh the information provided in oral histories? Did the respondent, for example, stretch the truth? Did he or she *really* walk three miles to school every winter through three feet of snow? Does he or she remember only the pleasant things? By compiling all oral histories that the class has gathered and comparing them, your students should be able to determine those areas on which most respondents agree. If there is a local historical society, its members may be able to confirm or disagree with some parts of the material you have collected. Finally, your class will have a valuable picture of what life was like in earlier years—of *history*—and they will have acquired it through active participation in the process of historical research.

Oral histories can also be found on the Internet. The American Memory Project of the Library of Congress (http://lcweb2.loc.gov/ammem/ammemhome.html) is the premier site to make oral history available to students. Most of the oral history archives' interviews, however, are in a written format (i.e., transcriptions), although photographs are available. Students can explore social history by reading the interviews of people in the oral history collections. Please check the reading level before embarking on a particular interview for your students. Sometimes using just a quotation from a source will be enough for students to create a hypothesis on what it means instead of trying to interpret a more difficult reading.

Family History

The same kind of active participation can be achieved through creating family histories. Many teachers use units on immigration, urban life, or other topics that actually depend on students' family histories for part of their content. Data from student family histories in effect are used to support or disprove generalizations.

Encourage students to make their own histories. When and where were they born? Have they seen their birth certificates? What do other family members remember about them as they were growing up? What do they remember about themselves? Are there photographs to analyze? What about written reports? Report cards? Certificates?

Have these historical documents been saved along with "artifacts" such as baby shoes? Students can make grade-by-grade time lines and the whole class can correlate them with historical events for each year. High interest will be generated if you ask students to describe the most important event in their lives and why it was important.

Usually, your job in creating family histories is to structure the necessary data. Do you want to record birth dates and addresses of parents and other family members? The various jobs held by all family members, including grandparents? Use prepared worksheets showing the information to be gathered, such as family trees with blanks to be filled in. Determine what data you need and then structure a way to report the data. This helps students complete their tasks and makes analysis of the data simpler.

Do not make family trees a painful experience for students. Some students and parents become upset when they feel they must choose between charting the biological lineage or the adoptive one. Instead, it is probably best to allow options such as including whoever is important to the students instead of demanding that they fill out the blanks for a mother or father who may not be there. Or give students more freedom in telling their personal histories by using essays, family orchards (more than just trees), and notify the home in advance, asking parents if the assignment of a family tree presents a difficulty.

To supplement the family tree activity, you can ask students, sometimes with the help of their parents, to do a search of their last name using an Internet search engine. This works best for more uncommon names, not Smith or Brown, to find clues of long-lost relatives. After usually finding many e-mail addresses, a general letter to their potential relatives is in order. Families have been thrilled by the links they have made. Also check out "My History is America's History" (http:www.myhistory.org), a National Endowment for the Humanities Web site for tracing family history.

Looking at Objects of Historical Significance and Field Trips

In addition to learning from oral histories and family histories, students can gain insights from seeing historical objects. To understand the community's roots, cemeteries, especially the old, historical ones, can be remarkably useful classrooms. If one is near your school, walk through it with your students. Provide guidelines about the information they should gather; a worksheet can be useful. Look at the headstones and monuments of the oldest graves. Ask students to list the name, gender, age, and occupation, if it is given, of the person buried in each grave you look at. Have one student write down interesting inscriptions from headstones. Students may be surprised to note, when the data are collated, that many more infants and children died in the past than do so today. This observation may lead to a discussion of mortality rates and the reasons for their change. Did husbands generally survive their wives or did wives outlive their husbands? Did occupation, if it is provided, seem to affect the age of death? How and why?

In addition, a walk through an older section of your community or a trip to view historical buildings can be valuable if it is well planned. You might also want to visit your local historical society or museums where artifacts represent what the community was like years ago. Often it is best to visit such museums at the end of a unit so that students will have learned something about the tools or other objects they will see.

Students can also be encouraged to bring to the class artifacts that their families may have. Families may have written records, such as a relative's discharge from the army, or a penmanship book written by a student many years ago. Students can also bring to class manual tools from the past such as a meat grinder or a nonelectric iron for pressing clothing. School yearbooks are also interesting (have students note changes in the school yearbooks in clothing, hairstyles, uniforms of athletic teams and the marching band) as is old clothing, especially hats. Warn students to be careful, however. If the artifacts are valuable, replacing or repairing them is almost impossible if they are lost or damaged.

To conclude this project, children can create a family artifact report for whatever items they have chosen. This would include the following information:

- What is the name of the artifact?
- Who owned the artifact?
- What historical period is the artifact from?
- How was it used?
- Did most people at that time have or use the artifact? Who used it? Who did not?

A form for analysis of a photograph or picture might ask what people are doing, what things are shown, and how different or similar the scene is to the present time.

Teaching About Faraway Historical Places

Via the Internet, students can easily visit Washington, DC, or a local historic place in their own state. The field trip has gone electronic! You no longer need to order the school bus, get all those permission slips, or round up parent volunteers. With an online computer, you and your class can go on journeys around the world. A virtual tour is an Internet way of taking a firsthand look at the people, customs, sites, sounds, and lifestyle of a place without actually going there. Lesson plans for some sites may be available to teachers at certain historic places. But like all successful field trips, a virtual tour requires a clear objective or purpose and an outcome that you want your students to accomplish before they take a tour (see also Chapter 10 on technology).

Children's Literature and Magazines

A fourth strategy to bring history or any of the social sciences to life is the use of children's literature or trade books. Literature can bring past events into the lives of students. Literature is usually more people centered than text material and can give fresh insight into the ways of life in our culture—past and present—as well as cultures of other places and times.

Biographies and novels are especially powerful. Stories can combine historical incidents with emotion and conflict. Kieran Egan suggested that, for students up to the age of seven, stories with clear conflicts between good and evil and fear or security are best.[3] Students from eight to thirteen are in the romantic stage and prefer to read about people who struggle courageously with real problems. Children want to know how Sojourner Truth felt in the face of great odds, for instance, and will often be interested in books depicting human suffering. Today, more emphasis is placed on reading books that have content themes instead of isolated books unrelated to each other.

[3]Kieran Egan, "What Children Know Best," *Social Education* 43, no. 2 (February 1979): 130–139.

Where can social studies teachers find good books? Each year the journal *Social Education* publishes a list of notable children's trade books in the social studies field. These books are selected because they (1) are written for readers from kindergarten through the eighth grade, (2) emphasize human relations, (3) represent a diversity of groups and are sensitive to a broad range of cultural experiences, (4) present an original theme or a fresh slant on a traditional topic, (5) are easily readable and of high literary quality, and (6) have a pleasing format and, when appropriate, illustrations that enrich the text. The number of good books is increasing. Who would not be excited by a book on the Salem witch trials, such as *Priscilla Foster: The Story of a Salem Girl* by Dorothy and Thomas Hoobler, Silver Burdett Press, 1997, or *Passage to Freedom: The Sugihara Story* by Ken Mochizuki, Lee & Low Books, 1997, a true story of a Japanese consul to Lithuania who risked his job and family's safety to provide visas to Jewish refugees in 1940, saving thousands of lives during the Holocaust.

Biographies and autobiographies can be a hook to a time period. Books about people such as anthropologist Margaret Mead; Thomas Gallaudet, a pioneer in the education of the deaf; Rosa Parks on fighting segregation; Molly Brown, a survivor on the doomed ship *Titanic;* and others are always popular, as are folktales and legends of cultural groups. Help students by using the following class organizer for biographies and autobiographies.

Key Events/Dates	Obstacles Faced	Key Accomplishments

Remember to tell students that both biographies and autobiographies may contain inaccuracies. It is helpful to check the story with another source.

Use the following sources for social studies literature bibliographies.

Sources for Social Studies Literature Bibliographies

Adamson, Lynda G. *Reference Guide to Historical Fiction for Children and Young Adults.* New York: Greenwood, 1987.

Book Links. American Library Association. Chicago: American Library Association, constant updates.

Korbin, Beverly. *Eyeopeners! How to Choose and Use Children's Books About Real People.* New York: Penguin, 1988.

Norton, Donna E. *Through the Eyes of a Child: An Introduction to Children's Literature,* 5th ed. Upper Saddle River, NJ: Merrill/Prentice, 1995.

Spirit, Diana L. *Introducing Bookplots 3.* New York: Bowker, 1988.

"Notable Children's Trade Books in the Field of Social Studies," *Social Education* (annually in April/May issue).

Sutherland, Zena and May Hill Arbuthnot. *Children and Books,* 9th ed. New York: HarperCollins, 1997.

VanMeter, Vandelia. *World History for Children and Young Adults.* Littleton, CO: Libraries Unlimited, 1991.

Zarnowski, Myra, and Arlene F. Gallagher, eds. *Children's Literature and Social Studies: Selecting and Using Notable Books in the Classroom.* Washington, DC: National Council for the Social Studies, 1993.

Check Dean M. Krey's *Children's Literature in Social Studies: Teaching to the Standards* (NCSS Bulletin No. 95, 1998) for excellent children's books published from 1990 to 1997 that can be used for each of the ten broad NCSS themes of the social studies standards.

Consult your librarian to see what is available in your school library that is related to the social studies. Indicate your preferences for future orders. Some teachers will read aloud to the class a portion from an interesting book to entice students to read further. Take care not to kill student enthusiasm by assigning only dull reading reports.

There are also history magazines for young people. The most popular is *Cobblestone,* which focuses on U.S. history with articles on entertainers such as Annie Oakley and the Wild West; explorers such as Robert E. Peary, who went to the North Pole; Joseph, chief of the Nez Perce, and so on.

Cobblestone is found in many public libraries and the back issues may be of interest to teachers.[4] The same publisher also has a children's magazine, *Calliope,* which features world history; *Faces,* for world cultures/multicultural studies; and *Odyssey,* which has articles on space and astronomy. They also have the helpful series *Teaching with Primary Sources,* which includes historical documents combined with teacher-developed classroom activities.

These four strategies—collecting oral histories, exploring family histories, looking at historical objects and places, and reading historical literature—will help children get a sense of the past and make history come alive for them. Other techniques include role playing or dramatic play. Have children research various occupations in a New England town at a particular time and then set up shops (general store, blacksmith forge, print shop, church, jail, bakery, inn/tavern, furniture/cabinet shop, barber/doctor shop, and the like). Include in your debriefing discussion an analysis of how accurately the children played their roles. Try a *history day,* increasingly popular in some states, in which children portray life in colonial or earlier times. Or dress yourself as a character from the unit and invite students to ask questions about whom—you represent. These techniques require active participation from students and move well beyond traditional textbook teaching.

Geography

Geography and map making are changing. Maps are prepared directly from mosaics of satellite photography as dramatic technological innovations are transforming the science of cartography. In addition, due to more Web sites, you can call up a growing volume of maps and geographic data and create your own customized map. Although, some of the Web sites are free, others are not. You can also find where you are or where something is with the use of Global Positioning System (GPS) technology.

Geographers are now concentrating more of their research on the relationships between people and the environment as the human transformation of the globe goes on rapidly. They especially focus on the *interaction of people and nature.* In fact, some geographers think of their discipline now as being environmental studies. Another area of concern is urban geography with attention to changing urban forms, such as suburban areas now having as full a complement of urban functions as the city. Finally, the concept of *regions* is becoming looser because the boundaries of regions are not fixed. For example, is all of California part of the "West"? Or just the mountainous area of California? Do the people in Los Angeles perceive themselves as being part of the region of the "West"? You can see some of the problems regarding boundaries of regions.

[4]Published by Cobblestone Publishing, Inc., 30 Grove Street, Suite C, Peterborough, NH 03458; telephone (800) 821-0115; e-mail custsvc@cobblestone.mv.com and www.cobblestonepub.com

TABLE 6.1 The Geographically Informed Person Knows and Understands . . .

The World in Spatial Terms (Standards 1–3)	1. How to use maps and other geographic representations, tools, and technologies to acquire, process, and report information from a spatial perspective. 2. How to use mental maps to organize information about people, places, and environments in a spatial context. 3. How to analyze the spatial organization of people, places, and environments on Earth's surface.
Places and Regions (Standards 4–6)	4. The physical and human characteristics of places. 5. That people create regions to interpret Earth's complexity. 6. How culture and experience influence people's perception of places and regions.
Physical Systems (Standards 7–8)	7. The physical processes that shape the patterns of Earth's surface. 8. The characteristics and spatial distribution of ecosystems on Earth's surface.
Human Systems (Standards 9–13)	9. The characteristics, distribution, and migration of human populations on Earth's surface. 10. The characteristics, distribution, and complexity of Earth's cultural mosaics. 11. The patterns and networks of economic interdependence on Earth's surface. 12. The processes, patterns, and functions of human settlement. 13. How the forces of cooperation and conflict among people shape human control of Earth's surface.
Environment and Society (Standards 14–16)	14. How human actions modify the physical environment. 15. How physical systems affect human systems. 16. The changes that occur in meaning, use, distribution, and importance of resources.
The Uses of Geography (Standards 17–18)	17. How to apply geography to interpret the past. 18. How to apply geography to interpret the present and plan for the future.

Source: Geography Education Standards Project, *Geography for Life: National Geography Standards 1994* (Washington, DC: National Geographic Society, 1994).

Responding to the criticism that most Americans are poorly educated in geography, the Geography Education Standards Project published its eighteen national standards, setting out what students should know and be able to do in geography from kindergarten through the twelfth grade. Its publication, *Geography for Life: National Geography Standards 1994,* emphasizes the value and importance that the council places on geography for all citizens throughout their lives.[5] The groups involved in developing these standards were the American Geographical Society, Association of American Geographers, National Council for Geographic Education, and the National Geographic Society. These eighteen standards were then organized into six clusters shown in Table 6.1.

[5]Geography Education Standards Project, *Geography for Life: National Geography Standards 1994.* (Washington, DC: National Geographic Society, 1994).

Almost every state has developed or revised its geography standards. Some of the states have been more thorough in their coverage than others. In general, borrowing from the national geography standards, the state standards in geography emphasize the physical and human features of the given state plus how people have interacted with the natural environment in the state's growth. This same pattern of interaction of environment and people is then shifted to regions of the United States and other places in the world. At all times students must strive to be able to interpret maps and other geographic tools.

However, geography as a separate subject has almost disappeared from the elementary school and middle school. Furthermore, most teachers themselves have had few or no courses in geography. This means that the geography standards will have to be integrated across the curriculum, most likely with history courses. In effect, geography has a supporting role to history. This approach can make for a rich history but may not do justice to the spatial perspective of geography. To help implement the geography standards, the Geographic Alliance Network has sponsored teacher workshops and supplied materials.

SAMPLE LESSON PLAN

USING STANDARDS TO TEACH REGIONS

The regions of the United States have been a traditional geography topic for the fourth grade. Let us briefly explore how the geography standards can provide help in teaching this topic. The United States is typically divided into six regions—Northeast, Southeast, Midwest, Southwest, Rocky Mountains, and Pacific—classifications that can be used in the classroom.

Start this unit or lesson with any region of the United States other than the students' own region. Ask if they have lived or visited in the region. What images do they have of the region? What do they want to find out more about in this particular region?

Give each student a blank outline map of the United States and ask them to identify this one region on their maps. You can then present data about the region—using videos, textbooks, pictures, trade books, and so on. Have students make inferences from these materials by asking questions: Could this scene take place elsewhere in the United States? What appear to be the distinctive physical and human characteristics of the region? Have them sketch the major landforms and states of the region on their blank maps and then ask them to list evidence of what people have done to change and modify the physical environment. You can conclude by asking students to compare their original images of the region with what they now know. Was there misinformation before?

You could repeat this exercise for another region. Students can work individually or in groups.

To see how geography standards could be used, let us look at South Africa as an example.

1. *The World in Spatial Terms.* What images or mental maps do you have of South Africa? Where is South Africa located? Is it closer to Brazil or India?
2. *Places and Regions.* What are the physical characteristics of South Africa? How is South Africa different from or similar to your community?
3. *Physical Systems.* What are the different climates of South Africa? How has mining changed the physical environment of South Africa?
4. *Human Systems.* Where do most people live in South Africa? How do people earn their living in South Africa?
5. *Environment and Society.* How have the people of South Africa changed their environment? What are South Africa's nonrenewable resources?
6. *The Uses of Geography.* How is South Africa changing? Do you think South Africa will have more conflicts or fewer conflicts with its neighbors?

You might ask: Where are map skills? Chapter 10 provides more detail on teaching the interpretation and making of maps. But note that a critical concern about how geography is taught is that too often *only* map skills are stressed rather than all the major concepts of geography as outlined by the National Council for Geographic Education. Students may learn the topography of their state or nation but pay little attention to how that topography has been modified or how people have adapted to the natural settings. In studying Brazil, for instance, students often learn that Brazil has a large forest area and that its major cities are located on the coast but not that Brasilia, its capital, was carved from a high plateau once thought uninhabitable, or that the migration of the Japanese into Brazil has changed the character of the nation.

A second criticism of how geography is taught is that thinking skills are underemphasized and low-level memorization is overemphasized. Geographers strongly emphasized geography skills to try to correct this weakness. It is, thus, no longer enough to ask students where the Nile River is; they should also know the consequences of its being where it is and its connections to other parts of the world. Rather than having students simply locate cities on a map, have them find common elements about the locations. They may be surprised to note that some 90 percent of all major cities are located near waterways. For those that are not, such as Madrid or Phoenix, ask them to hypothesize *why* not. Do politics and technology influence the location of cities? Are newer cities more or less likely to be located near waterways? Why? Also, rather than having students learn only about the climate of their own region, have them compare it with other climates. How does climate influence the way we live? The way we dress?

There is no best way to teach *either* geography *or* history. As with history, however, you need to make geographical concepts concrete by designing learning experiences for your class that use their environment and fall within their range of readiness. Take your students on a walk around the school and then have them make a map of the route as they recall it. Walk the same route again, this time making maps as you go. How closely do their remembered maps resemble their actual maps? What problems do mapmakers face when confronting new territory? (Three-dimensional maps, with boxes or blocks representing buildings, can be fun to make but may take more time than the concept requires.)

Make students aware of how the place they are studying relates to the place where they live; let them locate on the map the places they are studying. Use the textbook maps to point out the major cities of your state for your fourth grade class, or the major sites of revolutionary battles for your fifth-grade class. Calculate how many hours it would take to get from your community to Philadelphia, where the Constitution was written, by horseback or carriage and by plane; measure it off. If you live four days by horseback, talk about it on Monday, and on Thursday remind your students that they would just now be arriving at their destination.

In addition, try to tap as many actual student experiences as possible. Ask your students where they have lived or traveled, and have them talk about those places. Ask where the students in the class were born and plot these locations on a map. Or investigate and map the local shopping center or main street, classifying the types of stores and shops found there. Students can also map the interior of a supermarket, indicating aisles, major food categories, and other sections. A "Supermarket Rubric" that can be used is shown in Table 6.2. In addition, students can find items from the supermarket that come from other parts of the world and plot information about imports on a map. Talk about your travel experiences as well.

Using controversial issues also helps to bring life to major geographical concepts. Some ecology or environmental issues lend themselves naturally to a consideration of major concepts of geography. Should a given piece of land in the community be developed? How should it be developed? Should it be made into a shopping center or housing for low-income groups? Such discussions can lead to a better understanding of the advantages and disadvantages of using a land site for different purposes as well as showing how people can modify their environment. All these techniques, and especially using the local community as a concrete illustration, can help to improve geography education by moving beyond the textbook. In addition, the newer technologies allow teachers and students to link their classrooms to other classrooms in several parts of the world.

TABLE 6.2 Supermarket Rubric

The supermarket includes:

- produce, dairy, frozen food, bread, canned goods, and other appropriate sections
- checkout area
- loading dock or delivery area
- cold storage areas
- meat and poultry display
- meat processing/packaging area
- bakery (optional)
- manager's office
- restroom
- grocery cart area
- parking lot, including handicapped parking

ON YOUR OWN	**YOUR POSITION ON GEOGRAPHY**
6.1	*What do you remember about your own exposure to geography in elementary school? Jot down some things you remember about how geography was taught then. How comfortable do you feel about teaching geography? Have you had a college-level course in geography?*

Economics

Economics is the study of how human beings choose to use scarce resources to achieve personal and social goals. To increase economics literacy, the National Council on Economic Education issued twenty content standards for the field in 1997.[6] Borrowing from the national economics standards, state economics standards stress that students should develop economic reasoning skills to apply basic economics concepts, assess problems, make choices, and evaluate the choices of others as consumers, workers, and citizens participating in local, national, and global economies. The state standards stress that knowing about the economic world is essential for every student, especially as fundamental economic trends are redefining work and changing lives in a new economic context composed of complex global markets, currency movements, and almost instantaneous electronic communications. In state testing, economic questions are only a small portion of any test, but the inclusion of economics standards encourages teachers to now devote more time to this subject than previously.

All students will eventually need to have knowledge and skills to be able to earn a living. In addition, economic or financial considerations invade almost every decision we make—large or small. Students face the problem of whether they can afford to buy a new scooter or a pair of shoes. Governments as well as families face the problem of what to do with limited financial resources and the government's decisions influence decision making in everyday life. Scarcity and limited resources are always a problem and are the main focus of economics. Therefore, economics education is necessary if one is to be an informed citizen.

Teachers can take directly an economics standard such as "Different methods can be used to allocate goods and services." Students could then discuss what distribution methods are used to allocate a variety of goods and services, such as parking spaces, access to a new drug treatment for cancer, seats on a bus, tickets to a popular concert, use of classroom computers, and so on. They could then move to compare methods used to allocate work responsibilities at homes and work responsibilities in businesses. The comparison could go further with a discussion of the advantages and disadvantages of economic systems in determining different methods to allocate goods and services used in different countries and at different times.

However, because economics, like geography, is normally not taught as a separate subject or in special units at the elementary or middle school, most teachers cor-

[6]National Council on Economic Education, *Voluntary National Content Standards in Economics* (New York: National Council on Economic Education, 1997). Address of the National Council on Economic Education is 1140 Avenue of the Americas, New York, NY 10036. Phone (212) 730-7007; e-mail nces@eaglobal.org. Web site is www.economicsamerica.org for the standards, curriculum materials, and links to economic education.

relate economics standards into their history units, especially American history at grades 5 and 8. Such topics as Native American economies, early exploration, colonial economies, and the westward expansion offer multiple opportunities to examine economic concepts. Economic factors were important in the early explorations of the Americas by Europeans, the economic structure of the three main regions of colonial America, and economic factors were important as causes of the American Revolution. Too often these economic concepts are glossed over. In a similar manner, the impact of inventions, such as the cotton gin, McCormick reaper, and steamboat, can influence how price incentives affect people's behavior and choices. In summary, teachers must recognize the possibilities of including specific economics standards into history units that warrant increased attention. Otherwise, economic concepts in history units may not be identified or taught with any depth. If not taught in American history, economics standards are likely to be neglected.

The National Council on Economic Education, like the Geography Alliance, has state centers on economic education in almost every state. The workshops and courses offered by the State Economic Councils can help support teachers in teaching economics.

Economic concepts such as interest rates, unemployment, inflation, and the like can be made more concrete by starting with the economic knowledge students have already gained from their families and from community experiences. Economic policy decisions address ideological issues. The distinction between facts and values in economics is critical in evaluating policy proposals. Students should be prompted to look for points of view and opinions when using free materials such as videos and publications from business, labor, or other groups. The controversial nature of economics should lead students to engage in thinking critically. How much money should be allocated for defense or research on cancer?

Getting up-to-date information on economic topics such as the current population of the United States or any other country, unemployment rates, and inflation rates is now made easier by the Internet. These data often give good experience to students on how to interpret data, tables, and graphs. Students, however, need to evaluate the Web site. Is the site maintained by an insurance company? The securities industry promoting stock?

Field trips and resource people can help students understand local businesses. Some teachers have students make and sell some product of their own, such as school T-shirts, cookies, or holiday gifts.

Students have run an in-school bookstore. In a few classes, instead of pooling the money in an activities fund (the usual procedure), the school sets up individual accounts for each student, reflecting how much money each has raised. Then students can withdraw money out of their account for school activities. Some students have more, some less, and others nothing at all. Do you like this idea of individual accounts? What lesson does it probably teach to students?

Two areas reflecting a more practical or personal side of economics are consumer education and career education. Often these areas are integrated into other curriculum areas. For example, should the unit on how to write checks be part of a math unit or a social studies unit? Your district may have guidelines about teaching them; if not, you will want to decide how much to include in your own curriculum. For both, but particularly for consumer education, you will need to determine whether a specific unit should be included each year or whether the topic should be integrated into other units. Many experts feel that unless they are taught as separate units, these topics will get scant attention.

Consumer Education

Consumer education lends itself well to correlation with subjects such as math and language arts. Students can make price comparisons of similar products at the supermarket. They can become more aware of the intent of advertising through analysis of commercials on television and ads in newspapers and magazines. Consumer education can be linked with the study of nutrition and ways to improve our food buying and eating habits. Consumer education helps students develop skills to live more intelligently in the real world. Students can compare prices in printed grocery store advertisements with those found at grocery store Web sites. They can discuss the advantages and disadvantages of purchasing at a local store, a mall, online, or from a catalog. What is the "best" way to buy clothes, software, shoes, or music CDs? Web sites designed by businesses can also include information such as creating a budget, part-time employment, shopping, banking, and taxes.

Career Education

In a similar manner, the rationale for career education is that all adults need to be self-supporting, and this need usually involves employment. Some argue that regardless of gender, ethnicity, or geographic factors, all students need career education. Today's rapid changes in job structures suggest that *everyone* has to be prepared to make work and career changes and, therefore, must have a flexible attitude toward change as well as the capacity to readily acquire new knowledge and skills to compete in an increasing global market.

Career awareness and exploration can take many different formats. For the primary grades, parents who have various careers can bring what they wear to work and what they use as tools or equipment when they tell about their work. In grades 4 through 8, field trips to institutions such as hospitals may show the wide range of skills that a hospital needs to be able to offer its services. Students should move from the more familiar doctor and nurse to a consideration of people such as the X-ray technician, the dietitian, and the nurse's aide. Visits to hospitals, stores, offices, or factories can also illustrate the division of labor that is necessary in our modern society. Do not visit a factory or business that is too complex or abstract for your students. Generally, visiting an office or computer center is not as useful as visiting a place that makes a single product such as soft drinks. Services that are more difficult to "see" such as banking and finance also may be poor choices. Students can also "tour" several manufacturing sites on the Internet.

Along with increasing your students' focus on the wide range of occupations that exists in our society, be certain to include the affective domain. By the upper grades of middle school students can handle a variety of value exercises on what they like to do. Then they can think of how their individual abilities and values may lead to possible career choices. At the primary and middle school levels, however, no student should feel that something is wrong if he or she does not have a career choice. Students should be encouraged to be tentative about career goals and to be aware that each person has the potential for success and satisfaction in any number of occupations.

SMALL GROUP WORK	THE ROLE OF CONSUMER AND CAREER EDUCATION
6.2	*What role do you think consumer education and career education should have at the elementary level? Write down your ideas and compare them with those of others in your class.*

Civics/Government

Knowledge about the key concepts of government is essential for citizens to participate in our society. Formal instruction in civics or government has been part of the elementary public school program for well over a century. The goal in civics and government programs is to produce informed, responsible participation by competent citizens committed to the values and principles of the American democratic system. What standards should be used to see if students understand our political systems and the roles of citizens?

The Center for Civic Education issued in 1994 *National Standards for Civics and Government,* a K–12 curriculum, including specific standards for K–4 (see Chapter 5) and for grades 5 to 8.[7]

The organizing questions for grades 5 to 12 are these:

1. What are civic life, politics, and government?
2. What are the foundations of the American political system?
3. How are the values and principles of American constitutional democracy embodied in the government established by the Constitution?
4. What is the relationship of American politics and government to world affairs?
5. What are the roles of the citizen in American democracy?

Few would disagree with these standards. How to assess completion of the standards is more of a problem. Ideally in civic assessment, written responses, oral discourse, group discussion, and portfolio presentations should be included along with more traditional achievement test items.

NAEP 1998 Civics Report Card for the Nation primarily used the national civic standards in designing its civics test, which had more open-ended questions and more writing responses than in the past. At the fourth- and eighth-grade levels, about 30 percent lacked even the most basic knowledge of the system or the role citizens play in it.[8] Experts reacted to the new report by stating that too many students are simply not getting an adequate education in civics and government.

[7]Published by the Center for Civic Education, 5146 Douglas Fir Road, Calabasas, CA 91302-1467; telephone (800) 350-4223, www.civiced.org

[8]National Center for Education Statistics, *NAEP 1998 Civics Report Card for the Nation* (NCES Report 2000-457) by Anthony D. Lukas, Andrew R. Weiss, Jay R. Campbell, John Mazzeo and Stephen Lazer. Washington, DC: Author.

The Center for Civic Education and many other individuals and groups want civics to receive more attention as a subject equal with other subjects and stress the need for systematic treatment for civics and government from kindergarten through twelfth grade. This subject is too important to be left just to the last year of high school. The center feels that students, especially those from less privileged socioeconomic families, need both the formal school curriculum and informal activities, such as practicing democratic procedures, to acquire the knowledge and skills necessary for informed and effective citizenship.

Chapter 7 focuses in detail on citizenship education, both in the school and beyond the classroom, and addresses topics such as teaching the Bill of Rights. But here we briefly discuss *law-related education,* a promising development to help improve the teaching of civics and government. Law-related education seeks to promote an understanding of society and its system of laws so that students learn how they may effectively function within the law. In addition, law-related education tries to teach critical thinking skills regarding laws and issues facing our nation.

Law-related education makes use of case studies that focus on fictional or simplified versions of actual cases. Case studies have been constructed from fiction such as William Golding's *Lord of the Flies,* in which boys isolated on an island by a plane crash deal with the problem of trying to govern themselves, with some very unfortunate consequences. Case studies appeal to human interest because they show individuals caught between conflicting demands or facing a real crisis, such as a prison sentence. A good case study should illustrate some principle or concept; otherwise, students may miss the point of the exercise. In addition, students must accurately understand the facts in the case so they can make a good decision about what action should be taken.

Again, as in the teaching of history, geography, and economics, the local community can be an important resource in law-related education. Field trips can be arranged or guest speakers invited from the following agencies: the local police, the state police, and the Federal Bureau of Investigation; the local, state, and federal courts; the offices of the public defender and the public prosecutor; and the various people and facilities connected with corrections, such as probation officers, work camps, and detention halls for juveniles. In addition, lawyers are always a good resource. The use of action-oriented problems in the community, such as getting out the vote or cleaning a public park, can also be promising.

Substance abuse in the school and community can also be used as a topic. The school has a responsibility for developing plans to deal with drugs in the school. Students can think about how to evaluate rules concerning illegal drugs in their own school. Can a principal or an administrator search student lockers and bookbags? Should students found having illegal drugs be suspended from school? These questions of protecting the welfare of the group while respecting the rights of the individual are an important topic of law-related education and can be related to the students' lives.

The use of field experiences and guest speakers can help enliven dry textbooks. Speakers reflect current views. As always, using these resources effectively requires planning and helping students to observe and to ask good questions. Debriefing students and summarizing the experience are always worthwhile in assessing what students have learned. To make the social sciences and history meaningful in the context of a student's own interests and experiences, teachers need to be careful planners and use a variety of methods.

■ CURRENT EVENTS/CURRENT AFFAIRS PROGRAMS

What is the role of current events or current affairs programs in the elementary school? Part of the rationale for such programs is the assumption that all citizens must eventually be aware of current issues in order to vote and make intelligent decisions. One of the purposes of teaching current events, then, is to begin arousing student interest in what is happening in the world.

In your own classroom, current events can be the glue that binds all other social studies elements together. A newspaper article about an earthquake in Costa Rica can bring together history (have there been earthquakes there before?), geography (where is Costa Rica and what region did the earthquake affect?), economics (what will be the long-term economic damage to the people who have lost their homes?), and political science (how will the government respond?). Frequently, current events can be related to whatever unit you are studying, or, in reverse, you might ask students to look for newspaper articles about the country or period you are studying. It makes sense, if you are studying China, to have your students be aware of what is happening today in China.

Current affairs programs are not limited just to the upper grades. Primary students can also be encouraged to become interested in current events. However, as reading and viewing abilities become more developed, older students are more likely to have the skills necessary to find and to locate information about current events. Because current events programs serve multiple purposes, different teachers use different formats for them, as the following cases illustrate:

1. Barbara Carpenter, a fourth-grade teacher, has a current events period every day after lunch. Students are encouraged to bring in newspaper articles that are of interest to them to share with the class. There are no specific criteria for what should be brought in, so the items range from what is happening in the Middle East to local crime reports. There is only coincidental correlation between current events time and what is happening in the social studies program.

2. Maria Gomez, a fifth-grade teacher, has current events every Friday. She has a set of classroom newspapers, *The Citizen Edition,* published by Scholastic for the fifth grade, that is distributed and read during the social studies period. Ms. Gomez likes to use the Scholastic Junior classroom newspapers because many of her students come from families in which not much attention is given to current events. Few if any newspapers and magazines are delivered to their homes. In addition, the Scholastic series tries to coordinate some issues that are commonly taught at the fifth-grade level. Ms. Gomez thinks the students enjoy reading the junior newspapers and she finds the suggestions for the teacher helpful.

3. Sam Bronski, a sixth-grade teacher, has current events every Thursday. At that time he uses the previous day's local newspapers, which are delivered to the school free of charge. Mr. Bronski never forgets to have current events day on Thursday because the stack of newspapers becomes a nuisance if they are not removed. His last social studies class of the day gets to keep the newspapers. Sometimes Mr. Bronski finds that certain sections (e.g., the sports section) disappear before the last period of the day. Throughout the year Mr. Bronski has explained the different sections of the newspapers to the students. To be certain that they read more than just the comics, Mr. Bronski prepares a few questions for each

student to answer during the current events class period. He thinks the students enjoy having and reading the adult newspapers.

4. Andrew Oleson, a seventh-grade teacher, coordinates the current events program with the unit he is teaching. When the class is studying Russia, only items from newspapers or magazines that pertain to Russia can be brought to the class to be reported on. The items then are put on the designated bulletin board under the heading "Russia." Students get extra credit for the news items they bring as their class reports. Current events teaching occurs only within the regular social studies period.

5. Ann Bronstein, an eighth-grade teacher, has current events every Friday. At the beginning of the year, five categories are chosen: international news, national news, state news, local news, and sports. The category of sports is a concession to students' high interest. At the beginning of each week, five students are given one of the preceding topics, which they report on in class on Friday. All students eventually have a turn, and every five weeks a new cycle is started. The students use the format of a television show, with each specialist reporting on his or her category. Students are encouraged to make use of magazines such as *Time* or *Newsweek*. Students are motivated to illustrate or use the chalkboard in their reports as they each receive a grade based on content *and* delivery.

ON YOUR OWN	**YOUR VIEWPOINT ON CURRENT EVENTS PROGRAMS**
6.2	*Which of the previous current events cases do you like the best? What appear to be the strengths or the weaknesses of each program?*

Again, you see that your values make a difference in the teaching of current events. Regardless of your point of view, teaching current events requires a rich array of resources and materials.

Some teachers use current events as a separate subject with little or accidental correlation with the social studies program; other teachers use current events to supplement or reinforce what is going on in the regular program. Only in very rare cases would a teacher use current events as the basis for actual social studies units, since it is difficult to plan units around unpredictable events. However, a teacher could start a unit, especially on a given nation such as Japan or Israel, by focusing on that nation's current events.

A second area of difference among teachers is the sources used by both the teacher and the class to get current events data. This decision can be affected by the teacher's knowledge of the background of the students' families. Students from families that have a wide range of printed material probably do not have to use the junior newspapers prepared specifically for the schools. However, there are several advantages of using commercially prepared classroom newspapers published by Scholastic and Bruce Seide Publisher (*My Weekly Reader* [K–6], *Current Events* [7–8], *Scholastic News* [K–5] and *Junior Scholastic* [6–8], and *News-Currents* [3–12] and *Time for Kids (The Big Picture for K–1), News Scope for 2–3,* and *World Report for 4–6*). If these newspapers are in the class, you are more likely to use them.

Also they are objective and contain articles that are within the range of interest and comprehension of children. But some teachers do not use the commercial junior newspapers as a learning experience. Instead, they distribute them when there are only ten minutes left in the day. Students then get the message that current events are just a fill-in for killing time. It is little wonder that they learn to seek out the more enjoyable features of the commercial junior newspapers, such as the cartoons.

A new source of news information are current-events online programs such as *NewsCurrents Online*. Through this program, the teacher downloads the teacher's guide and previews a week's issue. The teacher can select the news items that are of interest. There are three separate vocabulary and concepts levels to choose from along with useful web links, and possibilities of a dicussion-based format.

Ideally, as they grow older, students should move into using adult sources of information. For this reason, the use of newspapers can provide an opportunity for learning valuable skills. Students can profit by exercises showing how an index such as "Today's Contents" or "Inside" helps to locate specific features of the newspapers. Reading headlines is important, and it is especially helpful if your community has two local newspapers so that students can compare the headlines of the two newspapers on a given day. Occasionally, bringing in a well-regarded national newspaper such as the *New York Times* or the *Los Angeles Times* is helpful; compare them with local newspapers. Bringing in foreign newspapers as well as specialized newspapers such as the *Wall Street Journal* can also help students see the wide variety of newspapers available.

Distinguishing between an editorial and a news story is another important skill. Give students a news item that is accurate, fair, and objective and an editorial on the same topic. Ask them which article wants action to be taken; which article best describes what is happening; which articles tells the writer's feelings.

An increasing number of people depend on television and the Internet as their sources of news. It is likely that more of today's teachers will tape parts of current news programs on their VCRs to show to their students. Some schools are also using the controversial Channel One broadcasts, which have commercials, in their classrooms. CNN Newsroom and CNN Newsroom Worldview have thirty-minute blocks of commercial-free news and features that air for videotaping at 4:30 A.M./E. T.[9]

The top news stories of the day are also easily accessible on the Internet. Major magazines and newspapers also have their own Web sites. Here are some starting points:

CNN Interactive: www.cnn.com

USA Today: www.usatoday.com

U.S. News and World Report: www.usnews.com/usnews/home.htm

Newsweek: http://school.newsweek.com

The Associated Press: www.apalert.com

NewsLink: www.newslink.org/news.html

ABC News: www.abcnews.go.com

[9]To obtain information about enrollment and licensing rights, call (800) 344-6219 or e-mail www.cnn.com/newsroom. The CNN Web site also indicates how to get more information on a given topic.

In addition, the New York Times Learning Network (www.nytimes.com/learning) has a free daily current events mini-lesson for grades 3 to 5. The Lesson Plan Search allows teachers to search the New York Times Learning Network's archive of more than 300 lesson plans free of charge.

Current events may be related to the teaching of controversial issues, as many items of current events at the local, state, national, and international levels are controversial. Here again, teachers must decide what role they will take in teaching controversial events. Having access to a wide variety of information sources such as newspapers and magazines will help students see the emotional impact of a division of opinion on a given issue as well as the differences in viewpoints. Many teachers encourage students to bring news items for a bulletin board. If this is done, students should change the news items frequently.

Using Television for Critical Thinking

Television is the main source of news and information as well as entertainment in our society. Almost all U.S. households have at least one television set and about half of all children have a television set in their bedrooms. Around 87 percent of U.S. households have a VCR. Children aged 2 to 11 are spending an average of twenty-three hours a week watching TV, although there are social class and ethnic differences with minority children and lower-status children spending more time watching TV than other children.

Television newscasts are lively, superficial, fast-paced reports of unconnected events. They do not offer enough context for viewers to grasp the complexities of issues that result in a disaster, a congressional vote, a change in the stock market, or a citizen protest. Frequently the lead story on the evening news is a violent event. The high dosage of violence in the media can lead to a callous acceptance of violent behavior and create fears in children of being victimized. Increasingly emotional, personal vignettes in TV news oversimplify complex issues. To assist students in extracting more meaning from such programs and newscasts, teachers need to use TV fare as springboards for critical thinking and values exploration as well as learning more about current public issues. The following are some activities that can promote media literacy and develop skills in processing information. Some are more appropriate for older elementary students.

- Ask students to keep a record of how often they watch television and to list their favorite programs and to write why they like them. Graphs can be used to present some of the data. What alternative activities or other choices did they give up by watching TV?
- Discuss what characteristics make a character likeable or unlikable.
- Survey plots for examples about honesty, fairness, and respect.
- Develop a list of shows in which the characters regularly cooperate with each other, and list the advantages of cooperation.
- Ask if a character on a TV show could have made a different decision. What might have been the consequences of such a decision?
- Compare different channels and newspapers' presentations and interpretations of the same news event.
- Count and time the news stories (crimes, local events, the weather, etc.) in a thirty-minute news program. What is the average time per event?

- Discuss which kinds of events tend to be used to start a program. Why?
- Explain how an event in the news may affect them or their families.
- Discuss whether violent action is rewarded or punished in TV programs. How are conflicts handled?
- Look at ads critically.

Many middle-grade teachers use TV as an ongoing current events resource that can serve as a prompt to help students choose issues to study in greater depth. Current events programs can be used in combination with cable television programming such as the History, Discovery, and Learning Channels.

■ TEACHING CONTROVERSIAL ISSUES

As students become older, they become better able to discuss controversial issues, of which there is no shortage in our society; economics and government policy, for example, have always provoked differences among citizens. Drugs, AIDS, and abortion generate strongly held views among citizens. What should be done to improve the economic well-being of our nation? There is certainly a wide divergence of opinion among citizens as well as between groups such as business and labor. What should be our policy on foreign aid? Again, a wide difference of opinion exists.

Among social studies educators, there is much debate over what role teachers should assume in the teaching of controversial issues. Teachers' methods have been criticized in their communities. There have been court cases in which the question of academic freedom to discuss controversial issues for both teachers and students has been considered. In general, the courts have ruled that teachers can discuss these controversial issues if they are appropriate to the academic subject area. This means that a math teacher would probably not be protected by the courts if he or she discussed abortion during a math class.

Here are four typical cases involving teachers presenting controversial issues:

1. Gloria Young does not discuss any topics that she thinks are controversial in her fourth-grade class. She believes that the classroom must be a neutral place and does not like it when students argue and bicker among themselves. Ms. Young thinks it is best to shield students from unpleasant topics that may upset them. She believes children have a greater sense of security if they can think that all is well in their community and that they should not be unduly concerned about local or world events. Ms. Young also thinks that her principal appreciates her not posing a problem for parents who might be upset to learn that controversial issues are being discussed in the classroom.

2. In the next room, teaching the fifth grade, is Carol Taylor. She is a civil rights advocate and a feminist and has a deep commitment to educating students on the injustices that women and other minority groups have suffered in the past. In her teaching of U.S. history she emphasizes how these minority groups were unfairly treated.

   Ms. Taylor believes she knows the right position on controversial issues that come up in the classroom and made it clear to the parents at an October open house how she feels. She argues that all Americans should have equal rights. Unlike Ms. Young, Ms. Taylor does not ignore controversial issues and actually welcomes their inclusion, especially as they relate to her teaching of U.S. history.

Ms. Taylor is constantly bringing up questions on how the budgets of governmental units should be changed, with more emphasis on job retraining and antidiscrimination efforts.

If a student with a different viewpoint suggests another idea, Ms. Taylor calmly ignores it and proceeds to present her point of view. She thinks that students hear and learn more in the media about accepting the status quo than making changes to improve the position of women, African Americans, and other groups. She feels her job is to free her students from these "false" ideas.

3. Marianne Ash teaches seventh grade in the same school. She believes that controversial issues should be discussed in the classroom. However, she also believes that she should be neutral and downplay her own views on certain issues. Even when students ask her how she will vote on a certain issue or what she thinks about a policy, Ms. Ash does not think it is appropriate for students to know. She is afraid that some students might accept her position without considering it carefully or that a few students who are not fond of her might immediately take the opposite position.

   Ms. Ash encourages her students to present a variety of viewpoints on a given controversial issue. She tries to guide the discussion, toward which people will benefit from a given issue (e.g., pollution) and which people will be the losers. Ms. Ash believes that with rational discussion students can clarify their own positions after hearing a variety of viewpoints.

4. Nicholas Baker is a teacher in the eighth grade in the same school. Like Ms. Taylor and Ms. Ash, Mr. Baker believes that controversial issues should be discussed in the classroom. But unlike Ms. Ash, Mr. Baker gives his own point of view on issues. He tells students how he will vote on certain issues. On his car is a bumper sticker indicating his viewpoint on ecology. In his classroom, Mr. Baker thinks he should be a model of a politically active citizen. He tells the students about the organizations he belongs to that have a political focus. In the classroom, Mr. Baker brings in a variety of speakers with different points of view. He also uses a combination of other methods such as library research and group discussions to help students clarify how they feel on a given controversial issue.

SMALL GROUP WORK	**VIEWPOINTS ON CONTROVERSIAL ISSUES**
6.3	*Which position do you think is the best of the four previously described for the teaching of controversial issues? Which one would you like to model? Give your reasons for your position to your group.*

As you can see, there are many opinions on the proper role of an elementary teacher in teaching about controversial issues. But in the previous four cases, there is another person whom we may have overlooked. That person is Dr. Jane Menshi, the principal of the school. She keeps hoping that the school district will issue some guidelines on the teaching of controversial events and the role of academic freedom for teachers and students. She knows that her teachers are handling controversial issues in many different ways. She has received a few complaints from parents about Ms. Taylor's strong position but was able to tell them that at least Ms. Taylor is open about her principles. If the parents want to bring up additional facts to teach to their own children what they think is right, they should do so. Dr. Menshi always points out to parents that the research on political socialization indicates that parents and the family are the most important factors in influencing what children believe about political issues. Dr. Menshi's discussions with parents have satisfied them and no parent has complained to a higher administrator.

Dr. Menshi, however, is a little concerned about the social actions that Mr. Baker wants to take. Mr. Baker believes that students need the experience of working in their community areas. He wants students to help support the local political candidates of their choice. The students would attend meetings of these political candidates and do tasks such as handing out political literature for the candidates for office. No student would be forced to do this community action, but students who want an A in the class probably realize that Mr. Baker is apt to look with favor on those who participate actively in community affairs. Mr. Baker even suggested to Dr. Menshi that students help in the political campaigns of school board members. What would the board members think of that? Dr. Menshi was very worried about this but did not know what she should do. What do you think would be the best position for the principal to take with regard to outside political action on the part of the eighth graders in her school? Can your class role-play some of the alternatives?

In looking over the four teachers' positions on teaching controversial issues, you can see that each has its advantages and disadvantages. The four positions move along a continuum from the teacher who does nothing about controversial events to the teacher who would like students to take social action in the community. Social studies experts themselves disagree on the proper position for teaching controversial events, but most of them would not support Ms. Young's total avoidance of controversial issues in the classroom. This is simply an unrealistic position in an age in which students are bombarded by the media with news of their community, nation, and the world. Children are aware of problems and controversial issues outside the classroom, and sheltering them from these real problems, especially as they are growing older, does not make sense. The experience of the Persian Gulf War showed that in families and classrooms where the war was not discussed, children were more anxious and concerned about their well-being than when the war was openly examined. To become effective citizens, students need to be able to make judgments on issues. Furthermore, even if Ms. Young does not realize it, she is teaching values. Her stance as a person unconcerned about controversial issues is probably not a good model of what a teacher should be (see Figure 6.1).

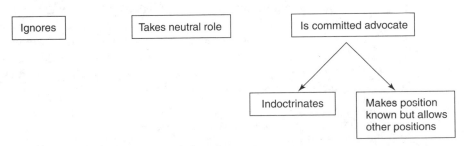

FIGURE 6.1 The Teaching of Controversial Issues

Ms. Taylor is trying to get students to accept certain positions. In effect, this is a form of indoctrination. Viewpoints different from hers are not given much attention. In this case Ms. Taylor is supporting a liberal position; however, advocates of indoctrination can range from Marxists to conservatives, all of whom believe it is their duty to pass on their particular ideology. These true believers are really authoritarian teachers with regard to the teaching of their own value systems. They are not giving students the opportunity to hear other points of view.

The advantages of Ms. Ash's position are that students are exposed to a wide variety of viewpoints on a given issue, and Ms. Ash uses a variety of methods with which students can study the issue. Mr. Baker's position is similar to that of Ms. Ash, except that Mr. Baker gives his own position on issues. He makes his positions clear to the class.

Is this good? At least students know what Mr. Baker believes. In many cases, students are perceptive enough to guess where teachers such as Ms. Ash stand by reading verbal and nonverbal clues. For example, without realizing it, teachers often do not write on the board the ideas suggested by students who disagree with the teacher's viewpoint.

In effect, Ms. Ash and teachers like her want to play the role of a nonpartisan referee. This position probably receives the most support in the teaching of controversial issues. It is also a noncontroversial point of view with the community, which normally does not object if the teacher plays this role. Advocates of social action such as Mr. Baker are likely to find themselves being attacked for pushing young, "impressionable" students into political action. This is especially true when the action involves local issues. In some cases, however, teachers have been rewarded with praise and publicity, especially if the social action takes the form of doing something popular such as cleaning up the local beach or getting out the vote.

The proper role of the teacher in teaching controversial events is not likely to be settled in the near future since it is basically a values issue. Topics such as abortion are highly sensitive in many communities. Students may feel offended by certain topics and are likely to complain to their parents. Teachers can be accused of being insensitive or biased. Court cases on the rights of teachers and students continue to define the limits of academic freedom and free speech. Policy statements by local districts on the teaching of controversial events are helpful, as these statements generally support academic freedom. The National Council for the Social Studies has issued a position paper on academic freedom and the social studies teacher, which treats explicitly the teaching of controversial issues.[10] The guidelines outline the rights and responsibilities of teachers, the selection of educational materials, and visiting speakers. These guidelines also encourage teachers to introduce controversial issues in their teaching. School guidelines are also needed for student use of the Internet. Many schools have both students and their parents sign statements that they understand the rules in using the Internet. All parties involved—students, teachers, administrators, and the community—need to know the guidelines that the school is using in the teaching of controversial events.

[10]National Council for the Social Studies, "Academic Freedom and the Social Studies Teacher: NCSS Position Statement," *Social Education* 55 (January 1991): 13–15.

■ SUMMARY

Most states have curriculum standards available for history, geography, civics, and economics. Moving beyond the textbook in the middle grades means making the content of history and the social sciences (geography, economics, political science) more relevant to students. Oral history, family history, community history, children's literature, field trips, and law-related education speakers can add zest to social studies programs. In addition, teachers must decide how they will teach current events and controversial issues and how new discipline standards may change their teaching.

■ SUGGESTED READINGS AND WEB SITES ■

Bradley Commission on History in Schools. *Building a History Curriculum: Guidelines for Teaching History in Schools*. Washington, DC: Educational Excellence Network, 1988.

Suggestions of historians for teaching history.

Brophy, Jere, and Bruce A. Van Sledright. *Teaching and Learning History in Elementary Schools*. New York: Teachers College Press, 1997.

The authors synthesize the most current research on children's historical learning and thinking.

Center for Civic Education. *National Standards for Civics and Government*. Calabasas, CA: Center for Civic Education, 1994.

Report on civics and government standards.

Cheney, Lynne V., and Albert Shanker. "Mutual Suspicions." *The New Republic* 212, no. 6 (February 6, 1995): 4.

Edinger, Monica. *Seeking History: Teaching with Primary Sources in Grades 4–6*. Westport, CT: Heinemann, 2000.

Ideas on how to use primary sources.

Geography for Life: National Geography Standards 1994. Washington, DC: National Geographic Society, 1994.

Report on the geography standards.

Haas, Mary E., and Margaret A. Laughlin, eds. *Meeting the Standards: Social Studies Readings for K–6 Educators*. National Council for the Social Studies, 1997.

For the history standards, seven articles ranging from using customized photographs to the value of children's homes and neighborhoods. For the geography standards, seven articles ranging from environmental education to creating an outdoor learning laboratory, and for the economics standards, another seven articles ranging from the cupcake factory to little tykes become big tycoons.

The best single source of journal articles for help in meeting the standards.

Hickey, Gail. *Bringing History Home: Local and Family History Projects for Grades K–6*. Boston: Allyn & Bacon, 1999.

History projects for elementary students.

Jorgensen, Karen L. *History Workshop: Reconstructing the Past with Elementary Students*. Portsmouth, NH: Heinemann, 1993.

Children create historical meaning as they interact with others.

Levstik, Linda S., and Keith C. Barton. *Doing History: Investigating with Children in Elementary and Middle School. 2nd ed.* Mahwah, NJ: Lawrence Erlbaum, 2000.

Sociocultural perspective showing students doing history.

Nash, Gary B., and Ross E. Dunn. "History Standards and Culture Wars." *Social Education* 59 (1), 1995, 57.

Codirector and coordinating editor for the world history standards answer critics.

National Center for History in the Schools. *National Standards for History: Basic Edition*. Los Angeles: University of California, 1996.

Revised report on history standards.

Provenzo, Eugene, Jr., and Asterie Baker Provenzo. *Pursuing the Past: Oral History, Photographs, Family History, Cemeteries*. Menlo Park, CA: Addison-Wesley, 1984.

Good on past oral history.

Ravitch, Diane, and Chester Finn, Jr. *What Do Our 17-Year-Olds Know? A Report on the First National Assessment of History and Literature*. New York: Harper and Row, 1987.

A critical report on the poor achievement of American students in history.

Web Sites

Center for Civic Education

www.civiced.org

e-mail: center4civ@aol.com

Standards, K–12 curriculum materials, newsletter.

Constitutional Rights Foundation

www.crf-usa.org

e-mail: crf@-usa.org

Materials for all grade levels, grants, and newsletter.

GOVSPOT

www.govspot.com

Collection of government and civic resources. Designed to simplify the search for the best government sites and documents.

The National Council on Economic Education

http://nationalcouncil.org

The economic standards, resources, and lesson plans. Some of the NCSS-affiliated Centers for Economic Education also have developed very useful resources. For example, see various state councils on economic education.

Teaching with Historic Places

www.cr.nps.gov/nr/twhp

National Park interpreters have lesson plans by location, theme, and time period.

Chapter 7

Elementary Citizenship Education

In this chapter we view citizenship education from a broad perspective. Citizenship is defined and examined moving outward from the classroom, the school, the community, and finally the global community.

- Defining Citizenship

- Classroom Citizenship

- Instruction in Democratic Citizenship

- Citizenship in School

- Linking Schoolwide Citizenship to the Community

- Global Citizenship

What do you think of when you hear the term *citizenship education?* Does it sound abstract, adult, and far removed from the elementary classroom? It is true that children entering school have twelve years before they can exercise full citizenship rights. It is well to recall that preparation to exercise these responsibilities has been the primary argument in favor of public schooling since the beginning of the American republic. The experiences children have in elementary school directly influence the attitudes and ideas they gain about citizenship. School and classroom events that involve seeking fairness under rules and cooperative problem solving give students tangible contact with democratic values that they may not have opportunities to experience in other facets of their lives. More formal study of what democratic values are and how they evolve provides a context for critical thinking about how we can organize our lives for the greater good of all people. To better understand the power of schools in citizenship education, we need to explore two issues. First, we must consider what values, knowledge, and skills the citizenship role requires. Second, we must consider how children can best acquire these attributes.

■ DEFINING CITIZENSHIP

What does a citizen do? Often the answer we give depends on our frame of reference. Unfortunately, schools have often put into practice a narrow, almost authoritarian model of citizenship in their award and recognition systems. To be labeled "good citizens" in many elementary schools, children need only to obey and cooperate. What they learn to value under these contexts may be the opposite of critical thinking and democratic problem solving. By contrast, "good citizens" in our local communities are those who not only obey laws but also seek to conserve public property or come to the aid of someone in distress. They may strive to help the homeless and raise issues of fairness in public, even when doing so is resisted by the majority. They vote and participate in community organizations.

For teachers, the orderly classroom frame of reference can lead to a focus that is entirely on the rule-following, obedient side of citizenship. In their anxiety to create environments where students can get on with the business of learning, teachers are prone to skip over the necessary step of exploring democratic values—fairness, equality, dignity of the individual, caring for each other, cooperation for the good of the group—that classroom order should knowingly uphold. We need to develop a definition of citizenship in classrooms and schools that promotes an active rather than a passive citizenship. We have to keep in mind the aspects of good citizenship that promote justice seeking and critical thinking: Good citizens protest misuse of authority by police and public officials. Good citizens seek new laws as a way of making desirable change. Good citizens complain when they see examples of government wasting taxpayer money. Active citizenship is not necessarily "orderly."

The active as well as the orderly component should be present in our definition of citizenship. We need to use the basics of democracy as guidelines for the system of school citizenship we devise. Some basics of democracy are stated clearly: Each person has one vote and equal protection under the law; decisions are made by majority vote; decisions and laws can be reviewed and amended by lawful process; decisions and government acts are based on law; and individual rights to religious beliefs, privacy, and speech are protected by the government. Classic democratic theory and practice as well as contemporary research support the centrality of the school's role in imparting these basic values and skills. Educational theorists such as John Dewey have demonstrated that children learn from experience to plan their own learning and consider how best to organize their classroom environments. The Lab School that Dewey directed at the University of Chicago in the early 1900s promoted children's learning by projects and group planning and research.[1] Longitudinal data from the High/Scope preschool curriculum project suggest that when at-risk children have experience in the area of planning and evaluation of daily activities, they achieve greater sociopersonal success as young adults and become contributing members of society.[2]

[1]John Dewey, How We Think (Boston: Heath, 1933).

[2]W. S. Barnett, "The Percy Preschool Program and Its Long-Term Effects: A Benefit-Cost Analysis," *High/Scope Early Childhood Papers*, no. 2 (Ypsilanti, MI: High/Scope Press, 1985).

These two illustrations speak directly to the importance of developing citizenship in classrooms. They suggest that citizenship development based on democratic values should guide the way we organize our classrooms and learning experiences. Knowledge about the way children learn suggests that care must be taken in the way citizenship attributes are developed. The old adage "do what I say, not what I do" is pertinent to acquiring these skills. Being told about democratic citizenship is not the best learning mode for children. Nor will they learn to be active citizens by following a set of rules and behaviors prescribed by the teacher or school that requires absolute, unquestioning obedience.

Currently, several discipline, or classroom-management, systems are popular in classrooms. These systems, whether advertised as such or not, are versions of citizenship education. And each should be evaluated using the broader term *citizenship* rather than accepted under the apparently benign title *classroom management*. Each one has its own merits and can be helpful in making us think about and organize the way we handle our students so they can have an orderly and pleasant place in which to learn. However, when we consider adopting any classroom-management system, we should ask ourselves citizenship education questions about it:

Does it promote self-regulating behavior?

Is it consistent with the way children learn?

Does it promote critical thinking and decision making?

Does it promote positive self-regard?

Affirmative responses to these questions are good indicators that a classroom-management system is consistent with the goal of developing democratic citizenship capabilities of children. Most teachers find that no one classroom-management system meets all their preferences and settings. Being required to adopt an entire system with little or no discussion of the type of citizenship education it implies should be resisted. Obtaining schoolwide consistency in discipline and management of behavior makes sense in a bureaucratic way; but rules should contribute more than consistency of student behavior. Does the rule have democratic value for the students? What is the decision-making role of teachers in enforcing it? To accept the principle that discipline and decision making both need to be taught consistently does not resolve the issues of how to obtain discipline while promoting decision making in a particular school or classroom.

There is no magic solution for designing a classroom-management or discipline program. Discipline issues rank supreme among teachers' concerns in schools from coast to coast. Experienced teachers report they are now seeing significantly more verbal and physical aggression than in the past, even among young children. The past may look rosier than it actually was, but the media have highlighted violence in schools today. In many schools, there is now zero tolerance for weapons, drugs, and violence in any form.

When we consider how to organize citizenship education for the elementary grades, two components need to be included. Both are equally important. First is instruction, the more obvious and traditional mode of inculcating the social institutions and procedures we have devised to maintain order in our large, diverse group of individuals in society. For this component, direct instruction *about* our system of government and its underlying values such as justice and equality continues to be an important responsibility in the elementary curriculum. A second component we need to organize is how to do, or the *process* of, citizenship. To acquire the attributes and commitment necessary for this part of citizenship, students must be involved in constructing, monitoring, and modifying rules and their application. Without experiencing, from the earliest school ages, the processes of self-governance, students will have greater difficulty in assimilating the "book-learning" about citizenship as well as putting into action the skills they need in decision making on controversial issues as citizens.

■ CLASSROOM CITIZENSHIP

The major task elementary teachers have at the beginning of every new school year is teaching the classroom system to new students. Routines (for entering and leaving the classroom, for getting supplies, for getting information from the teacher, for keeping the classroom orderly) are modeled and practiced. In the first days of a new school year, teachers are "lawgivers." Children must learn to handle these routines for the business of the class to run smoothly. Once these routines are put into practice, the teacher needs to take the democratic step of helping children see that they are responsible for constructing the atmosphere of the classroom. This is easily done by leading the children in evaluating and changing or modifying the set of rules used to begin the school year. This process of evaluation, proposing change, trying it out, and evaluating again should continue until consensus is reached on rules that govern the class.

In addition to the ongoing plan for rule development, the following strategies are typically used to help children perfect these routines while fostering their active involvement with organizing their school day.

1. Begin a day or period by discussing and planning a schedule.
2. Reinforce children who perform the desired routines.
3. Conduct evaluation at the end of day or period that discusses "how we did with our routines," "what we need to finish tomorrow," and "how we can improve our work."

By following these steps students are learning to play the procedural, or disciplinary, side of citizenship in a classroom society. It is imperative, for everyone's benefit, that this discipline be taught and learned. Teachers should ask students why they think we plan and evaluate. How does this help us? Are we being fair to each other? How could we work together to get more done?

Roles and Responsibilities

For children to develop active citizenship skills, the class system must allow them to make decisions. Some teachers build student choice periods into their daily or weekly

TABLE 7.1 Student Choices of Activity/Role/Responsibility

Kindergarten	Third Grade	Fifth Grade
Sand table	Computer	Computer
Painting easel	Listening post	Experiment table
Bookcase/pillows	Library corner	Art project
Computer	Math games, experiments	Media/library
Dress-up corner		Listening post
Block corner		

schedule (Table 7.1). During these times students sign up for their choices. Teachers usually have a poster or bulletin board with slots where students may place their names to assist with traffic control and the negotiation of "equal access" to the most popular activities.

Organizing students to assume responsibilities for classroom duties is another important way to let children practice citizenship. Typically, duties include cleanup and leadership roles. The variety in this array of tasks depends on the student age and classroom design. Figure 7.1 is an outline of fourth-grade jobs developed by Joan Elston and Barbara Mumma.

Elston rotates children through these roles. Her goal is to permit each student to have practice in both leadership and "followership," starring and supporting roles. All who visit this classroom sense the ownership and pride the system gives these students.

President
Take attendance
Pass lunch tickets
Lead flag salute

Vice President
Do daily checklist
Substitute for president
Take attendance to office messenger

Secretary
Write thank-you notes
Keep field-trip checklist
Fill paper drawers

Treasurer
Record service points
Collect, count money
Distribute book orders

Room Maintenance
Wash boards
Open, close windows
Empty pencil sharpener
Empty wastebasket
Scour sink

Technical Engineers
Set up, operate equipment

Table Chairperson
Lead group tasks
Hand out supplies, handouts
Collect papers
Check desks for neatness

FIGURE 7.1 Classroom Citizenship Roles and Responsibilities
Outline of fourth-grade jobs developed by Joan Elston and Barbara Mumma,
Collins School, Cupertino, California. Reprinted with permission.

A Caring Classroom

What really is more important than the specific roles and responsibilities of students is the atmosphere or the climate that gets established in the classroom. How often have you walked into a classroom and "felt" that it was a friendly place? In the same school, in another classroom the ambience may be totally different. One teacher may appear to promote a positive classroom climate where learning occurs while another may not. The atmosphere or classroom climate may seem poor when there is frequent disruptive behavior that wears down teacher morale, depresses students' academic and social outcomes, and creates parental dissatisfaction.

We all want classrooms in which caring and learning prevail. Building caring classroom communities takes considerable effort on the part of both the teacher and the students, and it does not come automatically. An important first step, done with both informal and planned opportunities, is for children to feel that they are among friends. How did you feel when you entered a new class in September and did not know one soul in the room? We need to help students to get to know and respect one another and, thus, create a safe classroom environment that fosters learning and citizenship goals.

Classroom Meetings

Classroom meetings are another essential strategy for modeling decision making. Decisions about real choices must be the agenda.

Whatever the issue, the meetings should have the following criteria:

1. A signal for wanting to speak
2. A discussion leader (teacher for earlier grades)
3. A discussion of the choices that examines good and bad possible results of each choice
4. The possibility of seeking more information before voting
5. A way of voting secretly so that each child votes according to his or her own feeling
6. A way of following through to see that the vote is honored

Look for these criteria in the sample classroom episode. As you read, think about the payoffs for the citizenship skills children can gain from classroom time spent this way.

ON YOUR OWN	**DECIDING THE BOUNDARIES OF COOPERATIVE PLANNING**
7.1	*How would you change the roles if instead of a first-grade class thanking a fifth-grade class, the fifth graders were thanking the first graders? Should Mr. Cervantes have manipulated the situation when the children did not prefer his choice? Or did he follow the spirit of the class? Would the same method work with fifth graders?*

SAMPLE CLASSROOM EPISODE

LOOKING IN CLASSROOMS: CLASSROOM DECISION MAKING

Mr. Cervantes wanted his first grade to thank the fifth-grade students that had brought their puppet show on important U.S. presidents to the first graders. Mr. Cervantes opened the meeting with this question: "Who remembers some of the things we learned about the presidents from the fifth graders yesterday?" (Various children volunteer information they remember.)

Mr. Cervantes: What were some of the things you liked most about the show? (Various children describe what they liked.)

Mr. Cervantes: How could we thank the fifth graders?

Jesus: We could tell them on the playground.

Mr. Cervantes: Yes, that would be one way. Does anyone else have a suggestion?

Kerry: We could send them a letter.

Mr. Cervantes: Yes. Are there any more suggestions about how we could thank them?

Erin: We could go to their class and tell them.

Mr. Cervantes: Those are all suggestions I want us to think more about. What would be good about telling them on the playground?

Jake: It's easy to do.

Jenny: Not for me.

Mr. Cervantes: What are some problems with telling them on the playground?

Jenny: I don't know who the fifth graders are.

Mr. Cervantes: Well, let's think about the second suggestion. What are some good things about the idea of sending a letter? (Mr. Cervantes leads the discussion to cover all suggestions.)

Mr. Cervantes: You've given some good things for us to think about. Are you ready to decide? So that we each vote the way we think, I'm going to ask you to close your eyes and raise your hand when I ask for the choice you want. Are you ready? How do you show me?

Postscript

The class voted to go to the fifth graders and tell them, not Mr. Cervantes's choice. He wanted to use the event to write letters. Now he's thinking about how to honor the vote while capitalizing on the oral language opportunity presented by going to the fifth-grade class. What would you do?

Zooming our imaginary lens back into the classroom a few minutes later, we see that Mr. Cervantes is quickly leading them into preparing a choral reading "thank you" that will have all the children saying "we learned a lot from you," interspersed with individual children telling one thing they learned, such as "George Washington had false teeth made of ivory."

There is a moral to this episode. Teachers should not embark on class decision making unless they are willing to abide by the decision that the class makes. As the example showed, Mr. Cervantes structured the decision-making episode; he did not dictate the decision. He integrated language arts with the experience but not the element of language arts he had envisioned. As teachers, we choose issues that are appropriate to class decision making. How do you feel about allowing the class to decide whether to study math or social studies? We think that would be going too far. As teachers, our professional responsibility is to organize instruction in the different curricular areas. Making decisions about how to present their learning efforts and selecting from a list of choices are appropriate for elementary students.

Conflict Resolution with Groups and Individuals as Citizenship Skill Building

The second part of learning ways to live together goes beyond organizing students to assume classroom responsibilities and procedures. Disagreements and conflicts between individuals and groups will arise no matter how imaginative and thorough the system for making classrooms and playgrounds run smoothly. Two strategies for helping students learn how to work through these incidents complete the well-rounded plan for citizenship development. One is conflict resolution, which engages individuals involved in a dispute in finding a mutually acceptable alternative. The second is the class meeting, which leads the whole class to work out a solution to a generally felt problem.[3]

In using conflict resolution or mediation, it is first necessary to realize that not all conflicts can be resolved by this technique. Some individuals do not want or cannot easily change or give up what they feel is important. It is easier to resolve conflicts that are based on misunderstandings than to resolve conflicts over beliefs and values. The conflict resolution process requires a mediator or person trained in the steps in conflict resolution: opening, listening, creating options, and planning to solve the problem.

To implement a peer-mediation program or conflict resolution program requires the support of the administration and the selection of students and staff who are trained as mediators.[4] Peer mediators should be chosen from a cross section of the school community and be willing to learn, have good verbal skills, and have the respect of their peers. In many schools, peer mediators are assigned to work in pairs. This gives mediators a degree of support needed to conduct their "Peace Patrol" during out-of-class time as they try to stop conflict between two individuals before it escalates. The mediators try to be nonjudgmental and impartial. Schools have reported great benefits on all grade levels when conflicts are able to be resolved. Sometimes this is called "Peace Education."

If your school does not have a peer conflict resolution team, the teacher can take this role. Here are the steps to follow, which are similar to peer mediation.

1. Identify the problem without blame.
2. Brainstorm alternatives together.
3. Agree on a solution.
4. Evaluate the result.

[3]William Glasser, Schools without Failure (New York: Harper and Row, 1969).
[4]Conflict resolution is commonly a component of districtwide programs for reducing violence in schools.

TABLE 7.2 Strategies for Resolving Conflict

Between Individuals	Class Meetings
1. Both individuals stop, cool off.	1. Leader asks whether anyone has a problem group needs to discuss.
2. Both take turns talking about what is wrong.	2. When problem is volunteered, leader asks show of hands for agreement to hold meeting on problem mentioned.
3. Both listen to each other without interrupting.	3. Leader asks group to define what the problem issue is.
4. Each one tries to tell what he or she needs.	4. Group lists ways problem can be solved.
5. They brainstorm possible solutions.	5. Group evaluates and chooses solution.
6. They choose solution both like.	
7. They plan how to put solution into action.	
8. They "go" for plan by writing it out.	

The teacher, however, cannot be an impartial mediator after going through the preceding steps. For example, a school rule could have been broken and the consequences for such behavior are already spelled out. In addition, as said before, this process is not a cure-all for some individual children. However, one successful anti-violence program for young children required that *all* the parents of children in the program be trained in management, discipline, and supervision. Teachers learned how to better manage inappropriate behavior. Volunteer playground monitors learned how to supervise more effectively and reward behavior during unstructured lunch and recess periods. At the end of the program, it was found that even the most initially aggressive children were virtually indistinguishable from the average child in behavior. The important key was to influence all parts of a child's world and to include the entire population rather than selected "problem" students within that group.[5] In other words, it may take a whole village to educate a child.

Study the steps for both strategies in Table 7.2 as a guide to evaluating the classroom incidents that follow. Ask yourself if you agree with the strategy chosen to address the conflict in each.

1. **Bernie the Bully.** A fourth-grade class is just returning from a recess during which Bernie reportedly shoved Sharif to the ground when Sharif came up to take his turn kicking in the dodgeball game. The teacher, Ms. Stearns, convenes a meeting to discuss better ways of sharing on the playground. Ms. Stearns asks Sharif what happened during the dodgeball game. Sharif hangs his head and says nothing. Penny, the original reporter, raises her hand and repeats that Bernie wouldn't let Sharif take a turn and pushed him down.

   Bernie glares at Penny and grunts a noncommittal "Yeah" to Ms. Stearns's query for confirmation. Ms. Stearns turns to the class and asks, "How can we be certain that this type of problem does not happen again?"

[5]Henry Tama, "Targeting the Adults in Young Kids' Lives Helps Halt Aggression," *USA Today* (April 24, 2000): 1D.

Several children make comments to the effect that they don't have the problem, that Bernie has the problem. Ms. Stearns asks Bernie how he can change his behavior. Bernie screws up his face and spits out, "Let 'em play."

2. **Dodgeball Dodgers.** Several children request to stay inside during recess. After the rest of the class goes out, Ms. Stearns asks the group why lately they have chosen to stay inside. They make comments that recess is boring and that if you're not a superstar, it's better not to play in the dodgeball game. After recess Ms. Stearns convenes a class meeting with the question, "What could we do to make sure everyone has a good time during recess?" Children suggest various ideas, some of which are about sportsmanship on the dodgeball field. Having listed their ideas, Ms. Stearns asks the children to vote for the two most important ideas to put into practice during recess. One of the most voted items is to "stop calling other people bad names during dodgeball." The other is "don't keep the same team members every recess." After negotiating how to handle the team item, Ms. Stearns closes the meeting by charging everyone to put these ideas into practice next recess time.

Did you agree with the strategies chosen in each case? Our reaction is that a class meeting was appropriately used in the second case, but that individual conflict resolution might have better fit the situation in the first case. It is true in the first case that Ms. Stearns may have helped Sharif get a chance to play, but she used a sledgehammer to kill a fly as far as Bernie is concerned. And Penny had better watch out for Bernie next time they're on the playground! We must be cautious to ensure that in our zeal to promote class resolution of problems we are not creating more individual problems. In other words, individual problems are not the best topics for group decision making.

These examples also show the face of bullying. **Bullying** is defined as persistent teasing, name-calling, or social exclusion. It may also include physical acts, although it is more likely to include threats of violence rather than violence per se. Unfortunately, too often teasing and bullying are part of daily life for students. Research has found that boys initiate most of the teasing and bullying incidents, but both boys and girls are the recipients. However, boys are more likely to respond physically, whereas girls are more likely to respond verbally to incidents initiated against them. The prime area of bullying behavior is the playground where play is unstructured and competitive games can be a problem. Usually teachers and other adults do not intervene in these incidents, often because they are not aware and they are easily overlooked. "Bernie the Bully" is realistic because typically the "victim" does not report the problem to the teacher or principal. Furthermore, the other students, the bystanders, often do not speak out either.

If there are problems on the playground, students can discuss in a class meeting the value of noncompetitive games in the playground. In fact, dodgeball has been banned in some schools' playgrounds. For example, new games of "tag" are available in which the players are never permanently "out." Either their roles change or they can be released back into the game by other players. Many students, especially those not well coordinated in physical ability, might like to try out some of the noncompetitive games, and it could reduce the bullying incidents. However, although all students should be encouraged in physical activity, no students should be made to do an activity at free time recess and lunch if they are uncomfortable about it.

SMALL GROUP WORK
7.1

CONFLICT AND YOUR REACTION

We all have learned a set of norms that tells us what is appropriate behavior and what is not. These include our reactions to conflict. How were you taught to end a conflict? Do you think conflict resolution programs are a good idea?

Values in the Classroom as Citizenship Development

Besides conflict management, classroom meetings, and classroom citizenship, some parents and curriculum planners are calling for more direct education in the teaching of values. For example, the national civics standards call for content standards in "Fundamental Values and Principles" of American democracy. These **values** of American democracy are as follows:

- individual rights to life, liberty, property, and the pursuit of happiness
- the public or common good
- justice
- equality of opportunity
- diversity
- truth
- patriotism

How can you help citizenship development by teaching these values? From Chapter 1, we have discussed several values approaches. Let us examine more carefully the "Analysis Approach" in which students use logical thinking to decide values issues primarily by rational class discussion and gathering resources from a variety of sources.

Values Analysis Strategy

1. Identify the problem.
2. Clarify the values question(s).
3. Gather and evaluate the facts about the problem.
4. Suggest several solutions to the problem and the good and bad consequences of each solution. Older students can examine the short-term and the possible long-term consequences.
5. Decide among the solutions proposed.

Let us see how the values analysis strategy could be used in the classroom episode, "Spiders and the Assistant Principal." Ms. Torres could take the opportunity to discuss this values issue with the whole class following the outline of the values analysis strategy. If she does not, the class will see modeled a passive role on the part of an adult and wonder if justice, private property, and the common good are really respected. The problem can be identified easily. What should be done with the black widow spider? The values question is more complex. There are the values of the teacher, Ms. Torres, the values of the assistant principal who wants the school environment to be safe, and the values of the children who like the opportunity of looking at the black widow spider.

SAMPLE CLASSROOM EPISODE

SPIDERS AND THE ASSISTANT PRINCIPAL

Ms. Torres was considered the "nature lover" at her school. If an insect was in her room, the children watched it for a while, caught it, and released it outside.

One day a black widow spider was found by a child in another classroom. The child's teacher called Ms. Torres who caught the spider in a jar for everyone to see. She taped the lid on tightly and spent time with classes discussing spiders, black widow spiders, and what it means to be venomous. She decided this was a great learning opportunity. She planned to keep the spider for only a few days and then release it in a field away from the school. Everyone in the school heard about the spider and wanted to see it.

But on the next day the assistant principal told Ms. Torres she needed to take the spider away. They had called an exterminator to destroy the spider because school policy insisted that any animal that could be dangerous to the children must be destroyed. What should Ms. Torres do?

Source: Carole Basile and Cameron White, "Tad Poles and Tough Questions," *Social Studies and the Young Learner* 12, no. 2 (November–December 1999): 17–20. The scenario is condensed.

Is there further evidence needed to make a decision on this issue? Looking at the wording and authority of the rule about destroying dangerous animals is essential. How serious would it be if the black widow spider actually bit a young student? Is the black widow spider an endangered species? Does killing the black widow spider have any effect on the rest of the environment? Is having the black widow spider in a classroom such an "attractive nuisance" that a child or children might be attempted to play with it?

Then students and the teacher could suggest solutions to the problem. One solution is to disobey the rule and release the black widow spider. What would be the consequences then to Ms. Torres? Another is to move the decision making up another level to the principal or even higher or enlist the aid of parents to speak up on this issue. Ms. Torres and her students then could marshall facts to show why the black widow spider should not be killed. Or the assistant principal could explain her concerns about safety to the class. There are different possible consequences for each solution.

This values analysis case study shows that often there is not a clearly "right" answer, partly because of the differences in values of some of the participants. Nevertheless, how problems are handled in the classroom is a valuable experience for students and illustrates how lofty and abstract values such as the right to life (even for a spider), liberty, and the pursuit of happiness are played out on given issues. It also shows that events are shaped, in part, by people who make decisions about what should happen in a certain situation. Human choices make a difference and not being engaged in policy issues allows others to make decisions.

■ INSTRUCTION IN DEMOCRATIC CITIZENSHIP

Functioning effectively in our modern, complex society requires sophistication. We must understand what our rights and responsibilities are. We must be able to locate and deal with a myriad of public institutions. We must know how to seek and use information we need from the mountains of information that are available but not always easy to find. We must understand the rules of the game as they exist under our system of government. Beyond the classroom, school, and community arenas, children need instruction in three general topics—the rule of law, our justice system, and the global citizenship. This section contains suggestions for organizing these three topics.

The Rule of Law

Typically, the formal aspects of learning what the law is and how it can be extended or changed are reserved for segments of the fourth, fifth, and eighth grades. The basis for understanding our formal system needs to be constructed, as we saw in the preceding section of this chapter, by a link to community functions at every grade level as well as citizenship activities that become part of the daily classroom life. Young children, as well as middle graders, can profit from formal consideration of the need for rules.

Young children are socialized rule followers by the time they reach kindergarten. They need to discuss the rules they have at home or in the classroom, why these rules are important, and what the consequences are when rules are not followed. Questions such as "Why do we have to raise our hands in class?" or "Why do we have to put garbage in the garbage cans?" are essential beginnings to discussions in later grades about the documents that define our society's rule of law.

Ask students to suggest experiences in their own lives that exemplify freedom—choosing their own clothes in getting dressed and choosing their own friends. Then ask them to list what they cannot do—fishing limits, age requirements for organizations such as the Girl Scouts, and so on. Why the limits or restrictions? What would happen if the limit was changed?

Middle-grade children need to translate into everyday language the documents that establish the basics of citizenship in our society. Documents that should be discussed in this fashion are the Declaration of Independence, the Constitution of the United States of America, and the Universal Declaration of Human Rights. For example, asking fifth graders to read the Preamble (as follows) and give six main reasons that the representatives to the Constitutional Convention stated they needed a constitution can help to define the historical context as well as make the content of the rest of the document more meaningful.

> We the people of the United States, in order to establish a more perfect Union, establish justice, ensure domestic tranquility, provide for the common defense, promote the general welfare, and secure the blessings of liberty to ourselves and our posterity, do ordain and establish this constitution for the United States of America. (*Preamble to the Constitution*)

Unfortunately, not all of the Constitution is as easy to decipher as the Preamble. Middle-grade children need an overview of the structure that the Constitution creates

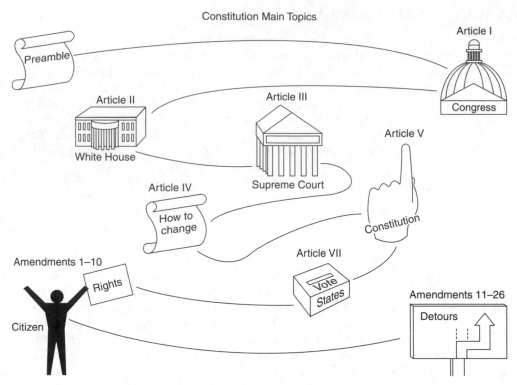

FIGURE 7.2 Advance Organizers as Instructional Aids:
Learning How the Constitution Can Be Changed

Source: From June R. Chapin and Rosemary G. Messick, *You and the Constitution*
(Reading, MA: Addison-Wesley, 1987), p. 62. Reprinted with permission.

for governing our society. One way to outline the main ideas contained in this document is through use of a visual outline or advance organizer such as that illustrated in Figure 7.2. Bulletin boards depicting main ideas about our system of government, such as the separation of powers and how a bill becomes a law, are keys to unlocking the lines of printed text for many students.

Making the Bill of Rights come alive for middle graders requires involving them in relating the document to hypothetical situations. Through lessons, such as the following sample lesson plan, students gain a knowledge-level awareness of their citizen rights.

This lesson requires critical thinking and discussion. When students examine situations that are familiar to them, they can readily see the relevance of the Bill of Rights to their daily lives. They may not be, and should not be, required to remember every detail of the first ten amendments to the Constitution. They will, however, gain a sense of the importance this document has. Pedagogically, note that small groups should read and discuss *before* the whole class discusses the lesson. Without the small group step, most children will miss the "opportunity" personally to read and discuss, thereby short-circuiting real contact with the material. The small group step is crucial to this lesson.

SAMPLE LESSON PLAN

BILL OF RIGHTS: CAN THIS BE DONE?

Objective
Students categorize hypothetical situations as being protected or not protected under the Bill of Rights.

Materials
For a class of thirty, one copy for each student of the Bill of Rights, one transparency of "Am I Protected?" and a chalkboard or butcher paper chart for recording answers.

Procedure
1. Explain that the Constitution gives each citizen certain protections or guarantees that the government may not take away. "Our task in this lesson will be to discover what our citizen rights are and to decide whether certain situations interfere with these rights."
2. Divide the class into groups of three and assign an amendment to each.
3. Distribute the amendment list, giving groups a minute to read their amendment and skim the others.
4. Explain that you will show a situation on the transparency and each group must decide whether (a) their amendment relates to that event and (b) whether the event interferes with their rights according to the amendment.
5. Show the events one by one, recording student decisions in category columns by event number (see recording chart).
6. Conclude by asking students to list what they learned about the Bill of Rights through this exercise. Ask how these events relate to real life.
7. Assign "I Learned" statement to be written and handed in within five minutes.

Evaluation
Did students relate the acts to the amendments? Could they generalize from the amendments and acts to make statements about their citizen rights?

Transparency
Am I Protected?
1. You own a hotel. The president calls and asks you to keep ten soldiers there because they are on duty in the neighborhood and have no place to stay.
2. You are opposed to a Supreme Court decision. You write a letter to the editor of your local paper stating your opinion.
3. You were freed by a jury decision from charges of robbery. Now, five years later, the bank that was robbed brings charges against you.
4. A policewoman knocks on your door. She shows you a search warrant and wants to come in to search your apartment.
5. You own a hunting rifle. Your neighbor says you have no right to have it at home.

(continued)

BILL OF RIGHTS: CAN THIS BE DONE? *(continued)*

6. You are asked to give evidence about a traffic accident you were involved in while you were under the influence of alcohol.

7. Arrested for driving while drunk, you are put in the county jail for a year and fined $10,000.

8. You are fourteen and want to get married.

9. The public school now begins each day with Bible reading.

Sample Recording Chart: *Am I Protected?*

Permits	Does Not Permit
1. _____	_____
2. _____	_____
3. _____	_____

The Justice System

Formal instruction is necessary to supplement the real and vicarious contact children have with our system of justice. They may have had real contact by riding in a car with a parent when a highway patrol officer pulled their parent over to issue a traffic ticket. Or they may have testified in a divorce hearing concerning child custody. Television provides them with a barrage of vicarious contact. These kinds of contacts need to be supplemented with classroom instruction. Increasingly, news coverage and reenactments of crimes cause children to become fearful. They need to have a forum that permits them to discuss their fears as it extends their knowledge of the ideals of the justice system: that a person is not guilty of a crime until proven so in a court trial and that people who become involved in crime still have civil rights.

Upper-grade students need specific instruction in the justice system. This instruction should include textbook study and classroom discussion. Possibilities for bringing textbooks to life include visiting courts in session, interviewing officials of the justice system, reading and dramatizing case studies, and participating in mock trials. Local bar associations and law school students are another resource for bringing the justice system to life. Associations are usually eager to send representatives to classes. Without getting into the finer points of contracts and torts, attorneys are able to illustrate how civil disputes as well as criminal charges are resolved. Teachers should take advantage of the resources law-related curriculum projects offer. These projects provide sample lessons and resource units that are free or available at minimal cost.[6]

[6]Following are law-related education centers: Center for Civic Education, 5115 Douglas Fir Drive, Suite 1, Calabasas, CA 91302; Constitutional Rights Foundation, 601 S. Kingsley Drive, Los Angeles, CA 99005; National Street Law Institute, 605 G. Street N.W., Washington, DC; Special Committee on Youth for Citizenship, American Bar Association, 1155 East 60th Street, Chicago, IL 60637.

Instruction about the justice system is a necessary complement to direct experiences that schools can provide young citizens. To round out their instruction in being citizens, children need to consider their roles as citizens of the world.

■ CITIZENSHIP IN SCHOOL

School student councils usually help a few students gain active citizenship skills. Those students who are bold enough to run for office and lucky enough to get elected will gain leadership practice. Typically, these students meet with an administrator and bring messages about schoolwide functions back to their classrooms. Children in such groups gain experience by participating in meetings and presenting messages to their classmates; in some schools, they vote on issues at the meetings. The rationale for having a student council is that learning by doing promotes growth in active citizenship. The issue is how to extend the benefits of student council participation to more than one individual student from each class. For example, one school created three branches of student government: a legislative branch, a judicial branch, and an executive branch. This increased both dramatically the number of students involved and the interest of students. The students had their own bill of rights, which was often used in cases that came before the court.

Beyond classroom responsibilities, some schools organize schoolwide positions and announce them in want ads. These positions include street and building traffic patrol, school lunch helpers, checkers for distribution and collection of noontime and recess equipment, librarian helpers and media center technicians, office helpers, playground cleanup patrol, and student council officers. These positions are mostly for middle graders. Students are not elected to these places but rotate through them periodically. Children apply for their positions by signing up for interviews. Teachers in charge of each job category check to make sure children understand the responsibilities involved. Children not selected for the first six weeks usually get a chance to serve during the second six-week period.

By giving their time and talents, children are contributing to making their school a place they own and can make better. Children can learn cooperative skills and see the benefit of working for a common cause when they participate in schoolwide campaigns. Fund-raising and cleanup drives are common to most schools. Class and individual awards for accomplishment help children recognize the value of their achievements and have pride in group effort.

Encouraging the expression of opinions about school events is a positive technique for building a sense of civic efficacy among students. Primary-grade classrooms can reserve a bulletin board with the heading "Citizenship: Success and Needs." Children can be encouraged to draw or write on the board about acts or situations they wish to compliment or ones they wish to improve by offering suggestions. Periodically, during sharing time, these contributions should be commented on and then removed to make room for new additions. Extending this idea is an effective strategy for focusing attention beyond individual classrooms. Directing students' attention to needed improvements in the school or local community can lead students to find out who is responsible for such things as repainting the traffic crosswalk or replacing the worn playground equipment. Students can write a class letter to comment on the needed change. Teachers and classes have been amazed to learn that such letters are read at school board and city council meetings.

We should not underestimate the power of student letter-writing campaigns. One middle-grade teacher, Mr. Garske, devised a system for counting the number of drivers not coming to a complete stop during school hours at the four-way stop crossing near the school. These data were used in a letter to a city councilperson as part of an argument for erecting an electric stop light at the crossing. The city councilperson contacted the teacher and came to the class to discuss the problem. Children were involved later in the conversation between the councilperson and representatives from the city departments of transportation and works. Some students attended the council meeting when the request was first proposed. The children involved continued to follow the process after they left Mr. Garske's room. Two years later when the light was installed, these first-year high school students returned for a class photo taken around "their" stoplight. The photo will remind them of the power of citizen opinion and of the patience and persistence required to move a bureaucracy through the process of change.

■ LINKING SCHOOLWIDE CITIZENSHIP TO THE COMMUNITY

Service Learning or Community Participation

Providing children access to the community outside of the school is an important element in the development of citizenship. Traditionally, elementary classes have learned about community helpers in ways that most often did little to involve the children in active citizenship. But this is changing by the increasing popularity in the schools for promoting service learning or community service. This movement reflects the grave concern that more has to be done to teach youth to participate in a democratic society. The declining adult voting turnout is often cited as a need for the schools to counter the current apathy and cynicism about government and political leaders. In addition, it is felt that volunteers are needed if national problems are to be addressed and young people are at a stage of their lives when attitudes are still being formed. Thus, volunteer service is seen as a tool for teachers to build both interest in social studies and to interact with the community.

Service learning is the integration of community service with academic learning. This means that students doing volunteer work need to do something in the classroom such as discussing their experience or giving an oral report. In service learning, students are to gain knowledge about their community, use skills such as acquiring information and evaluating it, and develop a sense of effectiveness in the community. In contrast, **community service** is giving back to the local community and is associated with charity and altruism. The purpose is to help those in need. Focusing on helping others is not necessarily tied into what is going on in a particular school course or topic. A visit by a class to a local nursing home might be an example of community service. The students may have prepared holiday decorations, visited in their Halloween costumes, or distributed Valentine candy. Often these one-shot activities, although very worthy, have little connection with the social studies program. However, one second-grade class "adopted" a nearby nursing home for a full year. Along with frequent visits, the students also communicated by e-mail with the residents because many nursing home residents now have access to the Internet. In practice it is often hard to distinguish between service learning and community participation, as when a class cleans up a public area such as a park.

For example, students may define a community problem—making it a safer neighborhood, helping the hungry, helping the elderly who are homebound, or protecting the environment—and follow up the class consensus by searching out community agencies that will be willing to work with the students to represent a bona fide program or institution in the community. These efforts have encompassed a wide variety of agencies. One school planted a garden to grow vegetables that were then sold on Saturdays at the local farmer's market; the money they made was donated to a soup kitchen where they were too young to work. This garden project went on during the summer even when school was out of session. Beautification/art projects also have been popular along with ecology projects. In doing these projects, students need to keep records of their hours and activities, maintain ongoing debriefing and planning sessions under teacher leadership, and reflect on what they are learning.

A difficulty with implementing service learning is the transportation problem. Unless children are able to walk to the agency's site, usually service learning or community participation is limited unless parent volunteers are willing to drive. Teachers also need to be careful that they are not forcing students into service activities that students do not want to do. Even when the difficulties in the implementation of service learning or community participation are overcome, service learning or community service is not a panacea for improving citizenship. However, classes using it have reported high satisfaction and a sense of accomplishment among students, which are both important in promoting citizenship in the community.

SMALL GROUP WORK	LINKS TO THE COMMUNITY
7.2	*What, if any, community service have you participated in? What individuals or groups organized the community service? What do you think are the problems and promises of community or service learning in the classroom?*

Mock Elections

One means that schools traditionally have used for linking children to the world of citizenship happens at election time. In some schools children read campaign literature and hold mock elections. Social scientists tell us that children replicate their parents' political orientations and choices. Even though the results of school mock elections may be interesting to teachers, the child receives little concrete citizenship development from such an exercise. In fact, the contrary is true. In voting for candidates, children typically get little information on which to make their decisions. They probably do not know what the candidate stands for or what the important issues are in the campaign. They are generally forced to rely on media images and home orientations. School elections then can take on the aspects of a horse race, where winning is the only issue. Teachers must ask themselves if this is the substance about elections that they wish to have the school propagate. Elections need to be studied and given attention in the classroom, but teachers should keep voting in perspective. Voting is the last act in a long process of making choices. It is the process, not the vote itself, that must be emphasized.

Middle- and upper-grade children are capable of following political campaigns. They should be encouraged to do so. Printed statements for and against ballot propositions and programs proposed by candidates make good critical thinking units. Keeping track of candidate statements over time and collecting facts about issues to display and analyze are essential current events activities. Analyzing the way candidates portray themselves and the issues on television, counting the number of times the candidate's name is mentioned, and noting the main and underlying messages alert children to how the media are used to shape our opinions and ideas.

Teaching Patriotism

Some teachers fear that students will become less patriotic as adults as a result of analyzing issues and questioning candidates. As teachers, we need to examine what we mean when we say that our goal is creating patriotic citizens. We have all been taught that patriotism is a good and necessary value for our nation to survive.

In most public schools, a love of one's country is instilled along with a reverence of national symbols—the flag that flies in front of the school; the reproductions of historical scenes and individuals, such as George Washington; the Minutemen's fife and drum corps; and the signing of the Constitution. Students routinely recite rituals of loyalty in the Pledge of Allegiance and sing the national anthem. Most of us believe that these symbols and rituals are appropriate, even essential, elements of school culture, as the activities create a sense of national identity and pride essential for young children living in this country.

Indeed, children seem to depend on these rituals in school as a necessary part of their daily routine. But what are our objectives in incorporating them? What are we looking for when we repeat these rituals every day? Do they accomplish our purpose? What are young children learning as a result of participating in these rituals?

Jean Piaget demonstrated that young children have great difficulty with the concept of country as an entity that is also part of, yet different from, the community and surroundings they know. In the late 1960s, Wallace Lambert and Otto Klineberg found that by the age of seven, children were specific about their own national identification.[7] Furthermore, they had internalized an international pecking order that included derogatory national stereotypes. At that time children of other nationalities tended to see Americans as a high-status group, as did the Americans themselves. Other studies have found that by the age of ten, children internalize an attitude about their own power within the political system. This sense of power was related to the socioeconomic status of the children's families. Teachers were found to modify their approach to citizenship-related activities according to the socioeconomic status of children in their schools. Teachers emphasized obeying laws and fulfilling responsibilities to children of poorer, blue-collar families. In contrast, teachers of middle- to upper-class children tended to emphasize problem-solving approaches to citizenship topics.

---

[7]Wallace E. Lambert and Otto Klineberg, *Children's Views of Foreign People: A Cross-National Study* (New York: Irving, 1967).

The recent results of the International Association for the Evaluation of Educational Achievement (IEA) confirmed this research. Textbook analyses and focus groups in the United States pointed toward little variation in the content students from one school to another receive. But students in urban schools serving families from lower economic levels were less likely to experience varied instructional strategies and a democratic school environment than students in schools serving more affluent families. This means that students in different school settings end up with different conceptions about democracy, national identity, and diversity.[8]

We have no evidence that the pledge to the flag, singing a patriotic song, or voting in a mock election is harmful to children's positive regard for national identity and citizenship. If, however, our purpose is to develop a love of our nation and a feeling of belonging to it, these activities are just the first step. To be effective, these rituals need to be accompanied by cognitively engaging activities that help children build their own positive connections to their schools and local communities. Without the practice of participating according to democratically oriented classroom procedures, we cannot assume that bridges of meaning and citizenship skills are built through the repetition of prescribed rituals. As we have seen, activities that can assist in this bridge building are planning and evaluating the school day with children, involving children with the responsibilities and decision making of running the class and school, and organizing exposure to community institutions. To reinforce links between symbols and rituals and understanding the ideals and functioning of civil society, children need direct instruction in the basics of citizenship under our system of government.

■ GLOBAL CITIZENSHIP

As our world community contracts to become a global village with nearly instantaneous communication and certainly eventual interconnection between all spheres of endeavor, our definition of citizenship must also change to fit this new reality. Sometimes this is called multidimensional citizenship. Children in our classes are, in fact, citizens of the world. As such, they need to develop a loyalty to and identity with their fellow world citizens.

Three Themes of a Universal Curriculum

Multidimensional citizenship requires more than just knowledge. It calls for viewing problems from a global perspective using critical thinking skills. It involves also a commitment to the following convictions.

1. We are all global citizens who share a responsibility for solving the world's problems and for creating the world we desire.
2. We are all members of the family of humankind. We are responsible for understanding and caring for people of cultures different from our own.
3. We are stewards of Earth, which is our home and life-support system.

[8]Carole L. Hahn and Judith Torney-Purta, "The IEA Civic Education Project: National and International Perspectives," *Social Education* 63, no. 7 (November–December 1999): 425–431.

First let us clarify some definitions. One is the distinction or difference between **global education** and **multicultural education.** Global education emphasizes the cultures and people of other lands whereas multiculturalism deals with racial and ethnic diversity within the United States. For other experts, global education examines global equity and multicultural education addresses national equity in the United States. This distinction is often not clear in the minds of students when students in a global education unit think the focus is going to be on Native Americans or Asian Americans. However, both fields have shared purposes to increase students' civic understanding and participation in national and global citizenship.

Global education is also often confused with **globalization,** a term which is increasingly used. Globalization includes both the objective sense of the compression or shrinking of the world plus the subjective feeling as consciousness of the world as a whole. Globalization also includes the following two dimensions:

Economic Dimensions

changes in technology and trading

changes in telecommunications—example, mobile phones, the Internet

reduced economic regulation spreading

effects on international economy

world not truly global; concentrated in N. America, European Union, and Japan

biggest losers—two-thirds of world population

globalization in part an ideology

Culture Dimensions

true global culture needs qualification

technologies encourage localism

national and local resistance to globalization

issue of human mobility and migration

idea of a common history and culture breaking down within a nation

every group is its own historian

with globalization comes fragmentation[9]

In other words, globalization is a controversial issue, but global education usually covers the four major areas shown in Table 7.3. Global education tries to cultivate in young people a perspective of the world that emphasizes the interconnections among cultures, species, and the planet.

Instruction that incorporates a global perspective on peace, environmental problems, international development, and human rights is a challenge. Teachers must make choices on how much harsh reality should be portrayed to children. The main

[9]David Reynolds, *One World Divisible, A Global History Since 1945* (New York: W. W. Norton & Company, 2000), 650–657.

TABLE 7.3 Problem Themes in Global Education

Peace and Security	Environment/Ecological Problems
war, terrorism, etc.	pollution of air and water
	depletion of rain forests, etc.
National/International Development	**Human Rights**
hunger and poverty	refugees, political and religious
population growth, etc.	persecution, etc.

question for all teachers to face is: Should children be shown reality or be shielded from it? Each teacher makes his or her own decision about this question and perhaps there is no single answer, only a balance. Yet from the media children are often aware of the problems.

Human Rights: Refugees and Gender Issues

Let us look at a possible unit on refugees. The United Nations High Commissioner for Refugees has a Web site (www.unhcr.ch) with units and lesson plans for three age groups, 9–11, 12–14, and 15–18, on this topic.

The unit objectives for the "Refugee Children" include knowledge objectives such as to understand the abnormal and trying conditions in which refugee children live and endure and to introduce the idea that people's basic needs are considered human rights. Other objectives are to encourage *empathy* and *respect* for refugee children in the world. The content may be a case history of Jacob, a Sudanese refugee child who fled Sudan without his family and had to walk across thousands of miles of barren land to the safety of a refugee camp in Kenya. Another case study could be Sybella Wilkes, *One Day We Had to Run!* (London, Evans Brothers, 1994). After listening or reading the case studies, students explore in pairs the wants, needs, and basic human rights of children. They can better understand that no one likes or chooses to be a refugee. Being a refugee means more than just being a "foreigner." It means living in exile and often depending on others for basic needs such as food, clothing, and shelter.

This unit could be further developed by reading the rich children's literature about American immigrants. Usually a distinction is made between voluntary and involuntary migrants. Voluntary migrants are those who have willingly left their homelands, usually with expectations of improving their standard of living. There are still groups coming to the United States that meet the definition of refugees—persons who fear being persecuted for reasons of race, religion, nationality, membership in a particular social group, or political opinion, and who are outside of their country.

Children need information and experiences that help them understand their relationship with all children of the planet. The goal in learning about refugees, global hunger, poverty, and ecological disasters is not to cause guilt feelings about the lifestyle possible in the United States. Rather, children need to see how global problems will affect them. It raises the question of what should be done to promote equity and fairness within and among nations. It is not enough to provide children with information about global problems. You must also show them avenues to personal efficacy in relation to these problems as part of the instructional sequence. However, children cannot be expected to solve the worldwide problems of millions of refugees. They may, however, see some connections about the refugee and immigrant experiences that apply to their own communities in terms of stereotypes and prejudice. Young children can make small and meaningful differences in their own schools and communities.

Another example from the United Nation's Web site (www.un.org/Pubs/CyberSchoolBus) appears in the sample lesson plan, "To Be Born a Girl."

SAMPLE LESSON PLAN

TO BE BORN A GIRL

My name is Maya. I was born fourteen years ago in a poor peasant family. There were already many children so when I was born no one was happy. When I was still very little, I learned to help my mother and elder sisters with domestic chores. I swept the floor, washed clothes, and carried water and firewood. Some of my friends played outside but I could not join them.

I was very happy when I was allowed to go to school. I made new friends there and learned to read and write. But when I reached the fourth grade, my parents stopped my education. My father said there was no money to pay the fees. Also, I was needed at home to help my mother and the others. If I were a boy, my parents would have let me complete school. My elder brother finished school and now works in an office in the capital. Two of my younger brothers go to school. Maybe they, too, will finish.

Many activities are suggested after students read this case study.

1. What important right does Maya *not* have?

2. The statistics taken from United Nations' reports and other reports on illiterate adults (two-thirds of whom are women) and on the years of education offered to males and females in certain nations or in the United States. Check the gender and ethnic/racial distribution in the professions such as medicine and law.

3. Bringing the case study to the local school level, survey the class on what students want to be. Are there gender differences?

4. Survey the class anonymously with only a check for gender by asking students how important education is: very important, important, somewhat important, or unimportant. Are there any gender differences?

Environment/Ecological Problems

Global citizenship is a complex, contradictory, and often controversial idea. Many Americans argue that global education activities undermine our national interests. Indeed, this may be the case if we define American interests as different from or antagonistic or superior to those of other countries. Nations, ours included, tend to see resource issues according to their own perspectives. Learning more about our connections with what may happen anywhere on Earth will help us evaluate both the costs and the long-term benefits resulting from seeing ourselves as citizens of Earth.

The ecological principles of balance and relatedness present endless opportunities for value analysis in this era of global citizenship that asks us to focus on the bumper sticker slogan "Think globally; act locally." It is easy for children, and adults, to thrill to the warm, protective sentiments of faraway campaigns to preserve environments and protect species as presented in films and the media. But students also should be aware of the balance between protecting the environment and meeting human needs. For example, valuable forests are being cut down (deforestation) on the justification of meeting human needs. Bringing these feelings to bear on issues closer to home is crucial for helping children to see the complexity and interrelatedness of defending the Earth. Every region is replete with "acting locally" environmental issues; see the following list.

Sampler of Ecological Conflicts

Hazardous waste dump sites versus acquiring attention and funds for removal

Logging economies versus endangered species

Species overpopulation leading to environmental degradation versus animal rights

Ranchers and sheep herders versus survival of predators such as wolves

Fishing industry (overfishing) versus protecting and limiting the resource

Housing development versus protection of green space or wetlands

Domestic animal birth control versus animal and individual owner rights

Species extinction and ozone depletion versus airborne pollutants and pesticide- and herbicide-bearing agricultural water runoff

When teachers involve their students in local environmental issues by organizing learning about these issues through observation, sampling, and other scientific processes, they are exhibiting the most responsible kind of global citizenship education. Long-term teacher and school involvement with a specific site can reap not only the rewards of student enthusiasm and learning but also a school role in community improvement. Global citizenship truly begins at home.

After reviewing this unit, you may feel that there is not enough of a global connection. More of a global emphasis certainly could be given, especially considering the amount of consumer goods that the United States, Western Europe, and Japan consume compared to the rest of the world. Nevertheless, the premise for this unit is that first each community needs to address its own local problems of protecting the environment before embarking on environmental projects outside the community. This unit also indicates that there is often no single solution to a given problem. Using landfills solves one problem but creates others. Incineration reduces volume and weight but, unless there are very stringent air pollution controls, it also creates problems.

WHERE DOES YOUR TRASH OR GARBAGE GO?

Grade Level
Grades 4 to 6; can be modified for other grades

Objectives
1. Students will identify the four main ways garbage (or solid waste, trash) is disposed of in their community.
2. Students will compare the costs and benefits of each of the four ways of getting rid of garbage in their community.
3. Students will be encouraged to be more environmentally responsible about their own family's and community's garbage.

Time and Subject Areas Integrated
Younger students will need more days; also depends on how much science is incorporated into the unit. Social studies, economics, science, and language arts integrated.

Big Questions
1. Why is it necessary to reduce family trash?
2. How can we educate ourselves and others to recycle, reuse, and compost?

Resources
1. Go online for *EPA's Solid Waste Fact Book* Internet Version (www.epa.gov/students/municipal_solid_waste_factbook.htm). You or the students can find a state profile of their own state. It will give information on how solid waste is disposed of in their state: amount landfilled, recycled, and incinerated as well as contact information. You also will need information about your local community's solid waste program.

Suggested Activities
Now and Not So Long Ago Garbage Disposal
1. Ask what garbage is. What are your images of garbage or trash? Draw a picture of garbage. Why does Oscar the Grouch only love trash?
2. What would happen if your garbage was not picked up every week?
3. Ask students if they know what happens when they "throw away" their garbage. Go through the process from their homes, their school, a supermarket, a restaurant, an office building, a construction site, and so on to the disposal site. Make flowcharts or diagrams to illustrate where the garbage goes from the curb or source point. Point out since garbage or trash is considered "unpleasant," it is often hidden from view.
4. The technical term for garbage or trash is *solid waste* or *municipal solid waste*.

5. Have a guest speaker from and/or secure the literature of your local solid waste collector. Gather data on the total amount of solid waste generated in the community in a year. Collect information on the composition of garbage by contributors (households, industry, and so on) and by content. Create graphs to illustrate the process. What are the projections for solid waste for the next five or ten years?

6. Secure bills for the cost of garbage service. Why are costs going up?

7. Using the literature of your local solid waste company, what sorting of solid waste is now required of your family? How many different containers do you have? Why?

8. Discuss what happened to garbage or solid waste long ago. What did pioneer families do? What kinds of things made up their garbage compared to today's family garbage?

9. To better understand what happened to garbage long ago, have students interview an adult, ideally an older adult.

Adult Interview Guide for Long Ago Garbage Disposal

1. Did you ever see leaves in the fall, garbage, or agricultural crops being burned when you were young? Was this a frequent practice?

2. When you were young, did your family's garbage have to be sorted in any way with different containers?

3. When you were young, did you ever visit the local garbage dump? If so, what kind of trash was there?

---

10. Chart the interview data. What is similar and what is different from what is now tossed away? What might explain the changes in garbage disposal?

11. Search the Internet with such Web sites as www.thegateway.org and use the terms *garbage, trash,* and *solid waste* for up-to-date information on this topic.

Source Reduction

1. Do we see all the garbage we use? No, waste is produced in making all the things we buy and consume.

2. Why is it necessary for all to reduce the amount of garbage? Even if families and industries reduce, there are now more families in the United States and six billion people in the world. How is garbage a global problem? How are other nations taking care of their garbage problem?

3. Have students become more aware of the amount of trash each of us throws away each day by filling out the following chart. The average American generates four pounds of trash a day. Every time you throw something away, write down the name of the item and put a check mark in the column that says what kind of material it is made of.

(continued)

WHERE DOES YOUR TRASH OR GARBAGE GO? *(continued)*

My Amount of Trash in One Day

Item	Paper	Yard	Food	Plastic	Metal	Glass	Rubber Leather Textiles

4. Analyze the data from the charts. If you wish, have them guess the weight. Calculate how much waste each student is producing for a day, a month, and a year.
5. Students list for a class bulletin board ways to reduce waste, for example, repair an item, give clothing to a charity instead of throwing it away, having a garage sale, and so on.
6. Students can analyze what goes into their own family garbage cans and containers. What are the largest categories? Why? One-third of our trash is packaging.
7. What are the costs and benefits of source reduction? Make a chart.

Recycling and Composting

1. Discuss with students the steps of recycling: collection, separation, and processing so trash items can be used again.
2. What recycling programs at curbside or at special centers are available for your local area? What happens to old tires? Batteries? Paints? Why do they not want tires, batteries, and paints in a landfill?
3. What is composting? What is its value? Can your class make a compost column, compost bin, or compost pile? Can you visit and interview individuals who are composting?
4. Can you make a worm bin?
5. What are the costs and benefits of recycling and composting?

Waste to Energy Incineration (Combustion)

1. Burning experiment outdoors. With permission of your principal, demonstrate the effect of incineration (burning) of material on weight and volume.
   a. Weigh newspapers and record volume.
   b. Place newspapers in wastebasket.

    c. Ignite newspaper and allow to burn to ash.

    d. Cool completely in the wastepaper basket.

    e. Remove ashes and calculate weight of ashes.

    f. Compare to original weight and volume.

2. What is released by burning? (smoke, ash, and air emissions)
3. Why is pollution control necessary for incinerators?
4. What are the costs and benefits of energy combustion?

Landfills

1. Would you want a sanitary landfill (old name, *garbage dump*) near your home or neighborhood? Role-play where the landfill should be located. Where is the landfill located for your community? If possible, visit the local landfill. What is going into the landfill and how long will it stay there?
2. What improvements have been made in sanitary landfills? Are there laws regulating landfills?
3. What areas are likely to be sites of landfills?
4. What are the costs and benefits of landfills? Make a chart. Why is a landfill presently the most common way to get rid of garbage?

Culminating Activities

1. Students present a program on what they have learned about garbage to another class or their parents.
2. Students create and sign pledge cards listing ways their families can help reduce garbage.
3. As a result of their research, students write a persuasive proposal and give presentations to various government officials on how to mitigate the problem of solid waste.[a]
4. Throughout the year, students should be encouraged to reduce trash.

[a]Some ideas from "Planet Patrol," an educational unit on solid waste solutions by Procter & Gamble, no date.

Those wishing to go more global can definitely use the Internet to connect students with action projects. As one example, students can examine the origins of their clothing and the conditions under which the clothing was produced. Please remember that many of the Web sites represent advocacy groups promoting their own policies and plans, such as saving a rain forest in a tropical nation.

American Forum for Global Education, www.globaled.org

Amnesty International USA, www.amnesty.org/

Children First, www.childrenfirst.org

Hungerweb, www.bron.edu/Departments/World_Hunger_Program

UNICEF, www.unicef.org

World Resources Institute Environment Education Project, www.wri.org/wri/enved

Before inviting guest speakers into our classrooms, another check we as teachers must make is to review our responsibilities toward citizenship education. Are we providing the children with an opportunity to consider data from a variety of opinions about the issue we are studying? Do we ask them to question the opinions and data they hear and gather? We need to explain these responsibilities to guest speakers invited to present their perspective on the problem.

SMALL GROUP WORK	INTEREST LEVEL
7.3	*Do you think your students would find the unit on garbage interesting and motivating? What difference would it make if the community already was doing a lot to reduce, recycle, and protect the environment? Do you think it would appeal more to middle-class students? What units on promoting citizenship education do you think would work best for working-class students?*

■ SUMMARY

To summarize our exploration of citizenship education, we need to recall that it is the major historical goal of public education in our country. In this chapter, we have suggested concrete, direct experiencing of decision making in the classroom and learning about our system of rights and responsibilities are necessary to prepare responsible citizens. Moving out into the school with student councils and then further into the community with community or service learning broadens the citizenship perspective. Finally, global education looks beyond our nation. In global education, we have stressed the dictum of thinking globally and acting locally by examining environmental problems and the like. The key to internalizing the citizen role, for most elementary students, is active, personalized involvement.

■ SUGGESTED READINGS AND WEB SITES ■

Dinwiddie, Sue A. "The Saga of Sally, Sammy and the Red Pen: Facilitating Children's Social Problem Solving." *Young Children* 49 (July 1994): 13–19.
Detailed presentation of social problem solving with young children that, with other articles in same issue, amply illustrates the connection between building a culture of responsibility in school and preparing children for citizenship in an expressive, not repressive, society.

Fine, Esther Sokolov, Ann Lacy, and Joan Baer. *Children as Peacemakers.* Portsmouth, NH: Heinemann, 1995.
Teachers of downtown alternative school in Toronto relate development of peacemaking program that changed tone of the school.

Fountain, Susan. *Education for Development: A Teacher's Resource for Global Learning.* Portsmouth, NH: Heinemann, 1995.
Classroom guidelines for helping students explore global issues—violence, hunger, prejudice, environmental abuses—in a positive, empowering way that links local to global issues.

Girard, Kathryn, and Susan J. Koch. *Conflict Resolution in the Schools: A Manual for Educators.* San Francisco, CA: Jossey-Bass Publishers, 1996.
Book sponsored by the National Institute for Dispute Resolution and the former National Association for Mediation in Education gives advice to educators planning conflict resolution programs in their schools.

Heller, Carol, and Joseph A. Hawkins. "Teaching Tolerance: Notes from the Front Line." *Teachers College Record* 95, no. 3 (Spring 1994): 337–368.

Thorough and inspiring contextualization of citizenship goals through review of diverse educational programs that build bridges toward racial and ethnic unity by appreciating diversity and seeing similarity.

Isaac, Katherine. *Civics for Democracy: A Journey for Teachers and Students.* Minneapolis: Free Spirit Publishing, 1993.

Book-length discussion of necessity for linking goals of citizenship development with action in larger community, recounting broad range of actual school-based programs.

Lewis, Barbara A. *Kids with Courage: True Stories about Young People Making a Difference.* Minneapolis: Free Spirit Publishing, 1992.

Stimulating annotation of citizenship efforts that may begin in school but extend far beyond and return to change student lives and visions.

Miller, F. Gene, and Michael G. Jacobson. "Teaching for Global Mindedness." *Social Education* (March–April 1994): 4–6.

Argues that a global view is an extension of multicultural perspectives.

National Council for the Social Studies. *Mission Statement.* Washington, 1992.

Official statement by content area professional organization of centrality of citizenship to this subject and totality of schooling.

Nelson, Jane, Lynn Lott, H. Stephen Glenn. *Positive Discipline in the Classroom.* Rocklin, CA: Prima Publishing, 1993.

Details year-long program for positive approach based on class meetings and cooperative problem solving.

Parker, Walter C. "Assessing Citizenship." *Educational Leadership* 48 (November 1990): 17–22.

Argues centrality of citizenship in curriculum and presents ways to organize for assessing citizenship.

Web Sites

The American Promise
www.americanpromise.com/home.html

Organization endorsed by NCSS promoting civic education.

The Center for Civic Education
www.civiced.org

Civics standards, curriculum guides, and programs.

State and government information
www.statelocal.gov

U.S. Congress
thomas.loc.gov

U.S. House of Representatives
www.house.gov

White House
www.whitehouse.gov

Chapter 8

Social Studies and Diversity

As a result of reading this chapter, you should have a broad view of the ways that schools influence children's learning of culture and how we can pursue social studies goals as we organize learning about cultural diversity learning. **Multicultural** or **diversity education** are the terms most frequently used to refer to this aspect of social studies. Part of what these terms discuss brings a new emphasis to social studies. Part does not. Social studies tradition includes learning about cultures and democratic values. Insights from multicultural and diversity education broaden the more traditional social studies scope of learning about cultures and citizenship; this expanded scope includes conscious and positive learning of how to relate to and get along with individuals and groups of differing backgrounds while becoming more aware of the strengths to be recognized in one's own abilities, orientation, and heritage. Specific objectives for the chapter are for you to be able to describe how culture is learned in three spheres of schooling and to suggest various strategies for creating positive classroom cultures, for learning about cultures, and for resolving conflicts in a classroom. To help you toward these objectives, the chapter is organized in four sections.

- Describing Learning About Diversity

- Classroom Organization and Learning About Diversity

- Classroom Instruction About Diversity

- Classroom Intergroup Problem Solving

■ DESCRIBING LEARNING ABOUT DIVERSITY

Learning about diversity as part of the social studies can be seen from a variety of perspectives. To get a sense of these perspectives and to discover which ones you share, respond to these multiple-choice items.

SMALL GROUP WORK	DEALING WITH DIVERSITY ISSUES IN THE CLASSROOM
8.1	*With others in your group, take turns sharing your responses to these multiple-choice questions and the text commentary at the end of this section. Do you have personal experiences to share that these questions remind you of? What are your ideas about the teacher's role and responsibility for this aspect of schooling?*

1. *What is the most significant goal children can gain from learning about their own culture and other cultures?*
   a. *Knowledge about how peoples of various cultures live and what they value*
   b. *Appreciation for the diversity of peoples and their ways of life*
   c. *Ability to accept people from different ways of life or of differing appearances*
   d. *Ability to communicate and work together with others toward common goals*

2. *What is the best strategy for improving the ability of diverse children to live together in a positive way?*
   a. *Present lessons about differing religious, gender, ethnic, and ability groups*
   b. *Celebrate holidays of significant ethnic and racial groups*
   c. *Structure classroom tasks so that children must learn by working together*

3. *What is the best strategy for resolving differences between groups in the classroom?*
   a. *Prohibit discussion about these clashes in the class*
   b. *Read stories about conflicts that have "happy endings"*
   c. *Discuss racism, stereotyping, and scapegoating with the class*
   d. *Invite adult members of different groups to the class to present their points of view*
   e. *Role-play conflict situations that lead children to practice resolution*

Did you have difficulty choosing one best answer? Clearly, each item has more than one acceptable answer. Part of the difficulty you experience in this forced-choice exercise may be due to your uncertainty about the term **learning about diversity,** which has also been called **culture learning.** You may not be accustomed to the definition we use.

In addition, teachers vary in how "multicultural" an educator they are prepared to be. How much, what kind, for whom, and at what age differ among teachers. There may be levels of diversity starting with the beginning level of awareness of needs to be addressed concentrating on the "Five F's" of teaching about diversity: food, fashion, fiestas, folklore, and famous people. The next stage is moving to a commitment to increasing a wider use of multicultural materials and, finally, the idea that diversity is crucial in the education of students.

From our perspective, culture learning occurs at every grade level in two ways. First is instruction. Traditionally, we have concerned ourselves with culture and culture learning as content we learn. From the academic discipline of anthropology, social studies programs have incorporated facts and generalizations about peoples of various times and places as significant instructional information for transmitting the concept of culture. For example, children learn that Chinese cultures exist in many locations outside the People's Republic of China and that family loyalty is one of the most important elements in understanding Chinese ways of being.

Immersion is the second way that children learn culture. Children absorb unconsciously what will become their culture through the close contacts of their daily living. They may learn that their school values quiet behavior whereas their family values lots of verbal communication. They may have conflicting feelings about associating with some individuals and groups in school whose characteristics are not held in high esteem by their home culture. Culture learning, both positive and negative, occurs in schools as naturally as breathing. Anthropologists call this learning **acculturation** when a child is acquiring the culture of parents. They distinguish acculturation from culture learning known as **assimilation,** when an individual, usually from a cultural minority, assumes attitudes and practices perceived by the larger society as more powerful than those of the individual's original culture. Both processes are part of culture learning. Assimilating the official curriculum of the school and becoming acculturated to the ways and rules of daily living there as well as at home are both types of culture learning.

From our perspective, it is important to remember that there are many kinds of home life. Furthermore, there is not one superior culture, but many, often competing ones, each with its own values and history. And, furthermore, home life does not always account for individual differences in ability or sexual orientation. Both kinds of culture learning—becoming culturally knowledgeable with positive self-esteem and developing the ability to get along with "different" others—are essential and integral to social studies. We need to plan how to honor both ways of culture learning—to keep the virtues of our social studies tradition of transmitting knowledge about culture and cultures, and to add to this tradition a consideration of the way we live together in classrooms. These can be among the most powerful culture learning experiences a child has.

■ CLASSROOM ORGANIZATION AND LEARNING ABOUT DIVERSITY

You can plan for learning about diversity by examining the following three aspects of classroom life: *motivation*—the way you introduce, organize, and reward academic performance in your classrooms; *instruction*—the content you offer about the ways of life of groups of people; and *problem solving*—the ways in which interpersonal and intergroup problems are observed, discussed, and resolved.

Motivation and Classroom Organization

Classroom interaction teaches children more than the content of lesson plans. Children learn from the way a class is organized to get work done, from the way the teacher calls on students, and from the way students are seated and prompted to move about the classroom.

Unfortunately, what they learn from these aspects of classroom life may not be what the teacher intends. In many classrooms, boys tend to dominate the classroom discourse over girls. Students from certain racial/ethnic backgrounds may receive less attention from their teachers. Ideally, schools should treat students with respect and dignity regardless of gender, race, ethnicity, socioeconomic background, or sexual orientation.

Students may learn that being quiet and compliant earns them more teacher approval than when they ask uncalled-for questions or want to discuss fairness issues.

They may learn that to get ahead in school they must behave like the majority community, assuming its language and culture while repressing or denying their own. This kind of assimilation is known as learning the hidden curriculum. The culture of the classroom is the hidden curriculum. If the classroom culture serves to promote one group while ignoring others, the hidden curriculum amounts to institutionalized racism and sexism contradicting the formal, pro-justice curriculum of social studies. To use the power of the hidden curriculum in a way that is beneficial to all students, teachers must examine their assumptions about how to help children learn in positive ways.

Comparing our beliefs to what actually happens in classrooms is one way to uncover this curriculum. Teachers and future teachers agree that their basic goals are to guide children to realize their potentialities and to learn to live and work with others in a rewarding way. Yet the organization and management of many classrooms often denies the second goal. We use individual rewards for learning and group rewards for behaving. We give stars to individuals who complete work successfully and top grades only to those who do better than others. The message children may get from this situation is that learning and working hard are not related, that children who do not shine academically have reduced value. School routines are criticized as granting almost exclusive recognition and value to children who excel at individual academic achievement. In classroom settings with various groups represented, the children of "less value" are often members of social or economic minority groups that have less status in the outside community. If the reward systems of our school and classroom reinforce the divisions and inequities of the adult society, we do not help children attain the basic goals of realizing their individual potential as they learn to work together.

There is new research on what can be accomplished in classrooms toward the goal of educating children to relate positively to all people and groups and to improve their own academic performance. More students can develop a positive relationship with learning if teachers alter the ways learning is organized. Researchers concerned with intergroup relations and minority-group achievement have begun to verify that the way we structure expectations in the classroom can have a positive effect on intergroup relations and achievement. Basing their procedures on Gordon Allport's earlier theory that "prejudice may be reduced by equal-status contacts between majority and minority groups in pursuit of common goals," researchers organized nonsuperficial, noncompetitive, equal-status contact in classrooms.[1] These structures are known as cooperative learning groups, as described in Chapter 3.

ON YOUR OWN	TERMINOLOGY REVIEW AND CONTEXTUALIZATION
8.1	*The following glossary indicates the crucial yet elusive nature of preparing for culture learning in the classroom. There is societal disagreement about the relationship of these terms to instruction in schools. You will develop your own unique perspective about how these concepts relate to learning and instruction as you work with children. Our purpose here is simply to alert you to the pervasiveness and complexity of the issues of culture learning.*

[1]Gordon Allport, *The Nature of Prejudice* (Reading, MA: Addison-Wesley, 1954).

Review the terms in the box. Do they have specialized meanings to you? Do you disagree with these definitions? Can you give examples of each term? Note any additional terms that you believe should be included in a glossary about culture learning and discuss them with your group.

Afrocentrism: values and perspectives flowing from the continent of Africa, typically used as guides for organizing curriculum for African Americans.

assimilation: person of one culture merging his or her ways of living, or culture, into another, usually dominant culture.

bias: acts or attitudes that favor an individual or group over others.

bigotry: acts of intolerance based on an individual's belief in a particular creed or practice or opinion.

culture: way of life and belief of a group passed from one generation to the next.

Culture: examples of "high," or "capital C," art and literature esteemed by "educated" individuals of a shared culture.

discrimination: favoring or rejecting an individual because of his or her group identification.

diversity: typically used in contexts that seek to value individuals and groups for their uniqueness; those holding this view argue that not all need to be alike in order to form a viable social group.

empowerment pedagogy: instructional strategies that recognize and capitalize on or make a strength of minority-group cultures that come from differences in language, ethnicity, disability, sexual orientation, gender, or religion.

ethnic group: group that shares a distinctive culture for racial, religious, or historical reasons.

ethnic studies: units or courses that present the history, culture, and contemporary issues of an ethnic group.

ethnocentrism: belief that one's group or culture is inherently superior, leading to contempt for other groups or cultures.

Eurocentric: values and perspectives flowing from the European point of view, such as using the westward movement to present the settlement of North America, or Columbus's voyage to present the discovery of America.

institutionalized racism: accepted, often unquestioned, organizational practices or regulations that function as discriminatory norms against individuals with traditionally ostracized social characteristics.

multicultural education: multiperspective knowledge and processes of positive interaction between individuals of different groups that lead them to value their similarities and honor their differences.

nationalism: ideas that seek to bind individuals to an identity with a political institution based on symbols, myth, shared history, and usually a geographical territory.

pluralistic society: society composed of multiple ethnic and cultural groups.

politically correct: marked by or adhering to a typically progressive ideology on issues involving especially race, gender, sexual affinity, or ecology.

popular culture: activities and beliefs of people that may not be recognized by political or cultural authorities as "the" best or most significant representation of that culture. Popular music as of less value than classical music would be an example.

prejudice: unfavorable feeling about members of a group formed without knowing individuals of the group.

racism: attitudes, actions, or institutional practices based on the assumption that certain people have the right to have power over others solely because of their skin color or ethnic origins.

scapegoat: a person who is blamed and made to suffer for acts of the group to which he or she belongs or is seen to belong.

sexism: discriminatory beliefs and behaviors based on one's gender, especially discrimination against females.

sexual orientation: gender(s) to which an individual feels attraction.

stereotype: unchanging idea about a group that defines members of that group without regard to their uniqueness as individuals.

whiteness: awareness of the privileges of being white.

Cooperative learning can apparently improve intergroup relations when it is used in diverse classroom groups. Furthermore, there is evidence that when cooperative learning is used, students' average academic achievement improves also. Although this strategy can be employed productively with any school subject, cooperative learning can have special relevance for the social studies. The major purpose of the social studies is to help children become active, critically thinking citizens capable of working together toward their common welfare, and cooperative learning offers a positive approach to constructing a cultural milieu crucial to this process.

Cooperative learning strategies create a classroom culture based on mutual assistance, equality among group members, and role diversity in learning tasks. In other words, this process itself teaches one of the social studies' major goals—learning to live positively with others. But the content of cultures we teach about is important and requires our careful thought. How shall we organize what we want children to learn about a culture?

■ CLASSROOM INSTRUCTION ABOUT DIVERSITY

When we prepare to study a culture that may be foreign to us, we have sensitive decisions to make. Shall the traditional aspects of the culture be highlighted? Shall the aspects of a culture that are presented to tourists by representatives of that culture be questioned? When we focus on American immigrant cultures, shall we present the memories of the places of origin as immigrants prefer to recall them, or shall we examine a more objective contemporary version of the culture? Shall the culture study be coordinated with a cultural celebration of holidays as we know them? Does the historical background of the group in the United States matter? Should groups be studied separately?

To address some of these questions, put yourself in the shoes of a parent whose culture the school plans to study. Would a Mexican American parent, for example, want her children and other children to know about Cinco de Mayo? Hanukkah? St. Valentine's Day? The Day of the Dead? Would that same parent prefer that children experience some of the food, music, and folk arts and crafts of her culture? What would that parent want us to know? For what purpose would that parent want to have her culture studied in the classroom?

Possibly a Mexican American parent would want us to include study of her culture as an integral part of the curriculum so that her children might feel their group is valued as a regular component of the school and society. Possibly not. This particular parent may be upset with our labeling her as a Mexican American. We have defined her as Mexican American, a one-dimensional category, when in fact, she may also be divorced, a medical doctor, and a fifth-generation American whose ancestors had been ranchers in New Mexico long before it became part of the United States. Any one of these facets of her identity might be far more significant to her than her ethnic background. Obviously, we cannot know how all parents feel about the elements of their own identities they wish to have included in the classroom curriculum. What we can do is acknowledge an individual's preference about how he or she wishes to be identified. And always remember that most individuals prefer not to be labeled according to only one aspect of their background.

Each of us is culturally multifaceted. Elements of our culture are related to who we are sexually, how old we are, and our religious background. The interaction and conflict between these various facets, or microcultures, of our lives continually redefine and reshape our cultural identities. We also, to one degree or another, are shaped by and share in the national culture. Acknowledging our own many-layered reality should guide us away from presenting material that prompts children to draw stereotypic conclusions about people and groups they study. Children need to learn about themselves and others as complex, changing cultural beings. They need to learn that although the larger society may categorize individuals as part of a group, people in any group differ widely from each other.

The process of cultural becoming begins with self-naming. Exploring our own names invites us to confront openly what labels mean. At the beginning of each school year, teachers need to assist students in their continuous process of self-representation. Simply asking each child to tell the name he or she wishes to be called assists this process. At every age, students appreciate the self-affirming opportunity activities focused on finding out more about the names associated with them offer. The research-sharing starters in the sample activity "Exploring Our Names" can serve the dual purposes of helping students get acquainted with one another and of affirming students' home culture in any classroom.

SAMPLE ACTIVITIES

EXPLORING OUR NAMES

1. Request that students do research at home asking parents to explain why students' first and middle names were chosen. Draw a picture that incorporates student names and tells the story of how they were named for a class display.
2. Does student's first name have another meaning? What does the name mean in other languages? Make a class roll of names and definitions and names and their equivalents in other languages.
3. What do your students' last names mean? What part of the world do they come from? Make a class name dictionary and atlas.
4. How do different groups order names and pass them along? (Order examples: Hispanic: given name, father's last name, mother's last name; Chinese: surname, given names; Russian: given name, patronymic, surname.)
5. Do any students prefer a nickname? What does it mean?
6. Ask students to use one of these reference books to find something to share about their names:

   Dunking, Leslie. *The Guinness Book of Names.* Enfield, Middlesex, England: Guinness Superlatives, 1984.

   Hook, N. J. *The Book of Names: A Celebration of Mainly American Names, People, Places, Things.* New York: Franklin Watts, 1983.

   ———. *Family Names: The Origin, Meaning, Mutations, and History of More than 2000 American Names.* New York: Macmillan, 1982.

   Meltzer, Milton. *A Book About Names.* New York: Thomas Y. Crowell, 1984.

Beyond exploring their own names, middle-grade children need guided experiences in name-calling. The typical admonition "We don't use names that hurt" needs to be turned inside out. Rather than prohibiting name-calling with no discussion, many brave teachers have discovered that a good technique for defusing the explosiveness and pervasiveness of name-calling is to study the negative slang words students are using that year (see the sample lesson plan "Confronting Name-Calling: Names We Call"). In one class, even after all the sensitizing about name-calling, a student suggested that the class develop a book based on their experience and call it *Our Black Book of Names*. Of course, the teacher then had to ask the students to think critically about why this list would be called "black." A precocious student commented, "Using *black* is not politically correct!" Taken by surprise but excited by the teachable moment, the teacher challenged the class to further investigate the ways they heard words used to classify or stereotype individuals and groups before they started their book. In two more sessions of sharing, this class developed their own ideas about what being politically correct was all about and titled their book *Hurting Names*. Two caveats are in order for teachers as they use this strategy: Do not censor names students contribute. Prepare the class for this session by having the students recall how they act when they discuss topics that can hurt them or their friends.

SAMPLE LESSON PLAN

CONFRONTING NAME-CALLING: NAMES WE CALL

Objectives

1. Students define name-calling and its effects on the name-caller and the person named.
2. Students bring examples of name-calling and stereotyping to discuss in class.

Time

One to two 40-minute sessions.

Materials

Paper bag, slips of paper, chalkboard, or chart paper.

Procedure

1. Tell students they are going to have a real-life vocabulary lesson. Ask them if there are names they know about that they feel should not be used in the classroom. Why do we censor these names? Why do people use these names sometimes? "Let's act like linguists and see whether we can uncover the semantics and attraction of names we call each other." Ask students to write on slips of paper names they use or hear used that refer to groups of people.
2. Collect the anonymous slips in a box or paper bag.
3. Draw a slip and write its contents on the chalkboard, pronounce it, and ask the class to volunteer a definition.
4. For each, ask students to volunteer their thoughts about how a person feels when called by this name.

Evaluation

1. After exhausting the slips of paper ask, "What have we learned about name-calling?"
2. Conclude by asking for individuals to take turns coming up and erasing a name they wish they would never have to hear.

Providing a forum in which they can discuss their feelings is especially meaningful to students of mixed heritage. Often they need to articulate the cross-pressures they feel about being categorized into any one of their antecedent groupings. Exploration of these experiences is a real-life study of the changing sociology of groups.

ON YOUR OWN	**SOCIAL CLIMATE OF CLASSROOMS**
8.2	Teaching Tolerance *magazine surveyed teachers asking the following questions. How often do you hear these types of comments from your students?* *Racist* *Sexist* *Anti–gay/lesbian* *Biased against a religion*

The same question was asked, "Have you heard these types of comments from your colleagues in the past year?" Based on your experience, how would you answer these two questions? For students nationwide, the highest category of name-calling was sexist followed by homophobic comments, racist, and the lowest was religious groups.

You may want to tackle the problem of prejudice with a unit. Examine the unit "Understanding Prejudice."

SAMPLE UNIT PLAN

UNDERSTANDING PREJUDICE

The following excerpts are from a unit developed by the San Mateo, California, Elementary School District. The unit emphasizes the affective (emotional) domain. It is designed for the sixth grade and is intended to last almost four weeks. Notice the difficulties in writing objectives in the affective domain.

Unit Goal
The students will demonstrate an acceptance of human differences while engaged in activities in the classroom and in other situations.

Specific Unit Objectives for Students:
Define prejudice and give examples.
Distinguish between dislike and prejudice.
Recognize stereotyping, including male and female roles.
Recognize prejudgment against persons with disabilities, either physical or mental.
Understand the physical differences of ethnic minorities.
Describe differences related to socioeconomic, religious, and emotional factors.

Lesson: The Stranger
Objective: Students will define prejudice and give examples of it.

Procedure: Ask a visitor to come to the room dressed entirely in paper bags. The visitor comes in and sits down with no introduction or other attention directed toward him or her. After the visitor has spent about fifteen minutes in the room, he or she leaves and a discussion follows.

Possible questions: What did you think about the stranger when he or she first came into the room? Who can tell us about the stranger? (Record answers since they may bring out fears and stereotypes.) How did you feel with a stranger in the room? Would someone tell us about a time when you were a stranger in a group of new people? How did you feel? What did you think of the other people? Why? How do you react to words such as *the homeless* and words describing other groups?

(continued)

UNDERSTANDING PREJUDICE (continued)

Lesson: Stereotyping

Objective: Students will be able to give an example of stereotyping.

Procedure: Review the meaning of prejudice. Ask the students how they think children learn prejudice. Then do the following:

Instruct the students to close their eyes and imagine a Native American. Have them draw their idea on paper. Show some of the pictures to the class. Next show them some pictures of Native Americans without feathers, war paint, and so on. Ask them where they learned about Native Americans.

Discuss with the students how they might expect a typical person of another race, nationality, and so on to look. Discuss why they might expect these things because of stereotypes. Ask if stereotypes are good to have. Ask if stereotypes can make us treat people unfairly.

Lesson: Stereotyped Attitudes

Objective: Students will recognize and give examples of stereotyping attitudes.

Procedure: Discuss with the class the opinion of some people that most children are terrible. Have them give examples of things they have heard people say about their age group.

Ask the students what they think about these things. Are they fair? Why? Why do some people feel that way? Do the children have reason to be upset?

Point out that ideas are formed by our experiences, but we should try not to group all people by the actions of a few. Ask students to write a description of a teacher. When they have finished, read the descriptions and explain that all teachers are not exactly alike simply because they are teachers.

ON YOUR OWN	MORE UNIT EVALUATION
8.3	*What are the strengths of the sample unit plan "Understanding Prejudice"? From the lessons provided, do you see any weaknesses in this unit? What skills might a teacher need to make this unit work properly?*

Learning from Each Other

Each school year brings a new cultural configuration to many of our classrooms. Informal culture learning can be promoted if we take advantage of the cultures of children in our classrooms throughout the school year. Finding out who we are and

SAMPLE ACTIVITIES

DEVELOPING MULTIPLE PERSPECTIVES

1. Conduct research about the names groups give themselves and what they mean. Starter examples: Navaho—*Dineh*, Cheyenne—*Tsistsista*, Salish—*Sle'lign*; most Native American self-names mean "the humans," "the people."

2. Select any historic event—the beginning of a town, building of an interstate highway, development of a suburban mall—and have students decide which of these names apply to people of different groups involved in the situation: *native, indigenous, nomad, displaced refugee, pioneer, colonist, squatter, homeless, exiled, immigrant, legal alien, illegal alien, migrant.* Discuss how this exercise changes students' ideas about the past and history.

3. Consider what the act of naming a place means. Find meanings and/or linguistic origins of local names of streets, neighborhoods, towns, counties, rivers, mountains, and swamps. What do these names tell about the history of a place? Have the names changed? What did the name change mean?

4. Local history projects need not be confined to a particular grade level. Pursuing local history inevitably leads to uncovering multicultural roots. Good source books for project and process ideas include the following:
   Cooper, Kay. *Who Put the Cannon on the Courthouse Square?* New York: Walker, 1985.
   Jungreis, Abigail. *Know Your Hometown History: Projects and Activities.* New York: Franklin Watts, 1992.
   Wertzman, Davis. *My Backyard History Book.* Boston: Little, Brown, 1975.
   Westridge Young Writers Workshop. *Kids Explore America's Hispanic Heritage.* Santa Fe, NM: John Muir Publications, 1992.

where we come from serves to instruct us about others as well as make us feel valued for who we are. Promoting the children's exploration of who they are does not directly address the "learning-about-culture" issue; but by valuing individual children for who they are, we hope the self-esteem messages children internalize are "I am worthy and welcome," "My classmates are like me in many ways," "My classmates like me," "My classmates are different from me and that's interesting," "I have something from home that is worth teaching my friends about."

Kim Anh Vu is a social studies teacher at Steinbeck Middle School, an urban magnet school in San Jose, California, that has many limited-English-speaking students of many nationalities. She devised a multicultural unit that engaged every student in culture teaching and learning. Her objective was that all students should experience teaching elements of their own culture and learning those of another. To begin the unit, Ms. Vu gave each student a unit overview handout (see the sample unit plan "Unit Overview of Cross-Cultural Teaching/Learning").

SAMPLE UNIT PLAN

UNIT OVERVIEW OF CROSS-CULTURAL TEACHING/LEARNING

Student Guide for "Culture Vulture Club" Membership

Over the next two weeks you and your partner will be given some time during each period to work together on becoming eligible for the Culture Vulture Club. You will each be tested orally by an examiner of your partner's choice on your performance of the following tasks. Partners are expected to earn perfect scores and will be awarded Culture Vulture memberships at the Cultural Exchange Evening we will hold on October 15, our Back to School Night for parents. Teach your partner how to do these things:

1. Say and write his or her name, or a name similar to it, in your language and script.
2. Greet properly a friend, a parent, a teacher, a grandparent, a new person in your language.
3. Thank someone for a favor in your language.
4. Describe the right foods for various times during the day.
5. Tell how to prepare a simple dish using proper ingredient names.
6. Write an invitation for your parent(s) to attend the Culture Exchange Evening.

The plan involved pairing each student with a culturally different partner based on the students' dominant home language. The tasks each pair had to perform were apparently simple. As students became involved in the tasks they discovered that things may not be as simple as they look. They also learned (especially the only English-speaking American partners of the learning pairs) to respect the knowledge their partners had, which at first had not seemed to be an asset. Parents attending the exchange evening were amazed and touched at what their children had learned and what they had taught a "foreigner." Most of all, students felt bonded to each other and to this teacher, who had honored their cultures and languages in this manner.

Children of single-parent or blended families, or families in varied relationships with immigration and naturalization laws and in various phases of the assimilation process, often make up the majority of our classes. Classrooms are populated with children of families with same-gender partners, children in foster care, and children from families defined as dysfunctional by outsiders. Assignments requiring children to research their family connections need to be presented to parents in a nonthreatening, flexible manner. The last thing we want from a school assignment is to have it create dissension at home, insecurity, or even shame for the child. We need to inform parents and caretakers about forthcoming assignments that might involve family sensitivities and ask that they alert us if there are activities that might be uncomfortable for their child.

SAMPLE ACTIVITIES

PROMOTING SELF-ESTEEM AND
DIVERSITY AWARENESS

Primary Grades

Profile of the Week: Post paper silhouette or photo of child with "Things I like about . . . " comments from classmates about spotlighted child. You can collect and write statements during a sharing time.

The Way We Were: Put up baby pictures of class members, with birth information, favorite toy, and first words.

Our Gang: Display current Polaroid photos of children with name and favorite things such as color, food, activity.

Our Gang Variation/Extension: Number photos and have children draw a number. They write "What I like about . . . " sentences to display under the picture they wrote about.

Culture Cooking: Collect simple culture-related recipes and schedule parent to assist classroom-cooking session on monthly basis. Have parent describe ingredients and where to get them. Compile a class cookbook.

Body Prints: Have children trace each other on butcher paper. Outlines are colored by each child, cut out, and displayed in classroom. Discuss how we are alike and different.

Self-Portraits: Have children make and sign crayon drawings or tempera paintings of themselves. Display the drawings.

Intermediate Grades

American Rainbows: Make a bulletin board featuring a rainbow with seven colors. Write "food," "homes," "religions," "families," "styles," "languages," "appearances" on different colors. Have students collect or draw pictures that illustrate diversity and place them on the appropriate rainbow color.

We're Here: On a world map, connect student names or pictures to place of birth.

What's in a Name?: Put up a research bulletin board with each student telling what she or he discovered about her or his first name—why parent chose it, its meaning, origin.

Book of Origins: Have students do individual research on family that can include stories starting with grandparents' detailing where they lived and what they did, illustrated with time line and map of origins.

Our Résumés: Have students identify their favorite things, abilities or talents, and future goals. Collect these into a class book.

SMALL GROUP WORK	WHAT WOULD YOU DO?
8.2	*Ms. Mercer, a white woman in her thirties, taps on the classroom door and introduces herself, asking permission to give her daughter Julie the lunch she forgot. Julie is a curly-haired, black child. From the doorway you announce, "Julie, your mother is here to talk with you." Upon seeing Ms. Mercer, Brad calls out to Julie, "Julie, are you adopted?"* *Discuss how you would respond to this situation. What are the issues for Julie? For Ms. Mercer? For the class? Share your solutions with your classmates. How does this episode relate to teaching about diversity?*

Learning from the Community

Other sources of learning about cultures are parents and grandparents, sources we often hesitate to tap. We may feel that because of language barriers or social inhibitions, some parents would not come to our classrooms to share their cultures. Breaking down these inhibitions might be easier if we gave choices of times and tasks for parents and other relatives to come to the class to share. The sharing can be simple and brief. It can be a picture, religious object, game, song, story, newspaper. Accept anything and offer suggestions if a parent does not know what he or she has to share. The payoff of parent presentations is multiple. Parent and child feel valued and included. Other children begin to see similarities between their ways and those of their classmates. Having parents in the classroom provides face-to-face contact between parents and children from different groups. We know that this kind of contact reduces fear of the unknown for all involved.

Basic Goals for Primary Grades Instruction in Diversity

1. There are many kinds of families.
2. All kinds of people live in our community.
3. There are some ways in which we are alike.
4. There are some ways in which we are different.
5. We work together in our community.

Excursions into the community, such as field trips and walking tours, can also be used to highlight learning about local cultural or ethnic groups. As the children study their community, they should give attention to the stores, restaurants, theaters, churches, cemeteries, and clubs that are ethnically or culturally identified.

Often local ethnic organizations are willing to send a representative to classes to tell children about their group and share some of its local history. Children can get more from these visits if they discuss why the visitor is coming before the day of the visit. They should list the questions they would like to ask and decide how they will make the visitor feel at home in the classroom. Following the visit is a fine occasion for the practice of thank-you note writing and the further study of group issues that the visitor initiated.

SMALL GROUP WORK	
8.3	

MATCHING ACTIVITIES TO BASIC IDEAS

Categorize the activities in the following list according to the basic goals of diversity from the five listed previously. Then develop two more activities for each goal and share with a colleague or your class. When you have finished, you will have a good beginning for integrating the affirmation of cultural diversity in your social studies program.

_____ *Make a class book of individual pictures and stories of people in activities of different cultural heritages.*

_____ *Celebrate holidays honored by various cultures.*

_____ *Gather pictures of all kinds of families from different cultural groups. Ask children to find a family with a grandmother, two brothers, and so on.*

_____ *Talk about what children do when they are with their families. Make a chart story about the discussion.*

_____ *Take walks or trips to see community workers on the job; include a variety of ethnic, racial, and gender groups in your selection.*

_____ *Have children categorize pictures of people according to basic activities of eating, working, playing, worshiping, and homemaking.*

_____ *Share a book with children that shows a child cooking, making music, celebrating a holiday, carrying out a daily routine, or communicating in a culturally identifiable way. Ask students to point out how the activity is different from and the same as the way they would do that activity.*

When teachers take their classes to a culturally related community celebration such as Chinese New Year, Greek Festival Days, Japanese Obon, or an Indian Pow-wow, they need to secure the assistance of a member of the group whose celebration is being visited. This person should serve as a cultural interpreter. Children should learn what the costumes, foods, music, and dances represent. They should discover how that group came to the community and learn something of the local history of the group. They should find out what activities the group organizes to teach its children their traditions. Furthermore, the students should discuss why the group chooses to keep these traditions and whether the traditions are the same here as they are in the group's country or region of origin.

The excursion should be followed by a review and discussion of the event visited. Further interviews with the cultural interpreter may be needed to answer the questions children have about what they saw and experienced. Individual pictures or stories or newspaperlike accounts of the experience are appropriate ways for children to integrate the event into their experience.

Incorporating the language and culture of students in our schools tends to empower students. Teachers need to see their roles as adding a second language and culture to a student's repertoire rather than subtracting the primary language and culture. Additional ways that we can promote a child's pride and proficiency in a primary culture include ideas extending beyond our individual classroom to the entire school:

1. Provide signs in the main office that welcome and inform people in their own languages.
2. Encourage students to use their primary language in school in such settings as cooperative groups, assemblies, and other functions; let them use the language in some writing assignments.
3. Recruit people who can tutor students in their primary languages.
4. Create units of work that incorporate other languages in addition to the primary school language.
5. Acquire books and reading materials written in various students' primary languages for classroom and school libraries.[2]

Some of us come from regions and communities that are not currently nourished by the arrival of new groups or immigrants. Unless we have personal contact with someone of contrasting ways or appearance, we may grow up thinking of ourselves as not having a distinct culture. We say, "Oh, I'm just an American," or "I'm so mixed that I don't claim any ethnic group," or more sadly and erroneously, "I don't have a culture!" Our task as teachers in such settings is to help every child uncover the unacknowledged and taken-for-granted ways in which he or she is a cultural representative. All the strategies for self-naming and naming others that were discussed earlier are viable in communities that identify themselves as mainstream American. In addition, these students need to explore their own ideas about what they do and believe that makes them American. Some topics to pursue are listed in the sample activity " 'Being American' Bulletin Boards." It is probable during the course of this kind of exploration that every student will discover group connections that he or she can prize; students also should be able to identify some of the many ways we express our Americanness. Of course, the suggestions listed are even more essential to classes populated with newer Americans. Participating in class activities that affirm multiple ethnic, racial, or linguistic backgrounds helps many students feel that they belong to the larger society. Our goal is to find a balance between honoring distinctiveness and prizing what is shared and common.

[2]Adapted from New Zealand Department of Education, *New Voices: Second Language Learning and Teaching: A Handbook for Primary Teachers* (Wellington: Department of Education, 1988).

SAMPLE ACTIVITIES

"BEING AMERICAN" BULLETIN BOARDS

1. Collect pictures for an "American Culture" that can be categorized into sections on food, clothes, homes, shopping, churches, government, schools, entertainment, and transportation.
2. "America Keeps and America Lends and Sells" can serve as a theme for reconfiguring any of the cultural categories—food, music, architecture, words—used locally that have come from or gone to another culture. Use a world map and different-colored labels to identify "keeping" from "exporting." Food examples include pizza, taco, gyro for "keeping" and hot dog, Coca-Cola, cookie for "exporting." "Keeping" architectural examples include pillars, Romanesque circles within arches, kiosks, and for "exporting" tepee, glass and steel, freeway; "keeping" words—*schlepp, ciao,* and *cheri*—are legion, as are "exports" such as *jazz, jeans, basketball,* and *weekend.*
3. Divide an American map into regions—New England, Midwest, East Coast, Southeast, and so on. Periodically change the focus for the regions using natural resources, common foods, expressions, ethnic composition of population, favorite sports, and events. Have the students collect pictures that illustrate each focus and locate and compare geographic regions.
4. Display an American map labeled "American Name-Calling" that locates state nicknames, regional nicknames, city nicknames, different names for the same foods, favorite expressions, or greetings.

Learning About Cultures from Secondary Sources

Learning about a culture from books and films or other materials is like learning another language from a textbook and tapes. Being where the language is spoken makes all the difference, just as firsthand contact is the best way to learn culture and learn about culture. Because we are not usually able to take our students to live with other people, we are forced to rely on books and mediated images as sources for learning about cultures.

Selection of authentic and contemporary materials about cultures is a sensitive task. In recent years, publishers of major textbook series have made substantial efforts to include in their books a greater variety of cultural and racial group representations as well as to make those inclusions authentic, nonstereotypic portrayals. We must go beyond textbooks, however, if we want to gain a depth of understanding about a particular group. Most texts are organized as factual surveys, and children need more material than a text provides to investigate a specific culture. Teacher's editions may give us some leads to enrichment materials about cultures they include, such as trade books and films. Other sources of materials about various cultures and ethnic groups are listed in the bibliography of this chapter. To give students critical practice in analyzing information to which they are exposed, teachers should prompt students to find out when the source they use was published and, if possible,

SAMPLE ACTIVITIES

CORRECTING FOR STEREOTYPES BULLETIN BOARD

Images of Japan: How Do We Know a Culture?

Our Stereotypes	Traditions	Japan Today
kimono	kimono times	kimono times
cherry blossoms	spring festival	spring festival
hard work	duty, loyalty	work and play
tea, rice	tea ceremony	coffee, tea, soft drink
manufactured goods	calligraphy	revere art, technology
look alike	geisha, coman	Western, traditional dress

Have students use these three themes to categorize pictures cut from magazines focusing on a single culture or national group or combination of them. They should find some pictures that fit all three categories of the group and discuss how we develop our images of groups or nationalities. Do we get our ideas about groups within our own society in the same ways? Do our textbooks portray a culture's traditional way of life? Could this exercise be used for exploring stereotypes we have of other groups?

something about who wrote and published it. Asking whether the pictures would be the same if taken today and whether the author was a native of the culture being described should become part of social studies instructional routines.

Whatever secondary sources teachers select to study a culture, they should use several themes and questions to guide students in exploring them. Teachers can help students examine how the group being studied uses the resources around them and how these resources shape the culture. In other words, what do resources have to do with clothing, housing, and eating styles? Another watchword to observe in selecting and using secondary materials is perspective. Good history instruction causes students to try imagining how an event such as the Civil War or the Gold Rush would look and feel to the different groups involved in it. Using a book or video that portrays one point of view is acceptable so long as the teacher helps students imagine how the story might have been portrayed if told from another perspective. Looking at cultural practices to discern how they serve to bind the group together can move students beyond fascination with what is exotic or perhaps distasteful. Reflecting on changes groups suffer as a way to discover what group members do to help their cultures survive can assist students in understanding practices as diverse as Amish separatism and the African American use of kente cloth. Asking these reflective questions over time will work toward building the students' critical sense that automatically prompts them to question either-or concepts and unchanging answers when learning about the social world. All these suggestions can be woven into a multicultural frame of reference that teachers can use in instruction aimed at learning about other cultures.

Using Holidays as Critical Thinking Times

Another source for teaching about cultural diversity is holidays. Consider how we might celebrate them using a multicultural frame of reference. Examining the possible motivations behind our traditional holiday art activities can provide clues. For our national culture, why was it important for Americans to remember President Washington as a young boy who always told the truth? Once children have explored the cherry tree chopping as a morality tale, making cherry-festooned hatchets of construction paper can have more meaning for them. Showing connections between a holiday and children's lives necessarily takes us into the religious realm. For example, children might discuss preparation for giving up something as a way to remember what Jesus Christ gave up as an initial understanding of pre-Lenten celebrations known as Mardi Gras or Carnival in Catholic cultures. They can examine the Jewish Passover, Pesach, as a celebration of the Hebrew exodus from Egypt that recalls the hard times the Jews experienced while enslaved by the Pharoah. Jews commemorate these times by serving such ritual foods as *matzoh,* unleavened bread that reminds them their ancestors left Egypt with such haste they could not wait for the bread to rise; *moror,* bitter horseradish recalling the horrors of slavery; and *haroset,* a mixture of chopped apples, nuts, cinnamon, and wine recalling the mortar the Hebrews used to build cities for the Pharoah. Learning such symbols and their meaning can show students how people of other religions recall difficult or important times of their faith. The Muslim holiday *Eid al-Adha* requires that an animal such as a lamb, goat, sheep, cow, or camel be sacrificed and cooked; then part of the meat is eaten at home, and part is given away to the poor or to friends. This holiday ritual commemorates God's command to the Prophet Abraham to sacrifice his son Ishmael, and God's subsequent release of Abraham from this awful duty by giving him a lamb to sacrifice in place of his son.[3] Hearing this story allows children to learn that sacrifice for a belief plays an important part in holidays of many faiths. In exploring reasons behind religious holidays, we help children learn about other cultures and, possibly, gain experience teaching others about their own cultures and beliefs. In teaching about culture, include examples that help students understand the importance of ritual and celebration in all our lives.

The approaches to instruction about cultures presented here can help you move your students toward the multicultural goals of seeing multiple perspectives, expanding their worldview and their knowledge about their own cultures, and learning to value cultures as visions of how groups can survive and adapt to changing circumstances. Ideas and strategies described under the subtitles of learning about ourselves and naming can strengthen a cultural sense of self. Activities and ideas generated around the categories of learning from each other and community sources serve to recognize and include all locally represented cultures in the classroom learning community. Using bulletin board themes can spotlight collections showing how an American can be recognized. Questioning stereotypes helps students visualize what they all have in common and assists them in recognizing stereotyping that may be done for the purpose of excluding certain groups. Extending and enriching instruction about cultures

---

[3]An explanatory *Calendar of Religious Holidays and Ethnic Festivals* updated biannually is available from the National Conference for Community and Justice, 71 Fifth Avenue, New York, NY 10003. Phone (212) 206-0006; fax (212) 255-6177. Other curriculum materials dealing with intergroup conflict resolution are also available from this source.

with secondary sources helps to encourage the critical thinking we want students to cultivate when they consider other cultures as well as their own.

■ CLASSROOM INTERGROUP PROBLEM SOLVING

Are we doing all that is required to prepare children to live in our culturally and racially pluralistic society when we structure more equitable learning settings in our classrooms, celebrate ethnic holidays and heroes, and incorporate multiple perspectives in our presentation of the American experience? Each of these categories of classroom and social studies instruction opens vistas to the realities of our society. None, however, *directly* instructs children about ways to live and interact positively in situations where power, prejudice, stereotyping, and status create conflict in personal and group interactions. Bringing problematic and conflictual situations into the classroom for controlled explorations adds a direct, real-life dimension to preparing children to live in our diverse society. Learning to deal with new situations and people takes practice. Viewing alternatives is a learnable critical thinking skill, and looking at a situation from another point of view is an attitude we need to model.

To many of us, the idea of intentionally including conflict in our classrooms is threatening. We may be highly adept in conflict avoidance; we may prefer not to recognize conflict when we see it. By controlling the situation, we hope the reasons for the conflict will disappear. And sometimes they will. Or we hope that we can prevent conflict by instructing children to treat one another with respect. Surely, we need to communicate this message in the hope that conflicts will be averted. Still, conflicts will always arise. Our task is to decide what to do about the conflict we see that emerges from individual and intergroup interaction. Lessons in conflict resolution can assist us with this task.

ON YOUR OWN	**INTERGROUP CONFLICT IN SCHOOLS**
8.4	*Examine your feelings about conflictual classroom situations by choosing the one response that best matches what you would prefer as a response. These sample conflict situations are designed to prompt your thinking about where you stand intellectually and emotionally.*

Situation I

Anton, an African American child, comes to you after recess and tells you that Chad, a white child, called him a "nigger" while they were standing in the third-grade line.

1. *You tell Anton to ignore Chad.*
2. *You get the rest of the class to work and call Chad and Anton to the hall. You ask Chad why he would "name-call," asking him never to do it again.*
3. *You seat the class and give them a "lecture" on words that should not be used in polite society.*
4. *Later that day you use the event as a situation for the class to explore through two puppets, one black and one white, without mentioning the boys who provoked this role play.*

Situation IA

Would you choose differently if Maria Elena said Jorge called her a "bitch"?

Situation 2A

What would you do if the name-calling of "bitch" was between students of different racial identities?

Situation 2

Your fifth graders are buzzing about the new second-grade teacher, Mr. Todd, who is a dwarf.

1. *You discuss the term* stereotype *with the class.*
2. *You tell the class that they should treat others as they would like to be treated.*
3. *You invite Mr. Todd to your class to tell them how he feels about being a "little person" teacher.*
4. *You ask the children to write about how they would feel if they were suddenly transformed into dwarfs.*

Situation 3

A newly arrived, adopted Korean child enters your kindergarten. Chungsoon cannot speak English. This is a novelty to all the other English-speaking children. They are laughing and pointing.

1. *You ask children to think of ways they can make Chungsoon feel at home in the class.*
2. *You appoint Angeline to be Chungsoon's special friend.*
3. *You read the book* I Am Here: Yo Estoy Aqui *about Luz, a Spanish-speaking kindergartener who learns to communicate with the other children through a Spanish-speaking classroom aide.*
4. *You create a special place separate from the other children for Chungsoon to work and give her special, individual attention with gestures.*

Examine Your Choices

If, in the preceding exercise, you selected number one in the first situation, number two in the second situation, or number four in the third situation, you need to examine why you are more comfortable ignoring the conflicts involved in these situations. Conflict can be turned into a learning experience for you and your students only if it is examined. If it is ignored, it will not go away; it will become part of the hidden, nonpositive classroom culture. If you chose number two in the first situation, you should consider the effect of this method. It may keep Chad from name-calling in your presence, but it may also inspire Chad to call Anton "tattletale nigger." If you choose to lecture the class, you are in effect, telling them what not to do. Yet they need to know why. They need to explore how it would feel to be called a similar name. The choices that involve presenting the conflict as an exploration using different characters requires extreme readiness on your part to "seize the moment of teachability." Can you be that alert? Ready? Adroit? What if you do not observe situations that are auspicious lead-ins to these vital issues?

There is no course that can prepare you completely for the decisions you will have to make in handling individual and intergroup conflict. What you can do is discuss with colleagues the situations in this self-check and other situations in which you have been involved or that you have observed. Be assured that as a teacher you will have issues of stereotyping and name-calling and prejudice. Only experience, informed by your attentive eyes and ears and tempered by your sense of social justice, can give you the self-confidence and courage to handle this kind of culture learning in a positive manner.

Teaching About Interpersonal and Intergroup Conflict

Techniques and materials for the exploration of conflict usually fall into the bibliographic categories of role playing, problem solving, and critical thinking. Typically, more than a verbal prompt is used to initiate this kind of classroom episode. The initiators can take many forms: staged incidents, photographs portraying children in dilemmas, puppets that get into conflict situations, videos that lead into a crisis point, and trade books that portray social, racial, or cultural dissonance.

Using dolls dressed as people who have come to the classroom is another effective way to involve children in the experience of living with people who are different from them or people who have disabilities to overcome. "Persona dolls" are introduced by the teacher as people who have come to join the class, as portrayed in the sample classroom episode.

SAMPLE CLASSROOM EPISODE

LOOKING IN CLASSROOMS: EXPLORATION OF DIFFERENCES THROUGH FANTASY

Mrs. Lever announces she will introduce "Brian," an orthopedically disabled third grader, to the class one morning during opening exercises. She brings in a doll dressed as a third grader seated in a wheelchair.

Mrs. Lever: Class, we have someone who will be joining us. His name is Brian. He comes to us from Children's Hospital where he has just learned to use his new wheelchair. His mother tells me that Brian is eager to be in our class. He was hurt in an auto accident. He cannot use the lower half of his body. He will need our help to do certain things. Do you have any questions about our new classmate?

Vito: How come he's coming to our class?

Mrs. Lever: He lives in our neighborhood and finished second grade last year.

This line of questioning continues until children have discovered that Brian will need help with bathroom visits, with getting a drink of water, and with moving in and out the doors. Mrs. Lever then sets up a buddy schedule for Brian for the rest of the week.

A few days later, Mrs. Lever asks the children to share what they have learned now that Brian is in the class. Brian's buddies tell about their troubles in bathrooms and with doors. Mrs. Lever leads them to explore how they would feel if they were Brian. Finally, Mrs. Lever asks them to think about what they could do to make their classroom and school an easier place for Brian to be. She fully expects that the group will begin a campaign to prepare the school for children like Brian. She expects that they will speak with the principal and write to the school board about their concerns.

When individuals with obvious ability differences are present in the classroom or school, teacher-led inquiry regarding their special needs and constraints is imperative. Some children with special needs are willing to talk about their situation. Others are not. We need to talk privately with these students to learn whether they wish to discuss their needs with the group, or whether they are more comfortable, at least initially, being assigned a special classroom buddy to assist them.

Under the guise of fantasy, you can introduce explorations of real-life problems and conflicts. Classrooms can accommodate more than one persona doll. In settings where children would not have contact with certain "different others," the dolls can provide opportunities for empathy-building experiences that lead children to think critically about human variety that is outside their life spheres.

Staging classroom incidents is one of the most effective avenues to open discussion and to generate more personal insights about the effects of prejudice and stereotyping. The sample activities present four classic ideas that have proven adaptable to a variety of ages and settings.

SAMPLE ACTIVITIES

UNDERSTANDING PREJUDICE AND STEREOTYPING

The Museum
This experience is to help children recognize their stereotypes and consider where they came from. It is appropriate for middle graders. Ask children to discuss the purpose of a museum. Ask them to tell what would be in a museum about people. Ask children to close their eyes and imagine that they are in an ethnic museum. Their purpose is to imagine a display in the African American Room of the museum. Allow some silent time before proceeding.

After silent imagining time, ask children to describe what they put into the African American Room.

Then suggest that children move to another room. Use a group that has significance for the class for the next mental display. Repeat the same recording process followed for describing the African American Room.

Discuss whether members of the group being portrayed would decorate their room the same way. Record corrections or deletions on lists using another color marker or chalk. Now ask students to visit the museum again as though they were members of the group represented in each room.

Finally, ask students to tell what they learned from their museum tours. Record their contributions. Conclude by asking students to write ways to use what they have learned. Collect statements and display around original "Museum" lists.

What Did You See?
This is a dramatic illustration of how selective memory distorts the way we remember events and individuals or groups. With no warning, stage a classroom interruption that will be witnessed by the children. You could have two children from another class, preferably from differing ethnic or cultural groups, chase each other into your room shouting at each other, using derogatory names, over a playground argument that you end by sending them to the principal's office.

(continued)

UNDERSTANDING PREJUDICE
AND STEREOTYPING (continued)

Once calm is restored, ask the children to write about who they saw, what the people said, what happened first, and what the scene was about. Then have them compare their stories. Are they the same? What kinds of differences are there? Are there differences related to mixing facts with conclusions or inferences? Are there differences of interpretation that stem from the racial or cultural identity of the players?

This experiment is much broader than intergroup relations. It should inspire more critical thinking about what we see and read in the news.

Stereotypes: Generalizations That Hurt People

Ask students to identify behaviors they do not like and write them across the chalkboard. Next invent a fictitious name and have the group make up a sentence that connects the behavior to the name. For example, "Ximena always wants to be first" or "James stole someone's baseball glove."

Next, add a sentence that further identifies each character. "Ximena lives in East Los Angeles," "James comes from a poor family." Then ask students to compose a third sentence for each that puts the two previous sentences together in a way that says something general about the people identified in the first sentences. Various possibilities for each may be listed: "All girls want to be first," "Mexicans have to have their way," or "Poor kids steal."

Ask students to tell why these groups of sentences do not make sense. Explore how the individuals in these examples would feel if they heard them. Ask students to recall whether they have ever heard people making judgments about individuals that sound like the ones they have just invented. Discuss how they can learn to analyze this kind of thinking in their own lives. Teach them the categories—religion, race, ethnic or racial group, gender, age, mental or physical ability, amount of wealth, family situation—that are used when people make stereotypic comments. Practice making more examples and discuss why they are and are not true.

Advice Column

Cooperative groups can act as though they were editing answers to the following letters written to a newspaper advice column:

Advice Editor:

I am worried that I will not be able to make friends in my new school. My family is Muslim and when I told the class that I did not want to eat snacks during Ramadan, the kids just laughed and called me a dirty Iraqi. I feel that the kids in my fourth-grade class think all Muslims kill people. What can I do?

Sincerely,
Selina

Dear Advice Editor:

I feel that being Haitian is bad. No matter how hard I try, the kids in my building treat me mean. They call me names and tell me to get a boat and go back to where I came from. What can I do to make them understand that we cannot go back? How can I be more American?

Your friend,
Marcel

Each group should compose a letter giving Selina and Marcel suggestions. After reading the responses to the class, let students analyze the positive and negative elements of each response.

The composition of our classrooms and the consequent interplay arising from the differences between individuals presents us with a built-in curriculum. Differences each child brings represent potential contributions for the growth of the other children of the group. The challenge is learning how to take advantage of these opportunities. Curriculum guides, with lesson ideas such as the ones outlined earlier, can initiate but not complete your curriculum planning. Each class will bring you a new configuration of cultures to explore and incorporate into your daily activities. Business as usual will come to mean changing and adapting your approach to include and incorporate elements of your students' diversity as part of the curriculum. A wise immigrant grandmother, when asked by a teacher how to respond to the needs of her grandchild, gave this advice: "You must give her roots to grow and wings to fly!" Explaining, she continued, "I want her to know who she is and where she came from. These are her roots. But she must have knowledge about the American culture so she can go where she wants and become who she wants to be."[4]

■ SUMMARY

In this chapter we have reviewed three ways that culture learning can occur in the elementary classroom. The way we organize learning is potentially a positive culture-forming process. Cooperative learning modes appear to offer a powerful tool for building positive interactions between children who may perceive themselves as different from others. We may learn about cultures by taking advantage of the cultures that children bring with them to school. Recognizing that each individual identifies with a variety of microcultures can guide us in the way we orient children's study of groups of people. We may learn about dealing with differences in our own and others' cultures by practicing the skill of seeing a situation from another perspective and exploring alternative resolutions of conflicts. Finally, we clear a path for creating new ways to behave in our culture by seeking solutions to real problems related to individual and group identities.

[4]From "Addressing Needs of Immigrant Students," an address delivered by Laurie Olsen, Director, California of Tomorrow Foundation, in Santa Clara, CA, March 15, 1991.

■ SUGGESTED READINGS AND WEB SITES ■

American-Arab Anti-Discrimination Committee. "Reaching the Teachers." Washington.

Resource and action guide addressing needs of Arab American students highlighting history, culture, and current events of Arab world, 4201 Connecticut Avenue, N.W., Washington, DC 20008-1158 Suite 300; Phone (800) 343-5540.

Banks, James A. *Educating Citizens in a Multicultural Society.* New York: Teachers College Press, 1997.

Influential educator's prescriptions for educating students for a multicultural society.

Bennett, Christine. *Comprehensive Multicultural Education: Theory and Practice,* 3rd ed. Boston: Allyn & Bacon, 1995.

Broad conception of multicultural education in updated college textbook.

Boutte, G. S., and C. B. McCormick. "Avoiding Pseudo-multiculturalism: Authentic Multicultural Activities." *Childhood Education* 68 (February 1992): 140–144.

Presents set of authenticity checks teachers can use to evaluate their attempts to multiculturalize curriculum.

Byrnes, Deborah A. "Teacher, They Called Me a _____!" *Prejudice and Discrimination in the Classroom.* New York: Anti-Defamation League of B'nai B'rith, 1987.

Practical definitions and activities for classroom teachers. The same source also offers a study guide for *A World of Difference* program and many more pertinent resources.

Cohn, Amy L., ed. *From Sea to Shining Sea.* New York: Scholastic, 1994.

Multicultural collection of stories and songs related to all periods of American history.

Coles, Robert. *The Spiritual Life of Children.* Boston: Houghton Mifflin, 1990.

Respected child psychologist explores children's feelings and thoughts about spiritual issues.

Cortes, Carlos E. *The Children Are Watching: How the Media Teach About Diversity.* New York: Teachers College Press, 2000.

Looks at the ways that media present diversity and what the schools and parents can do to address the implications of the media.

Hakim, Joy. *The Story of Us.* New York: Oxford University Press.

Groundbreaking series that employs storytelling approach to U.S. history, highlighting interplay of conflicting cultures and connecting past to present events in ten volumes for elementary and middle levels.

Howard, Gary. *We Can't Teach What We Don't Know: White Teachers, Multiracial Schools.* New York: Teacher's College Press, 1999.

Personal experiences of a multicultural educator over the past twenty years.

McCracken, Janet Brown. *Valuing Diversity: The Primary Years.* Washington, DC: National Council for the Education of Young Children, 1993.

Sourcebook for resources and activities beginning with preschool years.

Muse, Daphne, ed. *The New Press Guide to Multicultural Resources for Young Readers.* New York: The New Press, 1997.

Reviews over 1,000 multicultural books and related materials, organized by theme and reading level.

National Council for the Social Studies. "Guidelines on Multicultural Education." *Social Education* 56 (September 1992): 274–293.

Statement by professional association listing ways pluralism can be integrated in social studies.

Ogbu, John U. "Understanding Cultural Diversity and Learning." *Educational Researcher* 21 (November 1992): 5–14.

Disagrees with widespread approaches to school reform efforts of core curriculum and multicultural education arguing that they do not address real difficulties of minority group students who have traditionally not done well in public schools.

Pang, Valerie. *Multicultural Education: A Caring Reflective Approach.* New York: McGraw Hill, 2001.

Applies Ned Noddings's caring approach to multicultural education.

Pilger, Mary Anne. *Multicultural Projects Idea Index.* Englewood, CO: Libraries Unlimited, 1992.

Indexes sources that detail craft, holiday, food, game, and historical projects.

Schniedewind, Nancy, and Ellen Davidson. *Open Minds to Equality: A Sourcebook of Learning Activities to Affirm Diversity and Promote Equity,* 2nd ed. Boston: Allyn & Bacon, 1998.

Activities appropriate for upper elementary and middle school.

Teaching Tolerance. From the Southern Poverty Law Center. Free periodical for teachers, replete with multiculturally related teaching ideas and experiences. 400 Washington Avenue, Montgomery, AL 36104; Fax (205) 264-6892.

See especially Spring 1994 issue containing interview with historian Ronald Takaki, "Reflections from a Different Mirror," pages 11–15. The article defends a pluralistic view of multicultural instruction and the opportunity schools have to "hold up a different mirror" in teaching students about our society.

Web Site

www.teachingtolerance.org

Low-cost books, classroom activities posted monthly of the school year plus free kits including videos of one per school.

Chapter 9

Social Studies and the Literacy Connection

This chapter explores the different ways instruction can help students overcome language and literacy barriers so that students can acquire social studies content and skills. Social studies learning is intimately tied to literacy and cannot be divorced from it.

- Typical Social Studies Instructional Activities and Literacy

- Meeting Special Needs: Mild Disabilities, ESL Students, and Struggling Readers

- Reading Difficulties

- Finding Information

- Relating the Social Studies and Literacy

Often the difficulties that students encounter in social studies spring from the mismatch between the presentation of social studies content and their abilities to listen, read, speak, and write. These causes have contributed to students disliking social studies as they become frustrated while trying to read and to understand the text.

◼ TYPICAL SOCIAL STUDIES INSTRUCTIONAL ACTIVITIES AND LITERACY

Before tackling literacy learning in the social studies, let us review what is happening in the nation's social studies classes. Along with testing students in the NAEP Civics test, their teachers also responded by filling out a questionnaire. The results of this survey can be generalized to all the teachers in the United States. Fourth-grade teachers responded about the frequency with which they used a selection of instructional activities for the social studies using the conventions of "every day" and "once or twice a week." The most popular instructional activities on a weekly basis were using the social studies textbook (83 percent); using quantitative data, charts, or graphs (81 percent); completing worksheets (68 percent); hearing a teacher's lecture (66 percent), and using books, newspapers or magazines (58 percent). Only 35 percent of students in the fourth grade received group activities or a project on at least a weekly basis. Ten percent or less of students in the fourth grade used weekly computer software, wrote a report of three or more pages, participated in debates or mock trials, or wrote letters on civics topics. Surprisingly, despite all the attention now given to cooperative learning, only 53 percent of fourth graders had small group activities in the social studies once or twice a month, which is a very low usage rate.

By the eighth grade, on a weekly basis, students used the social studies textbook (95 percent); used quantitative data, charts, or graphs (77 percent); completed worksheets (76 percent), heard a teacher's lecture (77 percent), and used books, newspapers, or magazines (55 percent). Small group activities in the social studies only occurred once or twice a month.[1]

Of course, these teachers' reports cannot capture what really happens in classrooms. These reports say nothing about the quality of the teaching. However, the teachers' reports do give a clue to what is occurring as teachers teach and students learn about the social studies across the nation. In general, it appears that more traditional activities are used by many teachers in their social studies programs. It should be noted that in no sense were these the "worst teachers." Forty-six percent of these fourth-grade teachers had masters or higher degrees whereas 43 percent of the fourth graders were taught by teachers with a bachelor's degree. Teachers rated themselves as well prepared in social studies instruction, classroom climate/governance, classroom management, and in the use of computers but not prepared in using computer software for social studies instruction. Almost three-quarters (73 percent) of fourth graders were in classes in which teachers indicated never or hardly ever using the Internet for social studies.

Note that both the traditional, popular instructional activities in social studies and the least used activities depend on literacy, narrowly defined as the ability to read and to write, and more broadly to include also oral communication, listening, and speaking (see Figure 9.1). Literacy in the social studies can include complex tasks such as problem solving and presenting information in a variety of formats. Sometimes computer literacy is now included in the definition of literacy.

Students in the social studies are frequently asked to do such tasks as reading textbooks and using writing to fill in worksheets. In fact, some of the least used social studies activities such as writing a three-page report, participating in debates or mock trials, and writing letters require a higher level of literacy, which is perhaps the reason that they are not found more frequently in classrooms.

However, even with the ever increasing power of the media in portraying images and information,

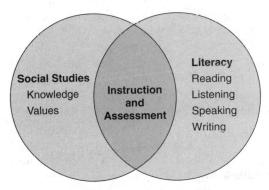

FIGURE 9.1 Relationship of Social Studies to Literacy

[1]U.S. Department of Education, Office of Educational Research and Improvement, National Center for Education Statistics, *The NAEP 1998 Civics Report Card for the Nation*, NCES 2000-457, by Anthony D. Lukas, Andrew R. Weiss, Jay R. Campbell, John Mazzeo, Stephen Lazer, pp. xii–xiii, p. 91.

reading, especially as students become older, remains a prime prerequisite for successful learning in the social studies. The use of the Internet generally requires a reading level at or above the sixth-grade level. There have been positive correlations between reading skills of students and social studies grades at all grade levels. A poor reader often is a poor social studies student. You can readily understand this by an examination of social studies test items that require literacy proficiencies. Even in the more popular open-ended questions, writing skills are important in answering test items. Learning social studies is directly connected with literacy (Figure 9.1). This is becoming even a more important issue with the standards-based reform efforts on increasing attention to concepts and methodologies. Furthermore, concepts at a higher level of abstraction, such as economic concepts, are now being moved down to lower grade levels.

SMALL GROUP WORK	**WHAT IS HAPPENING IN SOCIAL STUDIES CLASSROOMS?**
9.1	*Based on your experience, do you think the NAEP survey on teaching in the social studies is accurate? Why do you think teachers do not use more small group activities in the social studies? Why are teachers using worksheets, a practice most experts recommend keeping to a minimum?*

The Whole Language Approach

What is the present status of the teaching of reading, an important component of literacy or, as some believe, the most important skill in school for children to master? The 1980s saw the rise and acceptance of the **whole language** movement. Definitions varied on the term *whole language* but its basic premise is that children will learn language, both oral and written, best if it is learned for authentic purposes. The primary purpose of instruction is to motivate and interest children to become lifelong readers. Reading is perceived as responding personally to literature rather than seeing reading as information gathering. This means looking at whole texts and not looking at parts of language such as the sound–symbol correspondence or using artificial tasks such as worksheets.

Practical ways to implement the whole language approach are choral reading of Big Books, teachers reading aloud to children, sustained silent reading, the use of the writing workshop, use of trade books, integration of reading and writing, using invented spelling, and the use of an "author's chair." However, any of these activities could also be done by a teacher whose reading philosophy is not whole language. In fact, most teachers are eclectic in their practice. They use both a basal reader and trade books along with workbooks and worksheets. They use activities from whole language instruction in conjunction with skill instruction as part of a basal reading program.

However, the whole language approach did not appear to be successful with struggling readers. A backlash against the whole language approach developed in some states such as California and Georgia and in some districts when the public became aware of low reading scores. There is now a swing "back" to phonics and, in some cases, a more rigid reading program such as "Success for All" developed by Robert Slavin, a researcher in education at Johns Hopkins University, whose program has been used especially for Title 1 classes. Here in this particular reading program the teacher follows a script for ninety minutes. First graders learn to read from a series of forty-eight paperback storybooks, each of which stresses a different phonic sound. Beginner readers in this program spend a lot of time reading in unison and also daily time in teams in which peer pressure is expected to work.

So reading instruction appears to be in a flux. What is happening in the teaching of reading in your state or district? What are you being taught and what do you see happening in reading in the schools?

Social Studies and Whole Language

What impact did the whole language movement have on social studies? The whole language approach stresses children's responses to literature as opposed to their recall or comprehension of stories. Therefore, content area social studies textbooks were deemphasized and replaced by nonfiction trade books, or historical or other fiction relating to the content areas of social studies. Thus, research in 1995 showed that 85 percent of the primary teachers and 45 percent of the intermediate teachers reported using children's literature at least once a week in social studies.

Problems arise on the use of literature. Teaching history through a narrative approach using trade books has both advantages and disadvantages. A well-written story, especially about adventure or heroism, is usually much more interesting and easier to read than a textbook. But making characters heroic by overcoming obstacles as in pioneer stories sometimes leads to seeing other groups as hostile. There is also evidence that in using historical fiction children follow the narrative and the characters but often miss the factual information embedded within the narrative. Students do not approach the narrative with a critical eye. Rather they accept the story as "true."

This is most likely to happen if students do not read or hear about other counternarratives or compare the account with a textbook. Without these steps, students do not realize that history is interpretation. But often teachers feel that they do not have the time to search out counternarratives or differing interpretations of the same events and they cannot take classroom time to have students compare the trade book with other materials. The advantage of students seeing information from more than one source is that they must summarize, synthesize, compare, and evaluate. These thinking skills are harder to foster when teaching is organized around just one source.

Teachers may not stress the distinctions between historical accounts and fictional creations and that the literature may be inaccurate. In addition, from a story students may not see the "big picture" or why the American Revolution and Lewis and Clark's expedition were important. They just remember the patriots on Lexington Green or Sacagawea carrying her baby on her back.

Focusing on both social studies and literacy, what do we want students to be able to do? Recall that standards-based reform has placed greater emphasis on students understanding the major concepts or the big ideas of a subject area of history, geography, civics, and economics. In addition, students need to acquire the ways of thinking within the discipline and learn its particular methods of investigation that are used for establishing and evaluating knowledge. In other words, students need conceptual understanding of the subject area and mastery of those skills needed for expert performance. This means that the acquisition of skills is part of the larger picture of conceptual understanding. First, students are to develop research and information skills to answer questions, not as an end in itself. It is recognized that we are experiencing an information explosion that is unprecedented in human history. Knowledge is constantly expanding and students cannot possibly learn all that the academic fields, including the social sciences and history, have to offer. Even specialists can barely keep up with new ideas in their field. Instead, students will have to be able to find and to evaluate information as it relates to a given issue or problem. Of course, some background in any subject is necessary for a successful search.

Second, students need to develop presentation and communication skills, important for now showing in the classroom what they have learned as well as essential for living in our society. Student presentation strategies could include drama, oral presentation, posters with an explanation, and reader's theater as well as the more typical discussions in a classroom. Writing skills are essential to clarify one's own thinking and to communicate with others. And, finally, in the affective domain, we want students to accept responsibility for planning, developing, and executing their learning activities and seeing connections to other subject areas, real life, and citizenship. Eventually, they need to be independent learners who strive for excellence in information seeking so that they can gain knowledge for social studies problem solving and decision making.

In the teaching of reading and the social studies often the debate focuses on whether or when instruction should be *explicit,* with teachers leading students through predetermined lessons and activities, or *exploratory,* with teachers guiding children by responding to children's own questions and interests. This issue was already discussed on teaching social studies in the primary grades (Chapter 5) and on general methods (Chapter 3). Too frequently, this debate is framed as the traditional "teachers as knowledge transmitters" versus "teachers as facilitators." But instead of viewing these approaches as opposing camps, they could be thought of as complementary opportunities for teachers to move between these two perspectives. As a result, students could benefit from both explicit, teacher-led activities and from exploratory, teacher-facilitated activities. A certain amount of knowledge and skills is essential if students are to be able to participate in social studies classes and this is often gained by explicit direct teaching. In turn, students also need to learn how to make decisions about what to accomplish by posing questions and how to proceed, a more exploratory approach. Both approaches are essential and may be especially needed with students from diverse language backgrounds.

Thus, the premise for this chapter is that a balance is needed between the two approaches: the transmission model and the facilitator model in teaching literacy in the social studies. We first look at recommended approaches to teaching children with special needs and reading difficulties and then give attention to the facilitator model.

■ MEETING SPECIAL NEEDS: MILD DISABILITIES, ESL STUDENTS, AND STRUGGLING READERS

In thinking about teaching social studies and looking over your classroom, you are probably very much aware of two groups of students who may be having more difficulty than the rest of the class in developing literacy. In one group are students with mild disabilities or, as they are often called, students with disabilities (SD) or special education students. The aim for these students is inclusion in the classroom with general and special education teachers working together for the benefit of each and every student. Inclusive school practices embrace the idea that every student gets a learning experience that "fits." It also supports the idea that inductive, hands-on, active learning and more cooperative activities are desirable.

The second group is the increasing number of English as a Second Language (ESL) students. Other terms used for ESL students are *Limited-English-Proficient (LEP), Non-English-Language backgrounds (NELB),* and *English Language Learners (ELLs).* Both groups have often been underserved in the schools. These students have been at a disadvantage because instruction and assessment in the social studies are in a language not understood completely by these students. Sometimes the same strategies for helping these students work for both groups. Sometimes not. But they are not the only groups that experience reading difficulties since perhaps 40 percent of the total population experience reading difficulties.

Respect for student diversity means that today's schools must accommodate students from different ethnic and racial groups, language groups, cultures, family situations, and social and economic situations. It is important to make sure each student gets access to knowledge and skills because such access improves life chances, available choices, and the valued contributions of every person. This is one of the central purposes of education. Without effective instruction, struggling readers conclude that they can do nothing to improve. Often these students choose not to read and write, and are less likely to take control of their own reading.

Teachers can use multiple sources to gather evidence about each child's literacy abilities. It is important to view each child as an individual, not just as a member of a cultural group or a category with disabilities. This includes looking at how language is used in different settings and an awareness that background and prior experiences significantly influence a child's learning and interest. In looking at the child's age, personality characteristics, and the living arrangements of the child, teachers can gain insight on how to help the child. In particular, there is often a "silent stage" in which the newcomer does not speak initially in the classroom, giving a false picture of the child's abilities. Or when difficulties occur, they may be attributed to misconduct or learning disabilities rather than to a need for language learning or an understanding of social studies content.

First, all students bring different strengths to the classroom and it is up to the teachers to know both their students' abilities and disabilities. Typically literacy development can be seen on a continuum from no school and little exposure to literacy to the appropriate age and grade-level development necessary for social studies academic achievement. After assessment, the teacher can locate the available resources. Then the teacher can use teaching strategies that might work best with these students.

TABLE 9.1 Ineffective Strategies for ESL Students

1. Being forced to read in front of the class
2. Being corrected publicly by other students
3. Segregating ESL students from the rest of the class
4. Ignoring ESL students
5. Embarrassing students
6. Not providing adequate assistance
7. Covering information too rapidly

Here are a few suggestions that may be appropriate for these students or that may be used for all students. See Table 9.1 for ineffective strategies identified by former ESL students. These ineffective strategies apply to all struggling readers.

Buddy or Peer Pairs and Assisted Reading

Frequently an ESL student, a limited disability student, or a struggling reader can be placed with a "buddy" or friend who is a more capable peer. This is often a good commonsense solution, especially useful when a new student arrives. The ESL student can learn a lot both in language and social studies. The more advanced student practices the skills of having to explain, illustrate, and clarify language and ideas to another. The novice student is placed in a nonthreatening, friendly atmosphere that fosters a sense of belonging and self-esteem.

It is important to see that the task or assignment is one in which the pair can naturally support each other without the exchange being perceived as a hindrance to the more advanced student. For that reason and for giving opportunities for more friendships to develop, some teachers use a different buddy for different subject areas or many buddies for a given child in a given day. Nonetheless, in addition to supporting friendship, there must be individual accountability for both students. If possible, the novice student should be the one who reports back what has been accomplished.

Other Group Arrangements

Flexible grouping offers many opportunities for students with special needs in a social studies program. Cooperative learning produces more opportunities for content-related communication among students than a traditional, teacher-centered classroom environment. Cooperative learning can enhance academic learning, motivate students, and promote a positive climate (see Chapters 3 and 8). These qualities make cooperative learning a particularly appropriate strategy for diverse learners. Let us examine the pluses and minuses of different group arrangements.

Homogeneous English Competency Groups

Although recognizing that all groups are heterogeneous in that all students bring different strengths to the classroom, sometimes a teacher may wish to reduce the amount of heterogeneity within a group by establishing groups that share approximately the same level of English proficiency. The essential point is that the teacher must carefully avoid the negative stereotype that may result when students are grouped together because some are smarter and, therefore, more valued than others.

The advantage of this arrangement is that different tasks and materials can be assigned to different groups. Although all students may be learning about the Trans-Mississippi West Movement, the reading level of materials for each group can vary as well as the amount of visual representation. There can be different levels of material with a similar theme. Or materials can be on different themes within a topic, such as one group looking at routes the pioneers used and another group examining the lives of pioneer women. The students in each group may record their consensus information as they learn about the Trans-Mississippi West Movement.

Later, their information will grow with information provided by the other groups. This can be done by classroom discussion in which students develop and refine their understanding of the subject by finding out, comparing, and evaluating other students' knowledge and ideas. It is essential when students read different materials or do different tasks that they get the impact of other groups to complete their understanding of the subject.

Same Language Groups with Varied English Competency

Sometimes a teacher has several students who speak the same language (e.g., Spanish) and these students typically have varied English literacy. At times it is effective to organize them in a group or groups of the same native language when the teacher wants students in the group to efficiently convey key concepts, instructions, or information to their peers who speak the same language. The teacher knows that students may use their native language to teach the concept of government when students are to list the goods and services not privately produced and to explain how these goods and services are paid for. In most cases, students in the same language group will discuss first in their mother tongues and then, working collaboratively in English, will present their work to the whole class.

The advantages of this group arrangement is that there is assistance from more capable peers, students' knowledge and understanding, regardless of language background, are used and validated, and it usually takes less teacher time than explaining the work to all students. The disadvantage is that students may label some students as "the Spanish kids" and not promote integration of the classroom. In addition, students may not want to be defined by their parents' language and may not appreciate being put into a special language group.

Jigsaw or Experts Groups

The Jigsaw Technique (see Chapter 3) in which each group becomes experts in a certain subject area can best be done successfully with a diverse group of learners only if the teacher supplies each group with a wide range of reading and visual materials, audio books, fiction and nonfiction literature, and other ways to acquire information. Relying on a section of the textbook with the range of reading being "all over the place" may be too difficult for many students. However, many activities connecting to students' own experience of the content will help students to become experts in a certain area and to teach other students.

SAMPLE CLASSROOM EPISODE

PEER TEACHING

In the library, students from both the second and fifth grades are listening to Mrs. Anna Hamilton, a retired homemaker, who was raised on a farm. She describes her life as a child during the summertime. She stresses the time it took to do her chores: pumping water from outside, washing dishes and clothing, preparing vegetables, canning food, weeding and tending the garden, picking fruit, and doing housework. Mrs. Hamilton also talks about the fun she had with her four siblings, going swimming, and going to town once a week on Saturday to see a movie.

After her discussion and answering questions, the fifth graders and second graders go to find their buddy. The assignment is for the second graders to dictate to their fifth-grade buddies what they would like and dislike if they had lived on a farm at the same time as Mrs. Hamilton. One pair is Janeula, a second grader, and Stephanie, a fifth grader.

Stephanie: What were some of the things you would like the most about living on a farm long ago?

Janeula: Swimming. The horses, cows, the cats.

Stephanie: Were there any other things you would like?

Janeula: (softly) Don't know.

Stephanie: Did the family ever have any fun together?

Janeula: Going into town on Saturday.

Stephanie: Let me write that down. What did they do in town?

Janeula: She sometimes got to go to a movie. They liked that. No TV.

Postscript

Janeula continues to recount what she has remembered about what the speaker said. When necessary, Stephanie prompts and gives hints to Janeula to recall more. List the skills that were used by each student. What are the advantages of peer tutoring? What would happen if Stephanie did not prompt?

Teachers know that language learning is a social activity involving discussing and thinking of ideas. Understandings and capacities grow and deepen through interactions with others. Students who regularly engage in buddy or peer tutoring (see the classroom episode) and cooperative learning are able to share ideas with each other and respond to one another's thoughts. This contributes to language learning.

Summary in Working with Special Needs Students

Typically, students with special needs require more time and resources to meet the goals of a social studies program. Developing an atmosphere of trust and acceptance is essential. Sometimes a learning resource specialist and a librarian can help in assembling materials, but often these responsibilities fall on the teacher. Flexible group arrangements can help all students to learn, and greater use of cooperative learning is beneficial. Getting volunteers in the classroom and more peer tutoring situations including older students can also improve literacy and social studies knowledge and skills. See the sample classroom episode "Peer Teaching." Parent and home involvement of students with special needs as well as all students also pays off in big dividends. Try to make communication with parents a high priority.

■ READING DIFFICULTIES

You have or will have a course in teaching reading or language arts. You have been alerted that reading difficulties in the social studies are not limited to only ESL and students with mild disabilities. Starting around the third or fourth grade, children learn to use their reading skill to extract information from text. At this point, they are expected to learn from content area textbooks with increasingly less teacher guidance. Even students of average and above-average reading ability can be challenged by new vocabulary, longer sentences, lack of human interest, and high idea density in social studies materials. Reading primary source material that has an older writing style can be a real test of perseverance for students. Trying to make sense out of abstract content is extremely frustrating for students and their comprehension often is less than 50 percent accuracy. This is because the student has to shift mental gears from reading to learn what happens next to the need to read for specific ideas.

Teaching reading in the social studies can be divided into three areas: preexperience or engagement, development, and application. The preexperience is used to bridge student experience to content and to motivate the student. The development section helps students construct meaning from the text. The application provides the opportunity for students to "show what they know" after reading the text for the assessment process. Let us look over these three areas designed to help reading social studies texts.

Preexperience or Engagement

- *Survey*. Guide students through a survey of the text by reading the title, chapter headings, first sentence of a new section, key words, captions under pictures, and any questions at the end of the text.
- *Questions*. Encourage students to ask questions prior to reading.
- *Discussion*. By discussing, drawing, or writing, have students predict what the text will be about. This can be done in pairs.
- *Vocabulary*. Front load the key new vocabulary or concepts, not more than three or four words. Use short explanations and numerous examples to illustrate concepts.
- *KWL Chart*. Complete a KWL chart. What do you Know about the topics, what do you Want to learn about the topic, and what did you Learn?

Development Activities

- Avoid round-robin oral reading from the text.
- Have students read with a buddy. The more capable reader can assist with unknown words.
- Guide the reading by focusing on answering a few questions or seeking answers to a problem. Always orient students to what they are going to read.
- Encourage students to evaluate the content of their reading. Does it seem reasonable that people acted in a certain way?
- Use maps, globes, artifacts, photographs, and other manipulatives to supplement the text.

Application Activities

- Complete charts, graphic organizer, cause-effect diagrams, and Venn diagrams to compare and contrast information from the text.
- Dramatize part of the text.
- Create a time line.
- Journal writing. What happened? How did I feel? What did I learn?[2]

In summary, for all strategies as well as for reading there is always value in taking time to elicit students' ideas before, during, and following instruction. This can be done either informally or through structured methods such as KWL. Open-ended questions can be especially valuable in showing students' existing knowledge and misconceptions. Assessment then can focus on students' understanding.

■ FINDING INFORMATION

In social studies, students frequently have to find specific information. To do this effectively and efficiently, most have to be taught directly how, for example, to locate information from a book: how units, sections, and summaries are indications of organization, and how to make use of headings, topic sentences, and summaries to select the main ideas. In addition, students need to know how to use the index, table of contents, list of maps, illustrations, and appendixes. Have students look under several key words (cross-references) to make sure they have located the relevant information. In addition, alert students to use the title page and the copyright date.

Students also have to know how to use more specialized sources of information such as atlases, almanacs, and encyclopedias. However, the skills of finding information should be taught in a variety of ways. These skills may be taught directly at one point—out of context and as a lesson in itself. At other times, teachers can find a variety of creative and purposeful ways for the students to use the skills within the context of broader activities such as making a report. Usually these skills have to be taught in multiple types of lessons.

Let us look how Ms. Ishikawa's fourth-grade students studying diversity are given a structure to direct their reading. The use of projects and presentations at least once a semester is a well-recommended practice in the social studies.

By exploring together what they need to look for before they read, these students defined a purpose for reading that will give them a structure for recalling what they find. This careful guidance will provide students a structured transaction with infor-

[2]Thanks to Priscilla Porter, California State University, Dominguez Hills, California for these ideas.

SAMPLE CLASSROOM EPISODE

LOOKING IN CLASSROOMS: STRUCTURING READING PURPOSE

Ms. Ishikawa: We've been studying about diversity in our state. In addition to our general reading and study, we are going to do some personal investigation. One part of the investigation will be to interview people in our families. The part we want to begin work on today is our library research about our immigrant roots. Before we begin, we need to decide what kinds of information we all need to look for, even though we will be learning about different places. I will keep track of your ideas on the chalkboard. Who can get us started?

Cathy: My family came from Ireland and England. What do I do?

Ms. Ishikawa: I suggest you make one choice, but if you have time, you may want to research both. If Cathy chooses Ireland, what should she try to learn about it?

Lloyd: Maybe where it is?

Ms. Ishikawa: Good start. What else?

Cathy: What they wear.

Ms. Ishikawa: [Writes and uses body language to call on other children; different children add items such as language, kind of work the Irish do, the climate, the way the country looks, etc.] This is a good list. Now we need to look at it and see if there are certain things that could go together. Let's do some clustering. If I write *land* [she moves to another chalkboard segment], what would go with it? [She supplies *population* as a second category and asks students to supply others; they come up with *resources, famous places, way of life,* and *why people left.*] Tomorrow when you find your country in the encyclopedia, how can you use these categories?

mation-bearing texts. Giving students a teacher-made list of questions to answer as they read is a quicker but probably less effective method, as it does not involve students in its formulation.

Let us return to Ms. Ishikawa's fourth-grade class to see how she further prepared the students to gather information. This time we follow her lesson plan. Ms. Ishikawa wants the students to practice looking for details and main ideas before she asks them to work independently. She knows her students can find encyclopedia entries, on the library shelves, but in some schools students need to be taught how to get encyclopedia articles online. In both cases, she wants them to learn to paraphrase and summarize the information they find. The sample lesson plan is the lesson she used to follow the first project session.

Let us go through this process with students using the typical CD-ROM encyclopedias available with helpful and rich images in video and audio clips. The developers of these CD-ROM encyclopedias have learned that viewers do not like long written texts on computer screens. With the increasing amount of space given to images, this means that the amount of detail on a given subject or person is reduced compared to a volume on the library shelves. There may not be as much depth on a CD-ROM encyclopedia as found in the printed volume. Thus, there are both advantages and disadvantages

SAMPLE LESSON PLAN

DIRECT TEACHING LESSON:
USING ENCYCLOPEDIAS FOR MAIN IDEAS AND DETAILS

Objectives
Students will skim encyclopedia article for specific details. Students will read encyclopedia paragraphs and state main ideas.

Materials
Tape next to overhead projection screen a sheet of butcher paper with six sections on which categories are labeled (*land, population, resources, famous places, way of life, why people left*). Have at hand a magic marker, set of encyclopedias, transparency of Ireland encyclopedia entry, highlighter transparency pens, overhead projector.

Procedure
1. Move students to carpet facing overhead projection screen.
2. Tell students: "We are going to practice using an encyclopedia to gather information for our roots reports. There are two kinds of information we will need. One is specific numbers and facts. The other is more general ideas. Who knows how we go about looking for specific facts?" [Students review skimming.] "Who knows how we go about looking for general ideas?" [Students review process for getting main ideas.]
3. "Let's look at our category sheet. Which of these call for specific facts? Which seem to call for main ideas?"
4. "Now, let's pretend that my grandparents came from Ireland. What volume do I go to?" [Have students find Ireland entry.]
5. "So we all can work together, I have a copy of the Ireland entry on this transparency." [Lead group to entry overview by asking questions about subtitles.]
6. "We should read the whole entry for our report. After the first reading we should look at our papers and see which of the sections to return to for information we want to write down."
7. Take turns orally reading entry, pointing out along the way when paragraphs contain information pertinent to categories on sheet.
8. Have volunteers highlight detail sections of transparency while you record in appropriate category on sheet in front of class their rephrasing of facts and information. For "way of life," review entry for ideas and have students come up with and highlight main idea phrases. Discuss how reading for general ideas is slower than skimming for facts.
9. Use thumbs up or down to check for understanding: "First thing I do is look for details" [down]. "As I do the first reading, I make mental notes about what parts to come back to" [up]. "Main ideas must be copied word for word" [down]. "For the second reading I skim subtitles looking for places that should give me details" [up].
10. "Tomorrow we will begin our own encyclopedia reading. Who can review for us the steps for finding information from the article on our country?"
11. Continue independent practice using the encyclopedia next session.

to CD-ROM encyclopedias. Yet, given the cost of the printed volumes, eventually everyone will use a CD-ROM encyclopedia if they want to use an encyclopedia.

Using a CD-ROM encyclopedia, if the student types in the word *Ireland* or *Spain*, a list of topics under the nation appears. Typically, the categories of population, climate, resources, and the like are listed and the student can click to easily find the information. However, the category of "history" is often very long and most students do not have sufficient background to select the appropriate categories for more direct information. Furthermore, typically the way of life of a nation is described only as the present time.

Teachers need to anticipate these potential frustrations by going through the process of trying to locate the information in the six categories for a few nations. Teachers then can tell students that they may not find all the information from the encyclopedia and may have to use family recollections and other sources of data. Alerting students beforehand to possible problems is better than facing disappointed students who report that "they can't find the information" for certain categories. Furthermore, check the reading level of the encyclopedias. For most CD-ROMs and the Internet the reading level is at least sixth grade. Beware of CD-ROMs listing a very broad level as "Elementary, Middle, Secondary, Teacher." How are students below the reading level of the encyclopedia going to work independently? This presumes that your school does not have the more expensive synthesized-voice text reader's version of the encyclopedia. You may have to team them up with other students whose families have come from the same country or use some other strategy.

Speaking and Writing

What are the students in Ms. Ishikawa's class going to do after they successfully find their information? Individual oral reports are one option but they would not catch the richness and the comparisons of reports in which student data are combined and compared to other nations. Charting the relationships among the data is important. Usually the information needs to be written even if eventually it is to be given orally. The more learning experiences the students have in which they can gather meaningful information, the better they can support both their written and oral presentations. If the data can lead to a class publication, parents would be pleased and students would feel more rewarded for their efforts.

In the social studies, typically there are two purposes of writing. One is *information writing* in which the writer provides the reader with information. Information writing may involve reporting on events or experiences or analyzing concepts and relationships. When used as a means of exploration, information writing helps both the writer and the reader to learn new ideas and to reexamine old conclusions. The data may come from a variety of sources such as newspaper articles, charts, photographs, and specialized sources as well as students' own experiences.

Persuasive writing seeks to persuade the reader to take action or to bring about change. This type of writing involves a clear awareness of what arguments might most affect the audience being addressed. Writing persuasively also requires the use of such skills as analysis, inference, synthesis, and evaluation. Typical persuasive writing assignments may involve asking students to write letters to the editor or to friends, to refute arguments, or to take sides in a debate.

Using the "every student writing, every student thinking" strategy is recommended. For example, as a follow-up check after reading, instead of asking a few students to orally answer some questions, the teacher asks *everyone* to do a "quick write" by taking a couple of minutes to write why the Loyalists during the American Revolution did not support independence. After circulating around the room noting what students are writing, the teacher calls on several students to share and then asks who agrees or disagrees and why. In this way all the students engage in thinking, writing, and evaluating.

In writing in the classroom, we are seeing more computer use. Over one-third of fourth-grade students reported using computers for writing drafts or final versions of reports. Students who can type welcome the computer program's help in catching errors in spelling, grammar, and syntax and in being able to make corrections easily. Students with handwriting difficulties encounter less frustration by using computers. The big advantage of using computers for writing is to encourage students to write drafts, which improve writing ability.

Listening has become a neglected skill (see Chapter 3). Listening is one of the most important ways to acquire information to help in both speaking and writing skills. Yet keep in mind the amount of listening expected of students. Is it too long a time period? Are students helped to know what to listen for?

Asking students to reflect on their final products and to evaluate how well they have researched and planned them is valuable. This reflection, after having just finished the activity, serves to help students to see not just that they have done the assignment but whether they have actually done enough. Did they spend enough time researching, thinking, and reviewing their projects? How might they better approach their next assignments? In this way, students learn the strategies that help them monitor their own progress and cope successfully with new situations.

■ RELATING THE SOCIAL STUDIES AND LITERACY

Let us now turn to the whole language approach. Advocates of the whole language approach to literacy learning are helping us to see that good thinking and writing skills flow from well-developed oral language. They understand that good literature read by the teacher and discussed by the children builds a rich foundation for oral fluency essential to growth in literacy. A sharing or collaborative approach to these language experiences between the teacher and students and among the students themselves seems to lead to increased learning and heightened feelings of efficacy. This insight is as illuminating as it is demanding to social studies planning and instruction. Philosophically, whole language advocates remind us of the centrality of student participation and of starting instruction with what students know as the basis for further learning. The whole language approach can help us see that, from a psychological perspective, covering what is in a textbook by reading and rote recitation may not lead to greater student comprehension. Politically, we can see that whole language strategies require students to participate and collaborate in their own construction of knowledge; therefore, these tactics offer one means by which to progress toward one citizenship goal: engaging students in working toward solutions for issues that concern them.

Pedagogically, whole language specialists suggest that we think of listening/viewing/reading–speaking/writing connections as transactions with texts.[3] By expanding the

---

[3]Although it is beyond the scope of this book to detail the whole language approach, we include aspects of it that are crucial to integrative social studies instruction.

definition of text to include all the linguistic arenas, we can see more clearly the demands this redefinition makes on social studies planning and instruction. To engage students better, social studies instruction needs to incorporate a variety of textual transactions. Initially this may seem to be an overwhelming additional planning task. On more careful analysis, we can see that textual transactions have always been embedded in social studies instruction. Carefully exploiting them and becoming more discerning about how they are sequenced will help us overcome some of the frustration we feel when planning social studies instruction. To test this assertion, examine the following classroom episode and find the language opportunities inherent in this informally developed social studies theme. Read the sample classroom episode and look for these aspects: What social studies knowledge and skills were developed? What language/literacy skills were being developed? What sequence did the teacher use to develop them?

SAMPLE CLASSROOM EPISODE

LOOKING IN CLASSROOMS: GLOBAL EDUCATION IN KINDERGARTEN

Veteran kindergarten teacher Barbara Schubert, tired of the inanity of most sharing times, decided to introduce a global slant to the routine. She added a globe and a package of red stick-on dots. Children continued to bring in toys and other significant objects to share. Ms. Schubert directed them to look for where the toy, or object, had been made. Quickly, children learned the words *Korea, Taiwan, Japan,* and *Hong Kong* by sight and by location on the globe. After the children told about the objects they had brought, they placed a stick-on dot marking the place on the globe where the item had been manufactured.

Through initial structured questioning, each child was prompted to include the usual information of what I brought (naming and describing) and how I got it (sequencing), in addition to the extension of where it came from and where that place is on the globe (identifying origin).

Then serendipity entered! One morning a child asked, "What are we going to do about all the volcanoes?" Uncertain of the child's meaning, Ms. Shubert responded, "What volcanoes?" The child brought the globe to the circle and pointed to the mounds of red stick-on dots on Japan, Hong Kong, Taiwan, and Korea, which reminded him of red mountains about to explode. Astutely, Ms. Schubert moved into questions about what the dots meant. The students then were off and running, at their level of comprehension, on the implications of the balance of trade.

After some discussion, the children dictated the beginning of a chart story, with Ms. Schubert asking the children to tell what described most of the toys they shared. After listing several ideas—"mine has batteries," "it transforms," "from Japan," "orange and black"—they decided that none was true for all their toys.

Ms. Schubert: Then what is true about all? Think about the location of the volcanoes.

Children: Asia!

Ms. Schubert: Can we begin our story with a sentence about toys and Asia?

(continued)

LOOKING IN CLASSROOMS:
GLOBAL EDUCATION IN KINDERGARTEN *(continued)*

The children directed Ms. Schubert to write "Most of our toys come from Asia." Then Ms. Schubert asked them to tell her more details about the first sentence. They added: "Our toys are made in Korea, Hong Kong, Taiwan, and Japan. They are imported."

Ms. Schubert asked the children to talk about these facts with their parents and to come to school the next day ready to tell more facts and feelings about the significance of the red dots. Again, posing questions that follow the Taba model of concept formation (see Chapter 5), which substantiates expository writing, she led them to compose a paragraph starting with one general statement followed by two more sentences that added detail to the topic sentence.

As they wrote more about their investigation, Ms. Schubert had them find statements of fact and feeling in their writing. Every child could locate and name numerous countries as well as place them relative to continents and oceans. Beginning understandings of economic production, consumption, and trade were emerging. Many children brought their parents in to see the "volcanoes." The topic extended into looking at labels so the children could see where their clothes had been made. (At this juncture, had Ms. Schubert been working in a more formal, planned way, she might have led the children into a new line of investigation about the relationships between climate and clothing needs, and where cotton, rayon, polyester, ramie, and wool come from and the processes involved in transforming some of these materials into clothing.) Then Ms. Schubert asked the children to talk to their parents to learn of things other countries bought from the United States. The informal theme of global trade and interdependence produced several pages of chart stories that year. Children continued to bring parents into the classroom to read the results of the students' investigation into world trade. Parents were astounded that kindergarteners could become articulate about a topic that is usually part of a college-level economics course.

Source: Used with the permission of Barbara Schubert, Blackford School, Campbell, California.

This vignette illustrates our contention that young children can investigate apparently sophisticated social studies topics with great interest and profit. Furthermore, their language learning was strengthened, not by rote oral pattern exercises and routinized phonics drills taken from a teacher's manual, but by a horizon-expanding topic that generated opportunities for language skill development. To extend their oral exchanges about things within their experience, the teacher guided them toward the formation of concepts and generalizations while teaching them an expository paragraph composition form. By orally describing, categorizing, and drawing conclusions, and then putting the results into a group-written story, "reading" the story, and performing further oral activity followed by further writing and reading, the children developed literacy skills as a natural outcome of the integration of language practice with social studies content. This kindergarten episode also shows that through writing the results of their study, children are led to consider more consciously what they are learning. Ms. Schubert accomplished this by approaching the topic using concrete and emotionally meaningful objects and experiences. For young children, and for most of us, topics that best pique our interest are those with which we are familiar. Topics that build from the familiar to the unfamiliar are motivating as they permit us to sense our connection to a wider world.[4] The teacher built on the children's contributions and gave them a reason to explore further by involving their parents in the process of investigation and its findings.

Her strategy facilitated the children's development of expressive skills. She gradually helped them to make the transition from telling to writing, from idiosyncratic recall to recall based on facts, from stream-of-consciousness recall to a more logically considered relation of observations. All these are facets of thinking. Writing the charts was, in essence, a thinking exercise flowing from prolonged oral exchanges. Collaborative learning, always a keystone of primary-level, large group investigation, is increasingly seen as a literacy vehicle for older children as well. Small group work in social studies unit study and investigation, by virtue of the language activities required, generates collaborative learning opportunities important at all levels. If viewed from an integrative perspective then, social studies, and other subjects too, while focusing primarily on the knowledge and understandings of the content pertinent to the subject, automatically serve to enhance language and literacy learning.

Expressive Goals and Basic Instructional Strategy in Social Studies

We know that children who read and write with ease usually have previously developed oral-language facility. Recognizing this, a primary concern in our instruction is to provide all students with a rich oral-language environment. Children must be exposed to oral language from a variety of sources ranging from the teacher's own inventiveness to hearing stories read to them or watching and listening to media. Immersion in a content-rich environment supplies children with expressive ammunition from which they draw when they have opportunities to recreate their knowledge. Every time they recite rhymes, sing songs, assume roles in dramatic enactments, describe experiences, retell stories, discuss how to resolve problems, or make decisions, they are enlarging their language and thinking potential.

Developing young children's expressive ability is an ongoing, multifaceted, overarching goal. A good learning environment will have various and simultaneous expressive activities related to all curricular areas. The basic strategy, or method, used in social studies to develop these abilities is applicable to other content areas as well.

---

[4]Learning theorists call this *proximal development*. It involves capitalizing on what is known and bridging from that to more sophisticated understandings by contact with more knowledgeable students or adults. Planning instruction that creates verbal interaction between more and less knowledgeable students is applicable to every age and subject, but it is particularly important when you are planning for English-as-second-language learners.

The following list outlines this basic set of steps. At every step in the strategy the verbal exchanges between teacher and students and among students enhance both social studies and language learning.

Basic Steps for Prompting Language Expression

1. Eliciting student experience with topic to be introduced: concrete experience—exposure to picture, story, other information, experiment, visit, event
2. Discussing: making terms clear, outlining sequence, findings, questions
3. Motivating: considering purpose for using information, establishing need to organize information
4. Defining expression: deciding form for expression, making structure explicit, developing samples of structure
5. Providing time to develop expression: assisting expression development, providing time to share expression

ON YOUR OWN	**ANALYZING STRATEGIES IN A CLASSROOM EPISODE FOR LANGUAGE EXPRESSION**
9.1	*If you did the kindergarten sample classroom episode today, how would the range of countries where toys and clothing are made expand? You may find it useful to read the kindergarten sample classroom episode again to identify the basic strategy steps in the preceding list as Ms. Schubert employed them. What do you think was important in this episode for keeping the children's interest, enthusiasm, and expressive productivity going?*

When children produce less than adequately in expressive tasks, the difficulty can often be traced to a faulty instructional strategy. Teachers may omit or fail to develop sufficiently one or more of the basic steps—finding student connections to the topic, providing adequate input, framing the task, defining a motivation for the effort, providing models of the task, or supporting the process of development. Children who are enthusiastic about a task usually have an audience for their efforts in mind. Children who make a speech to tell why they favor or oppose letting pets roam freely in the community usually have been instructed about the form a persuasive talk should take. A class in which most children complete expressive tasks successfully has usually been provided instruction in all the steps in the basic strategy for developing expression.

Literacy and Long-Range Social Studies Planning

How do able readers, writers, and thinkers gain their abilities? Studies tell us that proficiency in literacy is positively correlated with lots of practice in reading, writing, and communicating. In other words, the best way to sponsor able readers, writers, and thinkers is to organize instruction and learning environments with high literacy expectations. Clear communication supported by enriched source materials are prerequisites to growth in social studies knowledge based on literacy development. Let us consider some ways of structuring literacy opportunities and some possibilities for providing enriched source materials as long-range planning issues in social studies.

Oral Reading by Teacher

Traditionally, primary grade teachers have read aloud to students, a practice that is often dropped after the primary grades. Teachers feel students should be reading independently by this age and may feel time constraints due to a building schedule that rotates students to various classrooms. Dropping oral reading by the teacher is unfortunate. For social studies content, teachers can use the daily oral reading time to read a novel related to the current social studies theme that can build interest and motivate students to do further reading. Usually, teachers choose books about the theme they like personally. Often, they select books that are above the reading level of most students but not beyond their comprehension. When novels are too lengthy for the time allotted to the theme being studied, teachers read the first several chapters, storytell the main events leading to the climax, and then resume reading the final chapters. Oral reading need not be confined to novels. Picture books, diary entries, news articles, and editorials are also sources that can prompt further questions to research, give human interest to text and other expository writing, and spark oral and written communication in response to the content of what was read orally by the teacher.

Sustained Silent Reading

Most schools have instituted the practice of using fifteen to thirty minutes a day for individually selected sustained silent reading (SSR). Teachers find that if they preview books that are within their students' decoding range during their oral reading sessions, students will avidly read the remainder. Teachers also increase social studies–related reading during SSR by making a selection of books available that are related to the current social studies theme.

Required Independent Work

Expecting students to do wide reading and recommended television viewing outside school requires that teachers provide students and parents with bibliographies and lists of programs. School media personnel and local library personnel can assist teachers in compiling lists of what is available on the current social studies theme. Television guides need to be scanned for specials and documentaries students can watch. Local and regional cultural events such as tribal dancing, local history walks and exhibits, and neighborhood civic activities should all become part of the outside-of-school work that teachers can expect students to seek out and become accountable for in their learning logs.

Structured Discussion Routines

Talking and writing about what we read is the best way to stretch our critical thinking. Setting up times in the daily and weekly schedule for student sharing should be part of a literacy-rich social studies program. Rationales for discussion groups can vary. Sometimes grouping students reading the same book is the best way to support less independent students. More independent students can profit from groupings that bring together students researching different sources related to the theme being studied. Activities in these sessions can vary from sharing written work to filling in information matrices using their different sources to debating issues from the different points of view gained from their research.

■ SUMMARY

Language and literacy skills are intimately tied to social studies instruction. A balance is needed between the transmission model and the facilitator model in teaching literacy and the social studies. Activities to help students with special needs as well as all students include using a buddy system, flexible small group arrangements, and helping students read the text. To access the literacy potential of social studies, children need instruction and guidance in reading, gathering, and communicating information.

■ SUGGESTED READINGS AND WEB SITES ■

Alleman, Janet, and Jere E. Brophy. "Trade-Offs Embedded in the Literary Approach to Early Elementary Social Studies." *Social Studies and the Young Learner* 6(3) 94.

Shorter version of book-length critique that examines limitations on social studies under some literature approaches.

Farris, Pamela J., and Susan M. Cooper. *Elementary Social Studies: A Whole Language Approach.* Madison, WI: WCB Brown and Benchmark, 1994.

Multiple-author methods text detailing social studies instruction from the whole language perspective.

Graves, Donald H. *The Reading/Writing Teacher's Companion: Investigate Nonfiction.* Portsmouth, NH: Heinemann, 1989.

This and the following book by Graves are two case study volumes that chronicle a writing-workshop approach to literacy and seeing the classroom as a community for literacy development.

———. *The Reading/Writing Teacher's Companion: Experiment with Fiction.* Portsmouth, NH: Heinemann, 1989.

Hoge, John D. "Improving the Use of Elementary Social Studies Textbooks." *ERIC Digest* 33 (1986): 2–3.

Lists ways to get more meaning from text reading.

Humes, Ann. "Putting Writing Research into Practice." *Elementary School Journal* 84 (September 1983): 3–15.

Suggests writing process steps from research for classroom application.

Irvin, Judith L., John P. Lundstrum, Carol Lynch-Brown, and Mary Friend Shepard. *Enhancing Social Studies Through Literacy Strategies: Bulletin 91.* Washington, DC: National Council for the Social Studies, 1995.

Fine overview of research on pedagogy made practical for middle-grade teachers.

Kornfeld, John. "Using Fiction to Teach History: Multicultural and Global Perspectives of World War II." *Social Education* 58 (September 1994): 281–286.

Author describes and analyzes personal experience of teaching sixth-grade literature-based unit including student bibliography.

Langer, Judith A. "A Response-Based Approach to Reading Literature." *Language Arts* 71 (March 1994): 203–211.

Overview of research on teaching and learning of response-centered approaches, from a constructivist perspective to literature highlighting differences in student reading purposes, distinguishes reading for exploring horizon of literary possibilities from reading for discursive purposes of maintaining a point of reference common in social studies that includes provocative integrative framework of teaching strategies.

O'Day, Kim. "Using Formal and Informal Writing in Middle School Social Studies." *Social Education* 58 (January 1994): 39–40.

Examples of using writing to learn in middle grades.

Yokota, Junko. "Books That Represent More Than One Culture." *Language Arts* 71 (March 1994): 212–219.

Categories of multiple cultures are presented separately; also includes comparisons/contrasts, interactions between/among cultures, multicultural curriculum thinking, and annotated discussion of children's trade books that deal with more than one culture.

Web Sites

Center on English Learning and Achievement (CELA)
http://cela.albany.edu
 Research center dedicated to improving student learning and achievement in English as a subject and in the other academic disciplines.
Children's Books Online
www.cyberkids.com/Launchpad/TextPages/Books.html
 Variety plus children's literature.
English as a Second Language Web site
www.rong-chang.com
 Web site links as well as other help for ESL students.

Inclusion Press International Home Page
www.inclusion.com
 Information on inclusion.
Internet Public Library
www.ipl.org
 Especially children's literature for librarians. Has a reference question section that may be helpful in answering questions.
The Internet TESL (Teachers of English as a Second Language) Journal
www.aitech.ac.jp/~iteslj/
 Games, conversation questions, and more for ESL learners.

Chapter 10

Teaching Social Studies Skills

Time, Space, Technologies

An information explosion of verbal, pictorial, and numeric facts is here. Information is a valuable and strategic resource, and students need the skills that will allow them to access and to understand it. Teachers need to teach specific social studies skills—chronological time, and map and globe skills—as well as to use new technologies, both as a teaching method and as skills for students to use. This chapter focuses on the following topics:

■ Learning About Time and Chronology

■ Map and Globe Skills

■ Technologies for the Social Studies

You already know that one of the important goals in teaching history is to help children develop a sense of time and chronology. We all operate in a time-space dimension and constantly view social phenomena in a time-space orientation. We describe events this way: "On July 4, 1997, the Mars *Pathfinder* arrived on Mars" or "Yesterday I attended the meeting of the local teachers' organization at Washington School." Individuals, influenced by their culture, determine the significance of historical events. Time and space are interrelated. For our purposes, however, we will consider them separately—first time (history) and then space (geography).

■ LEARNING ABOUT TIME AND CHRONOLOGY

How do children acquire the concept of *time?* Most children gradually recognize that events fall into patterns. From their home life, children learn that typically there is a time to get up, to eat, to play, and to sleep. Through the use of language and experience, they begin to distinguish among past, present, and future. In the Western model of time, the present is now, and it becomes past almost as soon as we think about it. The future is what will happen. *Yesterday* and *tomorrow* are early and important concepts.

A more mature time sense, *chronology,* allows us to move away from personal experience and to extend our understanding of time backward and forward. Dates become orientation points, and events fall into chronological order. We start to visualize how events a hundred or even a million years ago are related to the present. This perspective obviously involves more than simply memorizing dates. We begin to understand the concepts of cause and effect and of continuity. Individuals change, families change, social institutions change, nations change; the whole world changes. Most changes occur gradually; a child grows older, and the dynamics of her or his family shift a little each year.

In recent decades the awareness of time has undergone extreme contractions and enormous expansions. This is because the instruments for measuring time have become ever more precise. Computer-calculated time is measured in milliseconds and microseconds. On the other hand, our knowledge of the earth's history as well as the distances in the universe continues to be extended.

You know that when you are enjoying yourself, time seems to pass quickly. On the other hand, when you are waiting in the post office line or for a medical appointment, time seems to go slowly. We as adults know that these are *subjective* conceptions of time. However, children do not necessarily understand that the differences they experience in time are an illusion. They do not comprehend the uniform motion or velocity of a clock. They believe that the clock works more quickly or slowly depending on how they experience the time. Some children have reported that school time really seems to drag.

To make time *objective*, we organize units of time by a calendar. There are three distinct types of astronomical calendars. The one with which we are most familiar is the *solar* Gregorian calendar, which is used in the United States and also serves as an international standard for civil use. There are also a *lunar* calendar, such as the Islamic calendar, and the *lunisolar* calendar of which the Hebrew and Chinese calendars are examples. The importance of calendars is that they give shape to the passing of time by endowing certain days with special significance. They are signposts that give meaning to our lives. The calendar marks our birthdays, the holidays we celebrate, our appointments, and our work and vacation schedules. Being able to use a calendar and telling time are essential to function in our society.

This section on time and chronology is organized in the order that material is usually taught in the primary grades and then in the upper grades, as shown in the following list.

Learn meaning of day, week, month, year	K–third grade
Use calendar to find dates	K–third grade
Understand today, yesterday, tomorrow	K–third grade
Distinguish between A.M. and P.M.	K–third grade
Learn to tell time by the clock	K–third grade
Understand time lines.	First–sixth grades
Learn to translate dates into centuries	Middle-school grades
Comprehend the Christian system of chronology—A.D. and B.C.	Middle-school grades

However, there are no firm rules about when to introduce time and chronology. In addition, teachers often must reteach to maintain some of these skills.

The 1994 History Center (see pages 175–176) went beyond these recommendations on what students should be able to do to demonstrate chronological thinking. Examples of student achievement included the following:

In Grades K–2

On listening to or reading historical stories, myths, and narratives, students should be able to reconstruct the basic organization of the narrative: its beginning, middle, and end.

In creating historical narratives of their own, students should be able to establish a chronology for the story, providing a beginning, middle, and end.

In Grades 3–4

Students should be able to group historical events for broadly defined eras in the history of their local community and state.

Students should be able to construct time lines of significant historical developments in their community and state.

In Grades 5–6

Students should be able to construct multiple-tier time lines (important social, economic, and political developments).

Students should be able to interpret data presented in time lines.

The New York State Social Studies Framework asked the following for elementary-level students:

Create personal and family time lines to distinguish near and distant past and identify family origins.

Interpret simple time lines by recognizing correct chronological order of major events such as the Native American settlement of North America, Columbus's voyage of 1492, the American Revolution, and the writing of the Constitution.

Most children learn to tell time at home and in school, although the increased use of digital watches and clocks means that they are less familiar with the so-called face of the clock. There are, however, computer programs that teach children how to tell time. The program shows a digital 8:30 and then prompts that student to move the hands on an analog clock on the screen, using a mouse. Almost all children eventually learn to tell objective time through the use of clocks, calendars, and time-zone maps in their mathematics and science work. Their social studies classes provide the addition of the *cultural* aspect of time. Students learn the distinction between B.C. and A.D. and the meaning of the terms *decade, century,* and *millennium.* Teachers frequently use terms such as *ancient times, the Dark Ages, the colonial period, prehistoric time, several centuries ago,* and *the beginnings of modern times.* We need to make sure all students know what these terms mean.

Like all abstract concepts, time must be personalized and related to a child's experience if it is to be understood. One way to organize and understand time is through a *time line,* one of the simplest ways to organize historical information. Here is how it is done:

1. Draw a line based on a consistent scale of your choosing; each inch might equal ten years, one year, or a hundred years, depending on what information you wish to include.
2. Write in significant events at the appropriate places. A time line reads from left to right, with earlier events on the left and more recent ones on the right, so children are using a reading convention like that of English with which they are already familiar.

In the primary grades you can also make time lines for a week or longer. Put up the days of the week. Then have children draw pictures or symbols for what happened during the week such as special programs or holidays. Be careful not to have so much clutter that the concept of time is not obvious.

Students can also make time lines of their own lives or those of their families, noting important dates such as marriages, births of children, and graduations. Personal time lines are a good way for students to start the year. Ask them to bring favorite pictures of events in their lives to class and insert these at appropriate places on their own time line. Have students write about why events were significant in their lives. Time lines also can be made for a grandmother's life, a fictional character, a community, events in a story, or happenings in a given school day. Many teachers post several time lines around their classrooms and ask their students to add the dates of the events they study. Symbols (such as a train for the completion of the transcontinental railroad) make the meaning of the dates clearer.

Continue to introduce more and more complex time lines to students throughout the year. Vary the format by moving the earlier events to the top of the page and the more recent ones to the bottom, as shown in Figure 10.1.

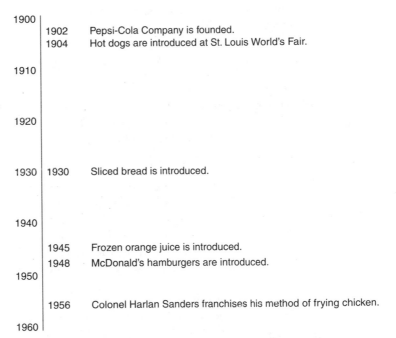

FIGURE 10.1 Time Line for American Foods

Ask your students to identify the year in which frozen orange juice was introduced. Then ask them how many years ago that was, but make sure that they are not simply calculating dates from the time line. Use time line exercises to introduce critical thinking about the data shown. For example, can students hypothesize from looking at the American foods time line what kinds of new foods might be introduced in the coming years? Also, you might ask them to talk about the impact that nationally available frozen orange juice has had on our society in terms of family roles or its impact on the orange industry or on our relationship with Brazil, the world's largest exporter of oranges.

Time lines can be used to teach about historical themes (a time line showing revolutions through the centuries) or about specific regions or nations. Children's encyclopedias such as the *World Book* often provide time lines about important countries. Consider, for example, the dates in the following list.

Important Dates in Mexico

1325	The Aztecs found Tenochtitlán (Mexico City)
1519–1521	Aztec Empire is conquered by Spain
1846–1848	Mexico is defeated in war with the United States; Mexico loses much territory
1910–1911	Francisco Madero leads a revolution that overthrows the dictator, Díaz

The preceding events are listed in chronological order rather than scaled as they are on a time line. What difference does this make in our reading of them? How does consistent scale teach historical lessons? You might provide students with a list such as this and then ask them to make a time line. How long, approximately, did the Aztec Empire exist compared with the Spanish occupation? Time lines can provide *visual* reinforcement of historical concepts.

Time lines are excellent aids in teaching American history or the history of specific states, as the periods involved in American history lend themselves to detailed time lines. A time line covering 200 years—or even more than 300 years, beginning in 1620 with the landing of the Pilgrims—enables you to include specifics about transportation, communication, and the development of industry as well as important dates in political history. Ask students to find or draw pictures of citizens in typical dress for each century or half-century, and paste them to the appropriate parts of the time line. Many students can calculate how many years ago the Pilgrims landed but have no real understanding of what life was like then or how long ago it was relative to the Civil War or the invention of the airplane. Why, they may ask, was setting out for the New World so frightening? After all, we now travel back and forth to and from Europe all the time. A time line can help them understand.

After using simple time lines, students may be more ready to tackle concepts such as *century*. A new century begins every one hundred years. In the year 2001, a new century began. Provide your students with a Western history chronology by centuries, such as the following:

Historical Events Classified by Century

1700	American Revolution
	French Revolution
1800	Industrial Revolution spreads
1900	World Wars I and II
	Computers
	Space exploration
2000	

Ask students to place specific events within the centuries. You can give them a random list of dates, including times such as 1776 (Thomas Jefferson writes the Declaration of Independence) or 1861 (American Civil War begins) or 1911 (Mexican Revolution). Don't use the dates of an individual's life, since these often overlap century boundaries. Now ask students what events happened in each century. In upper grades, you might ask whether two historical figures might have talked to each other. Students should get a sense that James Madison could (and did) talk to Thomas Jefferson but could not have spoken to Woodrow Wilson or Franklin Roosevelt.

When they understand centuries, students may be ready to tackle the difficult concept of A.D. and B.C. in the Gregorian (Christian) calendar and the contemporary secular designation for these same dates, B.C.E. (Before the Common Era) and C.E. (in the Common Era). Students may also see these abbreviations written as AD, BC, BCE, and CE without periods or space between the letters. They may see AD put before the year, as in AD 1492. In addition, students might encounter the use of B.P. (before the present) rather than B.C. (before Christ) when they study the beginnings of early society. B.P. is used by archaeologists and paleontologists when referring to dates earlier than 1000 B.C. The P is usually defined at 1950 A.D. The reason for this is that the techniques used to date ancient objects and fossils are based on analyzing substances found in those objects today. These scientists feel that they risk introducing errors if they try to conform to B.C. terminology.

ON YOUR OWN	TIME CONFUSION
10.1	*Do you recall any confusion you had in your youth about time concepts? Do you think that elementary teachers should use terms such as* nineteenth century *and* twentieth century *while teaching? Or do you think it is better to say that in the 1800s the railroad was invented or in the 1900s the airplane was invented?*

■ MAP AND GLOBE SKILLS

Maps, like graphs and charts, are specialized ways of presenting information. However, too frequently maps remain a mystery to adults. They have not benefited much from their experiences in elementary school learning map skills. Map and globe skills are often taught for a few weeks at the beginning of the year, isolated from the rest of the social studies program. This practice has been encouraged by publishers, many of whom have traditionally started textbooks with a concentration of map skills in the first unit. That situation is changing. More publishers now provide a well-thought-out sequence of map skills in their elementary social studies series. In fact, of all the skills of the social studies—listening, small group work, problem solving, and so on—map skills are probably receiving the most attention from textbook authors. In addition, of all the areas of elementary social studies, more computer software programs have been designed for teaching geography and map skills than for any other area.

ON YOUR OWN	MAP SKILLS AND TEXTBOOKS
10.2	*Check the map skills program in an elementary textbook series. If attention is being given in textbooks to map skills, why do you think so many children and adults have trouble using maps?*

Although geography and map skills have been taught for generations, the research in this area is still inconclusive, especially regarding the appropriate time to introduce students to specific skills. In other words, although charts on scope and sequence may state that children in grades 4 to 6 should use scale and compute distances or compare maps and make inferences, we are not really certain that all children are cognitively ready at these grade levels to learn map skills. Research has shown, however, that when teachers are well prepared and materials are carefully sequenced, most elementary students can indeed learn the basics of map literacy.

In teaching map-reading skills, you need to be aware of the differing levels of ability among your students. Map reading may be too difficult for some students, especially if the maps contain too much data. Evidence exists that girls at the elementary level might not perform as well as boys in map-reading skills and geography.[1] You should be aware of your own teaching methods and make sure that you give girls at least as much time and attention in reading maps as you give boys.

If there is one "magic" guideline in teaching map skills, it is to make the concept concrete. Relate what you are teaching to student experiences. Students in the primary grades, especially after exposure to globes, should be provided with the direct contact with landscape features. Every town has a landscape that includes some of the geographic, geologic, and cultural features that students find symbolized on maps. But simply taking students outside for a walk is not necessarily productive. To make effective use of outdoor time, you need to plan activities before and after the trip, as well as planning the trip itself. If you do not plan carefully, you run the risk that students will think your walk is simply free time outside the classroom.

First, know what you want to achieve. This means visiting ahead of time the sites your class will see and identifying the major features; it also means communicating the purpose of your trip to your students.

There are administrative considerations to any field trip, even a short walk to local sites. Make sure you inform your principal so that issues of legal liability and safety can be checked. To avoid trespassing, ask property owners for permission, even in the case of an apparently abandoned cemetery. For longer trips, your school will certainly have a policy about permission slips and number of chaperons.

During the trip, try to focus students' attention and help them understand concepts such as *swamp* and *treeline* and how these are related to symbols on a map.

[1]United States Department of Education NAEP *Geography: A First Look; Findings from the National Assessment of Education Programs* (Washington, 1998).

Symbols for cultural features (buildings, ruins, canals, dams, or even battle sites) must be explained; show students how the buildings they are seeing appear on maps. Finally, water and weather features are sometimes observable: dry salt lakes, tide pools, channels, coral reefs, ponds, warm and cold currents, and prevailing winds. You may want to have students take pictures or fill out worksheets. Anything students can touch (e.g., rubbing their hands against rock formations, dipping fingers into ponds) will make the trip more memorable.

Finally, plan posttrip activities and use the experience in future classroom activities. Ask students their impressions and observations; review your major objectives with them. Continue to discuss the field trip as a reference in future lessons. Students can make three-dimensional maps of the area they visited. Tabletop maps, clay or sandbox constructions, and paper maps on the floor can also help students demonstrate graphically what they have seen. You might want to have them use blocks or boxes to show miniature buildings, schools, or neighborhoods. The more effectively children can use their experiences, the better they are able to understand the basic ideas and concepts of any field.

In learning map and globe skills, primary-grade students begin with a realization that their local area is only a tiny part of the whole world and move to a broader conception of the world. Use students' trips to help them become more careful observers, as emphasized in the tips on having successful field trips. It is easy to pass through an environment without appreciating or noticing much about it, but all children can develop skills in observing cultural and physical features through short walks, field trips, and trips with their families. Learning to observe is especially important in the primary grades. (See Chapter 3 on observation skills.)

Because of the limitations of the local area, media—videos, Internet, and television programs—are usually needed to supplement students' understanding. But the importance of the local environment should never be forgotten at the elementary-grade level. Frequently, teachers concentrate on a national commercial textbook and ignore what is right outside the windows of their classrooms. Given a map worksheet with directions on it, students can usually determine location of key items. But many of these same students do not know the directions in their own community. Ideally, children should learn the cardinal directions (north, south, east, and west) by the position of the sun (or shadow). Outdoor exercises can be most helpful when they are introduced about the third grade.

We also recommend classroom signs or maps indicating north, south, east, and west. But what if you aren't sure where north is? This is not at all unusual. Many people drive freeways without any sense of direction; highway signs indicating east or west exit points mean little to them. Children who get perfect scores on map exercises in the classroom cannot walk or ride their bikes to a specific location using local maps because they cannot orient themselves to where they are. If you are not sure, ask a reliable individual, such as a police officer, or use a compass. Whenever you take students outside on walks or on field trips in a bus, indicate in what general direction you are all going. Using a compass can often be fun; let students pass it around. Just as students now often know more about computers than their teachers, students sometimes have better senses of direction than their teachers. Identify these potentially helpful students as soon as possible. Often they are children who score extremely high on nonverbal and spatial areas of intelligence tests. These children also can use a **GPS unit** (Global Positioning System), the latest technology, that can create a map as you walk and tell your place on the earth's surface.

Teachers should not forget to use the maps found in children's literature as characters move from one place to another. If there are not maps, some stories' characters such as Harry Potter go on journeys that children can map out as they read. Students gain meaning from reading if they understand better the geography of the novel.

Along with labeling and identifying aspects of the local environment, map teaching involves systematic, step-by-step presentation of a series of questions to help a student learn specific skills.

1. Locate places on a map and globe.
   a. Identify continents by shape.
   b. Identify hemispheres.
2. Orient a map and note directions.
   a. Find compass points.
   b. Use scale and compute distances.
3. Interpret maps and symbols.
   a. Use a map key.
   b. Visualize what the map symbols mean.
4. Compare maps and make inferences.

Each one of these skills may have to be explicitly taught. Although brighter students will absorb the concepts without much direct teaching, many others will need as much assistance as you are able to give. Working in pairs may be helpful for many students when they are doing activities or worksheets on map skills; it also makes these activities more fun. Because there is often a sense of accomplishment in completing a map exercise, students frequently report that they like geography and map work at the elementary level.

What can be done specifically to teach these map skills? You can show students silhouettes of the continents such as the ones in Figure 10.2. Ask them to label the

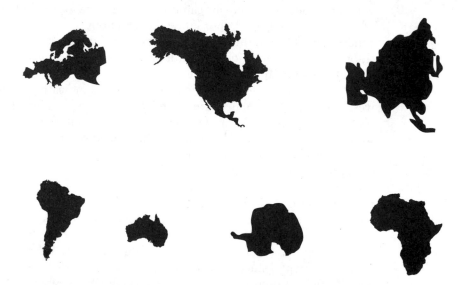

FIGURE 10.2 Silhouettes of Continents

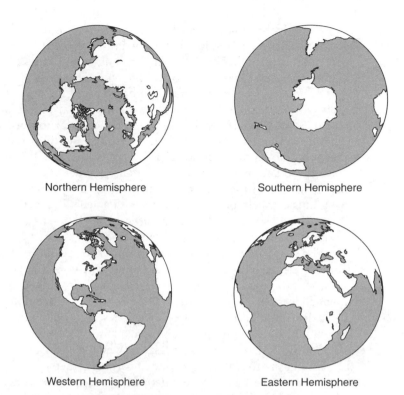

Northern Hemisphere   Southern Hemisphere

Western Hemisphere   Eastern Hemisphere

FIGURE 10.3 Maps of the Hemispheres

Source: "Teacher's Resource Binder-Level 3," *Communities Large and Small* (Lexington, MA: D. C. Heath, 1985). Reprinted with permission.

continents. Once you are confident that students really know the shapes of the continents, move on to identifying hemispheres and locating continents within them. Typically, students see maps only of the Western and Eastern Hemispheres. Occasionally, they are shown maps of the Northern Hemisphere but very rarely the Southern Hemisphere (see Figure 10.3).

Yet it is important to be able to recognize continents from different perspectives. In effect, this is what happens to the astronauts. Try to show your students maps that were produced in other nations. Maps printed in Germany or Britain, for example, have the prime meridian in the absolute center of the map. World maps made in China or Japan show those nations in the center with the American continents squeezed into the right-hand edge. (Good sources for these maps are the offices of consuls of different nations.) At first, students may say that something is wrong with these maps. This is a good lesson to show that people have different perspectives on what the world looks like.

The issue of perspective is important. Young children need to be shown that an object looks different if you view it from the top or from the foot of a mountain. In classrooms, a toy doll can be put on top of a miniature mountain and children can be asked to imagine they are seeing through the doll's eyes. Ask the children what they would see if the position of the doll changes. This is similar to exercises asking students to draw their own desks or their shoes as seen from an overhead position. Often students put in heels or other features that they really could not see from above.

As with chronology, specific map skills have to be taught and retaught, both as separate lessons or exercises and as integrated parts of other subjects. You cannot assume that students will transfer the learning of one map skill to another type of map skill or the use of map skills to real life without your help.

Almost every expert in the field has stressed the importance of introducing the globe to primary students and of explaining that globes are small models of the world. Some primary teachers bring in a model car to illustrate what they mean by a model so that students will not get confused and think that the world is the size of the globe shown in the classroom. Globes, and especially those with only water and continental land masses indicated, can help students visualize continents, a sphere, a hemisphere, and the equator. Furthermore, correlation with the science and math programs can help provide students with a general understanding of the rotation of the earth and seasonal changes. Photographs of the earth taken from outer space are also helpful in giving a new perspective on how the earth looks.

Flat maps are usually introduced in the intermediate grades, when students learn about scale, geographic grids, and the use of color and symbols in maps. Each skill must be taught and retaught separately. Students should become aware of the following ideas: (1) A map is flat and cannot show true roundness; (2) all flat maps have some distortion (although the technical reasons for different map distortions need not be explained); (3) the legend or key explains what each symbol means; and (4) the scale of the map controls the degree to which we can generalize.

Emphasize the information that a particular map provides. Intermediate-level students can be exposed to different kinds of maps: Students need to learn to interpret a temperature map, a time-zone map, a telephone area code map, a historical map (of the Roman Empire, for example, where the boundaries of Europe are different from what they are today), and a political map (of the United States, for instance, showing the number of members each state has in the House of Representatives).

Intermediate students must also learn how to locate places on a map. Most maps use a letter-number index to give the location of smaller cities or streets. Each student should have his or her own map with which to practice finding different places by using such indexes. Some teachers like to start this activity with small groups, but you must take care that each student learns the appropriate skill and that one student does not do all the work for the whole group.

An activity that is fun as well as instructive is comparing maps of Pangaea. Have students look carefully at a world map (top, Figure 10.4), especially the Atlantic coast of Africa. Tell students to think of the continents as pieces in a jigsaw puzzle. Where would Africa fit? This relationship among the continents was first noticed in 1912 by Alfred Wegener, a German scientist. He proposed the continental drift theory: that continents had moved and drifted from one large land mass, which he called Pangaea (center, Figure 10.4). Research has upheld Wegener's basic idea, although scientists have made some changes in his theory. The bottom map (Figure 10.4) shows how present-day scientists think the earth looked more than 200 million years ago. Ask students what differences they see among the three maps. Then ask them to explain a bumper sticker on a car reading "Reunite Pangaea!" and why the bumper sticker is really a joke. Students who want to learn more about continental drift can be advised to read about plate tectonics in encyclopedias and other sources.

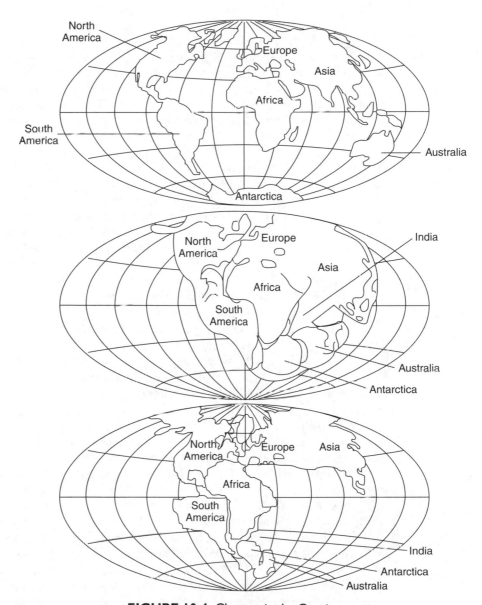

FIGURE 10.4 Changes in the Continents

Source: Adapted from A. Hallam, "Alfred Wegener and the
Hypothesis of Continental Drift," *Scientific American.*

Notice that we have been emphasizing map-*reading* skills. Map*making* (or making one's own charts, cartoon drawings, etc.) is more difficult than simply reading or interpreting a map or table. Making maps requires visualization abilities. Mapmaking is the supreme test of map understanding; it may be an appropriate activity only for selected students. With proper instruction, however, most students enjoy map production.

The steps in making a map are somewhat similar to steps in making charts and graphs. They usually include (1) collecting or observing data, (2) organizing or simplifying data, (3) planning the map (chart) in terms of scale, and (4) drafting or drawing the map or chart. Of course, computer programs can help students in making charts. Computer programs can eliminate a lot of the drudgery associated with steps 2, 3, and 4. One of the advantages of making maps (or charts) is that students can present what they have learned, especially local data, in a simplified format.

Primary children can make maps. Some teachers start with making a map of their own classroom. Children have to be told that they are looking down from the ceiling as they place desks and other room equipment in the classroom map. After this, children can be asked to make a map of their own bedroom or a room that they wish could be theirs. This activity can be expanded to include a map of their house or a house they would like. Finally a map of the local streets can be made, showing where the children's homes are located. Some teachers have used old shower curtains as the material for the local street map. The advantage of the shower curtain is its large size, making the streets visible in the back of the room. Note in all of these examples that the maps were local and personalized for the class. Usually, students must be taught each separate stage before they can draw the map.

Because of the time involved and the visual skills needed to make maps, many teachers ask students to place data on already assembled globes and maps. Unbreakable globes and wall maps that can be marked with crayons and washed off are especially useful. Even inexpensive outline maps (frequently found in teachers' guides for map exercises for students) that have a minimum amount of information on them can be used to real advantage.

As mentioned in Chapter 6, mapmaking has been revolutionized by technology. Your library may have the specialized software for atlases that will find a map after you type in the name of a place or country. There are maps with animated markers that show particular places. There is a street atlas of all the streets, roads, and highways in the United States with different levels of enlargement. In other words, with these tools it is easier than ever before to locate places with the use of an atlas. With these maps may come pictures, tables, charts of comparison data and articles, and Internet links. Never before have teachers and students had access to as many maps as they now do, but students still need some background to interpret a map.

We hope that the teaching of map skills will move beyond the rote-memory format that in the past has been typical of many map skills programs. Do you yourself recall the many hours you probably spent on longitude and latitude? How often in real life have you been asked to use these? We should not forget that most adults commonly use road, newspaper, and magazine maps and do not have to compute longitude and latitude. But more important, we should try to teach students that maps and globes are designed to help us think. Maps in textbooks as well as globes should be used throughout the year and not just during a September unit. In this way, teaching children map skills will enhance their critical thinking, an area that needs as much attention as possible in the elementary school.

■ TECHNOLOGIES FOR THE SOCIAL STUDIES

Today's technologies promise virtually unlimited possibilities to enrich and to enliven the social studies—from providing help and tutoring for individual students to engaging an entire classroom. When we speak of technology for the schools we can assume it to be the "new" interactive multimedia tools and computers rather than television, videos, and other media.

To take advantage of the new technology, American schools will need to undertake two tasks: (1) to engage continually in the expensive process of updating their computer systems and (2) to have teachers become experts in using the new systems so that they can set up learning experiences for students. Keeping up with the pace of innovations in technologies can be daunting for teachers, but the payoffs make it worthwhile.

Teachers and Technology

Before focusing on some promising practices in technology for social studies learning, let us first look at current reality. A U.S. Department of Education survey found that 95 percent of public school teachers reported they had access to the Internet in their schools. More than one-third of U.S. teachers from fourth to twelfth grades now have Internet access in their own classrooms. About three-fourths of all teachers also have a computer at home, leaving only about one-fourth of all teachers without a computer at home. Having a computer at home may be an important step in learning to use e-mail and to look for information on products, travel, hobbies, and entertainment on the Internet. Only after mastering these tasks may some teachers take the many steps needed toward using computers in the classroom.

For elementary teachers the most frequent use of computers in their classrooms was applications, mainly word processing. The second most often used computer activity by elementary teachers for their students was practice drills. These two most popular computer activities are probably not focused on social studies. Recall from Chapter 9 that 10 percent or less of students in the fourth grade use weekly computer software for the social studies, meaning that social studies is presently getting little or no attention in using technology.

Less than 10 percent of all elementary and secondary teachers reported using computers or the Internet to access model lesson plans or to access research and best practices. Newer teachers, however, were more likely to use computers or the Internet to accomplish various teaching objectives.[2] The net result is that profound changes in the teaching and learning of the social studies with the use of technology have not yet been made. The most widely adopted tools are those that fit easily within the existing classrooms. These include drill and practice programs that can be used by individual students without interfering with whole class activity, word processing,

---

[2]National Center for Education Statistics, *Teacher Use of Computers and the Internet in Public Schools* (Washington, DC: U.S. Department of Education, NCES 2000-090, 2000).

presentation tools that can replace overhead projectors, and tools for keeping attendance and grades.

Technology is not a panacea for solving problems in education but to have any effect it must be integrated into instruction on an ongoing basis. Of course, there are wide differences among districts and within classrooms. In addition, the data on teacher and student usage may be quickly out of date as usage increases.

Teachers vary widely in their familiarity and comfort with technology as well as their acceptance of its role in the curriculum. Again, teachers are at different stages of development in the use of computers. Some are at the beginning stage of "running the machines" and learning the basics. The intermediate group of teachers uses a variety of applications in their classrooms. The third advanced group is able to incorporate technology into learning activities. Still only about one-third of all elementary teachers reported feeling well prepared or very well prepared to use computers and the Internet in their teaching, referring to all subject areas and not just the social studies. Familiarity with social studies software and Web sites is probably much lower.

Besides the financial costs of technology, it appears that one very important obstacle to technology adoption in the schools is teacher time. Teachers report an average 47-hour workweek with their out-of-school preparation and grading. For many, there is simply not enough time to examine and to integrate technology into their teaching while keeping up with the daily responsibilities. Teachers have to identify and to evaluate software and Web sites, decide which to use, judge how they fit into the curriculum, and then organize classroom use. With all this work, teachers will only adopt technology if they think it is worth all the expended effort.

Computer Literacy for Students

The public believes that computers belong in the classroom. Parents and government and business leaders maintain that the information age demands that all students need to achieve computer literacy, although budget-constrained public schools have had much difficulty acquiring and upgrading computers. The reason for the national crusade to wiring classrooms is that half of new jobs that employ workers without college degrees require daily use of computers, often including use of the Internet. Furthermore, the income gap between those who use computers on the job and those who do not continues to widen.

Different organizations such as the International Society for Technology in Education (iste), school librarians, and individuals have proposed student standards in technology for guidance to teachers and schools. These standards can be divided more or less into three main areas.

1. *Basic skills or operations.* Use a word processor, use e-mail, use developmentally appropriate multimedia encyclopedias, find pertinent reliable data and information, use technology systems and software responsibly, operate equipment such as a VCR, audio tape player, interactive books, and so on.
2. *Critical thinking skills.* Select and evaluate information resources; distinguish between fact, opinion, and point of view; evaluate accuracy, relevance, appropriateness, and bias, and so on.

3. *Construction skills.* Use variety of media and formats to communicate information and ideas effectively, prepare publications, apply problem solving and decision making to the task, and so on.

These standards at first glance really seem a challenge to both teachers and students. Remember that more students, due to their home experiences, already have acquired many of the basic skills. Those without home experience will require more attention. In some cases, almost individual attention is necessary for students, many from historically disadvantaged groups, to meet these computer standards.

Thus, it is very important that all students become computer literate. Use proficient, computer-literate students as student tech mentors as well as any other volunteers to help all students to acquire computer literacy. One school calls this cadre of students "tech gods," as they come to the rescue of a frozen screen or a malfunctioning printer. Student mentors and volunteers can coach other students and serve as troubleshooters when the equipment malfunctions. When given the time and resources, the basic technology skills can be taught to almost all students. Students can also learn to be responsible by taking care of their work disks and filling out work logs on what they have accomplished, who used the computer, and what needs to be done next. However, teaching the critical thinking skills to be used in evaluating information resources is a far more difficult, although essential, task for computer literacy.

ON YOUR OWN	**TECHNOLOGY STANDARDS**
10.3	*Do you think elementary teachers can have their students meet the technology standards? Will it take too much time away from other curricular areas?*

Teacher Concerns About Technology

Teachers report three main problems in teaching computer literacy. One is access and location of computers. Unless available at a particular time, having a computer laboratory or a library/media center may not be very helpful if there is difficulty in scheduling computer use. Often labs are tied up teaching keyboarding and other skills. In addition, an Internet lab is not always ideal. Students often have difficulty staying on task because the temptation to play with the computer in front of them is so great when the teacher is explaining the task. Then, if several students try to access one Web site all at once, it can lead to long delays or even to system crashes. Students usually also like working with a partner rather than having a computer for themselves.

The second teacher concern is how many up-to-date computers are actually in their own classroom. Some experts recommend four or more computers per room or else students have very limited access in a given week. It has been found that teachers are more likely to use computers on a regular basis if they have them in their classrooms than teachers who have only access to computer labs. You may only have one computer, hopefully with Internet access. Remember that time—yours and your students'—is a valuable resource. If there is only one computer in the classroom, teachers usually have to set time limits for online computer use. Students will also need good planning skills before using the computer so they will not waste precious computer time. An advantage of one computer is that small groups of students can work together. Make sure that all can see the screen. Two students may be ideal or three with one at the computer and one on each side. After three, you may find students standing on chairs to be able to see, a poor safety practice.

The third concern of teachers is lack of support staff. Most elementary schools do not have a full-time computer support person to give necessary maintenance and troubleshooting assistance, as well as curriculum consultation and support. The "tech coordinator" often is a former teacher who has accumulated his or her expertise through informal study and usually is deluged with requests for help. Teachers are not unique in wanting someone to stand by their side to help them in using a computer. The business world recognizes the need to have computer support personnel available to get the job done. It is very frustrating to both teachers and students when software or equipment does not work. For teachers, the old adage about showing a video that may not work still applies: Have an alternative lesson plan should the Web site you need not be available or should the computer go down with technical problems. In reality, many schools trying to be high tech suffer from low-tech support.

The Internet in the Schools

The new gateway for learning is the Internet and its hypermedia part, the World Wide Web (WWW or Web), which form a vast information network spanning the world. The key to locating an address on the Web is its URL (Universal Resource Locator), the address of the data you are searching for on the Internet. The Internet's access to multimedia information resources is seen by parents, business leaders, government leaders, and teachers as the new way for students to develop skills for critical thinking, problem solving, and written communication and for learning to work collaboratively. Children with the Internet at home are at a distinct advantage, and teachers will constantly have to monitor that the key learning opportunities are not confined to the students already familiar with the technology. This will be especially important within small groups of students, where there is a tendency to allow those already knowledgeable to find the information resources and to favor males as well as higher-socioeconomic students.

Researchers have reported that e-mail has been the most useful Internet application used by teachers and the one that they have found to be the most motivating.[3] Teachers also felt that e-mail had the most potential of any Internet resource for them and their students, but actually used it more at home than at school.

Electronic Mail (E-Mail)

Because e-mail appears to be the primary application of the Internet for teachers, students tend to be steered toward this application. E-mail does not involve much teacher or student training to learn to use and requires few changes in the school com-

[3]M. D. Roblyer, "Predictions and Realities: The Impact of the Internet on K–12 Education," *Learning and Leading with Technology*, no. 1 (September 1997): 54–56.

pared with other reform efforts. The enormous popularity of e-mail with adults as well as students can be explained in terms of its many advantages: It is a convenient, relatively inexpensive, democratic, informal medium for conveying messages or just chatting. You can receive or send a message to your grandmother, your senator, or anyone with an e-mail address, anywhere in the world; you can also send your message to several individuals at one time. The volume of e-mail messages is now in the trillions annually and is increasing rapidly.

In the classroom, e-mail enables students and teachers to exchange data and share their experiences, or to send questions to government officials or to authorities in a particular field. Some teachers have noted that students who do not typically participate in classroom discussion often do participate in computer-based, classroom conversations.

Teachers use e-mail to contact other teachers and to provide emotional support and sociability as well as information, suggestions, opinions, and aid related to teaching. If they are planning a unit on pioneers or Native Americans in their own state, they can ask other teachers for help in activities and lesson plans. Student teachers in training, especially those far away from their university site, also use e-mail to exchange ideas.

Teachers can also belong to a *listserv*—an automatic mailing list for use by members of a special interest group. Updated messages are sent every day or so to all those on the list. Some teachers respond immediately to their e-mail from the listserv; others simply enjoy reading the messages or being "lurkers."

E-mail does have its disadvantages. Students, like adults, need to be cautioned about writing their messages with care and thought—not just speed. Their nonverbal reactions are not there for the recipient to interpret, and it is possible that the message could be taken the wrong way. E-mail may not be the best way to settle a conflict or difference in opinion. In addition, all users must remember that e-mail offers no privacy. It is in essence an electronic postcard; it is possible that others can read it.

Teachers must, thus, guide students to develop e-mail protocol and ethics so that clear directions are established about what is permissible and appropriate on a school-based system. Everyone should know what is off limits: criticism of students, teachers, parents, and administrators; grades or other personal materials about students; hate messages, sexually offensive materials or harassment, and profanity.

In the past teachers encouraged the idea of pen pals: Students would exchange letters and small photographs with students in other nations. Today this can be done easily by e-mail. Join a classroom exchange with students across town or across the world. A class can join anytime by using the following: (1) ePals (www.epals.com/); (2) Intercultural E-Mail Classroom Connections (www.stolaf.edu/network/iecc/) of St. Olaf College provides mailing lists to help teachers and classes link with partners in other countries and culture for e-mail classroom pen-pal and project exchanges; (3) KeyPals Service of the Educational Technology Support Center, Yakima, Washington, also allows teachers to send information about their classes and the type of project in which they are interested (www.esd105.wednet.edu/kp.html). Remember to have parents sign permission slips if they have not already signed for computer usage.

Sherry Field and her colleagues described a project in which third-grade students in Taiwan and Atlanta, Georgia, exchanged messages.[4] The exchange also could be just across the town and the future for all exchanges is more likely to include video-conferencing. In international exchanges, a translator or a bilingual teacher or parent may be essential.

When technology permits, teachers can attach files to the e-mail to exchange videos, photos, or sounds of what your classroom, school, and community looks and sounds like. Your students may be surprised that some students in other countries have very different classrooms than theirs. Here are other topics that spark exchange:

Write about favorite foods and graph the data.

Do projects gathering data on your community such as the jobs of parents in the classroom, favorite recreational activities, and typical classroom activities and send the information/research to the other classroom.

Make exchanges at a given time, say once a week, to allow the translator time (if possible, over a weekend) to do the translation. Students can compose questions and answers.

More ambitious pen-pal activities are organized by groups such as GlobaLearn, or similar groups in which a small group of real people take a trip, such as a 5,000-mile, twelve-week journey through major cities and small towns in Argentina, Chile, Bolivia, Peru, and Ecuador. At each stopping point, explorers in the field learn about the daily life of a local school child and explore the local community's culture, industry, history, and environment. The team of explorers in the field posts its discoveries as text, image, sound and video files to the GlobaLearn's Web site at www.globalearn.org/ for the vast number of students who were not on that trip. The files include student profiles, daily journals, expedition logs, and investigations. Using the company's free online services, students and teachers in the United States are able to communicate and collaborate with other participating schools and offer insights into their own local communities for comparison with those along the expedition route. Teachers also need to critically evaluate whether the expeditionary learning promotes an ethnocentric perspective or the biases of the explorers. Although the Web site is free, you must register. A fee is charged for the Teacher's Companion. Other similar global learning groups are also charging a fee.

Internet/Web Research

The vast resources on the Internet provide immediate access to a galaxy of information on almost any subject, but users need skills to evaluate the sites they find. Ideally, the teacher should be familiar with any Internet site before sending students to search for information on it. The sage advice to preview a video or any other media selection before using it continues to be valid. Be alert for sites—some of which may sound innocent enough—featuring pornography or hate groups. Along with infor-

[4]Sherry L. Field, Linda D. Labbo, and Cheng-Hsiung Lu. "Real People, Real Places: A Powerful Social Studies Exchange Through Technology," *Social Studies & the Young Learner* 9, no. 2 (November/December 1996): 16–18.

mation on the Internet comes porno, ads, crazies, and cookies. Teachers as well as parents may need to turn to content-rating systems and the use of blocking software. Teachers need to know what filtering does and does not do. Motivated students can bypass secure controls and nothing is really 100 percent safe.

SMALL GROUP WORK	**WHO SHOULD BE DENIED ACCESS?**
10.1	*All agree that the computer is a tremendous resource but it also has the potential to harm students. Under what conditions do you think students should be denied access to the Internet?*

Like learning any other skill, learning to search for information on the Internet is a gradual process and teachers need to be aware of developmental needs of their students. Because most of the material on the Internet is on the sixth-grade reading level or higher, it is not usually appropriate for primary children to even try to search the Internet. By the fourth and fifth grades, some students can be guided by the teacher. In these cases, the students typically go to Web sites "bookmarked" by the teacher before class, or they can research sites by using as a guide a sheet printed out from a previous search by the teacher or other students.

It is only in the middle school that students should be introduced to search tools and begin searching themselves. The advantage of using the Internet for research is that it may take less time than the traditional library search. Still a computer search can waste a lot of time as an individual explores unrelated topics and leads. In some cases it is easier to go to the library, if it is nearby, where the information and a reference librarian are quickly available. It is still all right to use more traditional sources such as textbooks and reference books. If not in a rush to get information, LookSmart (www.looksmart.com) and ExpertCentral.com (www.expertcentral.com) use people to uncover information but you usually have to wait a day to get results. Always check first if the information is available on CD-ROM references.

The first stop for a computer search is to check if your library subscribes to one of the online indexes, such as *Reader's Guide to Periodical Literature,* or has any of these indexes on a CD-ROM. The second step is to use URLs, but most of the time neither the teacher nor the student has these available. The third step is to use online directories that are compiled especially with the needs of students and teachers in mind. Younger students may benefit from search directories designed for kids such as "Yahooligans!" (www.yahooligans.com) and "AOL NetFind for Kids Only" (www.aol.com/netfind/kids). Only then take the fourth step of using a big search engine with the full realization that using different search engines will locate different resources. Popular search engines are Alta Vista, Lycos, and Yahoo! with their user-friendly, convenient categories. Choose your words wisely. Usually increasing the number of search words will enlarge the scope of your query. A free software agent, Ask Jeeves (www.askjeeves.com,) allows you to type a simple question.

In doing research on the Internet, teachers should urge their students to keep track of where they get their information. Too often students may be careless about the source of the information. In addition, plagiarism with cutting blocks out of a text and pasting into a word processing program is common (see class episode in Chapter 1). But most importantly, students need to understand the content that they have put in the report. One student's project on the Amazon jungle reported that the temperature there was on the average 30 degrees. When asked if that wasn't too cold for a jungle area, the student replied he found it on the Internet and, therefore, it was accurate. He did not realize that the temperature in his source had been reported in Centigrade scale rather than Fahrenheit. With regard to content, too often students think that visual appeal (i.e, showing pictures of the jungle) is more important than understanding the concept of a jungle.

Once students have gathered the data, analysis of the data is the heart of the research project. Here students can compare, predict, conclude, evaluate, and go beyond mere regurgitation of the information compiled. Finally, after finding the information and doing analysis of the data, students need to communicate their data. Besides the standard research report, this might include an editorial, diagrams, posters, e-mail, Web pages, speeches, letters, multimedia, and presentations.

SMALL GROUP WORK	HOW DO YOU USE THE INTERNET?
10.2	*Describe in your group how you use the Internet for personal reasons and for professional reasons. If possible, check with elementary students to see how they use the Internet.*

WebQuests

A WebQuest is designed to be an inquiry-oriented activity in which at least some of the information by learners is drawn from the Internet (edweb.sdsu.edu/webquest/webquest.html). WebQuests are developed to help the busy teacher and students to use time well and to focus on using information rather than spending a lot of time looking for information. In effect, they function like an unit with a problem or task, activities, resources, and evaluation. Familiar topics such as Ancient Egypt, Living in the Middle Ages, and Cinco de Mayo are examples of the many specific WebQuests topics. Within a given topic is usually found a variety of tasks or projects. For Living in the Middle Ages, students can choose a construction/art project, such as building a catapult or battering ram or making a coat of arms; a dramatic presentation, such as a day in the life of a serf; a presentation on medieval food or medicine; or writing assignments, such as a diary of a noble lady or a letter from a university student in London to his parents.

As you can see, some of these activities really are not new. The advantage of Web Quests is that they provide resource links and often a rubric for students to evaluate their work. Some of the WebQuests guide students first to find books from the classroom school or local library, locate experts, and then to do an Internet search. As expected, the quality of WebQuests varies but like other Web sites is expected to continue to grow in popularity because of its usefulness.

Evaluating Web Sites

Some excellent resources for teaching social studies are now available on the Internet, and they are expanding. However, so are the junk and the stale sites that have not been maintained or have unreliable and inaccurate information. Unfortunately, for many teachers finding the good stuff takes more time than they have, which means that the searching process will also be a frustrating one for students.

Because of the time constraints on teachers, teachers often depend on reviews of promising Web sites found in education journals or books. The National Council for the Social Studies' *Surfing Social Studies: The Internet Book* edited by Joseph A. Braun, Jr. and C. Frederick Risinger, NCSS Bulletin 96, has some helpful chapters listing many Web sites, but some of those are now obsolete since the 1999 publication. The International Society for Technology in Education (iste) has been publishing *The Best Web Sites for Teachers* (Eugene, Oregon, iste) that includes all subject areas as well as social studies. Other sources for locating good sites include ED's Oasis at www.classroom.com/edsoasis, which describes and more importantly evaluates Web sites. Other sources also exist for locating the most promising sites for teachers but the various Web guides or books need to be updated quickly. The Internet is constantly changing.

After finding a Web site, you can ask the following questions in order to evaluate the site.

- What is the purpose or intent of the site?
- What persons or organizations develop and maintain the site?
- What is the copyright date or last update to check if the material is current?
- How well does the site work? Is it suitable for your students to access? Is it easy to navigate around the site? What is the reading level and interest level? Is it appropriate for your grade's curriculum?
- Is it a site for teacher ideas but not for students?

Evaluating Software

Where do teachers find advice about the best software? The answer is usually the three C's: colleagues, catalogs, and conferences. Colleagues, especially those on the same grade level and with a similar type of class, are great on what seems to be working, but they may not know the full range of products available. Of course, the catalogs only will tell you how wonderful everything is! Unfortunately, most teachers can only go to one conference a year. What other help is available?

The best guide to finding software to preview is the annual *Educational Software Preview Guide* published by the International Society for Technology in Education (iste)[5]. This software guide is divided by curriculum areas such as social studies, multicultural studies, and various areas of the language arts. Teachers may appreciate the section on special needs that features software with big, colorful visuals and high-quality speech, or software available in non-English languages such

---

[5]International Society for Technology in Education, *Educational Software Preview Guide* (Eugene, OR: Annual), www.iste.org or customer service office is cust_svc@iste.org.

as a bilingual TimeLiner. For each software program, there is the title, publisher, platform (Mac, Win), an annotation, mode (bilingual, creative activity, problem solving, reference, simulation, education game, tutorial, etc.), grade level, and price. Approximately 150 social studies software programs are listed. The advantage of this guide is that all the social studies material is in one place. Otherwise, teachers have to depend on the various commercial catalogs such as Tom Snyder Productions (www.tomsnyder.com), Social Studies School Service (www.socialstudies.com), or Clearvue/eav (www.clearvue.com).

Teachers who want a rating or recommendation on a given product can use reviews of thousands of software programs from journals or from Web sites, such as Clearinghouse Online (www.clearinghouse.K12ca.us) funded by the state of California. Teachers should also check what their state has available in the way of recommendations by teachers. This is especially important in about half of the states where textbooks and the associated media are approved by the state because purchases of software not approved on the list may not receive state funding.

Some software is designed to assist in teaching students a set of facts or concepts. This is closer to what teachers typically do but the software can often provide more interest with auditory, visual, and multimedia effects. Original music of the time period or culture, poetry, speeches, political cartoons, photographs, and interviews can bring people and their history alive. Ultimately only the teacher can make a judgment on the usefulness of a given software program. Again, it is always wise to preview software before either using it or purchasing it. Look at it carefully from these two perspectives: How does it help me as a teacher and how does it fit into the curriculum? Too often, software is interesting but is tangential to the curriculum.

More bilingual software programs are becoming available. A computer software program can cost from $500,000 to $1 million to produce. To sell more copies is desirable. A program with more than one language can be sold in more countries. For example, the storybook of Marc Brown "Just Grandma and Me Deluxe" is available in English and at least one other language. This trend can be helpful for teachers with diverse linguistic populations.

Types of CD-ROMs

Sales of CD-ROMS, a special form of software that presents information in an audiovisual format, have been growing. With CD-ROMs, teachers do not have to worry about students wandering into pornographic sites or wasting time ("World Wide Wait") searching for information. DVDs (digital versatile discs) or video discs, although more expensive than CD-ROMs, will increase in popularity since they can carry four times more text and audio-visual material. However, because production costs are high for CD-ROMs, makers look beyond selling only to the education market to recoup their costs. This means that the educational CD-ROMs available are a crossover product aimed at both the educational market and the general consumer with broad historical overviews. This content may not exactly fit what teachers are looking for. This points out the need for teachers to view the material carefully.

In general, educational CD-ROMs fall into three categories.

Reference

The most common CD-ROMs in the school are reference materials: encyclopedias, atlases, biographies, dictionaries, and indexes. For some encyclopedias, a Teacher's Guide is available at extra cost. These guides usually have lesson ideas, activities for students, and a quiz to assess student success. The next most popular CD-ROMs for social studies are the content areas of U.S. history and world history/world culture. Reference CD-ROMs should allow a search by keywords. If there is not an easy way to locate specific items, the CD-ROM is not very useful. Although the encyclopedias are relatively inexpensive, other CD-ROMs can be expensive, especially the indexes.

Simulation

The best of these CD-ROMs focus primarily on decision making, with students having to use curriculum-related information to make their decisions. High ratings have generally been given to simulations as compared to other CD-ROMs. The fifteen or so of the "Decisions, Decisions" (Tom Snyder Productions), covering such topics as Ancient Empires, Building a Nation, Feudalism, and Prejudice, puts students in roles as leaders of an ancient city-state in control as a new nation emerges from colonial rule, dealing with a food crisis and growing rebellion against the king in feudal society, and learning how to identify prejudice and how to deal with it. Popular both at home and at school have been the SimCity (Maxis) simulations: SimAnt, SimCity 2000, SimCity Classic, SimFarm:School Edition, and SimTower where students use problem solving in a simulation format to grow crops or to manage a city.

Documentary Style

This generally denotes CD-ROMs that use video clips, narrated slide shows, animations, and other similar features to create a computer experience similar to watching a filmed documentary. Typically, these have focused on individuals such as Franklin Delano Roosevelt or Leonardo da Vinci (Corbis Multimedia) and may be more appropriate for older students. The documentary-style CD-ROMs often work effectively to introduce a topic with a presentation in front of the classroom by the teacher. The teacher can show a short portion of the CD-ROM and ask students what questions it raises.

CD-ROMs can be useful if they increase children's attention and interest and are helpful to the teacher with lesson plans and student materials. They should have something special to distinguish them from the more traditional classroom materials. Rainbow Multimedia Series (Curriculum Associates, Inc.) is representative of this genre. It consists of an interactive CD-ROM, student books, teacher guides, and audiocassettes on three topics: "A World of Hats," "Walk in My Shoes," and "The House I Live In." Children practice reading and writing while exploring geography and learning about cultures of children in other lands. In a subtle manner this software can increase the multicultural awareness of children without them even knowing it. The printed reproducible materials geared to the CD-ROM's content make it more expensive but can be a timesaver to the teacher and a useful means of assessment.

SMALL GROUP WORK	**ARE PEOPLE LOSING CONTACT WITH OTHER PEOPLE BY USING THE INTERNET?**
10.3	*There is concern that some Internet users lose contact with their family and friends because they spend hours on the Internet. Do you think this is a problem as more students use the Internet? Are chat rooms a good idea for the young?*

Multimedia Projects

Multimedia—the combination of sound, text, and images within a single information delivery system—can be classified into two areas: (1) commercial packages and (2) student-developed projects. Of course, in practice, a commercial package can and sometimes does have as part of its program students developing their own multimedia presentations. But the sources of data, for these student projects, although extensive, typically are restricted by teachers to just what the commercial product has made available.

Before purchasing a commercial multimedia program, think about the following questions:

- Do you have the necessary technology to run the program?
- What is the point of view, bias, or perspective of the commercial product?
- Will this product really help my students to learn?
- Will it help in my teaching?
- Does it align with my curriculum?
- What will be the student assessment?

The greatest single advantage of commercial multimedia programs is that they are user friendly. Good examples are Encyclopaedia Britannica Education Corporation's *Paths to Freedom: The American Revolution* and *Paths to Freedom: The Young Republic*. These two products are an interactive multimedia approach to teaching U.S. history at the elementary and middle school levels. *Paths to Freedom* features a variety of CD-ROMs, videodiscs, and print materials for students to explore historical materials that include illustrations, maps, primary sources, biographies, famous speeches, and historical narratives. The videodiscs have a bar code guide and bar code reader/remote control so that the teacher or students can easily access the material. After using these resources, the students work on projects and create multimedia presentations for portfolio review. The student readings (except primary sources), audio tracks, and glossary terms are in English and Spanish.

The second use of multimedia projects are those developed by students. For example, in community studies, students could be placed into small groups where the assignment is to create a multimedia presentation of a place of interest in their community—a library, tourist destination, point of historical or cultural interest, or any other place of general importance. The first step is to use a wide variety of sources—Web sites on the Internet, print material, and interviews. In this particular example on the community, students would be expected to visit their topic of interest, collect data in a variety of media formats, and then organize the information on the computer. Individuals can create their own file with a text, graphics/photographs, and sound. The group then puts together the contributions of all members and designs a home page, an initial display of the Web site, and a video. Grades are based both on a group grade (home page and video) plus their individual work. A rubric made by the teacher is available outlining what is excellent (A), good (B), basic (C), and beginner (D).

Based on the preceding description, a multimedia project of this type will normally take at least a month or more. Students may need a worksheet to keep track of what steps they need to do and check off when they are completed. Categories on the worksheet may include:

Historical background research

Write rough draft

Revise with another student

Word process corrections, spell check

Get teacher's approval

Copy

In addition, when visiting the community, transportation will have to be arranged by parents or teachers for students and their equipment. But the results may be worth the time and the effort. Think about the following questions before starting this type of assignment:

- Does your school have sufficient technology resources to product multimedia projects, especially for a whole class?
- What skills are needed by students to use the multimedia tools?
- Does it help me as a teacher in achieving objectives for the students?
- In assessment/evaluation, how much will count for content and how much on technical production? There is a tendency to focus on the whistles and bells in the technology, not on content.

Virtual Field Trips to Museums and Historic Sites

Forget those buses and parent permission forms and have your students go traveling almost anywhere in the world by using Web sites. From virtual museums, students can learn to "read" and interpret artwork, symbols, photographs, and buildings. Outstanding is the J. Paul Getty Museum in Los Angeles (www.artsednet.getty.edu/) with its incredible works of art and fully developed lessons plans and units. Lesson plans and curriculum ideas are sorted by grade level. Examples of valuable units are women artists, arts of India, architecture, and Native American artifacts. Smaller museums may also be helpful, especially if you do not have to sort through thousands of images.

More popular with elementary teachers are historic sites where students can visit cities, states, countries, and continents. Using Web sites, students can go on virtual field trips to a museum or a historical site such as Ellis Island, Plimoth Plantation, the *Mayflower,* walking about Philadelphia's Historic Mile, and the White House. However, virtual field trips vary a great deal in content and usefulness.

Many of these sites contain valuable information and pictures relating to a specific place but no insights about how to use them. Teachers who already have a curriculum, for example, on the Revolutionary War, and are looking for online enhancements will find these sites an added bonus. To make them more useful, teachers need to develop lesson plans with the site in mind. Students will need to feel an involvement or interest in order for the site to work. Thus, "White House for Kids" offers a tour using a White House cat and a dog as the guide to generate interest.

Probably the most successful are the interactive field trips where students can interact with researchers as they travel through cities and historic sites. However, using virtual field trips, like CD-ROMs, does not automatically convey key information to the students. To get the most out of the virtual field trip, teachers often devise worksheets including open-ended questions that require students to reflect on what they have learned. Some Web sites also include their own test questions but some of the best questions are those without a simple "right" answer. Questions requiring critical thinking on why the viewer should believe the facts about the site can be valuable. In other words, students have to ask how credible and accurate the facts are. Is there any reason to suspect bias in the source? How would a Native American look at the facts and interpretation? How much data were on women and families?

Online Communities

An online community is a group of individuals of different ages and expertise who use computer networks to share ideas and information about a given theme or topic. In an online community such as a chat room you see messages others are typing. Participation in such a community offers new avenues to share ideas with experts outside of the local school. Usually the focus of collaboration in the classroom is with experts such as scientists, scholars, and other professionals. Increasingly, some schools are enlisting community members such as lawyers who pledge to answer questions that students have. Students are, thus, exposed to and draw on the expertise of others. The usual problem-solving method can be followed: Students ask questions, gather data, interpret their findings, and draw conclusions. This technique has been most used in elementary school science instruction but elementary students can tackle with success problems such as how different communities are dealing with transportation difficulties. How is traffic congestion defined in your community? How much of congestion is caused by accidents? The potential of graphing the data appears suitable as students exchange data. The future may include more real-time videoconferencing for the exchange of ideas with more sites to ask the experts. There are also specialized sites for asking experts such as "Ask an Expert" (www.askanexpert. com/cat.shtml), which has a list of people who know about everything you cannot figure out from the text or library. The National Park Service's *Teaching with Historic Places* at www.cr.nps.gov/nr/twp is also valuable.

Hints to Teachers

In order to keep up with ongoing changes in technology, you should try to take advantage of any training that your school offers and seek help from those around you—other teachers, technology coordinators, parents, and students. Learn to use any technology that will simplify your teaching responsibilities—from report cards, assessment, and attendance records to communications with parents.

Do not try to do all things at once. Perhaps the best strategy is to learn how to use one piece of software or one Internet site at a time. You can then teach a few students in your class who can then practice peer tutoring with the rest of the class. If you have the Internet available at home, a relatively easy task is to get on lists for catalogs so that you can participate in the upgrading of your school's technology. The International Society for Technology in Education (800-336-5191 or www.iste.org) is a good source. Its publication, *Learning and Leading with Technology,* offers information on new books, Internet guides, software tools, and other resources on how to use technology in the curriculum areas. Or use a Web site to find educational software in the social studies (e.g., http://esi.cuesta.com).

In the future better communication and collaboration between the school and parents/community may also be possible with the use of digitized records of student work and parents' questions and ideas about what is going on in the classroom. Some classes have designed their own Web pages.

Some teachers require students to bring written permission from their parents stating that they understand that their child will be on the Internet or that their child may be exposed to controversial or sensitive issues by using technology. Many schools require student and parent signatures that students using technology will follow the basic rules of courtesy and respect. If you think an assignment might be controversial, write a memo to your principal expressing your concerns.

ON YOUR OWN	**THE BEST USE OF TECHNOLOGY?**
10.4	*What is the best use of technology that you have seen for the social studies? What features made it effective?*

■ SUMMARY

We want students to have a blend of computer literacy and critical thinking skills. Students must learn to understand chronology and time and to develop map and chronological skills as well as the ability to use technologies. If all students are to be technologically literate, teachers will constantly have to upgrade their knowledge and skills in technology. Technologies can broaden students' involvement in challenging activities that require active participation and application of knowledge. Technologies can also provide multiple perspectives on issues and facilitate cross-cultural communication. Technology is a tool that can greatly enhance the social studies classroom by increasing resources, developing interest, and promoting student problem-solving and critical thinking skills. It can also be a time waster and a burden to teachers. With careful consideration, technology can enrich the teaching and learning experience for everyone. As technology continues to improve and becomes easier to use, it offers a promising place as a tool in the social studies curriculum.

■ SUGGESTED READINGS AND WEB SITES ■

Teachers will find it helpful to get updated books on such topics as *Internet Lesson Plans for Teachers, Elementary School Version, All Aboard! The Elementary Internet,* and so on.

Braun, Joseph, Phyllis Fernlund, and Charles White. *Technology Tools in the Social Studies Curriculum.* Wilsonville, OR: Franklin, Beedle, 1998.

Excellent collection of journal articles on the different types of technological resources for teaching social studies and how to plan and evaluate these resources.

Buggey, JoAnne, and James Kracht. "Geographic Learning." In *Elementary School Social Studies: Research as a Guide to Practice,* Bulletin 79. Washington, DC: National Council for the Social Studies, 1986, 55–67.

Good for showing that the research base on teaching geography is limited.

Laughlin, Margaret, H. Michael Hartoonian, and Norris Sanders, eds. *From Information to Decision Making: New Challenges for Effective Citizenship,* Bulletin 83. Washington, DC: National Council for the Social Studies, 1989.

Marker, Gerald. "Social Studies and the Internet: Developing a School Policy." *The Social Studies* 87, no. 6 (November/December 1996): 244–248.

Helpful ways to avoid problems.

Martorella, Peter H., ed. *Interactive Technologies and the Social Studies: Emerging Issues and Applications.* Albany, NY: State University of New York Press, 1997.

Six articles on the application of interactive technologies along with a consideration of social and practical issues.

Natoli, Salvatore J., ed. *Strengthening Geography in the Social Studies,* Bulletin 81. Washington, DC: National Council for the Social Studies, 1988.

White, Charles S. *Social Education* 61 (March 1997).

Excellent special section on technology and the social studies.

Web Sites

International Society for Technology in Education. *The Best Web Sites for Teachers,* 3rd ed. Eugene, OR. International Society for Technology in Education, 2000.

www.iste.org/

800 sites evaluated by teachers that offer lesson plans that can be adopted to content areas such as social studies.

U.S. Geological Survey

www.usgs.gov/education/

Lesson plans by grade level and topic available on teaching map skills. "Exploring Caves" and "Map Adventures" for the primary grades may be of interest.

Index

Academic freedom, 197–200, 303
Acculturation, 19–20, 236
Activities. *See also* Lesson plans
  Being American Bulletin Board, 251
  Confronting Name Calling: Names
    We Call, 242
  Correcting for Stereotypes Bulletin
    Board, 252
  Exploring Our Names, 241
  Developing Multiple Perspectives,
    245
  Promoting Self-Esteem and
    Diversity Awareness, 247
  Understanding Prejudice and
    Stereotyping, 257–259
Advance organizer, 179, 272
Affective domain. *See* Values
  education
AIDS, 19, 163, 197
Alignment, 40–41
Alleman, Janet, 26, 50, 134,
  170, 282
Allport, Gordon, 237
Alternative assessments, 108–109
American educational assessment. *See*
  National Assessment for
  Educational Progress
American national holidays, 26
American Psychological Association, 5
Anthropology in the social studies
  curriculum, 6, 174, 235
Assessment
  alignment, 40–42
  alternatives, 110
  performance-based assessment,
    108–110, 116–117
  techniques and tools, 110–115
Assimilation, 238

Attitudes. *See* Values education
Authentic assessment, 110

Banks, James, 260
Barr, Robert, 19, 31
Barrett, W. S., 204
Barth, James L., 19, 31
Basal textbooks. *See* Textbooks
Basics of democracy, 20, 204–206
Behavioral objectives. *See*
  Instructional objectives
Bennett, William J., 15, 31
Bibliographies, 161, 182, 241
Biographies, 181–182
Bigelow, William, 170
Bill of Rights, 216–218
Bloom, Benjamin, 40, 124–125, 126
Brainstorming, 77
Brophy, Jere E., 26, 50, 134, 170, 201,
  282

Calliope, 183
Cardinal directions instruction, 151,
  291–292
Career education, 190–191
Caring classroom, 208
Case studies, 192
CD-ROMs, 273–275, 303, 306–307
Cemeteries, 180
Censorship. *See* Academic freedom
Center for Civic Education, 191–192,
  201, 202, 218
Centuries, 288–289
Chance, Paul, 100
Character education. *See* Values
  education
Charts, 262, 272, 296
Checklists, 130

Chenney, Lynne, 176, 201
Child-centered approach, 23
Child development and social studies curriculum
  middle grades, 172–174
  primary grades, 133–135
Children's literature. *See* Literature
Children's periodicals, 183
Chronological history, 284–288
Chronological skills. *See* Time
Citizenship
  approaches, 19–23
  in classroom, 206–208
  community, 220–221
  definition, 203–206
  global, 223–232
  school, 219–220
  skills, 4, 152–154, 213–214
  transmission approach, 19–21
  values, 4
Citizenship transmission, 19–21
Civic education standards, 191–192
Class decision making, 208–210
Class meeting, 208–210
Classroom discipline. *See* Classroom management
Classroom environment, 167–168, 208, 236–237
Classroom Episodes
  Cheating by Using the Internet, 17
  Classroom Decision Making, 209–210
  Exploration of Differences through Fantasy, 256
  Global Education in Kindergarten, 277–278
  Spiders and the Assistant Principal, 214
  Structuring Reading Purpose, 273
Classroom management, 205
Classroom responsibilities, 206–207

Classroom tests
  essay, 116–117
  matching, 112
  multiple choice, 113–115
  short answer, 111, 119–120
  true-false items, 112–113
CNN current events materials, 195
CNN Newsroom, 195
Cobblestone, 183
Cognitive development
  middle grades, 173
  primary, 133, 276–277
Cognitive style, 68, 133
Cohen, Elizabeth, 87, 100
Commercial prepared units, 47–48
Community resources, 45, 309
Community study, 43–43, 308–309
Compasses, 291
Computers
  CD-ROMS, 273–275, 303, 306–307
  computer literacy, 298–299
  e-mail, 300–301
  general, 297–298
  online communities, 310
  online instruction, 304
  virtual field trips, 60, 309–310
  WebQuest, 304
Concepts, 21–22, 28, 49, 71–73, 128, 135, 154
Conferences as evaluation techniques, 129
Conflict resolution, 210–213
Constructionist learning, 22, 60, 75, 128, 177, 276
Consumer education, 190
Content, grade level allocations, 25
Content selection criteria, 239–240
Controversial issues, 140, 187, 197–200
Cooperative learning
  evaluation, 91
  intergroup relations, 87, 239

Jigsaw, 92–93
organizational decisions, 89–92
room arrangement, 91
Core curriculum, 173
Critical theory, 23
Critical thinking. *See* Thinking
Cuban, Larry, 32
Cultural identity, 240, 250–251
Current affairs. *See* Current events
Current events, 46, 193–196
Curriculum alignment, 40–41,
126–127
Curriculum definitions, 8
Curriculum guides, 34, 39, 162

Daily lesson plan. *See* Lesson plans
Darling-Hammond, Linda, 132
Data gathering, 80–82
Debriefing, 96, 98, 183
Decision making. *See* Thinking
Definitions of social studies
child-centered approach, 23
citizenship transmission, 19–21
informed social criticism/reform, 23
reflective inquiry, 22
social science/history, 21–22
Democratic beliefs and values, 20,
204, 215
Dewey, John, 75, 204
Direct teaching strategy, 70–74, 206,
272–275
Digital versatile disks (DVD),
46, 306
Discipline, 205–206
Discovery learning/thinking, 74–82
Discussions, 86, 209, 271
Diversity
classroom organization, 236–237
definition, 235–236
holidays, 249, 253–254
instruction, 239–251
problem solving, 254–259
secondary sources, 29, 251–252

Dramatic play, 95
Drug abuse education. *See* Substance
abuse education

Ecology, 227, 228 231
Economics and economic standards,
188–190
Educational technologies. *See*
Technologies
Egan, Kieran, 142, 171
Eisner, Elliott, 66
Elections
mock, 221
student council, 219
E-mail (electronic mail), 300–301
English as a second language (ESL),
110, 111, 129, 158, 244–246,
267–271
Environmental issues. *See* Ecology
ERIC, 33
ESL. *See* English as a second
language
Essays, 116–117
Ethnic diversity, 31, 239–242
Ethnocentrism, 238
Evaluation
formative, 126–128
function of, 101–104, 124
parents, 102
summative, 128
Evans, Ronald W., 32
Expanding horizons curriculum
model, 28–29, 134

FACES, 183
Fairness, justice seeking, 210–211,
215, 218–219
Family histories, 150, 179–180
Fantasy as content source, 142–144
Field trips, 45, 180–181, 189,
290–291
Fill-in-the-blank test items, 111
Five-step lesson plan, 71–72

Gardner, Howard, 68, 134
Gelbart, Elizabeth, 54–56
Gender inequality, 31, 225–226,
    242–243
Generate ideas, 77–78
Geographic Alliance Networks, 185
*Geography for Life: National
    Geography Standards,* 184, 201
Geography methods, 186–187
Gilligan, Carol, 13–14
Glasser, William, 210
Global citizenship, 223–232, 277–278
Globe skills. *See* Map skills
Goals for the social studies, 3–5, 38
Grades, 129
Graphic organizer, 179, 208–209, 272
Graphs, 296
Grouping, 89, 268–270
Guest speakers. *See* Speakers

Haas, Mary E., 32, 201
Hanna, Lavonne, 134
Hickey, Gail, 201
Hidden curriculum, 12, 237, 255
History debates, 6, 174–177
History in middle grades
    content, 173, 245
    methods, 177–183
History standards, 174–177
Holiday curriculum, 26, 164–167,
    253–254
Humanities, 4
Human Rights, 225–226
Hypothesis testing, 86

Indoctrination, 20, 199
Inductive teaching, 74, 77
Informal teaching, 169–170
Informed social criticism/reform
    approach, 23
Informational gathering skills, 80–81,
    272–275
Inquiry as instructional strategy, 74

Instructional objective, definition of,
    40
Instructional objectives, 40, 42
Instructional sequence. *See* Task
    analysis
Integrated thematic instruction,
    49–52, 155–158, 173
Intelligences, multiple, 68
Interact, 99
Interdisciplinary approach, 5, 50
Interdisciplinary thematic unit. *See*
    Integrated thematic instruction
Internet, 9, 181, 195, 300, 302–304
Internet sites. *See end of each chapter*
Interviews, 82, 178–179

Jarolimek, John, 13
Jigsaw strategy, 92–93, 269–270
Johnson, David W., 100
Johnson, Roger T., 100
Journals, 272
Junior High. *See* Middle grades

Kiefer, Barbara Z., 156, 201
King, Rev. Martin Luther, Jr., 165–166
Knowledge, 4
Kohlberg, Lawrence, 13–14
Krathwohl, David, 125

Language. *See* Whole language
    approach; Literacy
Laughlin, Margaret A., 32, 201
Law-related education, 192
Learning style, 68
Lecturing. *See* Direct teaching strategy
Lesson planning definition, 63
Lesson plans. *See also lesson plans
    within units, activities*
    Bill of Rights, 217–218
    Confronting Name Calling, 242
    Deciding Which Ideas Are Best,
        78–80
    To Be Born a Girl, 226

Using Encyclopedias for Main Ideas
and Details, 274
Using Standards to Teach Regions,
185
Levstick, Linda S., 156, 171, 201
Listening, 84, 274
Listserv, 301
Literacy
fundamentals, 263
planning, 280–281
reading, 135, 264–267, 271–272
related to social studies, 263–265,
276–279
Literature, 159–161, 181–183
Long-range planning, 37–40, 280–281
Loyalty to institutions. *See* Patriotism

Map skills. *See also* Geography
methods
cardinal directions, 151, 152,
291–292
continents, 292–293
flat maps, 294
globes, 152, 294
interpretation, 294
map making, 295–296
primary grades, 151–152
Marker, Gerald, 312
Martorella, Peter H., 312
Marxism, 23
Matching test items, 112
Media, 45–46, 158, 222
Media literacy, 196–197, 222
Methods
cooperative learning, 87–94
direct teaching, 70–74
general, 67
role playing, 94–97
simulations, 95, 97–99
thinking, 74, 82
Middle grades
children's characteristics, 172, 173
curriculum, 173–174

Minority groups. *See* Diversity
Moral dilemmas, 14
Moral education, 12–15
Multicultural education.
See Diversity
Multimedia, 308–309
Multiple choice test items, 113–115

Names, 241, 243
National Assessment for Educational
Progress, 105, 132, 262, 290
National Center for History in
Schools, 175–177, 201
National Council for Geographic
Education, 184
National Council for the Social
Studies (NCSS)
definition of social studies, 18
integrated social studies, 18
themes and standards, 6
Web site, 32
National Council on Economic
Education, 188, 202
National goals, 5
National social studies curriculum
patterns, 25
*National Standards for Civics and
Government,* 25
National Standards for History, 25,
174–177
*Nation at Risk: The Imperative for
Educational Reform, A,* 5
NCSS. *See* National Council for the
Social Studies
Need for rules, 12, 152–153, 206
Newspapers, 195
News publications for
students, 194
Noddings, Nel, 13–14, 32

Objectives. *See* Instructional objectives
Objective test items. *See* Paper-and-
pencil tests

Observation
  skills, 82–84, 291
  teacher, 121–124
Odyssey, 183
Oral history, 178–179
Organization and scheduling, 64–65
Orlich, Donald C., 100

Paper-and-pencil tests, 110
Pappas, Christine, 156, 171
Parent and family resources, 39
Parker, Walter C., 171, 223
Patriotism, 20–21, 222–223
Performance-based assessments. *See*
  Authentic assessments
Piaget, Jean, 222
Planning. *See also* Lesson plans; Task
  analysis; Unit plans
  content standards, 40–41
  goals, 37
  importance, 34–37
  instructional objectives, 40
  long-range planning, 37–40
  resources, 34–35, 39, 44–46
  scheduling, 64–65
  sequence, 42
  skills, 37
  units, 46–63
Political science, 6
Portfolios, 108–109
Potter, Gladys, 134
Preamble of the U. S. Constitution,
  215
Prejudice, 239, 252–253, 257–258
Presentations, 59, 263, 275
Primary grades
  children, 133–134
  citizenship state standards, 252–254
  curriculum, 134
  economic state standards,
    144–148
  geography state standards, 149–151
  history state standards, 135–137

  integration, 155–157
  scheduling, 168, 169
Primary sources, 136, 178
Problem solving. *See* Thinking
Project SPAN, 25
Proximal development, 279
Psychology, 5, 8, 22, 174
Public issues-centered approach, 22

Questioning techniques, 85, 271
Questionnaires, 179

Reading, 135, 264–267, 271–272
Real-world problems approach, 22
Reference books, 272–273
Reflective inquiry, 22
Religious issues in classroom, 25, 165
Research projects, 53, 75, 263
Resource units, 62
Reynolds, Robert, 134
Role playing, 94–97
Roles of teacher, 8–9, 12, 69–70, 107
Rubric, 123, 187

Saxe, David Warren, 32
Scheduling social studies
  options, 64–65, 168–169
  primary grades, 168–169
Scope and sequence issues, 28–29
Self-evaluation, 117–118
Service learning, 220–221
Sexism. *See* Gender inequality
Shaftel, Fannie, 100
Shaver, James, 20
Sherman, S. Samuel, 19, 31
Short-answer test items, 111,
  119–120
Simon, Sidney, 13–15
Simulations, 95, 97–99
Skills. *See* Listening; Map skills;
  Observation; Thinking skills;
  Time; Writing
Slaven, Robert E., 100

Social action, 13, 15, 199
Social Education, 32, 159
Socialization, 19–20
Social participation. *See* Citizenship
Social science concepts. *See individual social sciences such as geography*
Social science model, 21–22
Social skills. *See* Cooperative learning
Social studies
    definition, 18
    images, 1–2
    goals, 3–5
    legal requirements, 26
    national curriculum, 24–26
    scope and sequence issues, 28–29
Social Studies, The, 32
Social Studies and the Young Learner, 32
Social Studies School Services, 99
Sociology in the curriculum, 8, 22
Speakers, 45, 93, 198
Special needs students, 93, 257, 267–271
Spiral curriculum, 30–31
Stahl, Robert J., 100
Standards
    civics/government standards, 191
    debate about, 9–12
    definition of, 5
    economic standards, 188
    geography standards, 184
    history standards, 6, 175–177
    influence of, 8–10, 103, 105
    NCSS themes/standards, 6
    state standards, 10–12
State legal requirements, 26
State standards, 7–8, 105, 135–154
Stereotypes, 161, 252–253, 258
Storypath, 142
Student center approach, 23, 169–170
Student characteristics, 68, 133–134, 172–173

Substance abuse education, 13, 192
Summative evaluation, 128

Taba, Hilda, 30, 100, 154
Task analysis, 126, 130
Taxonomy of educational objectives, 125
Teachable moment, 169, 241
Technologies, 70, 297–312
Television, 196–197
Tests, 7, 105, 106–107
Textbooks
    national editions, 27–28
    in primary grades, 158–159
    as resources, 262
    for unit planning, 39, 47–48
    ways to facilitate reading of, 271–272
Thanksgiving, 26, 166–167
Thematic curriculum, 49–51
Think-Pair-Share strategy, 77
Thinking
    accept or reject hypothesis, 86
    define problem, 77
    gather data, 80–82
    generate ideas, 77–80
Thinking skills, 74–86, 100, 154
Time (chronological skills)
    learning, 284–286
    primary, 141, 286–287
Time allocations for teaching social studies. *See* Scheduling social studies
Timelines, 136, 137, 272, 286–288
Tradebooks. *See* Literature
True-false test items, 112–113

Unit
    commercial, 47–48
    definition of, 46
    elements of, 46, 61
United Nations, 226

Unit plans
  Culture Vulture Club, 246
  Food, 62
  Grasslands, 53–54
  Historical Thinking Grade 1,
    137–140
  Hospital, 163–164
  How Things Change, 160–161
  Life in the Colonies, 127
  Living in Hawaii, 57–59
  Travel Day to Hawaii, 55–57
  Understanding Prejudice, 243–244
  Where Does Your Trash or Garbage
    Go? 228–231
*Universal Declaration of Human
  Rights,* 215
URL (Universal Resource Locator),
  300

Values analysis strategy, 213–214
Values clarification, 13–15

Values education
  character education, 15–16
  debate, 13
  democratic values, 20, 215
  major approaches, 12–15
  values exploration, 213–214
Van Sickle, Ronald L., 100, 201
Virtual Field Trips, 309–310

WebQuest, 304
Web sites, 305. *See also end of each
  chapter*
White, Charles S., 312
Whole-language approach, 264–266
Widening world scope and sequence
  model, 28–29, 134
Wiggins, Grant P., 132
Word processing, 298
World history/world cultures, 25–26
World Wide Web (WWW), 300
Writing, 130, 263, 275–276